FREUD IN ISTANBUL

FREUD IN ISTANBUL

Turkish Contributions to Psychotherapy and Psychoanalysis

Edited by

Salman Akhtar

KARNAC

firing the mind

First published in 2026 by
Karnac Books Limited
62 Bucknell Road
Bicester
Oxfordshire OX26 2DS

British Library Cataloguing in Publication Data

A C.I.P. for this book is available from the British Library

ISBN: 978-1-80013-320-4 (paperback)
ISBN: 978-1-80013-324-2 (e-book)
ISBN: 978-1-80013-325-9 (PDF)

Typeset by Medlar Publishing Solutions Pvt Ltd, India

www.firingthemind.com

MIX
Paper | Supporting responsible forestry
FSC® C011748
FSC www.fsc.org

Karnac Books is committed to a sustainable future for our business, our readers, and our planet.
This book is made from Forest Stewardship Council® certified paper.

To

VAMIK VOLKAN
in gratitude

IŞIL AND SİMAVİ VAHİP
in friendship

CEMİLE GÜRDAL
in generativity

and

MÜGE ALKAN
in love

Contents

Acknowledgments xi

About the editor and contributors xiii

Introduction xxiii

Part I
Historical backdrop

CHAPTER 1
Turkey psychoanalyzed and psychoanalysis Turkified 3
Kutluğhan Soyubol

CHAPTER 2
Crosscurrents between the development of psychoanalysis and self psychology in Turkey 17
Yavuz Erten

CHAPTER 3
Psychoanalysis, Turkey, and the IPA 27
Vamık D. Volkan

Part II
Developmental observations

CHAPTER 4
The nuances of the mother–daughter relationship in Turkish culture 41
Müge Alkan and Salman Akhtar

CHAPTER 5
Fatherhood and Turkish culture 59
Cüneyt İşcan and Süreyya İşcan

CHAPTER 6
The sibling relationship and some thoughts on siblings in Turkish culture 73
Pınar Limnili Özeren

CHAPTER 7
The absence of *adolescent-like* traits in the adult psyche 95
Talat Parman

Part III
Cultural studies

CHAPTER 8
The multilayered archeology of Turkish identity 107
M. Sağman Kayatekin and Z. Emel Kayatekin

CHAPTER 9
An exploration of hysteria through the Turkish movie *Nefret* (1984) 123
Elif Nisan İlkmen

CHAPTER 10
Suffering and memory of Holocaust survivors in Eytan İpeker's *The Pageant* (2020) 145
Bella Habip

Part IV
Clinical reports

CHAPTER 11
Incest and the role of silent mothers 159
Ülkü Elif Gürışık

CHAPTER 12
Art as a way of coping with the psychotic self 177
Ayla Yazıcı

CHAPTER 13
Some reflections on the psychoanalytic understanding of smells and sundry amorphous clinical material 189
Cemile Serin Gürdal

CHAPTER 14
Transforming the "enslaving mother" image to "liberating mother" image through the "analyst's womb" in transference 207
Gülgün Alptekin

CHAPTER 15
Technical challenges with bereavement in the course of an ongoing analysis 215
Işıl Vahip

CHAPTER 16
Spiritual elements in psychotherapy and psychoanalysis 233
T. Byram Karasu

CHAPTER 17
Some thoughts on tele-analysis in Turkey 249
Mine Özgüroğlu Çukurçeşme

Notes 263

References 271

Index 300

Acknowledgments

As any colleague who has put together a rather large edited volume knows, the effort and whatever gratitude is owed to it, belong not merely to the editor but to a number of other people who have helped him or her along the way. I too have been the beneficiary of such kind assistance by a number of fellow professionals, friends, family members, publishing house personnel, and secretarial assistance. First and foremost, I must mention those individuals who contributed original papers to this book and in the process, devoted their time and effort to this collaborative venture. Next, I wish to mention the academic and psychoanalytic colleagues who permitted me to reprint their previously published papers in this book; these individuals include Bella Habip, T. Byram Karasu, Kutluğhan Soyubol, Işıl Vahip, and Vamık Volkan. Still others helped me in subtle and not so subtle ways. Prominent among them are Yavuz Erten and Işıl Vahip, both well-known psychoanalysts of Turkey, my beloved muse and life partner Müge Alkan, our good friends Fisun Akdeniz, Ayşe Altan, Berrak Ciğeroğlu, Zehra Çalışkan, Nagehan Demiral, Ayhan Eğrilmez, Saniye Korkmaz-Çetin, and Simavi Vahip. My friendly and skillful publisher Kate Pearce, my stalwart copyeditor James Darley, my editorial guide Anita Mason, my book publicist Aimee Dexter, and my secretarial assistants Angela Williams and Jan Wright were each indispensable in their own ways. To all these individuals I am deeply grateful. Without their benevolence, this work would not have been accomplished.

About the editor and contributors

Salman Akhtar, MD, is professor of psychiatry at Jefferson Medical College and a training and supervising analyst at the Psychoanalytic Center of Philadelphia. He has served on the editorial boards of the *International Journal of Psychoanalysis* and the *Journal of the American Psychoanalytic Association*. His more than 450 publications include twenty-three solo authored books—*Broken Structures* (1992), *Quest for Answers* (1995), *Inner Torment* (1999), *Immigration and Identity* (1999), *New Clinical Realms* (2003), *Objects of Our Desire* (2005), *Regarding Others* (2007), *Turning Points in Dynamic Psychotherapy* (2009), *The Damaged Core* (2009), *Comprehensive Dictionary of Psychoanalysis* (2009), *Immigration and Acculturation* (2011), *Matters of Life and Death* (2011), *Psychoanalytic Listening* (2013), *Good Stuff* (2013), *Sources of Suffering* (2014), *No Holds Barred* (2016), *A Web of Sorrow* (2017), *Mind, Culture, and Global Unrest* (2018), *Silent Virtues* (2019), *Tales of Transformation* (2022), *In Leaps and Bounds* (2022), and *In Short* (2024)—as well as sixty-nine edited or coedited volumes in psychiatry and psychoanalysis. Dr. Akhtar has delivered many prestigious addresses and lectures including, most significantly, the inaugural address at the first IPA-Asia Congress in Beijing, China (2010). Dr. Akhtar is the recipient of the *Journal of the American Psychoanalytic Association*'s Best Paper of the Year Award (1995), the Margaret Mahler Literature Prize (1996), the American Society of Psychoanalytic Physicians' Sigmund Freud Award (2000), the American College of Psychoanalysts' Laughlin Award (2003), the American Psychoanalytic Association's Edith Sabshin Award (2000), Columbia University's Robert Liebert Award for Distinguished Contributions to Applied Psychoanalysis (2004), the American Psychiatric Association's Kun Po Soo Award (2004), the Irma Bland Award for being the Outstanding Teacher of Psychiatric Residents in the country (2005), and the Nancy Roeske Award (2012). He received the Sigourney Award (2013), which is the most prestigious honor in the field of psychoanalysis.

Dr. Akhtar is an internationally sought speaker and teacher, and his books have been translated in many languages, including German, Turkish, and Romanian. His interests are wide and he has served as the film review editor for the *International Journal of Psychoanalysis*, and is currently serving as the book review editor for the *International Journal of Applied Psychoanalytic Studies*. He has published eighteen collections of poetry and serves as a scholar-in-residence at the Inter-Act Theatre Company in Philadelphia. His *Selected Papers (Vols I–X)* were recently published and released at a festive event held at the Freud House & Museum in London.

Müge Alkan, PhD, is a clinical psychologist and psychotherapist in İzmir, Turkey. Dr. Alkan received her master's and doctorate in clinical psychology from Ege University Health Sciences Institute. She worked in the Department of Psychiatry of Ege University Medical School for nearly thirty years. She was a visiting fellow at Western Psychiatric Institute and Clinic at the University of Pittsburgh in 2002 where she was trained in psychotherapy for bipolar disorder patients and interpersonal psychotherapy. Dr. Alkan specializes in the psychotherapy of bipolar disorder and has made consistent and devoted contributions to the functions and activities of the Affective Disorders Unit at the Ege University Medical School's Department of Psychiatry. Dr. Alkan has coauthored a monograph titled *Kekemelik ve Kekelemek Üzerine* (1999) which deals with the treatment of stuttering. In addition, she has published several papers and book chapters on interpersonal psychotherapy and psychotherapy of patients with bipolar disorder. She has translated several psychoanalytic books, including those by Vamık Volkan and Salman Akhtar, from English to Turkish.

Gülgün Alptekin, MD, is a training and supervising analyst in Psike İstanbul (İstanbul Psychoanalytic Association for Training, Research and Development). She obtained her medical degree in 1991 from Ege University Faculty of Medicine in İzmir, Turkey and completed her residency in 1997. Following this, she completed a course of psychoanalytic psychotherapy training in İzmir Halime Odağ Psychoanalysis and Psychotherapy Foundation in 2000. She participated in the Vamık Volkan Study Group between 1997 and 2003 in İstanbul. When psychoanalytic training became available under the umbrella of the IPA in Turkey in 2004, she joined Psike İstanbul as a candidate and graduated in 2012. Since then, she has served on its executive board, Scientific Committee, and Education Committee and as the president of Psike İstanbul between 2014 and 2016. She is currently the chair of the Psike İstanbul Admission Committee and Progression Committee. She has presented at many psychoanalytic conferences and has authored a commentary on the Turkish translation of Salman Akhtar's book *Sources of Suffering*. Her areas of interest include cinema and psychoanalysis, femininity, female sexuality, and transference and countertransference interaction. In recent years, her study has focused on nonverbal aspects of transference–countertransference. She tries to deepen the understanding of nonverbal and preverbal interactions through representations of the womb and intrauterine life. Dr. Alptekin maintains a private practice of psychotherapy and psychoanalysis in İstanbul.

Mine Özgüroğlu Çukurçeşme, MD, is a training and supervising analyst at the Psike İstanbul (İstanbul Psychoanalytic Association for Training, Research and Development). She obtained her medical degree from Trakya University, İstanbul in 1986 and completed psychiatric training at İstanbul University in 1992. Later she trained at Psike İstanbul and became an IPA recognized psychoanalyst in 2010. She has been the former general secretary of the board of Psike, the chair of its Scientific Committee, and a member of its Ethics Committee. Currently, she is a member of the Education Committee and the Admission and Progression Committees. Dr. Çukurçeşme has chaired many study groups including those on "The first interview and making a formulation" and "Winnicott at clinical practice." She has published many papers in the Psike İstanbul Psychoanalysis Library Series, including those on "Ailing body: Psychosomatics" (2015), "Northern Cyprus: A country that does not exist" (2019), and a discussion of Maurice Apprey's paper on aggression (2014). In addition, she has made presentations at local and regional psychoanalytic conferences. She maintains a private practice of psychotherapy and psychoanalysis in İstanbul.

Yavuz Erten, MA, is a psychoanalyst and clinical psychologist based in İstanbul. He received his bachelor's degree in psychology and master's degree in clinical psychology from Boğaziçi University in 1987 and 1989 respectively. Between 1998 and 2003, he completed training in contemporary psychoanalysis at the National Institute of Psychotherapies (NIP) in New York. Between 2004 and 2009, he had his psychoanalysis training at the International Psychoanalytical Association (IPA) and became a psychoanalyst. In 2015, he was appointed by IPA as a training and supervising analyst. He is a founding member of Psike İstanbul, former president of this association, and currently the chair of the Scientific Committee. He is also a member of the International Association for Psychoanalytic Self Psychology (IAPSP). Mr. Erten has published a number of authored, edited, and coedited books on diverse topics within psychoanalysis. These include the solo-authored *Images in the Dark Room* (2010), the coauthored (with Cahit Ardalı) *From Psychoanalysis to Dynamic Psychotherapies* (1999), and the coedited *The Other Side of Psychoanalysis: Heinz Kohut* (2003) and *Knowledge of Psyche from the Perspective of Science and Philosophy* (2006). He has also published many papers in various Turkish professional journals. He published a collection of his poems titled *A Tabby Who Can Do Yoga* (1993). Mr. Erten serves on the editorial board of *Suret*, a prominent journal of psychocultural studies and maintains a private practice of psychotherapy and psychoanalysis in İstanbul.

Cemile Serin Gürdal, PhD, is a clinical psychologist and psychoanalyst based in İzmir. She is a member of Psike İstanbul (İstanbul Psychoanalytic Association for Training, Research and Development), the International Psychoanalytical Association, and a founding member of İzmir Psychoanalytic Psychotherapies Association. She has worked in Ege University, Faculty of Medicine, Department of Psychiatry, Psychotherapy Unit between 2003 and 2013. Currently she is a part-time instructor in Tınaztepe University Clinical Psychology Postgraduate (MA)

Program. She is one of the Turkish translators of Salman Akhtar's books: *Quest for Answers*, *Turning Points in Dynamic Psychotherapy*, *Psychoanalytic Listening*, and *The Damaged Core*. More recently, she has translated Stefano Bolognini's book, *The Vital Flows Between Self and Non Self: The Interpsychic*. She maintains a private practice of psychotherapy and psychoanalysis in İzmir, Turkey.

Ülkü Elif Gürışık, MD, FRCPsych, was born in Adana, Turkey, in 1939. She completed her medical training at İstanbul University in 1962 and her psychiatric training at Ankara University in 1967. After qualifying, she worked as a fellow of Hacettepe University from 1967 to 1969 and as a clinical assistant at the Fulbourn Psychiatric Hospital in Cambridge, UK between 1970 and 1972. She trained with the Contemporary Freudian Group at the Institute of Psychoanalysis from 1973 to 1976 and was privileged to be supervised by Joseph Sandler, Anna-Marie Sandler, Hannah Segal, and Malcolm Pines. She joined the Tavistock and Portman Clinic Trust in London as a senior registrar, becoming a consultant in 1989, and served as vice president of the Portman Clinic from 1997 to 1999. She organized a conference on incest in London in 2001 in the wake of the Butler-Sloss Independent Inquiry into Child Sexual Abuse, co-organized a major international psychoanalytical conference in Turkey in 2011, and has spoken at many major psychotherapy conferences around the world. During her time at the Portman Clinic, Dr. Gürışık set up a study group on domestic violence to further the psychological understanding of lawyers, judges, probation officers, and social workers, and lectured psychiatrists and nurses at Rampton High Security Hospital about the causes of and responses to violence. Her previous publications include "Speech and silence" (*Bulletin of the British Psychoanalytical Society*, 1986), "Challenges to the ambulatory treatment process and how to survive them, a case study" (In: *Challenges in Forensic Psychotherapy*, ed. H. J. C. Van Marle, 1988), and "Female prostitution and the Munchausen syndrome by proxy" (in: *A Practical Guide to Forensic Psychotherapy*, ed. Estela V. Welldon & Cleo Van Velsen, 1997). Dr. Gürışık is a founder member of the International Forensic Psychotherapy Association, a fellow of the Royal College of Psychiatrists, a fellow of the British Psychoanalytic Society, and a member of the International Psychoanalytical Association.

Bella Habip is a training analyst, supervisor, and a member of the Paris Psychoanalytic Society (SPP) and the International Psychoanalytical Association (IPA). She has completed her undergraduate studies in psychology and graduate studies in clinical psychology at Grenoble University in France. She is a founding member and former president of the İstanbul Psychoanalytic Association for Training, Research and Development (Psike İstanbul). She is a former member of the publishing committee of the *International Journal of Psychoanalysis* and the first editor of the *Turkish Annual* between 2009 and 2013, and remains a member of the redaction committee of the same annual. She is the author of *Psikanalizin İçinden/ Through Psychoanalysis* (Yapı Kredi Publishing, 2007, 2012), *Klinik ile Kuram Buluşunca/ When the Clinical Meets the Theory* (Yapı Kredi Publishing, 2012), and of *Kültür ve Psikanaliz/*

Culture and Psychoanalysis (Yapı Kredi Publishing, 2018), and the editor of numerous volumes from the Emerging Issues in Psychoanalysis series published by Ithaki including *Bensizbiz/Iyouus* (2002, edited volume); *Kadınlık, Yeniden/Femininity, Again* (2003, edited volume); *Neden Psikanaliz/Pourquoi une Psychanalyse?* (Roger Perron, 2003); and *Çocukluk Çağının Sıcağında/Au Vie de l'Infantile* (Florence Guignard, 2010). She is also the editor of the Turkish translation of M. Klein's *Love, Guilt and Reparation* (Kanat Publishing, 2008). Since 1996, her articles and interviews have been published in journals such as *Cogito, Defter, Tarih ve Toplum*, and *Doğu-Batı*. She has also contributed to edited volumes: *Yüzyılın Psikanalizi/The Century's Psychoanalysis, Freud Konuşmaları/Freud Lectures, Cinsiyetli Olmak/Being Gendered, Tuhaflık ve Yaratıcılık/Strangeness and Creativity* (Yapı Kredi Publishing, 1996, 2008, 2007, and 2024). In addition, she has published a number of papers in prestigious psychoanalytic journals including *Revue Française de Psychanalyse* and the *International Journal of Psychoanalysis*. She maintains a private practice of psychotherapy and psychoanalysis in İstanbul.

Elif Nisan İlkmen, PhD, LMFT, is the clinical training director and assistant professor of marriage and family therapy at Northern Illinois University. Dr. İlkmen's teaching and clinical interests are related to attachment in romantic relationships and issues of social justice in the field of psychotherapy. Dr. İlkmen grew up in Turkey, has lived in Canada, and now resides in the US. Her immigration experience and multicultural background has allowed her to become a culturally sensitive clinician and professor. Her clinical approach is the attachment-based model, emotionally focused therapy (EFT), a model that permeates her clinical practice as well as her teaching and supervision methods. Her approach to therapy is informed by psychodynamic models, helping each individual to understand their unique struggles in the past and present in order to facilitate internal change. She moved to Canada to pursue her studies and completed a bachelor of arts degree in psychology and French literature at the University of Ottawa. Dr. İlkmen then received her master's and PhD degrees in couples and family therapy from Adler University in Chicago, Illinois. As her clinical internship, she completed the two-year doctoral fellowship program at the Couples Clinic and Research Institute in Geneva, Illinois. In 2021, she completed the psychodynamic psychotherapy training led by Dr. Otto Kernberg. Dr. İlkmen is an active presenter at various conferences in the field at regional, national, and international organizations such as the International Association for Marriage and Family Counselors (IAMFC), and the Illinois Association for Marriage and Family Therapy (IAMFT). Dr. İlkmen identifies as a social justice qualitative researcher with a focus on the experiences of women across identities and dimensions of culture.

Cüneyt İşcan, MD, is a board-certified psychiatrist and psychoanalyst in the Boston metropolitan area. He earned his medical degree from Ankara University School of Medicine in Turkey. He had his residency training in psychiatry at the University of Michigan. His studies continued at the Austen Riggs Center in Stockbridge, Massachusetts, a center specializing in treatment-resistant psychiatric conditions and application of psychoanalytic treatments.

He pursued his psychoanalytic training at the Boston Psychoanalytic Society and Institute. He is currently on the faculty and an active member of this institute and the American Psychoanalytic Association. He has been an assistant professor of psychiatry at the University of Massachusetts Medical School since 2001. He has numerous publications in the form of books, book chapters, and scientific papers in English and Turkish focusing on psychoanalysis, applications of psychoanalytic theory in clinical work, and personality disorders.

Süreyya İşcan, PhD, earned her MA in educational psychology and her PhD in developmental psychology at the Ankara University School of Psychology in Turkey. She went on to earn a second MA and PhD in clinical psychology at the Fielding Graduate University of Santa Barbara. She was a postdoctoral research fellow at the University of Michigan and at the Austen Riggs Center, followed by a fellowship in psychoanalytic research training at the Yale Child Study Center and Anna Freud Center. She is also a graduate of the Boston Psychoanalytic Institute. She is the associate director for psychotherapy education at Umass Chan Medical School and also a faculty member at the Boston Psychoanalytic Society & Institute and Advanced Psychoanalytic Psychotherapy program. She was the recipient of the Paul B. Barreira Teaching Award in 2016, 2019, and 2020. She has published several research articles in the area of psychodynamic psychotherapy and psychotherapy outcomes.

T. Byram Karasu, MD, is a distinguished professor emeritus at Albert Einstein College of Medicine, and the Silverman Professor and University Chairman Emeritus in the Department of Psychiatry and Behavioral Sciences at the Albert Einstein/Montefiore Medical Center. Dr. Karasu is editor-in-chief emeritus of the *American Journal of Psychotherapy* and cofounder of the Annual Tarrytown Leadership Conference. Dr. Karasu is a widely renowned psychiatrist, educator, master coach, psychotherapist, and best-selling author whose work has been translated into many languages. He has published more than twenty books, including the seminal *Treatments of Psychiatric Disorders* and *The Art of Serenity*, which became a *New York Times* best seller. He gave the Harvard Bicentennial Lecture at Massachusetts General Hospital and is the recipient of many awards including the A. H. Stanton Award of the McLean Hospital, the Harry Stack Sullivan and Sigmund Freud Awards, the American Psychiatric Association's Presidential Commendation Award, and the Distinguished Alumni Award from the Department of Psychiatry and the Yale University School of Medicine.

M. Sağman Kayatekin, MD, is an adult psychoanalyst and psychiatrist, who worked as a clinician and teaching faculty member in diverse cultures—USA, Turkey, and China. He is currently living in Houston, Texas. Throughout his long professional career, Dr. Kayatekin worked in prominent psychotherapeutic hospitals like the Austen Riggs Center and the Menninger Clinic, in addition to working as a psychoanalyst and family therapist. He is also interested in the liaison of psychoanalysis and social sciences/humanities. He has taught, written papers and chapters for books, presented, and lectured extensively on his areas of interest in English and Turkish. His book *Psychoanalytic Conversations: From the Psychotherapeutic Hospital to the Couch*, about his individual, family, and hospital work was translated to Chinese. He has won numerous teaching awards in several institutions where he worked. At this phase of his professional life Dr. Kayatekin continues to work as a faculty member at the Menninger Department of Psychiatry, Baylor College of Medicine. He carries on a small private practice, and provides consultations to individuals and families and psychotherapeutic hospital systems. He continues with individual and group supervisions and teaches nationally and internationally. He has been lecturing on organizational dynamics at the international Business Administration department of Koc University, the most prominent private university in Turkey, located in İstanbul. He is actively writing papers, chapters, and working on book projects in psychoanalysis, humanities, and social sciences. Dr. Kayatekin is also in the process of developing psychoanalytic affiliations with Central Asian countries and Vietnam.

Z. Emel Kayatekin, MD, is a psychiatrist, family therapist, and psychotherapist, currently living in Houston, Texas. She has worked as a faculty member in USA, Turkey, and China. She has taught, presented, and written extensively in Turkey, China, and USA in addition to treating patients and doing research. She was instrumental in bringing formal family therapy to the Department of Child Psychiatry, Ankara University Medical School in the 1990s and establishing a research department at the Department of Psychiatry, Berkshire Medical Center (affiliated to University of Massachusetts Medical School). Her interest gradually shifted into psychotherapeutic hospital treatment, and she worked at the Menninger Clinic leading the team at its Young Adults Program for more than a decade. She continues to be on the faculty at the Menninger Department of Psychiatry, Baylor College of Medicine, in addition to working at intense outpatient and psychotherapeutic hospital programs.

Pınar Limnili Özeren, MD, is a training and supervising analyst at the İstanbul Psychoanalytic Association for Training, Research and Development. She is also an instructor at the IPA-affiliated psychoanalytic training program for the candidates. Dr. Özeren is the former president of the İstanbul Psychoanalytic Association for Training, Research and Development, the former chair of its Ethics Committee, and currently president of the Education Committee. She is a member of the European Psychoanalytical Federation (EPF) Ad Hoc Group titled "Psychoanalysis in Literature-Literature in Psychoanalysis". Dr. Özeren has worked with adolescent and adult patients in both inpatient and outpatient clinics at the Mazhar Osman Research and Training Hospital for Psychiatry, Neurology and Neurosurgery, İstanbul. She has published many papers in Turkish psychoanalytic journals. She maintains a private practice of psychotherapy and psychoanalysis in İstanbul.

Talat Parman, MD, is a founder of the İstanbul Psychoanalytical Association where he also serves as a training and supervising analyst. He is a member of the Paris Psychoanalytical Society and the International Psychoanalytical Association. He received his medical education at İstanbul University, İstanbul Faculty of Medicine, and psychiatric training at René Descartes University in Paris. He worked with children, adolescents, and their families at İstanbul University Child Health Institute for twenty years. He is an associate professor of psychiatry. He has written many books including *The Adolescent Passion* (2020), *The Reel Game of Sigmund Freud* (2020), *The Faces of Adolescence* (2021), and *Adolescence and Beyond* (2022). In addition, he has translated three books by J.-B. Pontalis from French into Turkish. Dr. Parman was the editor-in-chief of *Psychoanalytic Writings Review* for twenty years and is currently on the editorial board of *Psychoanalytic Notebooks Review* published by Yapı Kredi Yayınları, İstanbul.

Kutluğhan Soyubol, PhD, is assistant professor of sociology at Boğaziçi University in İstanbul. He also taught or held academic fellowships at the City University of New York, Tel Aviv University, and the University of Cambridge. His research articles have appeared in several academic journals, on subjects including but not limited to medical history, modern intellectual history, comparative studies of South Asia, Africa, and the Middle East, and Osmanlı Araştırmaları, as well as in edited books such as *The Oxford Handbook of Religion in Turkey.* He is currently working on a book project, tentatively titled, *The Republican Soul: Psy-sciences, Secularism, and Modernity in Turkey.*

Işıl Vahip, MD, is a professor of psychiatry and training and supervising analyst at Psike İstanbul, IPA Provisional Society. She served consecutively as chair of the Awareness in Ethics Working Group, and vice president and chair of the Admission Committee at Psike İstanbul. She is the former director of the Psychotherapy Unit at Ege University and the former chair of the Psychoanalytic Psychotherapy Section of the Psychiatric Association of Turkey. She was also trained as a group psychotherapist and has been conducting psychoanalytically oriented training groups and patient groups for more than twenty years. She spent one year at the Center for the Study of Mind and Human Interaction, founded and directed by Vamık Volkan, which shaped her future psychoanalytical training. She is the guest editor of the *Journal of Psychiatry, Psychology, Psychopharmacology* and *Journal of Update in Psychiatry.* She has written six book chapters and numerous articles in Turkish about psychoanalysis, the mourning process, some effects of cultural and ethnic issues on transference and countertransference, domestic violence, psychosocial aspects of bipolar disorder from a psychoanalytic viewpoint, and a model for teaching psychoanalytic concepts and their clinical applications to residents. She presented papers in the Multidisciplinary Conference honoring Vamık Volkan in Charlottesville, VA, USA in 2001, in the annual meeting of the German Psychoanalytical Society (DPG) in 2004, in the International Association of Group Psychotherapy, 2nd Regional Mediterranean Conference, Athens, Greece in 2004, in the 41st Annual Meeting of the American College of Psychoanalysts in 2010, and in the Members' Conference of the Australian Psychoanalytical Society in 2015. She is the founder of the İzmir Psychoanalytic Psychotherapies Association and maintains a private practice in İzmir, Turkey.

Vamık D. Volkan, MD, is an emeritus professor of psychiatry at the University of Virginia and an emeritus training and supervising analyst at the Washington-Baltimore Psychoanalytic Institute. He is the emeritus president of the International Dialogue Initiative and a former president of the Turkish-American Neuropsychiatric Society, the International Society of Political Psychology, the Virginia Psychoanalytic Society, and the American College of Psychoanalysts. He was a member of the International Negotiation Network under the directorship of President Jimmy Carter; a member of the Working Group on Terror and Terrorism, International Psychoanalytical Association; a temporary consultant to the World Health Organization in Albania and Macedonia; an inaugural Yitzhak Rabin Fellow, Rabin Center for Israeli Studies, Tel Aviv, Israel; and a Fulbright/Sigmund Freud Foundation visiting scholar of psychoanalysis in Vienna, Austria. He is a recipient of the Nevitt Sanford, Elise Hayman, Bryce Boyer, Hans Strupp, Sigmund Freud (given by the city of Vienna), and Mary Sigourney awards and the Margaret Mahler Literature Prize. He was nominated for the Nobel Peace Prize five times; letters of support were sent from twenty-seven countries. Dr. Volkan holds honorary doctorate degrees from Kuopio University (now called the University of Eastern Finland), Finland; Ankara University, Turkey; the Eastern European Psychoanalytic Institute, Russia; Eastern Mediterranean University, North Cyprus; and Kyrenia–American University, North Cyprus. Dr. Volkan is the author, coauthor, editor, or coeditor of more than fifty psychoanalytic and psychopolitical books, some of which have been translated into Chinese, Finnish, German, Greek, Japanese, Russian, Serbian, Spanish, and Turkish. He has written hundreds of published papers and book chapters. He has served on the editorial boards of sixteen national or international professional journals.

Ayla Yazıcı, MD, is a training and supervising analyst at Psike İstanbul (İstanbul Psychoanalytic Association for Education, Research and Development) and a member of the International Psychoanalytical Association. Between 1991 and 2011, she worked at Bakırköy Psychiatric Hospital where she founded the Psychoanalysis Unit. She also worked in the general psychiatry service and founded its Day Hospital and Rehabilitation Center in 2006. Dr. Yazıcı did therapy and rehabilitation work in this center with people with chronic psychotic disorders and retired from her job in 2011. She is the former chair of the executive board of Psike İstanbul, former chair of its Scientific Committee, and former member of its Education Committee. She is currently the trainer of the training group within the Psike İstanbul and continues her work on psychoanalysis in her private office in İstanbul. She is interested in psychotic disorders, community dynamics, creativity and symbolization psychoanalysis, and has written on these topics.

Introduction

Most books owe their origin to "sources from above" and to "sources from below," to extrapolate Freud's dictum about dreams. This book is no exception. Among its "sources from above" is my long-term interest in the dialectics between the internal world and external reality and the specific hues and flourishes of it in a given culture. This intellectual bent was fomented by my training in psychoanalysis as a "minority candidate" (I was the only Indian in my psychoanalytic institute and, to the best of my knowledge at that time, the only Indian candidate in the entire American Psychoanalytic Association) and later found expression in my books on immigration (1999, 2011) as well as my edited volumes on the people and culture of India (2005), Australia and New Zealand (with M. T. Hooke, 2007), the Muslim world (2008), China, Japan, and Korea (2010), and upon African Americans (2012b) and Hispanic Americans (with S. M. Bertoglia, 2015). Putting together *Freud in İstanbul* was thus an expected and logical step in my search for a genuinely anthropological psychoanalysis.

Now allow me to say a few things about the emotional origins or the "sources from below" of this book. Born in British Imperial India and raised in the newly independent, but tragically partitioned, nation as a member of a religious minority, I grew up sensitized to cultural differences, discrimination, and prejudice, the sustaining value of linguistic ancestry and festive rituals, and the evolution of amalgamated and hybrid identities. My immigration to the United States, during my late twenties, furthered such awareness, both on the conscious and the unconscious levels. In my newly adopted country, I encountered Professor Vamık Volkan, a Washington-based psychoanalyst and a prolific writer of Cypriot Turkish origin. A supervisor–supervisee relationship (1974–1979) grew into a long-term mentorship by him and then settled into a deep, ongoing friendship, though without the compromise of the generational difference between us. In 1999, he arranged for me to give a talk at a psychotherapy workshop sponsored by the Halime Odağ Foundation in İzmir, Turkey. There I met not only its founder, Celal Odağ (1931–2021), a patrician, dignified, and generous Turkish man who had trained in intensive psychotherapy in Germany, but also a number of fellow professionals who became my lifelong friends: prominent among them were Fisun Akdeniz, Gülgün Alptekin, Ayhan Eğrilmez, and Işıl and Simavi Vahip. Somewhat later I made acquaintance with the eminent members of *Psike* (the IPA recognized psychoanalytic group in İstanbul) including Yavuz Erten, and Ayla Yazıcı. I then started visiting Turkey often, becoming a "regular" at the educational conferences at the Odağ Foundation. I also supervised the work of a blossoming analytic candidate, Cemile Gürdal, and this put me in touch with the subjectivity of the younger generation of Turkish professionals.

Imbued with the beneficence of my seniors, the camaraderie of my peers, and tenderness for those who are much younger than me, I fell in love not only with Turkey as an inexhaustible font of history, poetry, political intrigue, and cultural admixture, but also with a refined Turkish woman of supple intellect and kind disposition. Now my life partner, Dr. Müge Alkan was a psychotherapist who had a great interest helping patients with bipolar disorder and who had translated a few of my books. The love between us became yet another "source from below" for editing this volume on psychoanalysis in Turkey.

The book is divided into four sections that deal, respectively, with the history of psychoanalysis in Turkey, child development patterns and family structure as these impact upon epigenetic psychic unfolding matters of Turkish culture-at-large, and clinical issues and challenges faced by Turkish psychotherapists and psychoanalysts. The first section is titled Historical backdrop, and has three chapters, each of which approaches the arrival, development, and blossoming of psychoanalysis in Turkey from a novel perspective. The second section, Developmental observations, consists of four chapters, dealing with the psychology of mothers, fathers, siblings, and the adolescence phase in Turkey. The third section, named Cultural studies, has three chapters, which address the complexities and nuances of identity formation, nostalgic rumination, massive trauma, and female aggression in the context of Turkish society at large. The fourth section pertains to technical issues and is titled Clinical reports. It consists of seven chapters dealing with matters as diverse as grief, spirituality in the context of psychotherapy and psychoanalysis, tenacious maternal transferences and the handling of amorphous nonverbal material in the clinical session, to name a few.

Three other comments about the contributors and the material included in this book seem warranted. First, while the book is intended to be psychoanalytic in its thrust and focus, not all its contributors are analysts; many belong to other fields including psychology, sociology, psychiatry, and cultural anthropology. Second, while all contributors (except the book's editor) are of Turkish origin, their "distance" from the native country varies; some reside in practice in Turkey, while others represent the nation's diasporic population. Finally, the level of clinical and academic experience of various contributors is also different. Some, especially T. Byram Karasu, Talat Parman, and Vamık Volkan, are established figures and prolific authors, with numerous publications to their credit; each of them has made profoundly significant contributions to our field and each of them has either founded or been the chief editor of a major journal of psychotherapy and psychoanalysis. Other contributors are relatively fresh to such academic discourse. In this context, therefore, representing such academic giants to the extent that they actually deserve became impossible. For this, I can only express regret and hope that the readers will independently pursue these authors' important works.

Before closing, I must mention a few prominent individuals, whose creative output and service to the cause of Turkish psychotherapy and psychoanalysis I was not able to include in this book. Some of them are psychoanalysts, others psychotherapists. Many are associated with IPA while others are not. Some reside and work within Turkey while others represent the diaspora spread over the United Kingdom, United States, Germany, and other countries. The contributions they have made vary in nature and scope, ranging from teaching, administrative activities, academic writing, community outreach, and, of course, clinical practice. Prominent among this group of individuals are the following. *Within Turkey itself*: Elda Abrevaya, Nesim Bitram, Banu Büyükkal, Levent Kayaalp, Ali Algın Köşkdere, Ayça Gürdal Küey, Serra Müderrisoğlu, Stella Ovadia, Mine Özmen, and Tevfika İkiz Tunaboylu. *Representing the Turkish diaspora*: Berrak Ciğeroğlu, Piyale Cömert, İlknur Girgin, Taner Güvenir, Yaprak Harrison, Ilgın Odağ, Özen Odağ, Fatema Sevinç, and Sumru Tüfekçioğlu.

All this having been put on the table, allow me to conclude this brief introduction by saying that the book in your hands, *Freud in İstanbul*, seeks to place Turkish contributions to our theory and practice on the international psychoanalytic stage from which it has been curiously absent. The extent to which its effort has been successful is for the readers of this book to decide, be they from other regions of the world or from Turkey itself.

Part I

Historical backdrop

CHAPTER 1

Turkey psychoanalyzed and psychoanalysis Turkified*

Kutluğhan Soyubol

In 1924, only one year after the proclamation of the Republic of Turkey, the new Turkish government assigned the deserted Reşadiye Barracks on the outskirts of İstanbul for the establishment of the first modern mental hospital that would provide novel (Western) forms of psychiatric care and services in the country.[1] The new regime's decision to launch a modern mental hospital, despite the war-torn economy it inherited from the Ottoman Empire, was emblematic of its determination in its project of producing a healthy and productive population. The project overtly included the sanitization of the field of mental health in Turkey, and it involved the reconfiguration of concerns such as what constitutes madness, the psyche, and the soul in light of Western psychiatric standards.

In the same period, two competing approaches dominated the field of psychiatry in the world at large. The first and better institutionalized among them was descriptive or biological psychiatry. This approach defined mental disorders as essentially brain and nervous system diseases and focused on observable symptoms and behavioral phenomena to classify them. The other approach, namely dynamic psychiatry or psychoanalysis, had a more nebulous definition of mental problems, and was concerned with examining and unraveling the psychodynamic processes that underlie mental and psychic disorders.[2] In its quest to sanitize the field of mental health from older metaphysical (and now so-called superstitious) beliefs and practices, the new Turkish state would invest in descriptive psychiatry to shape its policies

* This chapter was originally published as Soyubol, K. (2018). Turkey psychoanalyzed, psychoanalysis Turkified: The case of İzzettin Şadan. *Comparative Studies of South Asia, Africa and the Middle East, 38*(1): 57–72.

on social hygiene and mental health.[3] This decision and the consequent state policies proved it difficult for psychoanalysis to take hold in the country and hindered the possibility of the discipline to be institutionalized in Turkey until the initiation of the İstanbul Psychoanalytical Group in 1994.[4] Psychoanalytic discourse, however, was translated into Turkish almost simultaneously with descriptive psychiatry, and it posed an alternative—albeit more in the form of a discourse than a medical practice—to the state-sponsored descriptive psychiatry in both early republican and postwar Turkey.[5]

Focusing on the emergence of psychoanalytic discourse in Turkey, this chapter examines how psychoanalysis was culturally translated (and transformed) into Turkish within the context and problem-spaces of the early republic. To do so, the study addresses the work of İzzettin Şadan (1896–1970s), a psychiatrist and initiator of psychoanalysis in Turkey.[6] Attempting to promote and disseminate psychoanalytic knowledge in Turkey, Şadan went beyond the clinical practice of psychiatry and aimed to engage analytically with what he called the "collective Turkish psyche" through his psychoanalytic writings. In other words, he employed a psychoanalytic methodology to participate in—as well as to analyze—modern Turkish public concerns, including questions and discussions regarding the formation of a modern, healthy Turkish population (collective subjects) within the aspirational framework of the early Turkish republic.

While my focus is on Şadan's translation of psychoanalysis and his promotion and dissemination of it in Turkey, it should be reiterated that the importation and transplantation of a discourse and set of practices from one sociocultural setting to another is never a one-dimensional project. Put differently, by translation, I do not mean a word-for-word rendition between languages, but rather a conversion that involved a process of interpretation and cross-configuration among the different culture, contexts, and traditions.[7] Rather than being an emulation of the original, translation is here considered as the process by which "the original and translation complement each other to produce meanings larger than mere copies or reproductions."[8] The emphasis therefore is on how the psychoanalytic discourse passed through the sociopolitical filters of the early Turkish republican society while being effectively translated into Turkish. The process involved the transformation and rearticulation of psychoanalytic forms to accommodate the Turkish context, as well as the redefinition and reconstitution of Turkish society in accordance with the psychoanalytic interpretation of itself. In other words, the psychoanalytic knowledge passed through the lenses of its local interpreters (in our case Şadan), whose inclinations and subjectivities were constituted by their own locality (as well as temporality) and its conditions of possibilities. A consideration of this transformative process is central to my argument since it discloses the processes through which a different translatable psychoanalytic discourse emerged via Şadan's engagement with the perceived problems confronting the early republican society, including that of the role of religion and the historic origins of the modern Turkish nation.

The chapter also explores the ways in which Şadan's psychoanalytic translations and articulations posed a challenge to Freudian psychoanalysis by questioning its universality through a problematization of its conceptualizations of love and sexuality (eros)—which, according to Şadan, did not correspond with the dynamics of Turkish society. While scrutinizing Şadan's claim of his influence on Freud, the text invites readers to ponder the plausibility of evaluating psychoanalysis not simply as a Western formulation and franchise, but as a discourse shaped and developed within transnational and transcultural networks of intellectual interaction and influence.

İzzettin Şadan: a brief biography

İzzettin Şadan was born in İstanbul into a well-to-do family in 1896. He was educated first at Robert College and then in the İstanbul medical school (*Mekteb-i Tıbbiye-i Şahane*) during the Young Turk regime. In 1925, two years after his graduation from the medical school (and the proclamation of the Turkish Republic), he was assigned to Toptaşı, the major state asylum in İstanbul. Toptaşı during this period was undergoing a major structural transformation, which would culminate in the emergence of the aforementioned first modern psychiatric institution in the country, namely Bakırköy Mental Hospital. Şadan worked there as a psychiatric assistant until a dispute in 1927 with Mazhar Osman, the director of Toptaşı and later Bakırköy, compelled him to resign.[9] Following this incident, Şadan went to France to study neuropsychiatry in Pitié Salpêtrière and Villejuif Hospitals. Curiously, when he returned to Turkey in 1930, in spite of the fact that he was now a specialist in neuropsychiatry, Şadan could not find a position in any of the main psychiatric institutions in the country, including Bakırköy Mental Hospital. The only job he could find was a consultant in rural Anatolian hospitals and for a while as an inspector for the Ministry of Health.[10]

Being turned down from prominent positions in the main psychiatric institutions marked a shift in Şadan's intellectual interests, for he now grew more critical of descriptive psychiatry and more attracted to psychoanalysis. In this period, Şadan became the first Turkish psychiatrist to go through analysis to be trained as psychoanalyst. His training analyst was the German psychoanalyst Edith Weigert, who together with her Jewish husband, Oscar Weigert, took refuge in Turkey between 1935 and 1938 and obtained special permission from Mustafa Kemal (Atatürk) to practice psychoanalysis in the country.[11] It is important to note that Şadan's shift toward psychoanalytic discourse was what ironically brought his name to prominence if not fame. In fact, despite the wide range of his publications, including articles in medical journals, essay series in widely popular literary and cultural magazines, and psycho-sociopolitical commentaries in nationalist periodicals, Şadan's claim to fame was not accomplished during his lifetime, a period during which the field of psychiatry in Turkey was completely dominated by state-sponsored descriptive psychiatry. There is also no sign that Şadan was a practicing psychoanalyst or that any psychiatrist or psychoanalyst claimed to be a disciple or acolyte of his. Yet his name is still in circulation today as his contributions are being debated within the Turkish psychiatric circles and among the larger public, especially on questions relating to Turkish modernity and the formations of modern subjectivities under the early republic of Turkey.[12]

From descriptive psychiatry to psychoanalysis: a narrative of positivism

Before going into Şadan's psychoanalytic discourse, a few words are in order on his shift from descriptive psychiatry to psychoanalysis, a shift that was not in conflict or incompatible with Şadan's ardent belief in "positive science"—which for him is "the basis of any credible knowledge."[13] During a period of top-down secularization in Turkey, Şadan vehemently advocated the dissemination of scientific knowledge to counter prevalent "superstitious" and "pseudo-scientific" beliefs among Turks. A "conscripted" positivist from his early years, Şadan, in an article published in 1925, situated what he called "Freudism" within "philosophy" rather than "science." He harshly attacked the psychoanalytic method for holding "mystical and anti-positivist tendencies common to that era" and for straying away from "pure sciences." He concluded adamantly that psychoanalysis "prevailed only because of the [anti-positivist] tendencies of the era and society rather than scientific value it genuinely had."[14]

How is it possible for Şadan to switch his position completely to become the champion and the leading representative of psychoanalytic knowledge some years later? He tells us the story of his conversion with particular details in various pieces he wrote later on to introduce psychoanalysis to the Turkish public. In a 1925 article, Şadan points out that it might be difficult to distinguish psychology from philosophy if one starts with ancient Greece. "However," he emphasizes, "if one leaves this speculative, stochastic and abstract views behind ... he will see how psychology turned out to be a serious matter once the idea of experimentation became an essential part of it."[15]

When discussing Freud, Şadan stresses emphatically Freud's commitment to "causality and determinism." Causality (*illiyet*), although becoming the basis for understanding the physical world since the nineteenth century, was "never applied to decipher relationships between mental or psychic (*ruhi*) events and occurrences until Freud employed it for his analysis of the human psyche."[16] According to Freud, mental and psychic conditions (both normal and pathological) are the outcomes of the dynamic causal relations between the conscious and the unconscious as they manifest themselves in the struggles among the id, ego, and superego. Resorting to the unconscious to find out its effects on the conscious is, Şadan writes, an absolute break from the philosophers who proceeded him. While theorizing the unconscious, Freud left philosophical considerations behind, and stuck to the principle of causality. It is for this reason, psychoanalysis is absolutely determinist (*muayyeniyetçi*).[17]

Consequently, Şadan insists that Freud based his analysis on "various scientific proofs," such as the ones "taken from dream analysis, or the psychopathology of everyday life, as well as the results of scientific evaluations of the unconscious, the evidence taken from post-hypnotic situations, and the ones unearthed by free association during therapies."[18]

Convinced by Freud's emphasis on the scientific nature of psychoanalysis, as well as its compatibility with the secular-positivist intellectual climate of the early republic, Şadan might have realized the potential of psychoanalysis as a new space of operation within the field of Turkish psychiatry.[19] A turning point in his life, he tells us, came when he coincidently obtained *Traité théorique et pratique de psychanalyse*, a book by the British neurologist and psychoanalyst (and Freud's authorized biographer) Ernest Jones.[20] During that time, he began to delve into the writings of Freud as well as Carl G. Jung (1875–1961) and Abraham A. Brill (1874–1948).[21] Şadan consequently emerged as the interlocutor of this new—yet according to him, indisputable scientific—psychiatric trend in Turkey. However, his shift was clearly formalized on an intellectual level rather than clinically applied. Put simply, Şadan was more interested in preaching psychoanalysis than practicing it "medically."[22] As a matter of fact, his significance as a psychoanalyst lies mainly in his public engagement with historically embedded "Turkish neuroses" and his analysis of the "collective unconscious" of modern Turkey. In this regard, Şadan's publications on psychoanalysis in many ways resemble Freud's writings on society and neuroses, as in the *Totem and Taboo* (1912–13), *The Future of an Illusion* (1927c), *Moses and Monotheism* (1939a), and particularly *Civilization and Its Discontents* (1930a). Şadan's shift from biological psychiatry to psychoanalysis represents a momentous interpretational or methodological transformation. This significant shift from an understanding of psychiatric problems based on biology to a psychoanalytic interpretation of the individual subject and the collective whole constitutes the main theme of the rest of this chapter.

"Sickness of love": Libido, eros, and Sufism

In what follows, I address Şadan's attempt at the Turkification of psychoanalysis, a process of translation that includes a resistance to and a break from some features of Freud's psychoanalytic interpretations of society, civilization, the sex drive, and neuroses as they unfold within a Western context. In order to do so, I delve into what I call Şadanian psychoanalysis and discuss a series of Şadan's writing on love (eros) through which, I believe, we can trace his conceptualization of psyche, science, biology, and religion, among other things, more clearly. Although using Freudian psychoanalysis as his analytical framework, in this series of writings Şadan explicitly breaks away from Freud's formulation of and compliance with the idea of "libido as Eros."[23] Differently from Freud's Judeo-Christian notion of eros, which is not exclusively the sex drive, Şadan's notion of love is inseparable from sexual pleasure and the sex drive is by and large (consciously or unconsciously) predicated on the Sunni Islamic tradition and its discourse on sexuality.[24]

Thus, for Şadan, who never married or pursued bourgeois conjugal family relations as Freud did, it was time to raise awareness about this "sickness of love" and "save people from the tyranny and molestation of it."[25] While not targeting the sex drive or the libido, he nonetheless considers desexualized or romantic love (eros) to be an "abstract microbe, which constitutes a sickness like cancer, tuberculosis, and pneumonia, only a lighter one."[26] Even though to Şadan the sex drive can be "without a doubt, dissocial and treacherous," nonetheless it is a drive "embedded in human nature and cannot be disposed of." But to Şadan, love in the Freudian sense limited, if not detached, from sex (pleasure) is a notion that is primarily the "outcome of Catholicism, which itself is an overgrown child of Judaism. It is a product of the beardless, skirted and impotent priests of Jesus, whose own sex life could not go beyond crying on the lap of Mary Magdalena."[27] In his condemnation of romantic forms of modern Western marriage and love, Şadan concludes that the Western concept of love is "obviously masochistic" and one embedded in a Christian asceticism that "aims to extinguish the sex drive; and which in itself is pathological."[28]

In another article, Şadan revisits the idea that Christianity trivialized women's sexual drive and consigned men to impotency. Here he focuses his criticism on the (modern) bourgeois idea of conjugal love and marriage, which he characterizes as a form of "latent homosexuality":

> Any man who cannot view a woman as a source of pleasure is [ultimately] a homosexual—yet one who is unaware of his homosexuality. This is called "*homosexualité latente*." Our contemporary concept of marriage, consequently, is simply a homosexual one. And the reason for this is Christianity, which has pushed women away from [their] sexual worth .... Think of Virgin Mary for a moment: Mary is none other than a desexualized woman. She appears as a dominant woman that only loves and protects her son. She is the head of her family. The figure of the father does not even exist. The son, Jesus is simply his mother's pet. He is a weak, timid masochist, who preaches to offer your other cheek when slapped on your cheek.[29]

One might read Şadan's analysis within the framework of the psychoanalytic discourse that aims to track down neurotic themes situated within "religion" as Freud's work does.[30] Nevertheless, Şadan goes beyond Freudian psychoanalysis by stressing that the modern Western conceptualizations of love and marriage appear to be pathological since they are outcomes of a neurotic Christian understanding of sexuality. They reflect oedipal themes and hence should be construed psychoanalytically. Şadan furthers his arguments by asserting that Freud's sociohistorical analysis of the sex drive is valid principally within the framework of Christian civilization, since "Muslims do not confine the sex drive in such a strict way."[31]

One can see here that Şadan is questioning the universality and scientific nature of some notions of Freudian psychoanalysis with his reading of Freudian discourse as a set of knowledge and practices based on the emerging from a Judeo-Christian culture that is not universally applicable. Clearly, he is challenging Freud by suggesting that psychoanalysis is bound to be determined by its particular culture and is embedded in its own historical memory rather than being a universal, transhistorical knowledge and practice. As Şadan points out, certain aspects of Freudian psychoanalysis—in particular its definition of eros—are not applicable to Turkey and Turkish society. The Freudian understanding of eros simply has its roots in Judeo-Christian culture, and it cannot go beyond being a foreign importation for a Turkish society rooted in an Islamic culture.

Yet one should still pay attention to the strictly secular language he employs here, which assigns authority to Islamic civilization and culture but not Islam—the teaching of God—for the definition and formation of sexuality within Islam. Thus, he continues:

> When Islam obtains features resembling the masochistic proclivities of Christianity, it becomes masochistic and pathological. Sufism (*Tasavvuf*) constitutes the most significant example of that since it displays a strict monasticism and procreates mystical and introverted reactions such as self-torture and asceticism. Consequently, the sex drive loses its direction and moves from women, its real target, to man lover (*mahbub*); and the drama starts there.[32]

This reference to Sufism needs some deliberation. Apart from the explicit secularized language Şadan uses here, his interpretation of love (eros) is implicitly predicated on the Sunni Islamic cultural view of sexuality. The idea of sexual morality in Islam differs from that of Judaism and Christianity: Islam clearly considers sexual fulfillment (of both man and woman) a major principle, and unlike the Christian perception of "legitimate sex" sexual activity is not bound by the procreative purpose. Islamic marriage is polygamous and subject to easy termination. Moreover, Islam does not confine sex (for men) to marriage.[33] As a psychoanalyst informed by his own cultural memory, Şadan puts Sufism under the gaze of psychoanalysis, concluding that Sufis suffer from paranoia caused by the repression of natural worldly desires into pathologies, just as Christians do. Retrospectively diagnosing the "paranoid character" of Sufism, he emphasizes Sufis' implicit use of the "non-Islamic elements and artifacts such as 'feminine ornaments' and 'obvious homoerotic features.'"[34] It is clear from his analysis that Sufism is alien, a foreign importation (*bid'ah*) and a deviation from mainstream Islam. "It is for this reason," Şadan maintains, that a "Sufi is trapped in the mistake of defining the universe through love, or more correctly through a male lover [*mahbub*]."[35] He attributes this deviation to the influence of Greek philosophy on Sufism,[36] stressing that Sufism does not have a place in "pure" or "genuine Islam."[37]

It is within such a framework that Şadan's psychoanalytical evaluation of and resistance to the Freudian conceptualization of eros axiomatically transforms into a (Sunni) critique of Sufism formalized within a psychoanalytic language. Those moments of the unfolding of a veiled yet constitutive interaction between the psychoanalytic language and contentious Islamic debates on Sufism shed light on an intermediate zone (the *barzakh*) and/or a threshold (the *dihliz/dehleez*—in the al-Ghazalian sense) of the modern, and they reverberate with what anthropologist Stefania Pandolfo in a similar context defines as the thin line of modernity.[38] It is on this thin line of modernity, traceable in Şadan's psychoanalytic perception, that the cultural bearings of Sunni Islamic civilization haunt, and thus constitute, what is considered to be modern and secular Turkish understanding of the psyche.

One should keep in mind that Şadan's main goal in the aforementioned series of writings is to elaborate on the neurotic character and roots of imported romantic love, which he analyzes in a physiological and psychoanalytic manner. For Şadan, this kind of desexualized love is a sickness in which both physiological and psychic (particularly unconscious) effects are in operation. It has a social superstructure as well as psychic and corporeal reactions. Thus, it should be diagnosed by using scientific methodology based on causality that is used to diagnose infectious sickness.[39] Once such a method is employed, its symptoms can be traced accordingly, making it clear that the sickness of love proceeds in four phases that parallel the course of any infectious disease. These phases are the inoculation (*devri telkih*), infection (*devri istila*), standstill (devri tevakuf), and fading (devri inhilali).[40] Şadan's definitions of these phases rely on certain observable physical and behavioral symptoms of the lovers, such as being overjoyed, talking too much, and experiencing melancholia.[41]

Among the four phases of the sickness of love, the first one seems to be the most interesting since, according to Şadan, "it pertains to a period when the lover falls in love without determining the target of his love."[42] Thus, love does not start as a result of a physical attraction; it is a sickness that emerges within the psychic apparatus, then finds a target and develops instantly.[43]

However, there is a complete difference between Şadan's psychoanalytic diagnosis of love and the Sufi spiritual understanding and exaltation of love (for God and the beings God created that reflect no one but God). Şadan's conceptualization of love as a sickness, together with his absolute rejection of any spiritual and nonscientific rendering of the concept, directly targets the Sufi understanding of love—along with the Christian and romantic modern versions of it—declaring it to be an inherited sickness in modern Turkish culture.

This declaration indeed coincided with official government activities against the Sufi orders and institutions. The Turkish secular state's determination on dismantling all *tekkes* and *zaviyes* associated with Sufi practices in this period is well documented.[44] The official anti-Sufism policy of the early Turkish republican government seems to overlap with Şadan's views on the issue as a secular citizen, psychiatrist, and intellectual of the republic. At the same time, Şadan was clearly participating in the production of a psychological medical discourse that complemented the state's visions and actions. Concurrent with this, Şadan appears as an agent (albeit unsolicited) of early republican Turkey, drawn by its activities while actively producing a psychoanalytic discourse that engaged the state's "horizon of expectations" and its vision of a progressive modern Turkish nation made up of healthy, productive Turkish subjects.[45]

In addition to that, Şadan's analysis of Christianity (and not Sunni Islam) as pathological—that is, an outcome of the Oedipus complex, and hence repressive, masochistic, and neurotic—is apt to be read as a response to the cultural superiority claims of the West. Thus, it signifies a resistance to an all-encompassing discourse originating in Europe. What is striking about this gesture of resistance is the manner in which it constructs its arguments utilizing the rationality of positivism rather than employing local/indigenous forms of rationality to target the superiority claims of Europe. Yet Şadan still speaks within and through a Sunni Islamic cultural memory, hence producing a secular discourse predicated on an Islamic civilization (albeit Sunni) that is at odds with and different from the secular Judeo-Christian civilization.[46]

The power of science apparently provided Şadan, a secular, nationalist Turkish psychiatrist, the possibility to structure a different secular path informed by Sunni tradition and cultural memory to challenge the binarism of progressive (modern) scientific West vs. backward traditional East. Şadan, nevertheless, always operated within the secularist ethos of early republican Turkey.

Resistance to Western domination is also detectable in Şadan's other writings. For example, Şadan's conceptualization of a Turkish selfhood and psyche is considerably different from the Western self and its psyche. He did not, however, reject the idea of the individual subject. On the contrary, Şadan voiced criticisms of what he called the Turks' "hostility toward individualism" especially since he considered "individualism" to be an essential tenet for the production of a healthy society.[47]

Psychoanalysis, Turkish nationalism, and hallucinations of happiness

For Şadan, who was swept up by the nationalist fervor of the period, the major neurosis that the Turkish individual subject suffered from was none other than a crisis of confused identity. This confusion or neurosis is attributed to the *longue durée millet* system, a multicommunal system practiced by the Ottoman Empire that endured over many centuries and had been inherited by countless generations. What made things even worse, according to Şadan, were the futile and ineffective policies of Ottomanism.[48] As the title of his one and only book, *Birsam-ı Saadet* (*Hallucinations of Happiness*), boldly illustrates, according to Şadan, Turkish society was suffering from hallucinations of happiness, an outcome of historically embedded neuroses within Turkish society. He consequently delves into Ottoman history to trace the pathological effects of the multicommunal Ottoman system, as well as its attempted modernization under Ottomanism on the formation of an Ottoman and later on a Turkish subjecthood.

The concept of Ottomanism emerging in the late *Tanzimat* period, starting with the Imperial Edict of Gulhane in 1839 and culminating with the *Hatt-ı Hümayun* of 1856, introduced modern citizenship and common law to a multicommunal Ottoman Empire composed of different *millets*—that is, of communities based on religious denomination but not necessarily ethnicity. To put it simply, it was an ideology emerging at a time when another new, modern ideology called nationalism was shaking the very foundations of old multicommunal and multiethnic empires. Thus, it aimed to unite different communities living within the boundaries of the Ottoman Empire under the Ottoman banner.[49]

Following this historical trajectory, Şadan locates the origins of what he considers to be a characteristically Turkish neurosis back to Ottomanist modernization policies that, by undermining the notion of Turkishness, generated confusion over who is and what it means to be a Turk. Haunted as he was by the legacy of a multicommunal Ottoman past and a more recent Ottomanism that aimed to create modern Ottoman selves and citizens molded out of multiethnic and multicultural communities, Şadan found it only natural that Turkishness and the idea of Turkish selfhood could emerge only as a blurred category.

Moreover, Şadan traced back the neuroses of modern Turkish society (and the Turkish self) to what he calls the "disturbed" *Tanzimat* era that "exalted the Christian elements that never played a significant role within Turkish society under the auspices of its concept of Ottomanism."[50] Additionally, he points to "foreign enmity," as well as its effects behind the materialization of those confusions:

> Envying the unity of the Turkish World, some foreign elements attempted to break this unity. An example of this is the imaginary separation between Turks, Tatars, and Mongols. As the eminent ethnologist Loth [?] brilliantly proved[,] Turks, Tatars, and Mongols are exactly the same people. And the "Ottoman" concept that was added to this imaginary separation has no other purpose but to destroy national unity by using the "diviser, pour reigner" [*sic. Diviser pour régner*—divide and rule] principle.[51]

The ambiguity over what constituted a Turk and Turkish nation formed the basis of a major yet hidden neurosis within modern Turkey. This neurosis, Şadan continues, can only be overcome through an "empirically" well-defined Turkish nationalism.[52]

Determined to rely utterly on the scientific discourse of his own discipline to support his arguments, Şadan turns to Freud, whom he defines as a "deep nationalist."[53] Moreover, relying on, among other things, his claim of Freud's deep nationalism, he comes up with a prescription for Turkish society that constitutes the last chapter, "The sole cure: The feeling of nationalism," of his *Birsam-ı Saadet.*

Pointing to how the concept of nation (*milliyet*) has been "unfortunately arrested" previously among the Turks, Şadan once again turns to Freud, claiming that "as we have learned from Freud, the feeling of belonging to a nation does not concern solely the individual, but because of its integrative impact among society, it works as a mechanism to cure individual neuroses."[54] Thus, the feeling of nationality is "natural for human beings, and is an outcome of their narcissistic desires. Every acquisition on behalf of the individual satisfies him/her to happiness."[55] Accordingly, the "anti-nationalist communities appear to be communities of suicide."[56] In addition, says Şadan, nationalism works for the treatment of "inferiority complexes." He furthers his arguments by directly referring to Freud, whom he claims to underscore "the necessity of indoctrinating nationalism to the Jews."[57] He nonetheless fails to offer any substantial reference to Freud's works on the subject matter. Şadan's claims on Freud's arguments for the positive impact of nationalism on individual neuroses must be derived mainly from a highly subjective reading of Freud's study *Group Psychology and the Analysis of the Ego* (1921c), in which Freud postulates that the individual gains power and safety by association with a group (including a nation or ethnicity) at the expense of losing her/his own individual consciousness.[58] Yet one wonders (to no avail) what could be the source for Şadan's claims on Freud's proposition of introducing nationalism to the Jews.

Şadan further maintains that "the Turkish nation is the one nation that needs the feeling of nationality most." The "glorious Turkish history" constitutes the great example that must be traced in order to understand this:

> As one of the oldest, most united, and liveliest nations seen in history, the Turks dominated the world from time to time. And their dominion did not simply consist of plundering this and that on horseback as the West claims. They paved paths to make communities between Asia and Europe closer. They provided security for people by establishing orderly state structures. The best proof of this is the ongoing anarchy in the regions from which the Ottoman Turks receded .... Nevertheless, the connectedness of their language to Sumerian, "by all means the oldest language of the world,"—in tune with the principle of the most valuable is the most envied—put their enemies into an effort to belittle the Turkish civilization.[59]

Thus, Şadan adds, a "scientific approach to Turkish nationalism" should be developed, and the Turkish nation must be informed through such a mechanism against the "disinformation that was produced against itself and its civilization by its enemies."[60] This assertion again reflects a juncture point in which Şadan's ideas coincide with and are consolidated by the early republican regime's nationalist projects such as its history and language theses—which adamantly argued for the existence of a systematic body of disinformation in the West regarding the Turkish nation—and proposed Central Asian origins for Sumerians, and hence a Turkic origin for the Sumerian language.[61]

Turkish nationalism, Şadan consequently argues, should be formalized and promulgated as a "philosophical argument to protect and cure the Turkish society from social neuroses."[62] Şadan ends his arguments with an evolutionary reading of the natural human inclinations tending toward nationalism, the sole source of happiness of a society:

> Since the feeling of belonging to a nation satisfies the narcissistic inclinations of the psyche, then everything opposing this inclination would divert human beings into moral and psychic anguish. Anguish is a sickness and can only be diagnosed and treated by psychiatry. And this shows to me that happiness can be achieved only through nationalism.[63]

Since nationalism is the sole path to happiness, then other paths such as internationalism, antinationalism, socialism, the rejection of the existence of races and ethnicities, and the promotion of the idea of transcendental identities appear to be deceptions with hallucinatory effects.[64] For this reason, the "antagonists of racism almost always emerge among the religious, crypto-religious, mystic—Sufi cognoscenti, in other words, among the circles of pre-logical thought."[65] And such nonlogical thinking can only constitute hallucinations of happiness.

Moving even further from this secularist framework based on a binaristic understanding of what is real/healthy and what is hallucinatory/unhealthy, and ending up with a nationalist blackmail, Şadan concludes his *Birsam-ı Saadet* with the assertion that turns the possibility of standing against the idea of nationalism into rejecting the idea of *vatan*: "To blur the stream of nationalism is to blur the concept of the motherland."[66]

It is hard not to notice the constitutive effect of the nationalist fervor of the era on Şadan's own understanding of what constitutes a healthy society as well as his own rendering of psychoanalysis that aimed to help the "Turks" overcome their neuroses and reach a level of psychic stability. Suffice it to say that Şadan was and is often considered to be an extreme nationalist who was influenced by the ultranationalist (*Turancı*) circle of intellectuals of early republican Turkey, including figures such as Nihal Atsız, Rıza Nur, Zeki Velidi Togan, Fethi Tevetoğlu, and Orhan Seyfi Orhon.[67] He was a regular contributor to magazines such as *Çınaraltı*, *Kopuz*, *Toprak*, and *Büyük Doğu*, published by this group in the early 1940s. Clearly his nationalistic claims and psychoanalytic jargon fed and were fed by the Turanist movement. Şadan thus appears to be the psychoanalyst of that circle, bringing a diagnostic language to the social issues pertaining to nationalism as it was defined by Turanism. This group was so drastic in its nationalist claims and activities that it became the target of the nationalist republican government of the İnönü period, and some leading figures of it were imprisoned and charged with racism, fascism, and treason in 1944. The incident is known as the lawsuit of racism and Turanism (*ırkçılık ve Turancılık davası*), and although Şadan did not officially stand trial, his name was added to the list of ultranationalists in Turkey that was put into the file of the lawsuit.[68]

That being said, one must also stress the fact that Şadan's psychoanalytic thinking at some other points differed from and challenged the overall nationalist and Turanist understanding, especially on the issue of the sociohistorical roots of the Turkish "nation." For instance, Şadan refuted standard Turanist narratives—metastasized in the official history writing—that glorified Central Asian shamanic culture as the purest form of Turkish culture. To the contrary, Şadan identified Central Asian shamanism as a neurotic culture that carried within it homosexual tendencies, which it shares with Christianity and Sufism.[69] That is precisely why he rejected Central Asian culture and shamanic symbols as the foundation or origin for Turkishhood and the Turkish nation.

Provincializing Freudian psychoanalysis?

The emergence of a new form of psychoanalysis within the Turkish context also challenges the idea of psychoanalysis as a definitive, monolithic Western discourse. The reification of new renderings of psychoanalysis in different regions under different conditions prompts the question of the plausible impact of those new formulations on psychoanalysis as it was shaped in the first half of the twentieth century by Freud and other founders of the discipline in the West.

An article Şadan published in 1932 in *Imago*, the psychoanalytic journal under the editorial direction of Freud, offers a striking example of this issue. There, through an analysis of the Sufi legend of Merkez Efendi, Şadan points to the oedipal and castration complexes that are, according to him, apparent within the manifest and symbolic content of this particular Muslim (Sufi) legend.[70] In 1948, nine years after Freud's death, Şadan claimed in a letter to the *Psychoanalytic Quarterly* that some of Freud's ideas in *Moses and Monotheism* (published in 1939) postdated his own ideas on the dynamics of the unconscious underlying monotheistic religions. His ideas on the subject matter, Şadan emphasized, were previously admitted by Freud and were published in *Imago*; nonetheless, they were not publicly acknowledged in Freud's later work. This is how he put it:

> The first psychoanalytic study of monotheism was written by me (Izeddin, A.: Eine Mohammedanische Legende. *Imago*, XVIII, 1932, 189–213). There I showed—a fact admitted by Freud himself since he had the article translated into German—that psychoanalytic mechanisms discovered previously, and originating from polytheistic legends could be applied to monotheistic folklore. Freud's analysis postdates mine by six years, and no one during that period has published anything on that subject. So much for the question of priority .... I have written this letter not so much to criticize an author [Freud] whom I esteem, but rather to establish an outmoded fact, as well as to obtain justice for my work, meager as it may be. The facts are there.[71]

It might be easy to dismiss Şadan's claim on the issue, particularly since his *Imago* article did not deal explicitly with the question of monotheism in Islam. Nevertheless, a more nuanced consideration of Şadan's claim, which was also taken seriously by *Psychoanalytic Quarterly* in 1948, would be to evaluate it within the literature that reads modernity and modern science not as centered in the post-Enlightenment Western world or as one-dimensional—that is, flowing from West to the "rest"—but as multidimensional, thus lacking an exact center, and ensuing out of complex, multilayered, and yet asymmetrical relations between the different parts of the world.[72]

Apart from Şadan, Freud was in contact with many other psychiatrists and psychoanalysis in the world. The well-known intellectual exchanges that continued for almost two decades between Freud and Girindrasekhar Bose (1887–1953), an Indian psychoanalyst, is a good example. Although an admirer of Freud, Bose questioned the universality of some of Freud's foundational concepts, including the oedipal complex and castration anxiety, which, according to him, do not correspond with his own findings derived from his research and practice in India.[73]

I do not mean to lump Şadan and Bose together or to align the significance of their psychoanalytic formulations on their local or transnational communities. I instead attempt to ponder how (and in what ways) such conflicting findings and conceptualizations, as they were articulated within non-Western cultural settings, were reflected in Freudian and other early psychoanalytic formations in the West. Within such a framework, Şadan's case, despite being at times a far cry from the nuanced arguments of Freud, might enable us to shed some light on a small piece of what might be an enormous puzzle of intricate interactions and influences within psychoanalysis in the world at large.

Conclusion

Şadan's case displays the complex and convoluted layers of meanings and configurations of science, health, pathology, history, and society in Turkey through a historical account of the sort of psychoanalysis emerging in the early republican Turkish context. At the same time, it discloses the kind of psychiatrist and intellectual Şadan became in Turkey by and through his engagement with Western psychoanalytic discourse and its formative disciplinary mechanisms. Focusing on Şadanian psychoanalysis, therefore, is illustrative because it sheds ample light on the interactions, correlations, and mutual constitutive effects between various different structures and discourses in early republican Turkey, such as positivism, psychoanalysis, nationalism, secularism, and the Sunni Islamic tradition, many of which are believed to be contradictory, incompatible, and incommensurable.

Focusing on Şadan's psychoanalytic writings also provides certain indications regarding the possible impact of Şadan's new rendering of psychoanalysis on psychoanalysis at its European center and in the hands of its so-called father, Sigmund Freud. This novel Turkish interpretation of psychoanalysis, as we have seen in Şadan's analytic claims on the neuroses of Christianity and the Western world, challenges the universality of Freudian psychoanalysis as well as the cultural superiority claims of the West, even though it constructs its arguments utilizing Western forms of rationality and is constituted by a secular scientific approach par excellence. Şadanian psychoanalytic discourse, however, in contrast to a Western psychoanalytic discourse that is predicated on the Judeo-Christian liberal tradition, appears to be an outcome of the Sunni-Islamic trajectory, and shaped epistemologically within the context and problem spaces of early republican Turkish culture and society.

CHAPTER 2

Crosscurrents between the development of psychoanalysis and self psychology in Turkey

Yavuz Erten

In this contribution, I will first offer information about the development and institutionalization of psychoanalysis and self psychology in Turkey based upon my historical testimony and experience. Then I will give my thoughts on the reasons for the late arrival of psychoanalysis in Turkey. Finally, I will write about the current state of psychoanalysis and self psychology in our country.

Until the mid-1990s, there was no formal institutionalization in Turkey except for some informal efforts. In addition to the analysts who studied psychoanalysis abroad and returned to Turkey, a change began to occur when Turkish analysts living abroad started to train candidates in the country in shuttle format. Talat Parman, an analyst who was trained in the SPP (Société Psychanalytique de Paris), returned to Turkey and launched an IPA-affiliated effort, while Vamık Volkan, a Cypriot Turk living in the United States, visited Turkey regularly and started analytically training a group of psychiatrists. They called themselves the "Volkan Group." I decided to go down an entirely different path with a group of mental health workers who were not part of either group and who were interested in self psychology and relational psychoanalysis. That is how the story started.

I posted a message to Ernest Wolf on the self psychology website in 1997. I was not very hopeful about getting an answer. But at the same time, I was saying to myself "Why not?" A part of me was saying that I would not get any results, but another part was expecting a response from self psychology, the psychoanalytical school that stood out from others mainly with its "responsiveness." Our group originally consisted of almost thirty people: psychiatrists, clinical psychologists, child psychologists, psychological counselors, and social workers, who started coming together in late 1990s, who laid out the foundation of the group, participating in seminars, workshops, and supervision groups led by local as well as foreign trainers. Group members came from the three big cities of Turkey: İstanbul, Ankara, and İzmir. A significant number of them were interested in psychoanalysis and self psychology and were reading Kohut's books (1971, 1977) and papers (1972, 1982). They were willing to study psychoanalysis and self psychology thoroughly. On a sunny winter's day, the answer appeared on my monitor. Ernest Wolf had written a truly kind and supportive response and suggested that Dr. Allen Siegel would be a helpful resource to our group. The year 1998 was the beginning of the relationship between our group and Allen Siegel.

Together with Allen Siegel from the Chicago Psychoanalytic Institute who soon got in contact with us, I shaped the project of creating the opportunity for a psychoanalytic psychotherapy training in Turkey, and a training process ensued with a group of around thirty people through 1998 to 2004. This group of thirty people first called itself the Self Psychology Society and then assumed the name the Anatolian Group of Psychoanalytic Psychotherapies. Many analysts have come to Turkey as trainers within the scope of this training that was predominantly oriented toward self psychology. Teleconferences were organized via visual and/or audio links. Cyber-supervisions spanning years were conducted. During this process, nearly half of the group members started their analyses with local analysts.

Allen and Renee Siegel made their first visit in October 1988 and spent a week with the group. This first seminar, where Heinz Kohut's fundamental principles were studied, comprised a hopeful beginning to a long journey for the group. During their stay in Turkey, Allen and Renee Siegel also developed their first impressions of the shortcomings and needs of group members, the structure of the culture, and the condition of mental health professions in Turkey.

At that point, a decision was made to secure the continuity of training activities. Continuity and concentration could not be achieved through a couple of visits every year. Hence, technological equipment was obtained, and a tele-conferencing system via telephone link was developed. Dr. Allen Siegel and the group started two-hour meetings with the help of this equipment once every six weeks. These meetings, which were held over five years until 2004, started out mainly theoretically, but were largely allocated to case presentations in the last two years. These meetings were held on Sundays in İstanbul and Ankara, following a certain schedule. Every meeting takes seven hours. During the first two hours, Kohut's books were read and discussed chapter by chapter by the group. In the following two hours, the group read and discussed other important papers on self psychology. After a coffee break, Dr. Siegel was contacted by phone, and the training as mentioned above is carried out.

In May 2000, Dr. Allen Siegel and Renee Siegel were our guests in the first part of "Symposium 2000," which was centered on "narcissism." The guests for the second part of this symposium in October were Anna and Paul Ornstein. Each couple spent one week with us. These trainings, which were very satisfying, also proved to be rich and fiery opportunities to compare self psychology with other psychoanalytical schools of thought.

Meanwhile Dr. Siegel was also coming up with other resources of information for the group. Group members could list tape recordings of meetings of self psychologists held in the Chicago Psychoanalytic Institute. An important part of the group also subscribed to the *Journal of the American Psychoanalytic Association* (JAPA) with a special offer we obtained. Some of our members participated in the self psychology meetings in USA and represented our group. They were always received with great hospitality.

In June 2001, Dr. Joseph Lichtenberg visited İstanbul for a three-day seminar on motivational systems. In this warm meeting, conditions of membership for the International Federation of Psychoanalytic Societies (IFPS) were discussed with Dr. Lichtenberg. In November 2001, Dr. Allen Siegel visited İstanbul, and presented his paper "Heinz Kohut and co-created space and time in the psychology of the self" at one of what became known as "İstanbul Psychoanalysis Meetings." This meeting, which was mostly attended by classical analysts of the French school, witnessed a discussion between André Green and Allen Siegel. Within the scope of this visit, Allen Siegel and Dr. Chris Joannidis from the British Psychoanalytical Society made a comparison between self psychology and the object relations school based on a case presentation in a two-day workshop.

The year 2001 witnessed another major step for our group. Group members started to get supervision in subgroups of four or five people via email. Group supervisors were (in alphabetical order): Denise Davies, Connie Goldberg, Ruth Gruenthal, Sally Jenkins, Anna Ornstein, Allen Siegel, Renee Siegel, David Solomon, and Dori Sorter. With this new initiative, the basic need for supervision was met to a certain extent. By 2001, our group started looking for a name to represent its identity. The goal was to provide the group with an identity reflecting its activities and relationships on a national and international basis. The group chose the name "Anatolia" (Anatolian Group of Psychoanalytic Psychotherapies).

In the year 2002, Allen Siegel, Arnold Goldberg, and Connie Goldberg visited İstanbul to train Anatolian members. Allen Siegel, who was the director of the training, offered the resources of the Chicago Psychoanalytic Institute throughout this process. After 2004 the institute developed a distance learning model of psychoanalytic psychotherapy training linked to the Chicago Institute for Turkey. With this program realized via an advanced internet program yet another class of students was trained. Sibel Mercan who was one of the pioneering members of the group replaced me and assumed all responsibility in post-2004 activities for some years.

In the meantime, certain contacts and interactions were taking place within psychoanalysis circles in Turkey. In 2001 we had some first contacts with Bella Habip who was an IPA (International Psychoanalytical Association) member Turkish analyst and we began to give serious consideration to collaboration. Habip met with the Anatolian group members many times and conducted seminars and case studies. Habip was also the member of SPP (Société Psychanalytique de Paris). Thereby, after American psychoanalysis, the Anatolian Group also got acquainted with French psychoanalysis. Meanwhile the number of group members who were starting analysis was increasing well.

During this zealous period through 2001 to 2004, we developed a project of transforming this initiative into an association, and in 2003, Bella Habip, I, and Anatolian Group members

Melis Tanık, Berrak Ciğeroğlu, Leyla Tanoğlu, Pınar Koçak, İrem Anlı, and Sibel Mercan founded "the İstanbul Association for Psychoanalysis and Psychoanalytic Psychotherapies." This is how the association which is now called Psike İstanbul was founded. Almost half of the original Anatolian Group became members of this new association. These members were mostly ones who had been under psychoanalysis on the couch.

There are other details pertaining to these years that should not be left out. In 2001, the IPA commissioned Ülkü Gurışık and Marie Lise Roux to prepare a report on the situation in Turkey. The duo during their site visit met with the representatives of all groups in Turkey (and with me on behalf of the Anatolian Group). This is how I first met Ülkü Gurışık. Later that year, Gurışık contacted me and informed me that the American analyst Antoine Hani was responsible for starting a psychoanalytic training in Turkey, sponsored by the IPA. I met with Antoine Hani two times, first in 2002 with Allen Siegel in Washington, DC where Hani lived, and then in Estonia hosted by the East European School of Psychoanalysis, to which he invited me and the members of the Anatolian Group (Berrak Ciğeroğlu, Melis Tanık, İrem Anlı, Gökmen Tokgöz, Ayşe Özalkuş Şahin, and Alper Şahin). During these two meetings, Hani said that Vamık Volkan presented the project of a psychoanalysis school in Turkey to the IPA Training Committee and that the leadership, which included Hani, was evaluating this proposal. I thought it was very favorable toward the proposal. He also said that he was particularly impressed by the Anatolian Group and that we should take part in this endeavor. Vamık Volkan was also in Estonia. We met him both individually and as a group.

Later on, we got the information that the Turkish psychoanalytic school project would be realized in a format similar to that implemented in Eastern European countries, but it would include all the groups in Turkey. The IPA appointed a Sponsoring Committee for this project. The first two members of this committee, Abigail Golomb and Marie-France Dispaux, visited Turkey twice, at the beginning of the process. They held separate meetings with the groups in Turkey. We attended the first meeting as a delegation representing most of the Anatolian Group members named above and Bella Habip. In addition to us, meetings were also held with representatives of the İstanbul Psychoanalytical Association led by Talat Parman and the Volkan Group. The committee's conclusion appeared on the lines of opening separate classes for these groups. However, at the same time, the committee was also trying to understand whether these groups could come together through a certain agreement.

As I mentioned above, around the same time, the Anatolian Group was taking steps in collaboration with Bella Habip to become an association. It seemed that this association, just like the İstanbul Psychoanalytical Association, would become one of the local organizers of the psychoanalysis school in Turkey. What did members of the Volkan Group think? Through my meetings with Ozden Terbas who was the member of both the Anatolian Group and Volkan Group, I learned that they were also thinking of founding an association. Considering the wish of the committee for the groups to unite, could the association we have founded merge with the Volkan Group? There were no irreconcilable differences or incongruities between the two groups despite theoretical differences. Many people from both sides were friends personally.

Furthermore, individuals from both groups had collaborated in two symposiums organized by the Volkan Group.

In 2004, the IPA's Sponsoring Committee made its first candidacy interviews. And in the fall of 2004 the dream of many years came true: An initiative providing psychoanalysis training under the monitoring and supervising of the IPA was founded in İstanbul. By this development, a split emerged in the Anatolian Group. Almost half of the group took part in this new association and became the candidates in the formal IPA training; the other half chose to stay in the original group and out of the formal IPA training.

To clarify the situation, I must say that our journey with Siegel was shaped by the increasingly evident wish of group members to get analytic training and become IPA members. On the other hand, on our end, our work with Allen Siegel constitutes one of the most important parts of our process. Allen Siegel and his wife Renee Siegel have made extraordinary contributions to the training process of the Anatolian Group. Siegel's strong talent for organization, advanced adaptive talents, and emphatic personality are elements that should always be remembered and appreciated in terms of where we are today. Without Allen Siegel and his first six years of training, the former members of the Anatolian Group could have not taken part in the newly emerging project of the IPA in İstanbul. Without doubt we could not have accepted an invitation by the site-visiting committee of the IPA. By the existence of the Anatolian Group, though informal, we became a center which attracted the attention of the IPA.

With the parting from the Anatolian Group and the subsequent association foundation process, Anatolian Group members who did not partake in the IPA process continued to work with Allen Siegel. Sibel Mercan, who also participated in the IPA process, assumed the leadership of the Anatolian Group and managed the distant psychoanalytic psychotherapy school project together with Allen Siegel successfully. Additionally, this team was also the local partner of the International Conference on the Psychology of the Self in Antalya, Turkey, in 2010.

We must say that the separation we experienced with Siegel was difficult emotionally for both Siegel and us. We also experienced mourning and guilt regarding our friends from whom we separated with this process.

Why was psychoanalysis late to arrive in Turkey?

Thinking over why psychoanalysis was late to be institutionalized in Turkey, I would like to draw a historical conclusion first: though communist regimes were friendly in the beginning, especially after Stalinist policies became more victorious and dominant, psychoanalysis was ignored—or even suppressed—as a scientific discipline in the Eastern Bloc. Psychoanalytical knowledge was discarded from mental health education, the access to Freud's books was—almost—prohibited. By the collapse of communist regimes in the 1990s, psychoanalysis suddenly attracted an increasing number of people in Eastern Europe and Russia, and many psychologists and psychiatrists visited Western European countries through "shuttle analysis" and joined psychoanalytic training programs. Many analysts visited the United States and Western Europe regularly to provide training for these countries. This increasing interest was sown later in the first seeds of the psychoanalytic institutions in these countries. Though Turkey was not governed by a communist regime, it also exhibited the same developments in the arena of psychoanalysis in the 1990s almost simultaneously with the countries mentioned. Turkey implemented a mixed economic model, which was mainly state oriented until the 1980s. We could assume that this model was relatively disconnected from the global capitalism in much of the world. High protective rates, strict foreign currency policies, and low export rates considerably limited foreign investment, while low quality touristic activities, and restrictions meaning that Turkish citizens could go abroad very rarely or with difficulties, closed Turkey to the global world to a serious extent. Turkey, which had been influenced by global capitalism through liberal politics in the late 1980s, has experienced some transformations like that of communist countries. How can we relate this transformation, which can be evaluated positively or negatively depending on differing ideological perspectives, to the fact that psychoanalysis at last became an institutional organization? Is it just a coincidence? When we consider not only psychoanalysis but also other aspects of life, it is not easy to say that it is a coincidence. However, the developments in the late 1980s seemed to lead to liberalization in terms of economic freedom, which was not the only consequence. Turkey experienced novel developments which were not seen in the country before the freedom of thinking and religion in the 1990s and 2000s. After the late 1980s, ethnic freedom movements (covering culture and language and bringing about political conclusions) emerged.

In these periods, Turkish society was more encouraged to face up with its past. As Gürdal Küey (2009) said, we could not talk about a development of psychoanalysis in an environment where people did not face themselves and could not talk about their secrets. As in an individual psychoanalytic process, it must go back to the forgotten, to those who were forgotten, to embrace what was also forgotten, to embrace what was psychic, to mourn about unfinished processes, to pay for the unpaid, to be brave to face that avoidance of the process of sociopsychological research and coming face-to-face with oneself. In the 1990s, the official historical discourse that had dominated since the beginning of the century was evaluated through different perspectives; people could approach the issues critically. These developments caused what was hitherto suppressed, denied, and dissociated to emerge.

Habip (2004) wrote a good essay contemplating the answers to this question of "Why are we late?", reminding us of the fact that psychoanalytical knowledge and background can be formed within a psychoanalytical relationship. An essential characteristic of this relationship is that the transference is visualized and turns into insight within the psyche throughout the analysis. We can consider that the fact that there were few or no people learning psychoanalysis within this relationship of transference until the 1990s stunted the development of psychoanalytical background.

Therefore, psychoanalytical background cannot go beyond intellectual interest and institutional information. That psychoanalytical background could not be formed within the psychoanalytical relationship—and so through the development and analysis of the relationship of transference—did not render it possible to create a psychoanalytical tradition and culture to be transferred from one generation to another, which is essential to the establishment of psychoanalysis. Hence, an intergenerational relationship in which the analyzed ones became the analyzing ones in a later generation could not be formed until the 1990s.

At this point, I would like to focus on the language. The analyses of the first analysts could not be realized within this culture. The first analysts had to be analyzed by a member of another culture who speaks another language. Can the cultural background, where the relationship of transference occurs, and the cultural elements of this relationship be read totally by a member of another culture? Can a person reflect within another language system to achieve an analytical process that provides associative deepening from consciousness to pre-consciousness, and from here to unconsciousness, and traces the metonyms?

We can be hopeful to overcome this difficulty if we think that every psychoanalytical work is an anthropological participation both literally and metaphorically. If such a solution were impossible, there would not be a way for psychoanalysis to become a worldwide discipline. Nevertheless, as far as culture in Turkey is concerned, we should—by reconsidering the delay issue—take some points related to the case in this specific culture into account. In an overwhelming number of cultures where psychoanalytical institutions were rooted, Jewish and Christian elements should not be ignored. Historically speaking, psychoanalysis had met the "others," that is, some non-Christian or non-Jewish cultures before it met the culture in Turkey. In some of these, apart from individual participation of the analysts, institutional delay and difficulties are like those in Turkey. The institutionalization of psychoanalysis in Turkey is now one of the scarce examples apart from the Jewish–Christian bloc. In the vast geographical terrain of Islam, Turkey is an exception.

Habip (2004) underlines the issue that "the father couldn't be killed," related to the delay problem in the institutionalization of psychoanalysis in Turkey. A scion of every generation surmounts his father, predecessors, gains a critical distance, kills their images formed through the eyes of his childhood, describes himself and them in a new relationship within a process of acquiring his own personality and becoming mature psychologically. It is the very first step in the way adulthood is attained through opposition. If there are no challenges and reactions such as this, the subject cannot get rid of the huge gravity of childish dependence. He or she would be stuck in the earth like a rocket that would never be soaring from the world. If psychological maturing goes along with such a trajectory, realistic evaluations take the place of childish over-idealizations and adolescent deglamorization. In Turkish culture, both in the period of the Republic and in the previous periods, those founders, religious and political leaders, and administrators have an immunity that makes it impossible to grow in such a process. The individual and/or sociocultural process of analysis is not only possible when the subject analyzes his own deepening and his own psyche, but also when he analyzes the other he is connected to (with whom he narcissistically becomes united and wants to incorporate; whom he ambivalently disagrees with and wants to spit out; whom he oedipally fights and identifies himself with their defeat). In a situation where the other has some secrets, protects with his secrets, gains immunity, and turns into a taboo for a subject, we cannot talk about the existence of psychoanalysis.

Let's consider finally a point indicated by Tunaboylu İkiz and Arkonaç (2004). This point is related to the "father killing" issue, too. The Enlightenment-based modernization initiatives of the leaders of society in Turkey, going on since the "Tanzimat" (Reformation and Reorganization launched by the Ottoman Empire in 1839), developed with a reactionary quality and bore a formalism to get rid of the past and urgently gain a new identity and personality more than a work of quality with intellectual depth and significance. This approach was overstated in the period of the Republic as it tried to bury the father by repressing him into amnesia.

One of the important elements of this project is that positivism became an ideological reference immune to questioning (Tunaboylu İkiz, 2011). In the period of the Republic, especially through university reforms, all the doors were opened to Western science, but Eastern wisdom was imprisoned in the old coffins of the religious personalities. As underlined by Tunaboylu İkiz and Arkonaç (2004), positivistic, objective, and measurable techniques were relevant tools for experts working on human psychology in the universities of the young Turkish Republic. All hermeneutic disciplines dismissed by logical positivism were suspicious. No need to talk about "psyche" when the researchers have the brain and the nervous system in their scope.

Many losses, the sense of guilt and narcissistic hurt in the beginning of the twentieth century (especially by the defeat of the First World War, the defeat by the West also in respect of civilization and the collapse of its empires), had been pushed into the unconscious because there was no agency to work on and metabolize these. Later, when some mechanisms such as denial, projection, and dissociation were required to set up a nation state (the modern Turkish Republic in the 1920s), people got considerably away from the issues unmetabolized in the unconscious. Border walls were empowered with a new history and a new language.

After the first generation, the second generation did not seem interested in the missing part of the history/story either. The third generation started asking questions, was curious, did research. This movement of the third generation is concurrent with the efforts of questioning history and trying to break the taboos in the official history of the Republic of Turkey. During the time of the third generation, that is, in the final quarter of the century, various secrets, unanswered questions, traumas, crimes found at the crossroads of the nineteenth and twentieth centuries began to be questioned. Like the darkness at the social level, there were also secrets, taboos, and traumas in every family. It was as if the first generation had been forgotten and had forgotten that it had been forgotten. The second generation had abided by the law of silence but also had to deal with all the symptoms of this repression. Usually, that which was repressed was not remembered but was constantly repeated through enactments. That which was not remembered was being enacted with various castings. Like the Barangers (Baranger et al., 1983) we can name these resilient scenes as the "bastion." However, the third generation began to keep a certain intellectual and emotional distance from these scenes and ponder the meaning of these violent acts.

The third generation started asking questions and explored the issues they continued to encounter in their lives but could not symbolize. They faced an "enigmatic signifier" (Laplanche, 1989) about the origins and they tried to solve it (Micco, 2017). With the efforts of the third generation, the things that could not be spoken about would be voiced at the individual and social level. A mute history began to talk. We comprehended these on the social level, and on the individual level as analysts and analysands in the psychoanalytic rooms where we experienced the coming to light of various family secrets, laws of silence, and taboos (Erten, 2017).

By concluding this section, I am aware that I am giving a positive impression about today's situation in my country. This may be confusing if the reader is someone who watches TV and reads newspaper each day. Even though the social and political events of the last decade have assumed the image of a complication, I think this complication is still part of the above-mentioned developments. I believe that what Turkey is currently experiencing is a negative therapeutic reaction (Asch, 1976; Freud, 1923b; Olinick, 1964). Or I want to believe that. I am observing that the revived nationalism, dogmatism, and denialist approaches to history are but a repeated, exaggerated drift to the pathological pole in response to which has emerged, from the efforts of the third generation, the progress that has been attained; just as in negative therapeutic reactions. The pendulum will find time to find its center of balance.

Problem of timing: Being late or too early

The institutionalized mainstream psychoanalysis came to Turkey with a century's delay. The most recent school of psychoanalysis (self psychology and relatedly, relational psychology) came—maybe—too early in respect of the delay of the previous one.

The most active times of the Anatolian Group were especially concentrated in the late 1990s and early 2000s. The group got into a stagnation when almost half of the members participated in the establishment of an IPA-sponsored association (Psike İstanbul), with the members from the other groups in Turkey.

Why and what kind of recession did Anatolia live? How should we explain the revival after more than a decade? Of course, the most concrete and understandable explanation of the stagnation is the departure of some of the members of the Anatolian Group (these members were mostly executive ones, including me), who got into the IPA project and participated in the establishment of Psike İstanbul. But I think this separation is not a cause, it is a result.

Just as the entry of mainstream psychoanalysis into Turkey after one hundred years was a delay, it was also premature to start the process with self psychology and/or relational psychoanalysis for a professional group that had not yet fully understood mainstream psychoanalysis thoroughly, had not had any experience with it, and did not take it into its inner world with its positive and negative aspects in its practice—not only with what it reads from books, but also with its own personal analysis.

Mental health professionals who encountered all the earlier schools of psychoanalysis in the Western world on different planes, as therapists, analysts, supervisors, and supervisees, established contemporary psychoanalytic theories and practices with criticism, opposition, and alternatives that formed in their souls and minds as these experiences matured. Without these experiences in Turkey, the previous stages were suddenly intellectually omitted and reached the final stage.

What are my conclusions from the past twenty-three years? Self psychology and its sub-schools, which we are interested in at the beginning of the process and want to develop in Turkey, are the product of evolution and development in the one-hundred-year history of psychoanalysis in the Western world. It did not seem possible to import and apply these schools without comprehending the previous theoretical, institutional, and practical development of psychoanalysis and without traveling through various parallel processes of this evolution. For this reason, after producing, owning, and comprehending the theoretical, institutional, and practical experiences of mainstream psychoanalysis in these lands, meeting with contemporary schools again in the light of this experience makes this "second reunion" richer and deeper.

I strongly believe that self psychology and relational psychoanalysis have a future in Turkey. The roots of the past that created this future are the nuclei that Allen Siegel planted in the 1990s and continued to develop independently, as well as the fact that some of those first seeds then went through a mainstream formation and continued to develop within an IPA-affiliated institution.

Moreover, some of the theories and practices within today's mainstream psychoanalysis have come closer to the theoretical and technical propositions of self psychology and its sub-schools, which had been evaluated as an exit from psychoanalysis at the 1970s. I recommend anyone who suspects what I am saying to participate in an IPA or EPF (European Psychoanalytical Federation) scientific meeting to see the existence of the presentations which are very close to self psychology and/or relational psychoanalysis (sometimes giving references and credits to them, sometimes not).

CHAPTER 3

Psychoanalysis, Turkey, and the IPA*

Vamık D. Volkan

As I write this in 2010, there are sixteen psychoanalysts who are members of the International Psychoanalytical Association and two IPA-approved training centers in Turkey, both in İstanbul. Turkey is a secular country, with a population of about 73 million persons, of whom 99 percent are Muslims. Other analysts with Muslim backgrounds who are members of the IPA have been practicing in the United States, Europe, and elsewhere for many decades. As illustrated in Salman Akhtar's book, *The Crescent and the Couch: Crosscurrents between Islam and Psychoanalysis* (2008), some of these analysts have contributed greatly to psychoanalytic theory and technique. Even so, the IPA's initial involvement in a country with a Muslim population was groundbreaking. This chapter tells this story.

In order to have a clearer picture of how psychoanalysis evolved in Turkey, however, I will first go far back in history and provide a bird's eye view of how the Turks dealt with mental health issues under the influence of Islam, and then fast-forward to the 1930s to illustrate the initial reception of Freud's ideas in Turkey. I will describe how one German analyst escaping from the Third Reich played an especially significant role in introducing psychoanalysis in the new Republic of Turkey, which was founded in 1923 from the ashes of the Ottoman Empire.

---

*This chapter was originally published as Volkan, V. (2011). Psychoanalysis, Turkey, and the IPA. In: P. Loewenberg & N. L. Thompson (Eds.), *100 Years of the IPA* (pp. 419–434). Abingdon, UK: Routledge.

Turks and the Islamic tradition for caring for persons with mental problems

The Turks created two large empires in Central Asia before their Western migration during the ninth and tenth centuries. They filled the vacuum left by the fall of the Arabic Islamic Empire and adopted the faith of Islam and eventually established the Ottoman Empire, which lasted from 1299 to 1923. After its collapse at the end of the First World War, the Republic of Turkey was born under the leadership of Mustafa Kemal, who later took the surname Atatürk.

Let us go back to a book entitled *Kutadgu-Bilig*, which was written in Turkish in 1069. Passages in this book describe the *efsuncu*—people who warded off jinns (demons) and occupied a role just below *hekim* (medical men) in the social hierarchy. The same book gives an account of disagreements between efsuncus who treated their patients with "suggestions" and those medical men who scorned such methods (Gökay, 1969; Ünver, 1943; Volkan, 1975). When Yusuf Hasi Hacib wrote *Kutadgu-Bilig*, Avicenna (also known as Ibni Sina), the great Islamic physician, had been dead for thirty-two years. It is believed that he was a Persian, but in Turkey many scholars dispute his ethnic origin and often refer to him as a Turkish healer who, like other scholars of his time wrote in Persian (Gökay, 1969). Avicenna was aware of mania and depression and the importance of good child-rearing practices in preventing mental problems.

Before the Ottomans, Seljuk Turks had established an empire in Anatolia. They were great builders, and their principal innovation was the *madrassa* (or *medrese*) (Cahen, 1968). Today we associate madrassas in Afghanistan, Pakistan, and elsewhere with locations where future extreme fundamentalist Islamic terrorists are brainwashed and trained (Volkan, 1997; Volkan & Kayatekin, 2006) but during the Seljuk period the madrassa was an establishment for the teaching of the religio-judicial sciences (Cahen, 1968). Urban communities with schools, libraries, fountains, baths, and hospitals were established around madrassas, including several hospitals built between 1205 and 1308 that had sections for the care of the mentally ill. Besides these hospitals, *tekkes* (houses of sufitic beliefs) were erected throughout the country. *Tekkes* were religious and philosophical establishments that also offered humane treatment for people with mental problems, reflecting the traditional understanding of mental illness that grew from the belief that all goodness and suffering comes from God, and the reasons God inflicts pain on mankind are beyond human understanding (Volkan, 1975).

When the Ottoman Empire came to power following the disappearance of the Seljuk Empire, the Ottomans continued building madrassas and hospitals and erecting *tekkes*, and in most towns there were also separate hospitals for "infidels." In 1470 they opened a hospital in İstanbul for the exclusive use of persons with mental problems. This followed many similar hospitals in various locations in the Empire. Although Muslim Arabs had built institutions for the mentally ill before the Turks did, it was the latter who, by becoming the champions of Islam, not only carried out the Islamic tradition of benevolent treatment of persons with mental problems, but made further improvements in their care (Adasal, 1964; Erkoc, 2004; Öztürk & Volkan, 1971). For example, the hospital in Edirne that was built during the reign of Beyazid II (1481–1512) had individual rooms for the patients, with an open dome and a soothing fountain in the middle; at one of the dais musicians played to calm and distract the residents (Lewis, 1971).

During the final three centuries of the Ottoman Empire, every aspect of medical care declined, including that for the mentally troubled. Sultan Abdülhamid II, whose reign spanned the years between 1876 and 1909, was afraid of the "insane." Although this story might be exaggerated, we know that during this reign Topkapi Hospital, the main hospital in İstanbul for those with mental illness, became a virtual prison for those confined there. The patient death rate there was high, and at one time the Sultan's permission was required to visit the place. When Emil Kraepelin visited İstanbul and asked to see the hospital, he was unable to obtain permission to do so (Adasal, 1964).

There were also attempts in the Ottoman Empire at modernization. In 1898 the first modern neuropsychiatric clinic was opened by a Turkish physician named Raşit Tahsin, who had studied with Kraepelin. Following Raşit Tahsin, prominent Turkish physicians dealing with mental illness become followers of Kraepelin, among them Mahzar Osman, who had also studied with him.

During the First World War the allies occupied many parts of the Ottoman Empire, including parts of Anatolia, the heartland of the Turks. The Empire collapsed, and the Caliphate ended. Following a war of independence under Mustafa Kemal's leadership, the Turkish Republic was born. Even though Western powers were the enemies of the Turks, Mustafa Kemal Atatürk, as the first president of Turkey, led in westernizing and modernizing the new republic. His political/cultural revolution included the establishment of a parliamentary government, language and educational reforms, the closing of *tekkes* (Sufic houses), the emancipation of women, changing the dress style, allowing painting and erecting human figures (previously not allowed according to the Muslim tradition), creating the Turkish opera, and, most importantly, establishing secularism. In Atatürk's Turkey, interest in psychoanalysis began in Ankara, then a dusty little city that had become the capital of the new republic, rather than the capital of the now-vanished Ottoman Empire, İstanbul. The followers of Kraepelin in İstanbul, led by Mahzar Osman, dominated the psychiatric scene.

Mustafa Kemal Atatürk's Turkey and psychoanalysis

When Norman Itzkowitz and I (Volkan & Itzkowitz, 1984) were writing a psychobiography of Mustafa Kemal Atatürk, we learned that when he was Turkey's first president, he sometimes had severe problems with his teeth, and he had a special relationship with his dentist, Sami (Samuel) Gunzberg, a Turkish citizen of Jewish origin. We know that Gunzberg gave a great deal of information about Nazi Germany to the Turkish leader. Mustafa Kemal as a young man studied French and German and, prior to his becoming a national hero, had visited France and Germany. Ever since his days at the military college in İstanbul, he had been interested in reading the works of Western thinkers. He was a "reparative leader" (Volkan, 2009). Although we cannot attribute his aversion toward what was happening in Nazi Germany to his relationship with his dentist, nevertheless we believe that Gunzberg was influential. Some years after we published our psychobiography of the Turkish leader, during a trip to Jerusalem, I learned from Hebrew University historian Professor Gavriel Cohen that Samuel Gunzberg was the leader of a group of Jewish people helping other Jews to flee from Germany to Turkey.

A letter written by Albert Einstein on 17 September, 1933 to the president of the Cabinet of Ministers of the Republic of Turkey was discovered in October 2006. In 1933, Einstein lived in France and was the honorary president of OZE (Organization for the Protection of the Jewish Population). In his letter Einstein asks the president of the Cabinet of Ministers

> To allow forty professors and doctors from Germany to continue their scientific and medical work in Turkey. The above mentioned cannot practice further in Germany on account of the laws governing there now. The majority of these men possess vast experience, knowledge and scientific merits and could prove very useful when settling in a new country.

OZE would pay their salaries during the first year of their stay in Turkey. The letter ends in the following way: "In supporting this application, I take the liberty to express my hope, that in granting this request your Government will not only perform an act of high humanity, but will also bring profit to your own country."

On the document there is a handwritten instruction by İsmet İnönü, who was, at that time, the prime minister and Mustafa Kemal's right-hand man. This instruction sent Einstein's request to the Turkish Ministry of Education. The ministry rejected conditions to accept such an unusual request. But Einstein's request was accepted when Mustafa Kemal intervened. We have no document that illustrates Sami Gunzberg's role in Einstein's writing the letter and in Mustafa Kemal's positive response to it. We know only that the ten-year-old, very poor Turkish Republic had allowed some German-Jewish scholars to come to Turkey even before Einstein's request (Günergün, 2006). In 1933, thirty German-Jewish scholars and their families came to Turkey. Eventually 190 intellectuals and their families arrived, ultimately saving over 1,000 lives (Reisman, 2006).

Among the German-Jewish intellectuals who fled to Turkey was Professor Oscar Weigert. He would become a consultant to Atatürk in changing the attitude of Turkish men toward labor, bringing labor out of its feudal state and introducing such ideas as the eight-hour day, regular vacations for workers, workers' compensation, and the idea of organizing Turkish labor unions (Weigert, 1937). Professor Weigert's wife was an ethnic German, psychoanalyst Edith Vowinckel Weigert. She accompanied her husband to Turkey in 1935 and spent more than three years in Ankara before she and her husband went to the United States (Uşak-Şahin, 2009a, 2009b; Volkan & Itzkowitz, 1984). When I was accepted as psychoanalytic candidate at the Washington Psychoanalytic Institute in the mid-1960s, because I was a Turk, who had migrated to the United States a few years earlier, I was asked to start my training analysis with Edith Weigert, with the idea that she was familiar with the Turkish culture. I did not become Edith Weigert's analysand because at that time she had broken a bone and had to recuperate. However, during my last year of psychoanalytic training she functioned as one of my supervisors, and in the late 1970s, when Norman Itzkowitz and I began our training she functioned as one of my supervisors, and when Norman Itzkowitz and I began to write our psychobiography of Atatürk she was helpful by describing her life in Ankara, her perception of Atatürk, and her activities as a psychoanalyst in Turkey.

Edith Vowinckel Weigert was born in 1894 in Düsseldorf and settled in Berlin, where she was trained as a psychiatrist and psychoanalyst. She became a member of the German Psychoanalytical Society (DPG) and served on the board of the DPG as a training analyst as the Nazi regime began. The *Bulletin of the International Psychoanalytical Association* includes her name in the list of members of the IPA and gives her address as Ankara from 1935 to 1938. A report in the same *Bulletin* in 1938, written by Edward Bibring, states:

> In Ankara Dr. Weigert Vowinckel has given lectures and taken part in discussions on psychoanalysis in private circles; and as a psychiatrist, who is at present still in Training Analysis, has acquired a thorough theoretical knowledge of the subject and has translated Freud's writings into Turkish. (Bibring, 1938, p. 280)

In the 1939 *Bulletin* Edith Weigert Vowinckel is listed as a member of the Washington-Baltimore Psychoanalytic Society.

There is some ambiguity in Bibring's report since it states that Edith Weigert was still in training analysis. No one in Turkey was training her. Perhaps this statement refers to her continuing study of psychoanalysis. The report's reference to her giving lectures and discussing psychoanalysis in private circles is correct. Edith Weigert met Atatürk on several occasions, but during our interviews she did not say that Atatürk had been present when she was discussing psychoanalysis in private circles. Nevertheless, we have information on Atatürk's and some of his colleagues' interest in Freud. They were intent on modernizing Turkey, and knowing about Freud and psychoanalysis in general was of interest to them. For example, the second president of Turkey, İsmet İnönü, would, as Atatürk had done, sometimes gather Turkish intellectuals at the presidential palace for discussions. We know that in one such gathering Freud and psychoanalysis were the topic of discussion. When İsmet İnönü asked "Was Freud correct?" one intellectual—Hasan Ali Yücel, who was the Minister of Education—responded by praising Freud's finding and then added that Freud sometimes "went too far." Upon hearing this, İsmet İnönü replied, "I wish I could be like Freud and speak about the truth and go too far" (Küçükkaya, 2008, p. 129). With Atatürk's instruction, Edith Weigert was given a license to practice psychoanalysis in Turkey—thereby becoming the first formally trained psychoanalyst to practice there. Before and after her death in 1982, her Turkish license was exhibited at the Washington Psychoanalytic Association building to honor her.

While she was in Ankara, all of Edith Weigert's analysands, with the exception of one, were foreigners, most of them working at various embassies. The Turk whom she "analyzed" was a physician named Ahmet İzeddin Şadan Biril. İzeddin Şadan was born in 1893 and, after graduating as a physician in İstanbul in 1924, left for France in 1927 for three years of further training. In addition to French, he also spoke English, and later he would write three books, one titled, *Psikanaliz* (*Psychoanalysis*), as well as dozens of articles.[1] Certainly, İzeddin Şadan was someone who attempted to bring psychoanalytic theory and technique to the attention of Turkish psychiatrists and intellectuals even before he had met Edith Weigert. The parts of his memoirs that I have read mostly illustrate his struggles with better-known psychiatrists in İstanbul and the arguments between these psychiatrists, most of whom were influenced by Kraepelin. Mahzar Osman and others hesitated to be openly associated with Freudianism because in their minds it dealt with sexuality—a perception that would not be acceptable in their Muslim environment. İzeddin Şadan (under the name of A. İzeddin) studied a Mohammedan legend and published his studies in German in *Imago* (İzeddin, 1932). In this paper he basically deals with Sufi traditions and finds reflections of oedipal situations and castration anxiety in them. In 1948 his letter to *Psychoanalytic Quarterly* was published (İzeddin, 1948), stating that on account of the war he had lost contact with psychoanalytic centers and thus had failed until recently to read Freud's *Moses and Monotheism* (1939a). Then, referring to his German paper mentioned above, he declared that he had written the first psychoanalytic study on monotheism, and that Freud's analysis post-dated his by six years.

I recall that when I spoke with Edith Weigert, I got the impression that İzeddin Şadan did not undergo a proper psychoanalytic process. Reading the Turkish translation of his paper and parts of his memoirs, I came to the conclusion that İzeddin Şadan's approach to psychoanalysis was highly intellectualized. Furthermore, the nature of his personality organization, which made him known as an argumentative individual, is in my estimation what kept him from becoming a Turkish pioneer in initiating a deep interest in psychoanalysis in Turkey. Soon he was forgotten.

Interest in psychoanalysis in Turkey grew because of Atatürk's and his followers' intense efforts to modernize. After the Turkish Republic was born, the Turkish Ministry of Education had all major works of Western philosophers, thinkers, and novelists translated, one by one. Freud's writings began to be translated into Turkish in the late 1920s. During Edith Weigert's stay in Ankara, and because she was known to the Turkish authorities and diplomats mainly because of her husband's position, her discussion of psychoanalysis at private parties encouraged an interest in Freud's writings. There were not many Turks at these parties, but Turkish authorities and intellectuals' intent on cultural revolution were influenced by them.

Elsewhere, I wrote about my childhood and one of the reasons I became a psychoanalyst (Volkan, 1985). My father, a Cypriot Turk who was an elementary school teacher, used a huge black wooden box in my parents' bedroom in our house in Cyprus as his library. As a youngster, I was intently interested in what he kept in this box: the box, with its obvious symbolism, became an object of my oedipal curiosity. When I examined it I found Freud's *Three Essays on the Theory of Sexuality* (1905d) in it. To learn about Freud was to learn about my oedipal father, as well as to identify with him. Modernization in Turkey and Edith Weigert's activities in Ankara had reached my Cypriot Turkish home. Once I had established myself as a psychoanalyst, I would try to do my best to bring the IPA to Turkey. Atatürk died in 1938, but his influence and modernization continued in Turkey. The growing city of Ankara, with its medical school at Ankara University, remained a more fertile ground for the acceptance of psychoanalysis than did the medical school of İstanbul University, where followers of Kraepelin continued to dominate the psychiatric scene. When I went to Ankara in 1950 and started my medical education, some of the Jewish professors who had escaped the Nazis fifteen to twenty years earlier were still teaching there, and there were other such professors at İstanbul University. None of them, however, taught psychiatry. In 1950 the Turkish large-group identity had already greatly changed from what it had been during the Ottoman period. For example, one third of the medical school class were women. Seven years later, when I came to America, only a few female students could be found in any of the American medical school classes. Our psychiatry chairperson at Ankara University's Medical School was Rasim Adasal. He called himself the "Turkish Freud," even though he had no formal training in psychoanalysis. Adasal wrote books with references to psychoanalytic thinking. He was very charismatic and was well known by the public because of his interest in sports and sports medicine. Thus, Freud was popularized in Turkey.

In 1958 Donald Winnicott and Anna Freud were asked to write papers addressed to the Turkish audience on psychoanalysis and its role in medicine. I have not yet discovered who initiated this request, but both responded, and their papers, in Turkish translation, were published. Winnicott described some key points of psychoanalysis and stated that interest in psychoanalysis varies from one civilization to another. He added:

> When a medical journal in Turkey asked me to write a paper on psychoanalysis, I realized that there is yet another country that wants to place the investigation of the human psyche within the broad spectrum of science and that wishes to investigate the psyche, as we investigate the body, through a scientific method. (Winnicott, 1958c, p. 18)

He suggested that were those in charge of medicine in Turkey to decide to establish a psychoanalytic institute, they should find ways to send some bright Turkish doctors to foreign places, such as the Institute of Psychoanalysis in London, for at least four years. He then stated that when the time comes to start a psychoanalytic institute in Turkey, it should be established by both men and women. Anna Freud's paper is didactic and deals with the psychological processes in children when they experience physical illness or undergo surgery. It explains the importance of the mother–child relationship and a child's response to the loss of the mother (A. Freud, 1958).

Soon after I graduated from medical school and moved to the United States, another medical school, called Hacettepe Medical School, was opened in Ankara. Orhan Öztürk, who was still living and well respected, also studied in the United States before returning to Turkey and becoming the chairperson of the Department of Psychiatry of this hospital. While he was in the United States he worked for some years at the Austen Riggs Center in Stockbridge, Massachusetts, while Erik Erikson was also there, and he was influenced by Erikson. Öztürk did not go through a formal psychoanalytic training, but when he became a key figure in psychiatry in Turkey he also became a key figure in expanding psychodynamic views in psychiatric practice, and, following Erikson, he especially focused on interactions between individuals and their societies.

In 1974, as a psychoanalyst, I returned to Ankara University as a visiting professor of psychiatry for a little over a year. Also, there during the same time period as a visiting professor of psychiatry was Celal Odağ, who had been trained as a psychoanalyst in Germany. We joined forces and taught psychoanalytic concepts in a most intensive way. In 1994 Celal Odağ opened a training institution in İzmir called the Halime Odağ Foundation, named after her late mother. While this foundation did not offer traditional psychoanalytic training, it functioned as a forerunner of the IPA-sponsored schools that would later be established in İstanbul. I am grateful to psychoanalysts in Israel, primarily to the late Rafael Moses and the late Rena Moses, and, in the United States, to Salman Akhtar, Ira Brenner, and David Sachs—as well as other colleagues from Germany—who accepted our invitations and lectured at Halime Odağ Foundation, provided supervision for young therapists, and helped with the foundation's evolution. Through the activities of the Halime Odağ Foundation, psychodynamic training and interest in psychoanalysis spread in Turkey, especially among young psychiatrists and psychologists. The foundation's annual scientific meeting, where analysts from different countries spoke, was always packed with young audiences.

Starting in the mid-1990s, I began meeting one to three times a year, for several days each time, with twenty-one psychiatrists from İstanbul, who established themselves as a "psychoanalytic club" for the intensive study of psychoanalytic principles. I did this without any financial remuneration as part of my own desire to build a foundation so that Turkey could become a place where, in the future, formal psychoanalytic training would be available. Today some of these members, having gone through their formal education in psychoanalysis, are already IPA members, and others are close to becoming IPA members.

Others from İstanbul began training in France. Among them, Talat Parman would take the leadership role in creating the cornerstone of one of the IPA-sponsored training facilities in İstanbul. Still another group, again in İstanbul, established connections with the Chicago Institute of Psychoanalysis. This led to visits to Turkey by Arnold Goldberg and Allen Siegel and phone seminars that lasted for years. The emphasis of this group was on Kohutian self psychology (Siegel, 2003). Different groups interested in psychoanalysis in İstanbul did not have much communication among themselves. Nevertheless, the time was becoming ripe to start formal IPA involvement in Turkey.

While all this was taking place in İzmir and İstanbul, the IPA created a Middle East Committee, chaired by Antoine Hani from the Washington Psychoanalytic Society. Antoine Hani's personal connections to Lebanon and his knowledge of the Middle East were considered helpful to the committee's work. I, too, was appointed a member. Our task was to study psychoanalytic interest in the Middle East to try to see if there would be openings for formal IPA involvement and IPA-sponsored training facilities in this part of the world.

The story of the IPA's involvement in Turkey

The IPA was already well connected with the psychoanalytic scene in Israel. Accordingly, the IPA's Middle East Committee would be dealing only with countries in the Middle East where the majority of the population was Muslim. We learned that there were sixteen psychoanalysts in Lebanon but they were not trained in IPA-approved institutions. Antoine Hani's work with them apparently went nowhere, as they did not want further scrutiny or education and did not wish to become IPA members. Neither could we begin an IPA process in Egypt. Turkey remained the only country for our focus. We knew that those Turks who were being trained in France would be members of the IPA once their training was completed. Many other Turks in Turkey who wanted such training could not afford to be educated in France or did not know French, so our main problem in Turkey was that no training analysts were located there. We entertained the idea of finding training analysts from foreign countries who would settle in İstanbul and earn a good living because they would find many analysands. Attempts to bring this idea to fruition did not work out.

Talat Parman's and others' graduations were perceived as a major opening for the IPA's further work in Turkey. However, unfortunately a split occurred in this group: Bella Habip, who, like Talat Parman, had French training and, like Talat Parman, had graduated in 2000, separated herself from her French-trained colleagues and began to have her own followers. Antoine Hani's efforts to bring the Parman and Habip groups together failed.

In 1987 talks on the creation of a psychoanalytic training program for Eastern Europe began in Hungary. Eventually the Han Groen-Prakken Psychoanalytic Institute for Eastern Europe was established under the auspices of the IPA as well as the European Psychoanalytical Federation (EPF), but education in this institute was not offered to Turkish candidates. The IPA accepted what became known as "shuttle analysis" (Szönyi & Štajner-Popović, 2008) as part of psychoanalytic training. Eastern European candidates could have their training analyses by traveling long distances. Instead of seeing their analysts four times a week, they would lie on the couch many times, in what is known as "concentrated analysis," whenever they traveled to the locations where their analysis lived.

The IPA's acceptance of "shuttle analysis" opened a way to train other Turks who did not know French but spoke English or who could not afford to be trained in France. There were three individuals in İzmir who were willing to travel to a foreign country for IPA-approved training analysis. All of them were already very close to Rafael Moses and Rena Moses and could have gone for training analysis to Israel, but Greece was closer. This was a time of political tensions between Turkey and Greece. I contacted Peter Hartocollis, who had left the United States and settled in his home country Greece. He was most gracious and opened the way for three Turks to receive their training analysis in Athens, analyzing two of them himself.

I am indebted to Peter Hartocollis and other Greek colleagues. Two persons who had gone to Greece for their training analyses are today members of the IPA.

David Sachs, from the Philadelphia Psychoanalytic Society, matched Peter Hartocollis in going out of his way to help Turks. He was the chairperson of the IPA's International New Groups (ING) Committee. He had earlier participated in a Halime Odağ Foundation annual scientific meeting and had been exposed to the enthusiasm of many young Turks for psychoanalytic training. We prepared an official proposal to the IPA to start an IPA-approved school in Turkey. In January 2003 David Sachs and I were asked to go to Miami, where the IPA's Executive Council was meeting. We met with the council and presented data to show why it was time to start a training facility in Turkey, and how it could begin. At that time, we considered a modified Han Groen-Prakken Psychoanalytic model for Turkey until such time as some analysts in Turkey were ready to become training analysts. Our proposal that the IPA start a process of eventually establishing a training facility in Turkey was accepted, and then IPA president Daniel Widlöcher appointed an Exploratory Committee under chairwoman Abigail Golomb of Israel. At that time, Abigail Golomb and I were members of the IPA's Terror and Terrorism Committee, and she had been to Turkey when this committee met in İzmir. She consulted me and others who knew about the situation in Turkey and prepared herself well. Later, in 2005, Abigail Golomb would become the chairperson of the IPA Turkey Supervisory Committee. Nikolas Kouretas from Greece and Marie-France Dispaux from Belgium, both of whom know Turkish, also serve on the Supervisory Committee. The other two members are Betty Denzler from Switzerland and Milagros Cid Sanz from Spain.

Abigail Golomb and her colleagues had to find ways to deal with the split between the Talat Parman and Bella Habip groups in İstanbul. In the end it was decided that two schools would be opened in İstanbul, one under the leadership of Talat Parman and the other under that of Bella Habip. Those who had formed a "psychoanalytic club," those who had received education from Chicago Psychoanalytic Society earlier, and those who had their training analyses in Greece joined the Bella Habip group.

Many analysts from Europe and the United States were involved in training the Turkish candidates. The dedication of Maurice Apprey from the Virginia Psychoanalytic Society and Ilany Kogan from Israel in educating and supervising the trainees in the Bella Habip-led school needs to be acknowledged. Two years ago, the Talat Parman group, which had been guided by Bernard Penot in France and Yolanda Gampel in Israel, reached IPA Study Group status. This year the other group also reached the same status. Both schools already have graduates who have become direct members of the IPA. This year a new member of the IPA, Ayla Yazıcı, took the leadership role of the group that had originally been led by Bella Habip.

At the present time, IPA activities in Turkey exist only in İstanbul. There is only one IPA member in Ankara University, Elif Gürışık, who was trained in London long ago, and one in İzmir, Işıl Vahip. In 2010 Işıl Vahip was elected to become a fellow at the American College of Psychoanalysts, an organization that honors accomplished psychoanalysts with a medical background. There are dozens of young mental health professionals in Ankara and

İzmir eagerly awaiting IPA-sponsored psychoanalytic training facilities to develop in their cities as well.

In İstanbul, the split between the two psychoanalytic schools continues, and it has also played a role in creating some discomfort within the IPA and a "competition" between French and American "styles" of psychoanalytic training or thinking. Nevertheless, the IPA's involvement in Turkey has been successful, and one hopes that new graduates will, in the near future, bring an end to the split.

I will finish this brief story of IPA involvement in Turkey by recalling Donald Winnicott's 1958 advice when he stated that both men and women should work together in establishing a psychoanalytic institute in Turkey. He would have been very pleased to know that most candidates in both Turkish schools are women, the number of the IPA women who are members at the present time exceeds that of their male counterparts, and, while one school is led by a man, the other has been and is led by women.

Part II

Developmental observations

CHAPTER 4

The nuances of the mother–daughter relationship in Turkish culture

Müge Alkan and Salman Akhtar

Despite the pervasive phallocentrism and patriarchal undergirding of his viewpoint, Freud recognized the mother's central and formative influence on the development of her child. He noted, for instance, that:

- "I have found that people who know that they are preferred or favoured by their mother give evidence in their lives of a peculiar self-reliance and an unshakable optimism which often seem like heroic attributes and bring actual success to their possessors" (a 1911 footnote to *The Interpretation of Dreams*, 1900a, p. 398).
- "We call the mother the first *love* object" (1916–17, p. 329, italics in the original).
- "A child's first erotic object is the mother's breast that nourishes it; love has its origins in attachment to the satisfied need for nourishment" (1940a, p. 188).

These declarations are impressive. At the same time, it remains a fact that for a deeper and more meaningful study of the mother–child relationship, psychoanalysis had to wait for those clinician-theorists who worked with children on a daily basis and whose eyes and ears were closer to the sights and sounds of early ontogenesis.

The maternal turn in psychoanalysis

The great pioneers of this field were Bowlby, Spitz, Anna Freud, Winnicott, and Mahler. Before a raised eyebrow appears among the readers, we hasten to add Klein and Fairbairn to this list, even though the former was essentially a drive theorist and the latter paid greater attention to endopsychic structuralization than to relational scenarios leading to it. Nonetheless, it is to the landmark contributions of these seven pioneers that psychoanalysis owes its "maternal turn." The project—still in progress—found further momentum and refinement in the labors of Stern, Ainsworth, Beebe, Parens, Fonagy, Emde, Balsam, Kulish, the Novicks, and Chodorow, to name but a few among the later outstanding contributors.

Pooling the observations of these investigators together reveals that the development-facilitating tasks of the mother are multifaceted and involve many sectors of psychic functioning of the child. The most important of these tasks are the following.

Holding

"Holding" (Winnicott, 1960a) refers not only to the ordinary function of a mother holding her infant but also

> the total environmental provision prior to the concept of *living with*. In other words, it refers to a three-dimensional or space relationship with time gradually added. This overlaps with, but is initiated prior to, instinctual experiences that in time would determine object relationships. (pp. 43–44, italics in the original)

The mother meets the child's physiological needs and also takes care of the psychological needs. The mother remains reliable and does not abandon or impinge. Such an umbrella function of the mother is not directly felt by the child as emanating from an "object mother" that is outside of his omnipotence; instead it is experienced as a subjective "environment mother" that makes autonomous thinking and growth possible. As a result of "holding," the infant gradually becomes a person in his own right. Such "holding" extended beyond the infantile period to the broader caregiving functions of the mother in relation to the older child.

Containing

"Containing" (Bion, 1962) allows the child to put aspects of his or her experience in the mother's mental space till these can return and be assimilated. The maternal mind receives the projections of the child and, by that very act, makes it possible for the latter to discover his or her needs. The mother becomes the provider not only of literal and emotional nourishment, but also of the metabolism of the child's unpleasant feelings. Bion regards this process as the original prototype for the capacity to think. Thoughts arise in the child's mind as sense perceptions and subjective experiences but are not processed until the mother empathically deciphers them and returns them to the child as thinkable entities. Bion refers to such a receptive attitude of the mother as "container" in structural and "reverie" in functional terms. Gradually the child internalizes her attitude and develops the capacity to think about his or her own thoughts.

Protecting and nourishing

Motivated by a combination of love, narcissistic investment, identification with the "good" aspects of her own mother (Balsam, 2000), and hardwired animal altruism (Seelig & Rosof, 2001), the mother protects her child from physical danger. Her safeguarding is directed toward threats from the external world as well as those arising from the child's own uninformed or counterphobic valor. The mother assures that the child does not get overwhelmed by external stimuli (e.g., noise, heat, or cold) and by internal demands (e.g., hunger, fatigue); this, in turn, leads to the formation of a "protective shield" (Freud, 1895d), that is, the internal structure that precludes overstimulation throughout life. The mother also nourishes the child. Indeed, from the moment of conception through the nine-month-long period of gestation to the period of infancy and early childhood, the mother is almost solely responsible for providing nourishment to the child. Her nourishing the child, however, extends beyond the literal sphere. She also "nourishes" the child's internal world by her touch, smell, laughter, lullabies, rhymes, and songs. The "good breast" (Klein, 1933, 1937, 1948) is thus more iconic than actual.

Awakening the child's body's libidinal potential

One feature of "primary maternal preoccupation" (Winnicott, 1956) is the mother's deep investment in her child's body. She holds the child and protects him from injuries. She looks into the child's eyes and, with a twinkle in her eye, creates a joyous self in the infant. The mother kisses the child. She rocks the child in her arms. She feeds him with her breast, plays with his little hands and feet, and massages the back and front of his torso. She cleans him, bathes him, and dresses him. Through all these activities, the mother develops and sustains a profound connection with her child's body. Such ministrations—more marked during infancy and early childhood—awaken the "hardwired" libidinal potential of her child's body and familiarize him or her with its corporeal landscape.

Introducing the child to his or her inner world

The mother facilitates the child's awareness of his or her inner world. She does this in many ways. By "holding" (Winnicott, 1960a), she creates the possibility for the child to put bits and pieces of his subjective experience together and move from non-threatening states of "unintegration" (Winnicott, 1945) to that of psychic integration. A second manner in which the mother enlightens the child about his or her affective and cognitive goings-on is by "containing" (Bion, 1962) his un-mentalizable experiences and then returning them to him in suitably titrated doses of information. Finally, by empathic immersion in her child's experience, the mother discerns his moods and drives and then identifies them verbally ("Oh, oh, someone is really angry"; "Oh, oh, someone is feeling very happy"; and so on) or conveys her understanding by the nature and pace of her motoric responses. The child, in turn, comes to know not only that he is happy or angry or hungry or sleepy but also how angry or hungry or sleepy he is. The mother becomes a beacon of light and illuminates his inner experience for him (Burnham et al., 1969).

Evoking the core self and helping consolidate gender identity

The mother plays the most fundamental role in evoking and giving shape to the child's "basic core" (Weil, 1970). To be sure, the newborn is no tabula rasa. He or she gives evidence of possessing capacities, from birth onwards, that facilitate meaningful interaction with the mother. These include "a propensity for participating in eye-to-eye contact; a state-responsivity for being activated and soothed by human holding, touching, and rocking; and a propensity for showing prolonged alert attentiveness to the stimulus features contained in the human voice and face" (Emde, 1983, p. 171). Such "social fittedness" of the infant has a counterpart in the mother as well. She directs speech and gestures to her infant in a simple and repetitive pattern. But more important in the development of identity is that the mother conveys a particular theme to her newborn: "The mother imprints upon the infant not an identity, but an identity theme. This theme is irreversible, but it is capable of variations, variations that spell the difference between human creativity and a *destiny neurosis*" (Lichtenstein, 1961, p. 208, italics in the original).

A more specialized aspect of the child's subjective experience pertains to gender. The mother, building upon the child's anatomy and working in unison with the father, imparts a sense of core gender identity (Stoller, 1968) to her child. Under her care, a male or female newborn becomes a boy or girl, respectively. Naming, dressing, grooming, gazing at, touching, talking to, and playing with the child in culturally syntonic gender-specific ways, the mother consolidates the biologically rooted gender sense of her child and paves the way for his or her acquiring an era-appropriate "gender role" (A. Green, 1975). Mother's relinquishing the control of her son's body (Greenson, 1968) enhances the latter's sense of masculinity. Her drawing esteem and pleasure from her own body encourages her daughter to emulate her and thus strengthen her gender identity. By permitting "dis-identification" on the part of the boy and by encouraging identification on the part of the girl, the mother becomes an important agent of gender identity consolidation.

Imparting ego skills

In well-attuned synchronicity with the child's maturing motor skills, the mother begins to "teach" him or her the art of doing things. Thus, the way to hold a milk bottle or a cup, the movement necessary to produce the needed sound from a rattle, and, later, the use of spoon, fork, and knives as well as dressing, undressing, putting shoes on, and tying laces, etc., all come under the purview of mother's ongoing didactic efforts. Freud's observation that "ego is a precipitate of abandoned object cathexis" (1923b, p. 29) is a firm reminder of how the above-mentioned skills are at first external to the child's self and only by the internalization of efficacious others (mother being the first in this list) come to reside within it. The mother teaches skills of daily living and the child learns, gradually making them his own, as it were.

Seeing goodness in the child

Like the sculptor who can envision the statue hidden in a rock, the mother sees the potential strengths of her child. This has a developmentally salutary impact upon the latter who strives for correspondence and proximity with her "vision" of him (Loewald, 1960). The mother's capacity to see "goodness" in her child arises from a combination of her "healthy narcissism" (Kernberg, 1980), built-in altruism (Seelig & Rosof, 2001), and an overall attitude of generativity and care (Erikson, 1959).

Surviving

Yet another important, though relatively "silent," function of the mother is to "survive" the emotional disturbances stirred up by her child and to find her maternal self over and over again. The child inevitably develops destructive impulses toward her but whether these impulses actually end up being destructive or not depends on the capacity of the mother to retain her maternal attitude and not react in a retaliatory manner. If she remains a mother, so to speak, then there is no destruction in reality. Her "survival" makes her an object that the child can now "use" (Winnicott, 1969). Over the course of time the child internalizes this capacity of the mother and, later, as an adult, himself becomes able to survive others' attacks on him.

Letting go of the child

Although the "dual unity" of early mother–infant symbiosis blurs the boundaries between their respective psyches, even then there are moments when the mother "lets go" of the baby and allows him or her psychic space to be peacefully and creatively alone. During the "practicing subphase" of the separation–individuation process (Mahler et al., 1975), this space grows, permitting the child far greater autonomy and exploration of the world away from the mother. The mother "lets go" to a greater extent. Still later, in the "rapprochement subphase," the mother "lets go" at the intrapsychic level (of her own earlier representations of the "lap baby" of the symbiotic phase and the hypomanic toddler of the practicing subphase) while serving as the "container" (Bion, 1962) of the child's disowned self- and object-representation till these can be synthesized into their respective composite wholes. Mother's "letting go" also involves the child's body. Submerged into intimate and pervasive attention to her child's bodily care, the mother gradually hands over the responsibility of body-care to the child. Not only the kissing and hugging diminish over the passage of time, but also aspects of feeding and toilet care become increasingly the domain of the child alone.

Remaining available as a psychological "home base"

Even with increasing such acceptance of separateness, the fused infant–mother core (at the intrapsychic level) and the actual mother (at the external reality level) remain forever needed by the child for psychic retreat, haven, and stabilization. The thrills of pleasurable toddlerhood, the joys of latency, the rebellion of adolescence, and the seeming "independence" of adult life are only partial triumphs against the acknowledgment of this ego-need. And, a "good enough mother" (Winnicott, 1960a) knows the secret intuitively. Hence, she makes herself available as a "secure base" (Bowlby, 1988) to which her child can always return for emotional refueling. The anchoring role of "motherland," "mother nature," and "mother tongue" is similarly reassuring; their ego-replenishing attributes are, at least partly, symbolic stand-ins for an imperishable mother.

Helping the child bear the oedipal situation and teaching the child to respect the father

By being and acting as the father's romantic and generative partner, the mother introduces the child not only to the barriers to his or her oedipal aspirations. By her continued affectionate availability in all other realms, the mother makes her erotic non-availability tolerable to her male child. Correspondingly, by presenting herself as a barrier (somewhat permeable, though) between her husband and her daughter, the mother establishes a bearable limit of cross-generational sensuality. On a plebian and macroscopic level, the mother teaches the child to respect the father and to take his guidance and counsel seriously.

While covering a wide terrain and thus earning a certain claim to readiness for generalization, this list has been distilled from the observation of mother–child interactions in the West. The cross-cultural stability of its implicit nodal points, sequencing, intensity, and accommodations or alterations to fit the gender of the child has hardly been tested. Maternal interactions with infants and children from non-Western cultures, including Japan (Doi, 1962, 1973; Freeman, 1981, 1994, 1998), India (Kakar, 1990a, 1990b), South Korea (Choi-Kain, 2009; Kim et al., 2009), and China (Chao, 1994; Gu, 2006), have begun to add nuances and fresh concepts to this realm. And, it is at this point that we introduce our psychosocial mapping of the Turkish mother–child relationship, especially as it pertains to a girl's (and later, woman's) psychic growth and adaptation.

Before proceeding further, we wish to enter a few caveats. *First*, our clinical experience is almost solely that of working with adult patients; our portrayal of the mother–child relationship, especially in its earliest phases, is based on reconstructions. *Second*, our contribution has the weakness of a cis-gender inclination; this emanates not from our subscribing to gender essentialism but from the scope of our clinical experience and the limit of our scholarly oeuvre. *Third*, though we have attempted to learn from the scattered writings on Turkish motherhood (Açıkgöz et al., 2014; Bektaş et al., 2022; Oflu, 2020; Öğüt & Güvenç, 2023; Sunar, 2009), the psychodynamic dimension of this literature is limited, compelling us to fill in the needed conceptual blanks ourselves. *Finally*, both the coverage by the contributors preceding us and our own clinical material represents a particular slice of socioeconomic and regional population; in a vast country with considerable variations in monetary status, educational achievements, regionally normative practices, and extent of religious belief, observations such as ours might carry only a modest potential for generalization. It might therefore be best to begin with a brief foray in anthropology before delving into clinical perspectives and their psychodynamic underbelly.

Some data from social anthropology

Although demographically largely Muslim, Turkey is a secular country ruled by a constitutional social state of law. It has a wide range of ethnic groups, economic strata, and social idioms of life. Also, the norms of family structure and child-rearing practices have changed considerably over time. As a result, no ubiquitous and uniform parent–child relationship exists in the country. While the nuclear family structure is more common in big cities today, traditional extended and joint family structures are still prevalent in the rural and peripheral areas of the nation's wide geography. Located in a geopolitically pivotal location, the country has experienced the influx and influence of different cultures throughout its rich history, with various settlements dating as far back as the Stone Age. Turkish lands have been the locale of Hittite, Thracian, Hellenistic civilizations and elements of Roman, Byzantine, Persian, and Seljuk empires. Alongside this long and layered history of the country`s psychosocial context, the recent past and present are dynamic, ever-changing, and constantly evolving. Inevitably, dynamic cultural codes and sociopolitical imperatives act together and are reflected in evolving child-rearing practices in the family. The establishment of the current Republic in 1923 was a major turning point in the country's history and cultural evolution. It changed the family system and elevated the women's place in society. With these geo-historical reminders and caveats in place, let us turn to some specific features of the mother–daughter relationship in Turkey.

The "Value of the Child" studies

The "Value of the Child" research, one of the most comprehensive examinations of the family structure in Turkey, was a nationwide study carried out in Turkey as a part of a cross-national comparative study carried out between 1975 and 1979; it examined three generations for thirty years (Kağıtçıbaşı, 1980; Kağıtçıbaşı & Ataca, 2005; Kağıtçıbaşı et al., 2005). These investigations, carried out under the leadership of the eminent Turkish social psychologist Çiğdem Kağıtçıbaşı (1940–2017), reflect the changes in the sociocultural structure of families in Turkey over the years. In the 1970s study, it was determined that there was a hierarchical structure in which the role of women in the family was lower than that of men. It was observed that women were dependent on their spouses and stayed home, while men drew support from their original family members (parents, siblings, uncles, etc.). In such a family structure, the value given to the sons was higher than daughters since the parents expected the sons to support the family financially and socially. Daughters felt unworthy and insecure from a young age since all that was expected from them was housework and caring for the family members. During this era, a child's independence was perceived as a threat to the family which was a system that approved collectivism and support rather than individuality.

In the 1980s, women's status began to change with urban migration, westernization, higher education levels, and participation in the workforce. In parallel with this change, there was also an enhancement in the value given to girls and women. The psychological value of the child gained precedence over economic value, thus lowering the preference for a boy. Women, economically self-sufficient or not, began to regard their daughters as companions and rely more upon them than their sons during old age.

These earlier "Value of the Child" studies have been repeated more recently (Kağıtçıbaşı & Ataca, 2005) and findings now show a significant change in the expectations from the child. The financial and utilitarian value of the child is now lower and the psychological value of the child much higher than in the original study. Three decades later financial dependency between the parent and the child had decreased, yet psychological dependency remained the same. Through the years, the value of the female child has increased and there is the indication that she might even be favored more than the male child. Daughters who provide emotional closeness have become the desired child for the mother and, interestingly, among the grandmothers as well.

Although the value of daughters is rising in urban (and to a lesser extent, rural) families, true individuation for girls in a collectivist culture and a thickly interdependent family structure is laborious and painful. To be sure, higher education and joining the workforce have helped mothers to expect less from their daughters and yet it is not enough for them to let go of the latter; most mothers continue to see their daughters as an extension of themselves. The culture expects the continuation of the early mother–child bond and the daughter's identification with mother to the extent that is demonstrated in the famous saying, "*Anasına bak kızını al, kenarına bak bezini al*" ("Check the mother, then marry the daughter, check the seam, then buy the fabric"). This declaration that a daughter will turn out to be a carbon copy of her mother also contains a fetishistic devaluation of the girl by comparing her to bought and sold merchandise. The fact is that Turkish mothers still try to control and shape, according to their own needs, the life choices of their daughters.

Modulating the daughter's attitude toward her father

As is prevalent in other parts of the world, Turkish mothers also help their children develop a fond and respectful attitude toward their fathers. In a culture that still is largely patriarchal,

> The mother upholds the father's prerogative of imparting *Weltanschauung* (a vision of the world at large and how life is to be lived in it) to his children. She facilitates the

> "forward projection of narcissism" (Chasseguet-Smirgel, 1984a) on the child's part and thus gives credence to the phase-specific idealization of the father. In this way the mother participates in laying down the early foundations of the ego-ideal. (Akhtar, 2012a p. 10, italics in the original)

Such psychoanalytic speculations have been "confirmed" by a Turkish study (Çelik, 2020) of the implicit and explicit messages the mother gives to her children regarding the father's status in the family. These messages—both positive and negative—go a long way in shaping the image of the father in the child's eyes and imagination. This clearly has profound implications for the formation of the child's superego and, under fortunate circumstances, the ego ideal.

From adolescence through adulthood

Turkey is a predominantly Muslim country, in which the honor and virginity of the girl is a major concern. A daughter's dating men can bring shame to the family and since the mother is deemed responsible for assuring the honor of the daughter, maternally controlling behavior can ensue (Hortaçsu et al., 2003). Menarche, which is a major biological and physiological turning point in a girl's life, has major cultural ramifications as well. In rural parts of Turkey the tradition of slapping the adolescent girl when she has her first period is still common. This is rationalized by explanations like helping the girl overcome the shock of bleeding or giving her rosy cheeks as a beautiful woman; at deeper levels, it seems aimed at shaming the girl and "punishing" her for having become a woman. In rural parts of the country, the menstruating woman is regarded as "dirty" and is exempt from many daily activities like planting seeds, fermenting yoghurt, or making pickles. Dating is limited and the girl is often married off in her early twenties. Sex before marriage is not common. Sex is regarded as not for pleasure, but only for having children. Any licentious behavior on the part of the daughter is seen as bringing dishonor and shame to the whole family (Kandiyoti, 1996). It can be met with severe retribution.

Here we hasten to add that in the great majority of Turkey's population and especially in big cities, the norms and practices regarding menstruation, dating, and premarital sex are quite different: it is celebrated in the family. Most of the women in big cities date men, some have sex before marriage. Cohabitation with boyfriends is not infrequent in big cities.

Mother–daughter relationship after the daughter's marriage

After the daughter's marriage, the responsibility for honor is transferred to the husband and the parents feel relieved of this "burden." The mother now accepts her daughter's separate home, family, and life. Geographical separation expedites psychological separation between them. At the same time, the fact that even this marital home is often partially subsidized by the parents of the bride keeps the young woman in a relatively childlike position. The ensuing loss of self-esteem is compensated by the unconscious (or preconscious) knowledge that she herself would bequeath some form of living quarters to her own daughter.

Over time the marital home loses its conscious and preconscious links to parental largesse. The dissolution of this link permits the daughter to grow up further and acquire not only the status of a householder but a fully functioning adult woman. Paraphrasing Winnicott (1946), the breakdown of this marital home (in the unfortunate circumstance of divorce), often sends the daughter back to the bosom of the family in search of a feeling of security and belonging. This is especially true if she is not working. Once again, the duty of protecting the daughter's honor is transferred back to the family. Her getting divorced may be perceived as a failure and shame for the mother, as a divorced woman is looked down upon in society (Mottram & Hortaçsu, 2005).

Some five or six decades ago, the extended family model was common and though this has all but vanished from urban societies, most married children even now live in close proximity to their families of origin (Kongar, 1998). In such settings, daughters receive support from their mothers when they have a child. Meanwhile daughters care for their aging parents. Alongside this interpersonal ego benefit of mutual "holding," the everlasting mother–daughter codependency has some negative effects on the daughter's self-esteem as well (Onaylı & Erdur-Baker, 2013).

Mother–daughter relationship upon the mother's getting old

A final turning point in the mother–daughter relationship occurs when the mother grows old or is widowed. In these situations their roles are reversed; the mother becomes "the child," and daughter becomes "the mother." A survey of pertinent literature (Mottram & Hortaçsu, 2005) revealed that such "filial" obligation is "likely to increase with a decline in [maternal] health … [and] mothers and daughters grow closer after mother's widowhood" (pp. 475, 484). Significantly, while mothers felt more comfortable with such relational reversal, daughters found it to be a source of ambivalence. On the one hand, they felt proud at being efficacious and reparative. On the other hand, the fading and loss of the hitherto powerful mother was agonizing; this subterranean despair was compounded by the contemporary daughters' awareness that, owing to the increasing individualism in Turkish society, during their own old age they themselves might not be the fortunate recipient of such filial piety.

Summary

All in all, it seems that in collectivist cultures like Turkey, where interpersonal relationships play a crucial role, the mother–daughter bond is tight, multifaceted, and long lasting. There exists a dialectical loop of emotional discourse in which the two partners of this dyad continually attend to each other's needs. Not surprisingly then, women are viewed more as instrumental agents of an integrated family system rather than as autonomous individuals in their own right (Triandis, 1995). Some rural/urban differences continue to exist in the extent of interpersonal distance, sexual freedom, and personal autonomy at large. Rural daughters often sacrifice a Western style of "personhood" at the altar of family cohesion. Those who are urban, educated, financially independent, sexually liberated, and socially adept do "hatch out" to a greater extent from their "symbiotic orbit" (Akhtar & Parens, 1991) with the mother, though at the cost of carrying unconscious guilt.

Illustrations from clinical practice

Turkish mothers perform the customary maternal tasks of holding, containing, protecting, informing about the internal world, imparting basic ego skills, modeling era- and gender-specific roles, and establishing an oedipal barrier between the daughter and the father. In undertaking and sustaining such responsibilities, they appear little different from mothers around the globe. However, clinical experience (all cases cited below having been drawn from MA's practice and have been given fictitious names to protect their identities) suggests that subtle nuances of emphasis, tone, and texture in the way Turkish mothers relate to their daughters might carry some differences from their Western and Far Eastern counterparts. Such differences become more noticeable when the mother is caring for a male child alongside raising a daughter. The ever so slight discrimination against her female offspring might show up in a seemingly innocuous lack of empathy with her: an indifference that can actually prove to be quite traumatic.

Clinical vignette 1

Ebru, an internist in her mid-forties, recalled a particularly painful memory of her childhood. When she was five years old, her family went on a long road trip. Her father, a dignified man who was a car enthusiast, drove, and her self-absorbed mother sat by his side. Ebru and her older brother, Mustafa, occupied the back seat. As the car entered a scenic mountainous area, Mustafa saw a small white house up in the hills and immediately told Ebru that she will be sent there to live. Then noticing a nearby prison, he warned that its residents were dangerous criminals and Ebru would have to be very careful while living in that little white house. Little Ebru was terrified and protested against such "verdicts." This paradoxically intensified her brother's teasing.

As a grown-up professional engaged in psychotherapy with me, Ebru was pained by this memory but what troubled her more now was that her parents had not intervened on her behalf. They seemed utterly oblivious to the infantile cacophony unfolding behind them. Ebru wondered if her mother would have become actively protective had she been a little boy being teased by his older sister. Did she leave Ebru unprotected because of her being a girl?

Emotional neglect of such sort, especially if repeated over time, can result in the girl's questioning her value and her place in the family. A trauma, however, can cut both ways. It can increase competitive strivings and ambition but it can also result in low self-esteem, ego inhibition, and regressive clinging to the mother. The latter outcome is strengthened if further infantilization is faced by the girl during puberty.

Clinical vignette 2

> Seher, a thirty-seven-year-old computer programmer came for psychotherapy to work on her problems with opposite-sex relationships. While physically beautiful and well-coiffed, Seher had inhibitions in such matters. She had grown up in a traditional Turkish family, but was a noticeably "fancy" girl who was curious about sexuality from childhood onwards. When she was five or six years old, her parents would get upset or ignore her when she wanted to wear flashy and "girly" dresses and would pretend to sing on stage like famous female singers. When she wanted an Edwardian dress right out of the movie *My Fair Lady,* the family refused; this stayed with her and she felt that she was not allowed to be feminine. Seher did not receive any sexual education in her family and associated sexuality with shame, hiding her first menstruation from her mother; clearly, her early curiosity had undergone severe repression. As an adult, she lived on her own, but could have sex only in a hotel fearing that doing such things at home would defile it. She would not let her boyfriends stay overnight, fearing there might be an earthquake and they would be found naked under the rubble.

While this vignette demonstrates the long-term effects of the disparagement of a girl's burgeoning "femininity" during early childhood and latency, parental (especially maternal) anxieties about such matters during the girl's puberty and adolescence can cause even more severe harm.

Clinical vignette 3

> Tijen, a fifty-two-year-old divorced lawyer sought psychotherapy for profound feelings of unlovability and loneliness. She had married twice and her relationships with men were invariably disappointing. She had grown up in the setting of an unhappy marriage between her parents. Her mother was an outgoing and lively woman who was perpetually disappointed with her depressed husband. Tijen had an early puberty (around age twelve) and rapidly became an attractive girl, getting much attention from men. She was a popular, talented girl at school and was interested in art besides academic studies. Once when Tijen came home rather late after attending a boisterous party, the mother became furious and shouted at her "Are you going to be a slut?" They had a huge fight and next morning her mother took her to a gynecologist to check her hymen to see if she had been penetrated. This was a shameful and traumatic event which wounded her budding sexuality and later contributed to the disappointing relationships she had with men.

In contrast to overt maternal intrusions of such sort, subtly coercive relational scenarios between the mother and daughter can also impact upon the latter's acquisition of confidence in her body, mind, and social prowess. Physical beauty often plays a role in such developments. Mother's unenthusiastic, if not critical, attitude toward her daughter's appearance damages the latter's self-esteem and sows the seed of chronic self-doubt. Devaluing messages can be conveyed in myriad forms (e.g., "You look pretty from a distance," "You look nice when you don't have so much weight on"). Daughters of very good-looking mothers are especially subject to hurtful comparisons.

Clinical vignette 4

Arzu, a twenty-two-year-old graduate student at a prestigious university, constantly worried about her appearance. She was the daughter of an outstandingly pretty mother who was fair-skinned, blonde, and green-eyed. Arzu has a dark complexion and this frequently led to raised eyebrows in family gatherings. As she entered adolescence and then young adulthood, Arzu became "addicted" to taking selfies in a perpetual vigilance regarding her looks. None of the photos she took satisfied her, however. Despite her remarkable intelligence and outstanding academic record that far superseded her saleswoman mother's status, Arzu remained restless. She entered psychotherapy just when she was considering some cosmetic surgery. The reality factor in what was at its bottom severe oedipal competitiveness between her and her mother obfuscated the psychogenesis of her difficulties.

Mother's tension about the daughter's sexuality (regardless of its origins in oedipal competitiveness, voyeuristic impulses, and suppressed homoerotism) can gain great potency as the daughter enters full adulthood. Some mothers are unable to metabolize the separation such a development inevitably causes. Psychically renouncing the daughter to a man seems too painful and this, in turn, propels a domineering and controlling attitude toward the daughter who is becoming a sexual adult.

Clinical vignette 5

Ayşe, a thirty-two-year-old woman, was referred by a psychiatrist for psychotherapy for her intractable depressive proclivity. She was recently married and working at a marketing company. Despite a quite traumatic childhood, the patient was pleasant and psychologically minded. Her parents were divorced when she was twelve years old; father who was an eccentric man soon moved to another city and rarely saw his children. Mother was unemployed and depended solely upon alimony. She seemed to be mentally disturbed and paranoid. She saw the world as full of dangers. This fearful stance made her turn fiercely to Ayşe.

Upon finishing college, Ayşe moved out of town and started working. She was doing quite well when her mother started a business of her own and asked Ayşe to move back to their hometown. Ayşe who was meanwhile dating a man and trying to settle down with him

> could not decline the mother's invitation. She and her boyfriend moved to mother's city to facilitate the growth of this new business. Together they made strenuous efforts to help the mother who paradoxically got upset with Ayşe's attachment to her boyfriend. Eventually, the mother created a huge argument and their relationship came to the breaking point. Mother and Ayşe did not talk for years. Mother "ghosted" her, and did not attend Ayşe's wedding a year later. Clearly, she could not tolerate her daughter breaking their earlier symbiotic bond and leaving her for a man.
>
> Even though Ayşe had moved on with her life, from time to time she would regress and begin thinking she is not a separate person from the mother or that she is mentally disturbed like her mother. The self-doubt was especially marked when she observed her friends' cordial relationship with their mothers.

The symbiotic pull exerted by Ayşe's mother could have come from unresolved oedipal competitiveness with the daughter. However, it could also have emanated from a weak psychic structure (in the mother) that needed the child to function as an auxiliary ego. To be sure, structural and functional weakness on the mother's part impacts the daughter's psychic development in a decisively adverse manner. Besides, some mothers experience the daughter's striving to psychically separate as an attack and then retaliate against her.

Clinical vignette 6

> Gülsüm, a professionally successful daughter of a narcissistic-sadistic father and a weak mother, had witnessed her father beating her mother severely several times during her childhood. Gülsüm, whose academic life was successful, had insisted that her mother get divorced. She wanted her and her mother to live together in an effort to protect and save her mother from the father. Her mother was not keen on separating from her husband. Her "tolerance" of his beating her seriously damaged Gülsüm's bond with her. Gülsüm felt betrayed, a pain experienced even more piercingly when her father hit her and the mother did not come to her protection. Over years, the bond between them weakened and ultimately they stopped talking to each other altogether.

A relational conundrum of such a sort is far more intense when the daughter encounters a "dead mother" (A. Green, 1980). Not only is their relationship marked with hostile futility, the internal world of the daughter is desiccated and libidinally impoverished. Life is not simple, however. There are times that the daughter raised by a "dead mother" can survive the maternal emptiness and grow up to be a benevolent and helpful adult. Such an outcome is likely to happen when a kind and loving relative (e.g., an aunt, a grandmother) or even a neighbor takes the child under her wing and makes her feel worthy of attention and care. Turkish culture, with its emphasis upon communal bonds, is especially generous in its provision of such "rescue." The following illustration amply "confirms" this assertion.

Clinical vignette 7

Selin, an unmarried woman in her thirties, came seeking help for anxiety attacks. She was still living with parents even though she had graduated from college. Her developmental background showed a mother who was profoundly neglectful (rationalizing her attitude as that of granting freedom to her children) and a father who was a weak man, hardly involved in family matters. Selin had difficulty starting primary school and often fell "sick" in order to stay home. As a somewhat older child, she felt lost and forlorn. The one redeeming feature in her life was an unmarried paternal aunt who took special interest in her and showered her with love. Around this font of psychic nourishment, Selin built a core of forbearance and concern. Bit by bit, she grew into the caregiver not only of her mother but of her entire family. When there was an illness in the family, it was Selin who took the suffering member to the hospital. She remained celibate and devoted her life to becoming the mother of the family.

The remnant goodness in this case largely took the form of "altruistic surrender" (A. Freud, 1946) which is not an infrequent path for love-deprived daughters in Turkey to take. However, there are also instances in which the "sacrifice" is not the active choice of the daughter but extracted by a controlling and demanding mother.

Clinical vignette 8

Twenty-three-year-old Gül was a pediatric nurse who was diagnosed with bipolar disorder. She had a post-partum manic episode and had to be hospitalized for about one month when her baby was two months old. Gül's mother took care of the baby while she was at the hospital. Upon being discharged from the hospital she and her baby stayed with the mother for a while and eventually returned to work and her own house. Gül's mother kept looking after the baby and Gül would go and see her baby after work and then go back to her house to sleep. This went on for a year until she came for psychotherapy for managing bipolar disorder. Although she did not have any other episodes after the hospitalization and adhered to the treatment routine, she was made to think by her family, especially her mother, that she was not suitable to take care of her child.

Upon learning about Gül's staccato relationship with her baby, we worked on her anxiety about bringing him home and taking care of him; the baby had meanwhile begun calling Gül's mother "Mom." Gül and her mother were not well-informed about bipolar disorder and feared that she will have another episode when the baby cries and she wakes up at night or if she is stressed about the baby. As the negative aspect of such maternal overprotection was worked through, Gül decided to bring the baby home and take care of him with the help of her husband.

Even in the absence of an explicitly compromised ego (e.g., in the form of a bipolar disorder in the case cited above), discouragement from an overprotective and/or competitive mother can dishearten the daughter in regard to her mothering capacities.

Clinical vignette 9

> Serap, was a forty-year-old woman who came for mild depressive symptoms after having her first child. Serap was happily married and worked as a doctor at a hospital. Her parents were hardworking people who had saved money to provide good education for their kids. Serap's mother's life was devoted to taking care of her children. When Serap gave birth Serap's mother was quite helpful and supportive. However, Serap also recalled a painful dialogue between them. Her mother said, "Your milk is not enough for the baby. When I was breastfeeding I had plenty of milk." As a doctor, Serap was aware that the baby was gaining enough weight and healthy, yet she still felt she was not a good mother who can feed her baby. As she contemplated this conversation, she thought about covert rivalry between her mother and herself through the years. She realized that her mother was getting older and losing the role of being the needed and "too-good mother" (Shields, 1964), which was very important to her.

This case demonstrates that the mother's need to be needed, even if based upon consciously experienced love, can preclude her daughter's growth. The fact that the mother in this instance was also becoming a grandmother could have stirred up anxieties about aging and its attendant anxieties. Hesitation, inability, or refusal to advance in the developmental epoch of the life span are multiply determined, to be sure, and Serap's mother seems no exception in this regard.

A portrait of psychosocial synthesis

Our discourse has provided three sets of data on the nature of the mother–child relationship, focusing upon the mother–daughter bond and its vicissitudes. These sets of data emanate from: (i) psychoanalytic literature, (ii) Turkish anthropological studies, and (iii) anamnesis and reconstruction in clinical work with Turkish women. The composite profile of the mother–daughter relationship in Turkey that emerges from pooling such diverse sources of information reveals the following.

- Mother's emotional reaction at giving birth to a female child has evolved from mere acceptance to pleasure.
- Mother's response in this regard shows some rural/urban divide, with the positive end of the emotional spectrum being more commonly witnessed among urban mothers.
- Mothers maintain a keen vigilance on their daughters' whereabouts, interactions, and interpersonal connections.
- Mothers are very instrumental in helping their daughters form positive or negative attitudes toward their fathers. Mother's upholding the father as a reputable and strong figure while maintaining herself as a barrier against incestuous enactments facilitates the daughter's "civilized" (Freud, 1908d) sexuality. Mothers putting up with an abusive

husband can fuel the daughter's masochism or lead to a breakdown of the mother–daughter relationship.

- Mothers are keenly involved in their daughters' romantic lives. This manifests as control and anxiety-laden prohibition in the less-educated strata of society and as a gentle facilitation of femininity, dating, and "wifehood" in satisfactorily married urban mothers.
- The mother–daughter bond diminishes in intensity only slightly after the daughter's marriage. Mothers (and fathers) help acquire and sustain a post-marital residence for their daughters and maintain personal contact that is more frequent than in most Western nations, especially the United States.
- The mother–daughter relationship is quite symbiotic and separating from it is not easy for either member of the dyad. In the mother it mobilizes mental pain, and in the daughter, conscious or unconscious guilt.
- The mother–daughter relationship becomes even more strong with the birth of grandchildren and as Furman (1982) has observed, with the daughter's "return" to mother as the grandchildren enter adolescence and strive for separation.
- The mother–daughter relationship finds a rejuvenation, though in reverse, as the mother grows old and the daughter takes on a maternal role toward her.

Conclusion

By forging links between the psychoanalytic perspective on the development-initiating and development-facilitating tasks of the mother and the socio-anthropological data on the specificities of the mother–daughter interactions in Turkey, we have stitched together a sumptuous fabric of ontogenetic hermeneutics. Our endpoint is that the mother–daughter relationship at large not only shapes the latter's core identity but also impacts upon her body acceptance, era- and culture-specific gender role, self-esteem, separateness tolerance, attitudes toward men (derived considerably from the implicit and explicit messages she has received from the mother about the father), efficacy quotient, and her own potential to be a patient, protective, and loving mother. The universal applicability of this proposal does not detract from its veracity vis-à-vis the Turkish culture. What we have offered here is both generalizable and tightly focused upon culture-specific nuances. In effect, we have unveiled and underscored a triad of vectors that runs through the mother–child (specifically, mother–daughter) interactions spanning the years from the earliest infancy to the well-established adulthood of the latter. This triad consists of factors that are universal, factors that are culture-bound, and factors that are idiosyncratic. That our clinical material testifies to the truth of our proposal is the hope on which we conclude this contribution of ours.

CHAPTER 5

Fatherhood and Turkish culture

Cüneyt İşcan and Süreyya İşcan

In his acceptance speech for the Nobel Prize in literature, Orhan Pamuk shares his appreciation of his relationship with his father despite his prolonged absences in his childhood: "he'd never been a commanding, forbidding, overpowering, punishing, ordinary father, but a father who always left me free, always showed me the utmost respect" (www.nobelprize.org). His father was an avid reader and Pamuk grew up surrounded by his father's sizeable book collection (1500 volumes) at their home. Two years before his death, his father gave him a suitcase filled with his own writings in a slightly embarrassed, skittish way, suggesting to him that he might read them "after he was gone." Orhan Pamuk recounts his experience in this vivid, literary way, capturing the complex relationship between a father and his son:

> We were in my study, surrounded by books. My father was searching for a place to set down the suitcase, wandering back and forth like a man who wished to rid himself of a painful burden. In the end, he deposited it quietly in an unobtrusive corner. It was a shaming moment that neither of us ever forgot, but once it had passed and we had gone back into our usual roles, taking life lightly, our joking, mocking personas took over and we relaxed. We talked as we always did, about the trivial things of everyday life, and Turkey's never-ending political troubles, and my father's mostly failed business ventures, without feeling too much sorrow. (www.nobelprize.org)

The father, as a representation, as a symbol, takes center stage in human development and experience. Our experiences with our fathers in their presence and absence shape our personalities, our aspirations, goals, dreams. Fatherhood does not exist in a vacuum. As much as it is a psychological construct, it happens in the context of the family structure and the sociocultural context.

Preamble

In this chapter, the role of the father and fatherhood in the psychological development in Turkish culture will be explored mainly through the lens of psychoanalytic theories. We will try to explicate the role of the father as a psychic representation that has a strong presence in the psychological structure as well as the ever-evolving role of fatherhood in the cultural context. As we hope to demonstrate, the area of studying the role of the father in the cultural context is multifaceted and there is a need to draw from various disciplines. The historical and sociocultural perspective is especially important in terms of understanding the evolution of the role of the father and of fatherhood throughout the years. As can be imagined, such a study is not a simple task. An interdisciplinary approach to the study of a social construct requires several fields of the humanities, yet the study methods and the findings overlap, concur, and sometimes are in conflict and contradiction.

Psychoanalysis and its methods have evolved in clinical settings, where analysts work with individuals to study their psychological experiences as well as to alleviate suffering. Psychoanalysis is not the only method to study human psychology. Empirical research based on positivist notions has driven the field of psychology as a gold standard since its inception. Studying the social context within the historical context is complicated in a myriad of ways. The role of biological factors is hard to neglect when we think about gender differences and the role of gender in the fatherhood construct. In this chapter, we hope to demonstrate this complexity and stimulate interest in this rich area, a fertile ground in our view. We believe that what we don't know far exceeds what we know.

The role of the father and fatherhood has evolved throughout the years. The evolution of the theories in the psychoanalytic field reflects this evolution. Psychoanalysis came to life within the Victorian era in Europe at the turn of the twentieth century. Freud's ideas and his core concept, the Oedipus complex, have their roots in that era where an authoritarian, distant father who was not directly involved in child-rearing was normative. As the field evolved in the twentieth century, the focus shifted to the mother–child dyad especially after the Second World War (Etchegoyen, 2002; Fischer, 2004; Trowell, 2002). It is possible to see the nuclear family structure as the norm in this phase of the Industrial Age. The twentieth century witnessed many changes in the social structure as the family structure shifted and sociocultural movements changed the cultural landscape. Women entered the workforce more and more. The feminist movement had its impact on gender-based roles and values. Single-parent families, with an increased number of divorces, have become more common occurrences in this changing social landscape. We witness advances in information technology in the last several decades that have affected the world order drastically and paved the way to the era of globalization. Progressive movements such as LGBTQ have led to increased liberation in sexual orientation and gender preferences. Our views of the family and family structure continue to evolve in this context. An inevitable outcome of these changes is the way we think about fatherhood and the role of the father within the family and in society. The sociocultural context has another wrinkle in the study of fatherhood in the sense that the world is divided in the context of globalization along a fault line between the Western societies and the "Majority World," a term Çiğdem Kağıtçıbaşı, a prominent Turkish sociocultural psychologist, coined to replace the term "Third World." The religious, ethnic, racial elements all come into play in this context.

Our aim in this chapter is to apply psychoanalytic theories to understand fatherhood within Turkish culture. In the first section, we will approach fatherhood from the perspective of psychic development within the psychoanalytic framework. In the second section, aspects of Turkish culture will be explored in terms of the experience of fatherhood. In the third section, clinical vignettes will be presented to demonstrate the utility of these concepts in understanding the function of fatherhood in human experience.

Psychoanalysis and fatherhood

It is possible to surmise that Orhan Pamuk's father's suitcase represents the phallic object that contains the fountain of the words (literature) that Pamuk has already internalized as the function of the father. Here they are, his father is unsure of his own phallic power vis-à-vis his son, yet he continues to be present emotionally to allow his son to surpass him. His son, as a result, is eternally grateful: "Today, as I stand before the Swedish Academy and the distinguished members who have awarded me this great prize—this great honor—and their distinguished guests, I dearly wish he could be amongst us" (https://nobelprize.org/prizes/literaure/2006/pamuk/lecture). This brings us to Freud's most influential concept of the Oedipus complex and its healthy resolution, a pinnacle of sublimation that carries the son to the ultimate victory as a Nobel laureate.

The early psychoanalytic formulations of the role of the father in psychic development rely heavily on Freud's ideas of the crucial role of the father in the formation and resolution of the Oedipus complex. The term "Oedipus complex" makes its first appearance in Freud's paper "A special type of choice of object made by men" (1910h) where he states that the child "begins to desire his mother himself in the sense with which he has recently become acquainted, and to hate his father anew as a rival who stands in the way of this wish; he comes, as we say, under the dominance of the Oedipus complex" (p. 171). In this view, the father emerges as a rival. In the same paper, Freud writes that "all his instincts, those of tenderness, gratitude, lustfulness, defiance and independence, finds its satisfaction in the single wish *to be his own father*" (p. 175, italics in the original manuscript). As evidenced here, Freud sees identification with the father as a healthy outcome of the Oedipus complex. The oedipal father continues to preoccupy Freud's thinking and formulations in his other works, *Totem and Taboo* (1912–13), "The dissolution of the Oedipus complex" (1924d), *Civilization and Its Discontents* (1930a), and *Moses and Monotheism* (1939a).

In his view, the father represents the power, the authority, the prohibitions, and the punishment. Freud's view of the father's role is epitomized in his "castration anxiety" concept. The child's experience of the father is ambivalent in nature between the destructive urges (to fight his rival) on one hand and self-preservative urges (to submit to preclude castration) on the other hand. Freud's ideas around this "nuclear complex" (1908c, p. 214) have their vast developmental implications in superego formation and identification with the father.

The evolution within the psychoanalytic theory following Freud led to a shift in the focus toward the role of the mother in psychic development. Psychoanalysts began to focus on the mother–child dyad. This trend was especially marked between the 1930s and 1980s.

Klein (1921, 1932), through her analytic work with children, focused on the mother's role in development and spearheaded this shift in psychoanalysis. The Kleinian view postulates that the body parts in the early phase of development are intrapsychically represented. The breast is represented initially as the source of nurturance and in its absence as deprivation. The penis takes on a symbolic function as the infant's curiosity around body parts and functions develops. The penis inside the mother's body forms the crux of the Oedipus complex and it is perceived as attacking the nurturing breast as well as an alternative to the depriving breast. Later, Kleinian analysts emphasized the role of the parental couple as opposed to the singular role in development and the child's capacity to accept the parents' relationship as a developmental task. In his paper, "The missing link: Parental sexuality in the Oedipus complex," Britton (1989) emphasizes that the oedipal situation begins with the child's recognition of the parents' relationship and paves the way to the maturational step of acquiring the depressive position:

> In the phantasied tragic version of the Oedipus complex the discovery of the oedipal triangle is felt to be the death of the couple: the nursing couple or the parental couple. In this phantasy the arrival of the notion of a third always murders the dyadic relationship. (p. 257)

According to Britton (1998), separation is experienced as the mother retreating to the parental bedroom with the second object, the father. Kleinian notions ascribe a crucial yet representational role to the father.

Winnicott (1960a, 1971, 1974) also assigns a primary and fundamental role to the mother in psychic development. A "facilitating environment" is provided by the mother and Winnicott views the role of the father as "holding" the mother–child unit. According to Winnicott, fathers serve a maternal function in the early phase just like the mother and the paternal function comes into play in the later stages of development. He puts this succinctly: "Good enough mothering 'includes fathers but fathers must allow me to use the term maternal to describe the total attitude to babies and their care. The term paternal must necessarily come a little later than maternal'" (cited in Etchegoyen, 2002, p. 28). Etchegoyen also points to Winnicott's belief that this later phase is usually in adolescence and the crucial role of the parents' capacity to tolerate an adolescent's "murderous wishes and feelings of personal triumph on taking the parents' place" in healthy development (ibid.).

Attachment theories also emphasize the role of the mother and designate a role to the father in the later phase of the development (Ainsworth et al., 1978; Beebe & Lachmann, 1994; Bowlby, 1969). Mahler postulates that in the rapprochement subphase of separation–individuation, the infant has the need "to defend his own evolving, enjoyable and jealously guarded self-image from the infringement by mother and other important figures" (Mahler & Gosliner, 1955). These authors write:

> In boys as well as girls, around eighteen months (in some cases even much earlier), the father has become an important object. This relationship ordinarily has the advantage that the inner image of the father has never drawn to itself so much of the unneutralized drive cathexis as has the mother's, and therefore there is less discrepancy between the image of the father and the real father. (p. 199)

In this view, the role of the "real father" as opposed to the "symbolic father" is emphasized in the development.

Hans Loewald (1951) emphasizes the function of early positive identification with the father allowing the child to separate from the mother and as a protection against strong attachment to mother and engulfment (danger of the womb). The theme of symbolically destroying the parents as part of healthy development is also evident in Loewald's (1979) view:

> In an important sense, by evolving our own autonomy, our own superego, and by engaging in nonincestuous object relations, we are killing our parents. We are usurping their power, their competence, their responsibility for us, and we are abnegating, rejecting them as libidinal objects. In short, we destroy them in regard to some of their qualities hitherto most vital to us. Parents resist as well as promote such destruction no less ambivalently than children carry it out. What will be left if things go well is tenderness, mutual trust, and respect—the signs of equality. This depends on, more than anything else, the predominant form of mastery of the Oedipus complex. (p. 757)

In Winnicott and Loewald, similar to Klein, we see that the focus of the oedipal complex pivots to the parental couple as opposed to Freud's emphasis on the father.

Summarizing the aforementioned psychoanalytic theories, Akhtar and Powell (2004) identify four tasks in terms of father's role in the child's development:

> 1. By being a protective, loving, and collaborative partner to the mother, the father facilitates and enhances her ability to devote herself to the child. 2. By offering himself as a relatively neutral, ego-oriented, new object during early childhood struggles over autonomy and independence from the mother, the father provides the child stability, a haven from conflict and (in the case of a boy) an important measure of "disidentification" from the mother. 3. By appearing on the evolving psychic horizon of the child as the romantic partner of the mother, the father helps consolidate the child's capacity to experience,

> to bear and benefit from the triangular familial relationship and the conflict attendant upon it. 4. By presenting himself as an admirable model for identification to his son and by reflecting the budding femininity of his daughter with restrained reciprocity, the father enriches his children's gender identity and gives direction to their later sexual object choices. (p. 77)

As opposed to these psychoanalytic theories, Lacanian theory has the father back to center stage. Lacan returns to Freud's Oedipus complex and reformulates it in a way that it becomes the crux of his theory. According to Lacan, the father serves the function of a signifier or metaphor in symbolic structure. Similarly, "mother" is a signifier in the early symbolic structure representing "the other" in the child's experience. As the child emerges from the initial dependent phase to the mother, she or he is faced "with the enigma around the (m)other's desire" and must confront the question "What am I in the Other's desire?" (Homer, 2005, p. 53). Here is how Homer summarizes the process of transition from the Lacanian imaginary register to the symbolic register through the Oedipus complex: "Through the intervention of a third term, the Name-of-the-Father, that closed circuit of mutual desire between the mother and child is broken and a space is created, within which the child can begin to identify itself as a separate being from the mother" (p. 53).

Homer argues that Lacan radically reformulated the role of the father by replacing the actual father with a signifier, a paternal metaphor, "which substitutes the desire of the mother with symbolic law" (p. 64). Another important aspect of the role of the father in Lacan's view is "through the notion of the two fathers to the function of the superego, as at once the internalization of the symbolic law and the desire to transgress the law" (p. 64). The father can represent the law but at the same time can be subversive, above the law, and ruthless. We see the iterations of the symbolic father in the Lacanian view despite its central role in both the imaginary and symbolic registers.

What do all these theories have in common? All these theorizations seem to agree that the father has a role in psychic development. The father's role seems to follow the mother's role by providing an external structure holding the mother–child dyad. Father's role gradually takes on the task of breaking the bond between the mother and the child and furthering the establishment of the child's developing relationship with the external reality. The processes of identification and internalization seem to solidify the child's relationship with the external reality (society/culture).

We believe that the psychoanalytic field is at the cusp of a paradigm shift as we gain more insights and a better appreciation of the individual psychic structure within the context of social structure as we have a much more nuanced appreciation of sociocultural factors creating biases in our conceptualizations, our theories, our studies, and research in understanding the human mind. Cisnormativity shapes our thinking in such fundamental ways that unwittingly we seem to get caught in and fall back on gender-based attributions and binary thinking. Etchegoyen references Temperley coming from a feminist Kleinian perspective arguing that "Freud's and Lacan's theories, which made the penis/phallus the signifier, resulted in women being placed in disadvantageous and relatively powerless position, 'rendering them "objects" in a world of male signification'" (2002, p. 33). Temperley seems to agree on the significance of the father but suggests the father's use of his authority to preserve a creative relationship with the mother as an equal partner. Davids questions the idea that we need a father in development (Davids, 2002). This is an evolving area and understanding the function of gender in development in same-sex marriages can shed light and potentially modify our current views.

Another area of vulnerability in our studies is our conscious and unconscious biases based on our culture's normative views based on our ethnic, religious, nationalistic, and racial backgrounds. We will elaborate on this issue in the next section.

Cross-cultural perspective

While psychoanalytic theories seek generalizations and applicability across cultures, this proclivity creates a vulnerability for the field. Target and Fonagy (2002) in their critical review of psychoanalytic theories regarding fatherhood indicate that "psychoanalysts, particularly over the past quarter of a century, have evolved increasingly complex models of the role of 'the father' in normal development and in so doing made significant assumptions of homogeneity of family structure, individual behaviour and interpersonal relationships" (p. 45). Pointing to the dialectic between these generalizations and the psychoanalytic field's focus on individual differences, they suggest: "Nowhere is this dialectic so readily apparent as in the psychoanalytic literature on fathers, where generalisations about the role of the father are readily made but remain poorly integrated with the observations of individual fathers with individual children under their care" (p. 45).

Çiğdem Kağıtçıbaşı (2013), a Turkish psychologist who has devoted her career to cross-cultural psychology, has made important contributions to understanding fatherhood in Turkish culture. Her approach and her research offer ways to bridge the gap between the psychological constructs and the cultural context. Çiğdem Kağıtçıbaşı has a critical perspective of Euro-American psychology and brings a unique understanding of the cultural dynamics in the "Majority World" (term that she uses to replace the by now pejorative term "Third World" to refer to 80% of the world population). She challenges the Western-centric view of human development, which is based on individualistic values as opposed to relational, collectivist values. She refutes the ideas of the supremacy of Western values and that the "Majority World" cultures will gradually evolve to adopt those values. She offers a contextual cross-cultural approach to study human development and psychology in a manner akin to Roland (1988) and Kakar (2024) who as psychoanalysts stand out for their questioning the universality of an individuated, unitary self whose developmental hypotheses are firmly anchored in regional anthropologies.

Kağıtçıbaşı, in her book *Family, Self, and Human Development Across Cultures* (2013), challenges the Individualism-Collectivism model in studying culture and offers ways to conceptualize the development of the self within the family and in the societal context across different cultures. She approaches psychoanalytic notions of separation–individuation and autonomy and valorization of these theories through a critical lens:

> there is an emphasis on clear boundaries separating the selves (subsystems) within the family system. Thus, for healthy development of the self and for healthy family functioning, ***individuation-separation*** (emphasis on original text) and well-defined boundaries of the self are considered crucial in much of personality theory and clinical psychology ... Thus, Western psychology affirms one type of self—the separate self—as the healthy prototype. It is the prescriptive nature of psychology that empowers it; it can do more harm than good. This is what the critics of American psychology have complained about: that psychology is part of the problem, rather than the solution, of selfishness and lack of social commitment. (p. 111, italics in the original)

She proposes an "independence–interdependence" dimension in the development of "the related self" and "the separate self":

> The independence-interdependence dimension can be conceptualized at different levels. At the level of the self, it is equivalent to separateness-relatedness. It can also be studied at the familial or cultural levels, similar to the culture of relatedness-culture of separateness. At this level, it can be useful in understanding, for example childrearing and socialization orientations. It is at this level, especially that of the family, that an independence-interdependence dimension provides the links between the background (cultural, social-structural) variables and the self. (p. 110)

Kağıtçıbaşı sees the possibility of an autonomous self with the context of relatedness and that separation should not necessarily leading to individuation with clear personal boundaries as the Western psychological framework suggests.

Turkish culture with its long-standing bridging position between the Western and the Eastern cultures provides the richness in understanding the cross-cultural context. Bayrakçeken and Randall (2005), in their paper, point to the way Orhan Pamuk captures this complexity:

> Pamuk's individual characters, and by extension the cultural constructions he stages, are driven by need, the need to seek completeness and coherence in the field of otherness. Countering Kipling's "East is East, West is West", Pamuk states that "East should not be East and West should not be West". (pp. 191–204)

Stepping in and out of each cultural context assists in understanding the role of cultural context in social constructs, such as fatherhood.

Volkan and Çevik (1989), in their chapter about Turkish fathers, approach the rich historical elements in the evolution of Turkish culture, encompassing thousands of years, as a backdrop in understanding the cultural context within which the experience of fatherhood evolved. They illustrate how societal factors underpin the intrapsychic development in the specificity of Turkish culture. They return to the concept of the "satellite state," a term initially coined by Volkan and Corney (1968), that defines "a developmental compromise, a stable fixation in psychological orbit around the central figure from whose representation the individual fails to separate and achieve true individuation" (Volkan & Çevik, 1989, p. 354):

> A Turk living in the country, where traditional ways are the norm, is not fully liberated from his mother's representations by becoming a freestanding person, intrapsychically, in his own right. Although he must remain near it, he fears being engulfed by it and so maintains some psychic distance from it. Since he can differentiate her representation from his own, he does not enter into symbiosis but is drawn toward the center when it represents the "good" mother and is repelled when it is the "bad" one. Like the circling moth so often described in Ottoman poetry and folk verse, he is suspended between two dangerous possibilities: he can be destroyed by it flying into the flame or be lost in the darkness by fleeing in it. (p. 354)

The need to be in the orbit is a useful metaphor that Volkan and Çevik further expand that captures the traditional family structures in Turkey where the individual does not fully separate from their family of origin by living in close quarters or cohabiting with their extended family. The man being in the circle of women during his childhood years and the father being outside this circle reinforced by authoritarian, patriarchal family structure lead to rigid gender based internal representations of femininity and masculinity. The man's need to disconnect from his emotional side as a result of this social construct has its interesting intrapsychic repercussions, which are captured by Volkan and Çevik:

> The modern Turkish man has a fixed mental representation of a father figure that he shares with his fellow citizens and that directs them to become idealized and rather omnipotent. This process requires denial of painful aspects of manliness and realities of fatherhood. (p. 361)

The intrapsychic and social structure interface is a fertile ground. The evolution of the social structures throughout time further enriches the study of human mind. Social research provides interesting data to understand this evolution.

Kağıtçıbaşı (2017) spearheaded internationally groundbreaking research in Turkey to study family structure, parenting, and early child development as well as immigration and acculturation. Her Turkish Early Enrichment Project was a four-year longitudinal project involving early childhood enrichment and mother training in low-income areas of İstanbul. "Fatherhood in Turkey" Series (www.acev.org) is a group of reports including "Involved fatherhood and Its determinants in Turkey," the second, "Fatherhood in Turkey: In the midst of parenthood,"

"Masculinity and work," and "The states of masculinity and fatherhood in Turkey." These studies were conducted under the aegis of Anne Çocuk Eğitim Vakfı (ACEV) (Mother Child Education Foundation).

Akçınar and her colleagues (2017) studied 3235 fathers from fifty-one cities to shed light on how fatherhood was viewed under specific societal and cultural conditions in Turkey. Their results indicated that fatherhood behaviors were strongly related to gender roles and how masculinity was perceived by the fathers. Patriarchal masculinity led to the "traditional fatherhood" category which was the predominant group (49%) in the study. Traditional fatherhood represented a type of fatherhood which was characterized by behaviors such as resistance to change, authoritarianism, and distance toward children both emotionally and physically. The lack of maternal functions of the fathers was observed in this group and the participating fathers did not report being involved in feeding, caring, and emotional touching behaviors. These values were congruent with "patriarchy," which represented a model of masculinity where men are seen as the breadwinners of the family with a tendency for violence, whose authority cannot be questioned. On the other hand, 28 percent of the participants comprised what was called the "new traditional fathers," who resemble traditional fathers in their attitudes toward masculinity, but the fathers in this group engaged in behaviors to build affectionate relationships with their children. A third category of fatherhood, named as "keen fathers" by the researchers, had traditional views of fatherhood; however, they make a conscious choice to display behaviors resembling good maternal care (23%). These fathers fall into the "masculinity in transition" category which played a critical role in the transformation in society.

Understanding the sociocultural factors that shape fatherhood in Turkey, including the impact of modernization, urbanization, and changing gender roles, is important to recognize the diverse ways in which fathers contribute to family life and child development in the Turkish context. This research shows that a more nuanced understanding of fatherhood that considers the intersection of cultural, economic, and social factors and their implications for child development and family dynamics is emerging. Assigned gender (biological sex) is becoming less definitive as the traditional societal structure evolves.

In the next section, we will try to demonstrate how socially defined gender roles in Turkish culture shape and inform parenting and how these parental behaviors play a role in positively or negatively impacting development. We also hope to demonstrate the utility of the culturally informed psychoanalytic approach in understanding clinical phenomena. We do believe that gender fluidity ultimately has beneficial results in development.

Clinical insights

Clinical vignette 1

Mert is a middle-aged cisgender heterosexual man, who came to therapy to address his depression and problems in his romantic relationships. He had a failed marriage and was struggling in his current marriage. His parents were both physicians who after their training in İstanbul returned to their small hometown in southern Turkey to establish their practice and raise their family. Both of his parents were born in the modern Turkish republic and grew up with Western ideas and aspirations. Mert's father was a hard-working family man who lost his father at a very young age and was raised by his brothers. Driven by feelings of guilt and gratitude he felt obliged to help his extended family. His focus on his family of origin led to significant chronic discord between him and his wife. Mert's mother had a traditional view of family structure despite pursuing a career as a woman where the man was "the head of the household" and the woman was ascribed a submissive, dependent role. Although his mother subscribed to this worldview, she suffered greatly by not having agency in her marriage. His mother's absences due to her depressive states and her passive-aggressive engagement in her relationship with her husband shaped Mert's personality. He felt responsible to take care of his younger siblings to fill the void that was created by a hard-working, preoccupied father as well as a depressive and emotionally unavailable mother. His father was a compassionate man in his own ways but was not able to express his positive feelings. Mert had no recollection of his father telling him that he loved him. Mert in his relationships with women took on the role of the caregiver which left him with feelings of resentment and anger while withdrawing from relationships and focusing excessively on his career and work.

Despite higher socioeconomic status and education, we see traditional roles in operation in this example, both the man and woman being caught in traditional roles and societal roles accordingly, namely father carrying the responsibility of being the breadwinner, protecting the family, and serving the role of authority, and mother being responsible for child-rearing. These roles can continue to be in operation despite both partners having full-time jobs and careers. In this case, it is possible to see the potential benefit of equally shared roles of "maternal functions" and "paternal functions" allowing the child to internalize these functions in a gender fluid way. In Mert's situation, his parents' inability to break away from the traditional roles led to him getting caught in the "maternal role" of selfless giving and needing to break away, and swinging to the other end of the dialectic role by getting stuck in the "paternal role" outside the family.

In the next case vignette, it is possible to see similar themes in the experience of a cisgender woman.

Clinical vignette 2

İpek is a cisgender heterosexual woman in her mid-thirties who came to therapy due to her struggle with depression and problems in intimacy. Her parents were a high achieving professional couple. Her father grew up in the Eastern part of Turkey and was driven by aspirations of status and power. He married a woman of "higher status" who came from a family who held important positions in the palace during the late phase of the Ottoman Empire. She viewed her mother as weak, vulnerable, and dependent on her father and her father in the position of authority and having the last word in the family. In her teenage years,

> she became increasingly defiant in response to her father's controlling tendencies, and sexually promiscuous. Her parents' values were Western and secular. She grew up in a metropolitan area.

Her parents' adopted Western values did not provide protection to gender-based roles and Ipek was not able to internalize a solid core self-identity with fluidity in gender roles allowing for a healthy intimacy in adulthood. She was faced with identification with her mother as a woman in a submissive position vis-à-vis a man. Her identification with her father, all-powerful, all-knowing, authoritarian, was not culturally permissible due to strictly defined gender roles. Her adoption of Western egalitarian views like her parents' made it even harder to deal with the unintegrated aspects of rigid gender roles and was detrimental in the establishment of stable self-identity.

In the next clinical vignette, we see a more solidified aspect of identity in terms of functioning in the outer world, yet unintegrated self-experience again in the context of rigid parental gender roles.

Clinical vignette 3

> Aslı is a cisgender heterosexual female in her thirties who had a high-paying influential job in an urban setting in Turkey. She moved to the US in her college years for education and permanently stayed after securing a job as a postgraduate. She sought therapy to address her anxiety and depression, which was accompanied by intense feelings of emptiness and loneliness. She had a satisfactory work life, but her romantic life was a disappointment for her. She did not like online dating. She viewed online dating as superficial and for people who are seeking "hook ups." Several previous romantic relationships ended because of her partners' infidelity. She found herself being drawn to married men. She secretly hoped that a man who would have a genuine interest in her would leave his family and ultimately "choose her." Aslı deeply struggled with the idea of not having a family her own. She grew up in a midsize city in rural Turkey. Her mother came from a family with Western values and was highly educated. She fell in love with a man who was uneducated but with significant wealth who grew up in rural Turkey with traditional values. Her mother's experience of cold and distant family life with Western values led to her attraction to a man and his traditional family life and roles which was perceived initially as loving and warm. Her father was absent throughout Aslı's childhood. She remembered him proudly saying that he had never even put a sock on his girls and that he in his view represented a "real man." Aslı's father was very close with his brothers and older sister and his aging parents. They lived in a compound. He spent most of his downtime with his extended family. Aslı's mother refused to be with her in-laws to punish her husband's lack of interest in the nuclear family. Aslı felt as if she was not part of her father's extended family and felt that he valued his nieces and nephews more than her and her sister. Aslı's parents got divorced when she was sixteen years old after long and very tumultuous times over sharing the wealth of the father built during their long marriage and

father's extramarital relationships. Aslı's father moved out quickly from the family home. Aslı did not know where her father lived. She heard from her mother that her father had moved in with a sex-worker, his long-term mistress, and her son. She spent considerable time finding his address. She showed up on his doorstep one day. He cracked the door open and asked her to leave and that he would be in touch with her. She remembered painfully how it felt to be excluded from her father's life. She was not the one desired and cared for and felt that she could not be the chosen one.

Although emotional absence of any parent could create disturbance in development, when gender roles are strictly defined as in Aslı's family there is not much room for father's maternal caring. Children of both genders greatly benefit from well-balanced triadic constellations which means each parent despite their genders should carry both maternal (nurturing) and paternal (protection) caring responsibilities. The absence of maternal caring in fathers, such as feeding, bodily care, and nurturing, could lead to disturbances in self and self-representations. In Aslı's case, strictly defined masculinity and the absence of inclusion and nurturing by her father led to unstable romantic relationships. Her desire to have her own family and being in an intimate relationship with a man painfully failed. While what had been given to her by her father (financial success and freedom) was available to her in her adult life, what had not been given could not be accomplished for a satisfactory adulthood.

In the next clinical vignette, we see the parents' struggle around rigid gender roles leading to a deep sense of unhappiness and feeling at a loss in their family unit, pushing them to find solace in relationships outside the family.

Clinical vignette 4

Cem is a cisgender heterosexual man who suffered from intense mood dysregulation and anger outbursts. He sought treatment after being arrested for fistfights in intense traffic in İstanbul. He had road rage and was beaten up several times by cab drivers for attacking them. Cem was raised by a father who was lost in his artistic longings and sensitivities. Cem witnessed his father's humiliation by his mother for sexual impotence and his mother's infidelity mostly with a neighbor when growing up. He felt belittled by his mother's actions. When he went to his father with this information, his father dismissed his suspicions and said that he had imagined things, in order to avoid a confrontation with his wife. Cem's father lacked the ability to bring the man's authority and the protection to the family, which led to boundary violations.

Cem was angry and filled with rage most of his life. He physically and sexually abused his two younger sisters which caused him consequently to suffer from intense guilt. He found his mother tantalizing and dismissive. He wished to bring sanity, control, and protection to his family by overly relying on acting out and violent behaviors. Cem's terrorizing behaviors greatly harmed him and people who were close to him, which was a result of compensatory, exaggerated, aggressive masculinity.

These clinical illustrations highlight how the absence of a healthy triadic structure, with loving parents who both are fluently able to take up the role of protection and nurturing at the same time in the family, greatly inhibits a healthy psychic development. The emerging self can be harmed by the absence of both the maternal function of a father and the paternal function of a mother. Children need structure, security, and stability with attachment figures who can navigate the traditional gender roles which are culturally determined. The lack of fluidity of gender roles and parents' internalization of sociocultural constructs might interfere with healthy development and lead to early childhood trauma.

Conclusion

The triadic nature of internal family life emerges as the core theme for conceptualization of developing the human mind and its relationship with the larger sociocultural context in many psychoanalytic theories. Although the importance of the mother and the dyadic nature of the mother and infant relationship is highlighted, the healthy development of the human psyche depends on the successful resolution of self and other differentiation in the context of triadic relationships. The triadic nature of the human experience and the function of the parental couple renders the importance of the father's role in development inevitable. Binary and gender-based role descriptions in psychoanalytic theories have suffered from fully capturing the importance of the fathers and their willingness to carry out the duties that were traditionally assigned to the mothers, such as feeding, bodily care, and affectionate touching which are commonly considered as maternal functions. Also, the traditional psychoanalytic theories' view of the function of the father as bringing the "father's authority" for breaking the mother–infant dyad can be stifling in the theory and in need of reexamination. We believe that the fathers' fulfilling of maternal duties and mothers' ability to insert their authority and power lead to more competent and resilient human psyches with gender fluidity. The two parents, independent of their assigned gender at birth, carrying both maternal and paternal functions as equally as possible seems to be the key factor for a healthy psychological development. Sociocultural factors greatly impact traditional feminine and masculine roles and bring limitations, specifically for Turkish fathers carrying out crucial maternal tasks for their children. These sociocultural factors seem to be changing, as evidenced by the research we shared in this chapter. We are yet to see the impact of the further evolution of gender fluidity in human experience as well as a better understanding of same-sex marriages in child development. A lot has evolved and there is more to come.

CHAPTER 6

The sibling relationship and some thoughts on siblings in Turkish culture

Pınar Limnili Özeren

The sibling relationship has been suboptimally investigated by psychoanalysis despite its important place in our lives and in the structuring of our psyche. It is this lacuna in the psychoanalytic theory of development that I will seek to fill via this contribution of mine. I will begin by examining the place of siblings in Freud's texts in chronological order. Following this, I will summarize the views of Klein, Winnicott, and a few other subsequent analysts on this topic. I will also address the role of real or imagined sibling projections in shaping psychic development, clinical unfolding of transference and countertransference, group dynamics, and social life at large. Finally, I will make some comments upon the specific nuances of the sibling relationship in Turkish culture.

Freud's views

There is no separate section on siblings in Freud's collected works, and when he centered his theory on the Oedipus complex siblings remained a vague background in the psyche shaped around the parent–child relationship. He sporadically mentions sibling relationships and their influence on the psyche in his work, and yet he did not conceptualize sibling relationships and give them a decisive role in the development of the psyche. Siblings appear as equals competing for the love of the important other object, the mother or father, and their intense emotions toward each other were mostly defined through their parents.

The idea that early experiences with siblings and peers are important seems to have been in Freud's mind but did not find much place in his theory. However, we can see sibling images in Freud's dreams that he wrote in detail between 1895 and 1901 (Anzieu, 1984). In Freud's dreams, sibling images are manifested as peers that he competes with and he feels insecure around them. These were also the years when Freud started to develop his theory of psychoanalysis and tried to get himself and his theory accepted in the prestigious Viennese medical circles. In his dreams "Irma's injection" and "the dream of uncle Josef," his rivalry with his colleagues and his desire to prevail over them are evident (Freud, 1900a). Although Freud does not say anything directly about sibling rivalry, his associations with his dreams go back to his childhood memories and his close relationship with his nephew John, their games and fights (ibid., p. 424).

Freud does not say much about his own siblings, either. We do not hear about them except for the death of his younger brother Julius, and his youngest brother Alexander. The title "brothers and sisters" appears only five times in all of Freud's works (Colonna & Newman, 1983). Freud describes the sibling as an "unwanted intruder" (Freud, 1933a, p. 122). With the arrival of the sibling, he writes, the child loses not only the breast but also the mother's care almost completely, feeling as if he has been "dethroned, despoiled and prejudiced in his rights." The child expresses his resentment to the "faithless mother" with his disagreeable change in his behavior while harboring a jealous hatred for the new baby. Even if the child remained the preferred favorite of the mother, not much would change because the child could understand what was happening even if there is only an eleven-month age difference between the two siblings. He says that the child's jealousy is nourished with each new sibling in the following years (ibid.). It is hard not to recall Freud's own childhood here; although he was his mother's favourite, it seems that it was not easy to cope with the emotions created by his brother Julius, who was born shortly after him, and his other siblings born one after the other.

In rare instances where Freud mentions siblings, the sibling image is usually negative. The child's mind is filled with fantasies of hatred, rivalry, or even murder against the newcomer who has displaced him or her. How could Freud have arrived at this negative perception? What was the role of his own experience as a sibling? Agger (1988) suggests that the near-absence of siblings in psychoanalytic theory may be related to Freud's unresolved psychic conflicts with his own siblings. We might wonder about the impact of Freud's own sibling experience on his relationships with his patients and colleagues. Freud's sibling experience seems to have influenced not only his theory of siblings, but also his relationship with his rivals and peers. In his dealings with them within the psychoanalytic movement, his authoritarian attitude, his desire to prove his rightness, and his uncompromising personality are evident. Bank and Kahn (1980) argue that Freud's desire to retain absolute power within the psychoanalytic movement all the time was similar to his experience with his own siblings. They suggest that it is telling to think of his struggles with Adler and Jung, and of his refusal to compromise intellectually or socially in his role as leader, in terms of sibling dynamics (ibid.).

Although Freud never gives siblings a central role in his case histories, he often mentions them. In Freud's early case histories and texts, Freud states that incestuous relationships and sexual abuse between siblings will negatively affect the child's adult sexual life and mentions their possible psychological consequences. He argues that in most cases of hysterics, the brothers had years of sexual intimacy with their younger sisters, and that in adulthood these childhood experiences led to hysterical symptoms in the girl and obsessions in the boy (Freud, 1896b, pp. 157–185).

In *The Interpretation of Dreams* he explicitly mentions the desire to kill the siblings: "Many people … who loved their brothers and sisters and would feel bereaved if they were to die, harbour evil wishes against them in their unconscious, dating from earlier times; and these are capable of being realized in dreams" (Freud, 1900a, p. 251).

Freud was aware of the intense feelings toward siblings in his cases. He thinks that for the older child, the birth of a sibling is experienced as a kind of displacement and that the desire to destroy the newcomer is always there. At the same time, according to Freud, the younger siblings are not immune from these destructive feelings and are jealous of their older siblings. "The elder child ill-treats the younger," he says, "maligns him and robs him of his toys; while the younger is consumed with impotent rage against the elder, envies and fears him, or meets his oppressor with the first stirrings of a love of liberty and a sense of justice" (ibid., p. 250). In his *Three Essays on the Theory of Sexuality*, on the other hand, he argues that the child's curiosity about the foundations of his or her existence arises with the arrival of a new baby, thus attributing to the sibling a psyche-structuring role that stimulates curiosity and reflection (Freud, 1905d).

In the case of Dora, a case of hysteria, the elder brother of Dora is one of the erotic objects of her early childhood. When Dora was four or five years old, as she was suckling her finger, she was at the same time tugging the earlobe of her brother who was one-and-a-half years older than her. Freud, who defines the symptom of enuresis as a substitute for masturbation, points to the elder brother as an object of identification as he says that this habit was passed from her elder brother to Dora (Freud, 1905e).

In the case of Little Hans, Freud argues that the birth of Hans' sister had a decisive influence on the sexual psychic development of the little boy. Hans, who often said that he wished his sister had not come into the world, was afraid of his hostile desires toward his sister and repressed this desire by transforming it into a symptom of fear of bathing and of horses carrying heavy loads. In Hans' imagination, his mother's belly is full of siblings he wants to eliminate (Freud, 1909b). Returning to this subject in 1917, Freud says that children's rage at the appearance of an expected or real rival manifests itself in throwing objects out of windows and other acts of aggression and destructiveness. He argues that the child knows that the rival is in the mother's body, and that the heavy objects thrown out represent the mother herself, to whom the child directs his or her anger as long as the new baby has not yet appeared. Freud recalls Little Hans and his fear of heavily loaded cars here (Freud, 1917b, pp. 145–146).

In the case of the Rat Man, the themes of sibling jealousy and sibling loss stand out. The patient remembers fainting after shooting his younger brother in the forehead with a toy gun to harm him. Freud attributed the Rat Man's frequent attendance at funerals and his extreme empathy for those who have suffered loss with the death of his sister. He suggests that the guilt of his deadly childhood desires for his sister, which were realized when she died at the age of four, is one of the causes of the patient's obsessional neurosis (Freud, 1909d).

In the Wolf Man case, Freud describes in detail the patient's intense relationship with his dominant, intelligent, and seductive older sister. This sister had sadistically seduced the patient in childhood, skillfully rebuffed his sexual advances in adolescence, and made him feel humiliated. The older sister's seduction led to recollection of the primary scene by *après coup*, which formed the basis of the Wolf Man's neurosis. Freud argues that the patient's exposure to the sexual games of his older sister paved the way for his adoption of the passive role and some of his neurotic symptoms. According to Freud, the patient's sexual desires for his sister and his seduction by her in his childhood determined the choices of his sexual life in adulthood. In this case Freud also emphasizes the traumatic effects of power inequality as well as sexual seduction between siblings. However, while Freud's interest in the relationship between the two siblings does not play a decisive role in the neurosis of the Wolf Man, he emphasizes once again through this case that oedipal trauma is at the heart of neurosis (Freud, 1918b).

In *Totem and Taboo*, Freud gives examples of the prohibition of incest between siblings in primitive tribes and argues that the first incestuous object of the male child is the mother or sisters. The bond between sisters and brothers includes the prohibition of incest, whereas the bond between brothers, who have killed and eaten the tyrannical father, develops on the basis of the oedipal guilt. Freud refers to the alliance between brothers who emerge from the guilt of killing the father as the first step of the social order (Freud, 1912–13).

In "Some neurotic mechanisms in jealousy, paranoia and homosexuality," Freud emphasizes the importance of siblings in the choice of homosexual objects in men. He states that the male child shares the mother with his brothers in addition to the father, and that the intense jealousy caused by this leads to killing desires in the male child toward rivals, usually older brothers. These desires are transformed by repression and rivals can become the first objects of homosexual love (Freud, 1922b).

In Freud's later works, siblings play an important role in the construction and maintenance of social life. In *Group Psychology and the Analysis of the Ego*, he states that initially rivals, siblings can identify with each other thanks to the similar love for the parent, and thus hostile feelings may create a positive bond through identification and form the group spirit (Freud, 1921c).

Klein, Winnicott, and subsequent analysts

When we look at the place of siblings in Klein's theory, in her early writings she seems to give a special place to sibling relationships. She suggests that siblings promote emotional development and may help the child overwhelmed by the instinctual intensity of relationships with parents to take a distance (Klein, 1932). Pointing to the existence of sexual relations between children in early life as a very common incident, she gives many examples of destructive sexual relationships between siblings. On the other hand, she also notes that "where the positive and libidinal factors predominate, such a relationship has a favorable influence upon the child's object relations and capacity to love" (ibid., pp. 118–119). It is important to emphasize that Klein pays attention to the constructive effect of sibling love on the psyche without ignoring the envy and destructiveness in sibling relationships in which love and hate are side by side from the beginning. Competing for a parent's love brings with it envy and hatred of the rival, phantasies of killing, but sibling relationships are not limited to this. The prohibition of incest against intense love and eroticism between siblings is there from the beginning.

Considering the importance of early object relations in the structuring of the psyche in Klein's theory, it is surprising that siblings are not included among these early objects. Klein's case histories are full of siblings. She sees and hears siblings in her child cases, but she usually interprets the sibling issues through oedipal conflict and feelings of love and hatred toward the parents (ibid., pp. 113–117, 267–268). She emphasizes that the fear of parents can be so strong that the Oedipus complex could not be resolved without the help of a sibling as an ally (ibid., p. 118). She says that this "secret complicity" between siblings may relieve children of their anxieties about their phantasies toward their parents (ibid., p. 224). Klein also mentions sexual games between siblings in case histories, especially identifications with the older sibling, but does not give them an important role in the structuring of the psyche (Klein, 1957).

Klein thinks of projective identification as a phantasy in which bad parts of the self were split off from the rest of the self and, together with bad contents, were projected into the breast to control and take possession of the mother in such a fashion that she is felt to become the bad self. Is it possible to think that siblings, who are important early childhood objects, stay away from this mechanism? In *Envy and Gratitude* (1957), Klein refers to siblings as objects to which jealousy and envy can be directed. She also states that paranoid–schizoid anxieties can be projected onto the sibling. In this book, a patient's intense feelings of envy and rivalry toward her sister are analyzed through a dream and the patient discovers her own madness in this way. However, despite the richness of the case examples in her complete works, it is hard to say that Klein gave a crucial role to siblings as early inner objects (Klein, 1975). Siblings are both the objects of strong affections, and suitable objects for the child to project the parts of his or her self and inner objects. The good parts of the self are also projected, which leads to the enhancement of the ego and good object relations. In this context, can we not think that siblings with good relationships play a favorable role for psychic development?

As for Winnicott's approach toward siblings, we see that he emphasized the importance of the birth of a sibling in the child's psyche. He considers the appearance of some symptoms after the birth of a sibling in children up to three to five years of age as a part of normal development and does not define it as childhood psychoneurosis. He mentions cases of children who had been healthy until then, but who began to show physical or mental symptoms after the birth of a sibling. Winnicott talks about the traumatizing effect of the mother being unreachable for the child with the birth of a new sibling (Winnicott, 1931). In the famous Piggle case, he describes his work with Gabrielle, who had become a depressed, anxious, nightmarish child after the birth of her sibling at the age of two (Winnicott, 1978).

For Winnicott, in order for the child to overcome sibling trauma without it turning into a neurosis, parental attitude recognizing and empathizing with the child displaying these symptoms is very important. He states that the child's self-image will be enriched through identification with a loving, "good enough" mother who enjoys taking care of her baby (Winnicott, 1958a). Winnicott also emphasizes that sibling experiences can be positive and developmental.

Mitchell (2003) gives a central role to the neglected sibling dynamics in psychoanalytic theory, and underlines the necessity of looking into intragenerational-horizontal as well as intergenerational-vertical dynamics. In the foreword to the Turkish translation of her book, *Siblings: Sex and Violence*, she states: "I had been thinking about hysteria for many years when suddenly I felt as if I had stumbled upon the siblings in the dark. I looked around and realized that they were everywhere" (Mitchell, 2011, p. xii). She traces the siblings through a critical reading of some key texts and case histories of psychoanalysis and criticizes that the classical psychoanalytic approach overlooks the siblings because it deals with the psyche of patients on the Oedipus-centered vertical axis. According to Mitchell, the horizontal dimension is related to the search for a place and position rather than identity, and the presence of siblings removes the illusion of being single. The infant's psyche develops not only in its relationship with the parents but also simultaneously with his or her siblings. Siblings open space for the study of spiritual issues such as love, hate, jealousy, envy, as well as sameness, difference, and sexual difference. The horizontal dimension is an attempt to resolve the crisis of non-uniqueness. The new baby perceives a threat to his or her existence from the older siblings and develops a fear of being killed. This reaction also develops into hatred and love as well as friendship and rivalry. The presence of siblings also confronts children with the fact that they are not unique or even irreplaceable, but ordinary. The development of a positive sense of self depends on the child's ability to mourn this loss more or less successfully and to accept the state of ordinariness.

Mitchell suggests the prohibition of murder and incest comes from the mother, which she calls "the Law of the Mother" (Mitchell, 2013). The Law of the Mother provides vertical differentiation between the mother and her children and lateral differentiation between siblings. The Law of the Mother tells the child vertically that he or she cannot bear children and horizontally that they cannot kill their sibling, thus ensuring the acceptance of order and difference. One is a child in the same position as one's siblings in relation to one's parents, but one is also different: there is room for two, three, four, or more ... With this law, killing and incest between siblings are prohibited, and these desires are transformed into dynamics in peer and partner relationships.

Akhtar and Kramer (1999) listed the factors that determine the course of sibling relationships as parental availability, relationship between parents, parental behavior toward children, twinning, sex of the siblings, age difference, and specialness of a sibling (pp. 5–21).

Siblings and psychic development

The ambivalent nature of sibling relationships is shaped by their identification with their parents and shared experiences. Parents' attitudes toward each child may differ on conscious and unconscious levels. Each child has a different representation in the inner world of the mother or father and these representations are influenced by unconscious, and even transgenerational, phantasies. Two siblings may have the same biological parents but very different psychological parents. Each sibling has a psychologically unique mental representation for the others and for each of the parents. Siblings may be carriers of their parents' unconscious representations of objects or selves. Feelings toward a sibling, whether they are expressed in terms of competition or cooperation, jealousy or admiration, love or hatred, constitute the main factors determining how the sibling experience will unfold.

Through the concepts of replacement child, twinship, baby/phallus equality, and the existence of unconscious womb fantasies, Volkan and Ast (1997) argue that sibling representations and experiences in childhood play an active role in symptom formation and character structuring by creating pathological unconscious fantasies. Volkan states that unconscious womb fantasies may develop in children who experience the mother's pregnancy as traumatic and the birth of a sibling as a displacement. The child may have an unconscious fantasy of entering the mother's body, killing the fetus, and possessing the mother's womb alone. This fantasy leads to a conflict due to the guilt and fear of losing the mother, and this conflict leads to anxiety and can manifest itself in claustrophobia due to displacement and avoidance. Unconscious uterine fantasies can also be observed in the form of fear of conception, compulsive desire to enter closed spaces, hypersexuality, or intense envy and anger toward sibling representations of childhood (Volkan, 1999, pp. 115–133).

The mother's being physically ill or depressed when the sibling was born, or if the child was sent away before the sibling's birth, could have a traumatizing effect. The illness or death of a sibling could also be decisive in the child's psychological development. In this case, the child may develop unconscious fantasies that he or she was born instead of the deceased sibling, or that the child has to get sick like the lost sibling or even die in order to have the mother's love.

Siblings, like parents, could be the object of passionate feelings of love and hate, and the relationship between siblings may play a decisive role in adult relationships. The idea of siblings is innate, in Bionian terms a pre-conceptualization, which is always present in the child's mind, as to whether or not he or she actually has a sibling (Bion, 1965). Even if a child is the only child, in the imagination he or she may fear any future siblings and perhaps want to destroy them, or alternatively long for siblings. The only child may have unconscious phantasies about destroying the babies inside the mother.

The sibling experience offers the child the chance to have multiple identifications, identifications with the newborn baby, with oneself as an older child, or with a sibling of the opposite sex, and thereby enrich the psyche. Living with a sibling means being able to share experiences: parental love and care, creative play and imagination, and many years of closeness. The traces of these early bonds continue in friendship and love relationships, in work and family dynamics. According to Klein, siblings are important as allies in the resolution of the Oedipus complex; the existence of a kind of complicity between siblings can alleviate the fear of the parent and plays a fundamental role in every love relationship (Klein, 1932, pp. 118–119). Is our adult sexuality really only a stage reached through the resolution of our oedipal desires for the parent of the opposite sex? Can we say that sexual interest and attachment between siblings is not important in the formation of our own sexual identity and in our choice of partners?

Psychoanalytic theory frames the sibling relationship in the triangle of mother–father–child. There is always the image of a mother or father whose love is competed for. The parents' conscious or unconscious preference for one child makes it difficult for siblings to process the burning feelings of competition and envy. Both the favored and the unfavored child may experience guilt, jealousy, competition, and difficulties with closeness. If the parent allocates different aspects of self or objects between siblings through *splitting*, one child may be idealized while the other becomes the repository of all that is unworthy or bad. Counter identifications with siblings often clearly frame the boundaries of the self within the restriction of what is not like the other. The sibling relationship is as full of love, sharing, empathy, and understanding as it is of negative emotions such as jealousy, hatred, and competition. Sibling relationships can have a positive impact on curiosity, sublimation, and creativity in adulthood. Knowing that one has to share one's parents, having the burning feelings of rivalry and envy ingrained in one's psyche, going through the experience of producing and creating together, all affect the experience of becoming an individual as a part of society in later years.

Although not much attention has been paid to the positive and developmental aspects of sibling relationships in psychoanalytic theory, there are some notable exceptions. Vivona (2010), for example, argues that sibling relationships are indispensable to develop a sense of unique and valuable identity in a world of equals. Kieffer (2008) draws attention to the mirroring and regulating functions of siblings in identity development as they are accessible models for comparison and feedback. The mirroring function of siblings becomes more important especially in situations where parents are neglectful or destructive. Bank and Kahn (1980), and Akhtar and Kramer (1999) point to the function of the older sibling as a caregiver, emphasizing the importance of the child's age and mental maturity, and the anger caused by being forced to assume this role. When a parent is incapacitated or traumatized, siblings may come together more tightly and the importance of the sibling bond increases. Colonna and Newman (1983) argue that children who are not siblings, but who grow up together in such environments as orphanages or camps, form stronger bonds with each other rather than with caregivers and idealize their peers, and define this as "social siblings" (p. 303). Rustin (2007) argues that making room for a sibling in one's inner world contributes to the development of symbolic thinking.

C. Levin (2008) suggests that the traditional Oedipus complex should be considered as a broader metapsychological construct that includes sibling relationships with their conflicts and strengths. He argues that the oedipal triangle may be reconceptualized as part of an oscillating "structure" including not only a vertical triangulation but also lateral triangulations involving siblings. Referring to René Kaës, he states that the Oedipus complex is not the fundamental conflict of the psyche and that the sibling conflict (*le complexe fraternal*) cannot be underestimated. Levin (2008) argues that sibling rivalry is not only about possessing the desired object, but also, and perhaps primarily, about getting rid of unwanted and painful parts of the self. He says:

> Long before the child thinks of killing his father, he may already have killed his brother. Indeed, before the fratricidal moment, we may all have killed off the version of ourselves into which we had projected our psychic pains and failures—our psychic twin, or alter ego, who may still haunt us from birth. (Levin, 2008, p. 262)

J. Mitchell (2003) argues that sibling trauma is an organizer of mental life in the transition from narcissism to oedipal triangulation. According to her, when the desire to destroy the other who displaces us and the desire for sexual union with our double is forbidden by the Law of the Mother, there is a triangulation between mother and siblings. This triangle precedes, and prepares the ground for, the oedipal triangle.

Siblings are called to help when parents are physically or mentally incapacitated, they assist in the neutralization and displacement of aggression, and can play a role as supportive and bridging objects in the transformation of incestuous fantasies. According to Akhtar (1999), mental representations of siblings play a decisive role in our choice of spouse, the kind of parents we will be, and how we will relate to the "other." Internal sibling representations may be much more important in shaping our psyche than we assume.

Siblings in the clinical setting

In traditional psychoanalytic theory it is rare to think of the analyst–analysand pair as a sibling pair. In psychoanalytic theory, the psyche of the individual is basically shaped around the relationship with the parent and the resolution of the Oedipus complex. The reflection of this approach in the analysis room is the evaluation of basic transference dynamics in the context of the parent–child relationship. In the study of transference–countertransference, the dynamics of the sibling relationship do not attract much attention. As important objects of the inner world, is it possible that they are not in the analysis room?

We know that siblings have a real impact on a person's life, that they affect the child's future relationships, but what shapes the person's future life and relationships even more are the repressed or unconscious fantasies connected with their siblings. It is these fantasies that need to be addressed in the analysis. During the analysis, the focus needs to be on what kind of fantasies the presence, birth, illness, or death of the sibling have caused in the person's psyche.

Coleman (1996) criticizes traditional psychoanalysis for neglecting siblings and underlines the importance of the sibling dimension in transference–countertransference. He states that positive sibling transference facilitates the development of a working alliance between therapist and patient. Graham (1988) mentions that his own countertransference reactions led him to underappreciate the role of sibling representations in his adult patients. He suggests paying more attention to sibling dynamics in both transference and countertransference reactions.

Through two case histories Blessing (2007) argues that the analysis can only progress after the intense conflicts in sibling relationships are experienced through transference and countertransference. She draws attention to the influence of siblings on the organization of the ego and superego of the cases and associates this with pathological superego organization. Coles (2003) also states that the patient's overly rigid superego organization may be related to the internalization of a cruel sibling as an authority figure. She also states that the therapist's feeling of secret complicity with the patient in countertransference may be related to siblings uniting in complicity against their parents.

The first mention of a sibling in the analysis may be a sign that sibling transference has begun (Waugaman, 1990). Sometimes the analyst may get the impression that the patient is the only child in the family because he or she does not talk about siblings. Patients' feelings of jealousy and competition toward other patients may also be an expression of repressed competition and aggression toward siblings. Patients are often unaware of jealousy or rivalry toward siblings because it is repressed, and initially they do not acknowledge feelings of jealousy and rivalry toward other patients. However, working with intense feelings toward other patients and addressing them in transference can make room for siblings in the analysis. Other patients in the analyst's couch, the real or imagined children of the analyst, allow for the study of sibling trauma. Coles (2003) says that if a patient has severe existential anxieties and the analyst discovers that the patient may have had an overwhelming experience of sibling rivalry, it may be related to a fear of being annihilated by the other sibling and it must be taken into account.

Larmo (2007) states that the sibling rivalry and jealousy that emerge in the analysis may be a sign that the patient cannot withstand the disappointments of the oedipal universe and regresses to a more undifferentiated stage. In order to deny the separation from the mother, she argues, the child may identify with the mother or the sibling in her arms. The analytic relationship creates a situation in which the patient's feelings of jealousy and rivalry toward the siblings may surface, as the patient has to share his or her analyst with other analysands. The siblings entering the analytic situation give the patient a new opportunity for triangulation.

The analyst may not always play the role of parent in the transference; sibling images and object relations can be projected to the analyst and direct manifestations of sibling rivalry or incestuous desires may also occur in the transference. Siblings can also exist in the analytical room as objects through which painful and intolerable parts of the patient's self are projected. Siblings may serve as a repository for weak, worthless, or destructive aspects of the patient in order to protect the narcissistic structure of the patient.

It is a special experience when the analyst becomes pregnant during the analytic work. This period can serve as a fertile ground for working through for the earliest mother–infant relationships and conflicts related to femininity, as well as for the study of issues related to fraternity. It exacerbates the patient's pre-oedipal and oedipal conflicts as well as sibling conflicts, and can be a unique process for the analyst–analysand despite all its difficulties.

An analyst who is blind to their own sibling rivalry may find it difficult to hear their analysands' sibling transference or to observe their own countertransference reactions. J. Mitchell (2003), referring to Winnicott's concept of fear of breakdown, says that the breakdown experienced by the adult patient who is always afraid that "someone else will take his place" in the future has already occurred in childhood. According to her, it is not only the patient who cannot discover the source of his or her fear, but also the analysts who have failed to see the siblings who are always standing in front of them (p. 217).

The extent to which we have worked our sibling dynamics through transference in our own analyses will inevitably affect our work with our analysands. As analysts, giving siblings a place in our minds can help us to see more sibling dynamics in transference–countertransference and to understand our patients' inner worlds more coherently.

Sibling dynamics and group psychology

Psychoanalysis emphasizes the uniqueness of the individual, aims to discover his or her inner world, and to reinterpret their personal history within the analyst–analysand relationship. In this endeavor, the analyst is always aware that the individual is not alone. The individual is and has always been a member of a community. Freud argues that the psychology of the individual cannot be completely separated from the psychology of the community, since it is a derivative of the relations between two separate individuals, and the family is the first that underlies all communities.

In *Totem and Taboo* (1912–13) Freud takes the first step in his theory of the basis of society and culture. In the section entitled "The return of totemism in early childhood," Freud suggests that the birth of the group is linked to a common murder. He says:

> One day the brothers who had been driven out came together, killed and devoured their father and so made an end of the patriarchal horde. United, they had the courage to do and succeeded in doing what would have been impossible for them individually … The violent primal father had doubtless been the feared and envied model of each one of the company of brothers: and in the act of devouring him they accomplished their identification with him, and each one of them acquired a portion of his strength. The totem meal, which is perhaps mankind's earliest festival, would thus be a repetition and a commemoration of this memorable and criminal deed, which was the beginning of so many things—of social organization, of moral restrictions and of religion. (Freud, 1912–1913, pp. 141–142)

This is a formative murder, laying the foundation of sociality. Eating the father is the second important part of this myth and lays the foundations of brotherhood. By eating a piece of meat together, the brothers recognize each other unequivocally as brothers, and internalize the power and love of the dead father equally.

While dealing with the formation of the social in *Totem and Taboo*, Freud discusses the mechanisms of social functioning in *Group Psychology and the Analysis of the Ego* (1921c). After working on masochism and the death drive for a long time, in this work he tries to understand the factors that lead to social cohesion with the help of psychoanalysis.

In *Totem and Taboo*, the brothers were united around a foundational murder. Freud describes here the brothers as equals who, because they had to share the primary object of love, were filled with envy and destructiveness, and who compete with each other and are required to reverse these feelings. The father in *Totem and Taboo* is a father who forces his sons to conspire against him, depriving them of love and justice, whereas the father in *Group Psychology and Analysis of the Ego* is an almost hypnotizing father who loves all his children equally. For Freud, whether it is a father to be murdered or a loving father, in any case a group without a father cannot exist, otherwise chaos ensues.

In *Group Psychology and the Analysis of the Ego*, Freud argues that it is a desexualized libido that creates and sustains bonds in a group: He says: "love alone acts as the civilizing factor in the sense that it brings a change from egoism to altruism. And this is true both of sexual love for women, with all the obligations which it involves of not harming the things that are dear to women, and also of desexualized, sublimated homosexual love for other men, which springs from work in common" (Freud, 1921c, p. 102). We can think of this definition of love that enables the creation and maintenance of in-group bonds as similar to the love that exists between siblings.

When Freud wrote *Group Psychology and the Analysis of the Ego*, the effects of World War I were still very much alive, the years in which brothers in different armies, perhaps hypnotized communities, as Freud called them, adopted national identities and wreaked havoc. Freud had spent the last few years thinking and writing about the destructiveness of mankind. For Freud, when people become a group, they gain a sense of unity and security, but lose their freedom of thought and judgment. Freud, who wondered why masses could be more intolerant, irrational, and immoral than individuals, explains the change that a person undergoes in a group with the mechanism of identification. In *Group Psychology and the Analysis of the Ego*, he defines groups as organized groups, such as the church and the army, and ordinary groups. In ordinary groups, members identify with the charismatic leader of the group in a narcissistic and sublimating way. Underneath this identification, there is hypnotic submission, loss of individuality, and a primitive bond that could lead to all kinds of perversion and violence (Freud, 1921c).

While Freud was developing his theory on groups, sociality, and civilization, serious conflicts were taking place within the psychoanalytic movement, as, on the one hand, the movement was becoming widespread, and on the other, criticisms and attacks were increasing. The psychoanalytic movement was gaining the character of an organized group, and its glorified, charismatic leader was undoubtedly Freud. The members of the group were tightly loyal to each other and to their leader, whom they considered to be the ego ideal, and the outsiders were those who criticized psychoanalysis or his friends who had theoretical differences with him. It is safe to assume that Freud, while theoretically defining group dynamics on the one hand, had to confront the problematic sibling dynamics in his own inner world within the psychoanalytic movement on the other.

The "other" is part of our psyche. Our inner world is full of representations of the other. With each new relationship, the bond we have established with our important objects from the past comes alive and we create the "other" once again. What kind of other we create is determined by our relationships with our objects and self in our inner world.

J. Mitchell argues that "childhood sibling relations are an important place where we negotiate 'self' and 'other' but also where we, or through whom we, construct the other of ourselves" (J. Mitchell, 2006, p. 35). The sense of sameness and difference needs to be redefined over and over again in dyadic relationships, in small groups, in large groups, and finally, in this postmodern age, in our loneliness as individuals. According to her, the pair of self and other should be thought of not only in terms of mother–child and father–child pairs from the traditional perspective of psychoanalysis, but also in terms of sibling–sibling pairs.

How the sibling–sibling pair can turn into a peer–friend pair and into a group; how the interaction between self and non-self can take shape in groups based on the dynamics of the relationship with siblings, are important questions. In *Group Psychology and the Analysis of the Ego* Freud says, "in the individual's mental life someone else is invariably involved, as a model, as an object, as a helper, as an opponent" (Freud, 1921c, pp. 1–2). Freud talks about the inseparable link between the psyche and the object, and does so through the concept of the ego ideal, which he first defined in 1914 in "On Narcissism": "man has here again shown himself incapable of giving up a satisfaction he had once enjoyed. He is not willing to forgot the narcissistic perfection of his childhood …, as he grows up …, he seeks to recover it in the new form of an ego ideal" (Freud, 1914c, p. 94). In his work, the ideal ego remained within superego. The superego is the internalization of the authority of the father figure. Freud writes: "A primary group of this kind is a number of individuals who have substituted one and the same object for their ego ideal and have consequently identified themselves with one another in their ego" (Freud, 1921c, p. 116).

Freud discusses two highly organized groups, Church and Army, and the relationship with the leader in these groups. The leader loves all the members with an equal love. Each member binds themselves with libidinal love both to the leader-father and to the other members-siblings. Freud compares identification with falling in love and gives a central role to identification in group formation (Freud, 1921c). Identification is a fundamental mechanism in the development of the subject's personality and in the relationship with his or her objects and the external world. There is a continuous interchange between subject and object. Is it possible not to think that real or imaginary siblings, with whom we have been in a close relationship since the beginning of our lives, are our first objects of identification, just like our primary objects?

Chasseguet-Smirgel argues that the powerlessness arising from the infant's inability to take care of him- or herself forces the subject to recognize the non-self and that the narcissistic omnipotence that is torn away from the child is projected onto the object, the child's ego ideal

(Chasseguet-Smirgel, 1985, pp. 31–60). The ego ideal is essentially a narcissistic formation. There is a projected narcissism, which is then invested in other objects. For the male child, according to Freud, it is carried to the father during the oedipal period. Chasseguet-Smirgel argues that giving up of a certain number of satisfactions and successive objects prompts the need to find substitutes for them and to effect displacements. According to her, the symbolic activity, sublimation, phantasy life, the elaboration of a desire and language are all born from having to delay satisfaction (Chasseguet-Smirgel, 1985, p. 37). Siblings are suitable objects to replace the primary objects that the child has to give up, and in this way they contribute to the development of symbolic activity and the fantasy life of the child.

Identification itself is a complex process. In *Group Psychology and the Analysis of the Ego*, Freud exemplifies identification through the oedipal state and argues that the little boy wants to grow up to be like his father, the ideal object of the little boy being the father (Freud, 1921c). So where are siblings among these objects of identification? Perhaps in the image of an admired older brother or a caring sister in the nuclear family, or conversely, in the image of a critical older sibling, or perhaps in the infinite variety of identification possibilities for an adolescent …

Through the ego ideal, the child tries to regain the narcissistic perfection he or she has lost. During adolescence the ego ideal is reconstructed. We know how important it is for adolescents to have friends and to feel a sense of belonging to a group. It is as if with each new friend, with each new group, adolescents know a little better who they are, who they want to be like. They enter and leave many groups, have new identifications and changes. Thus, identifications with siblings and peers will be revived in every group formation in the years to come, and feelings of love, hatred, and envy may again become dominant in one's psyche. Freud argues that the bond between members of a group is in the structure of identification. Individuals give up their own difference for the group; they see the group as an important object of affection and a place where members reflect the same feelings. While group members want equality in the group, they also want to be led (ibid.).

Chasseguet-Smirgel claims that the regression observed in groups is shaped around the promise of the unification of the ego and ego ideal. The superego, she argues, separates the child from the mother, while the ego ideal drives the child in search of wholeness. The tendency of the ego to lose its boundaries facilitates identification not only with the members but also with the group as a whole. In this situation where everyone's ego extends to the whole group, the narcissism that was lost is regained. The group is now the ego, the primary object and the ego ideal all at once (Chasseguet-Smirgel, 1985, pp. 31–60).

Grouping is coming together, but at first it creates intense anxiety. According to Anzieu (1984), one of the deepest anxieties is that of losing the unity of one's own body and psyche, and group participation makes each member ask the question "Who am I?", which is one of the most difficult questions to answer, for being part of a group means giving up the previous self. Here we can recall what the birth of a sibling means for a child. With the birth of a new baby, the older child loses not only the mother, but also the old self-image that was unique to the mother, and must mourn this loss. This is a significant trauma and displaces the child, who is not who he or she thought until then. One can imagine that this trauma will tend to recur throughout life in moments of displacement or loss. Being a member of a group also means giving up one's uniqueness, just as a child has to give up the uniqueness that preceded the birth of a sibling.

For a child, the newborn sibling is both different and threatens sameness, and she or he feels a deadly hatred toward the intruder. The sibling is "the separate, the other, the not-me." Attempts to define the younger sibling as a creature, some kind of animal, an unreal toy, are perhaps related to the need to feel this difference. The child is overwhelmed by this threat of sameness and tries to think of a way to prove his or her difference.

Is the anxiety at the beginning of groups not partly related to this threat of sameness? The group member quickly feels obliged to make new identifications, to redefine the self. The way one copes with this threat of sameness is influenced by one's past experience with a sibling. For the person who has managed to abandon narcissistic self-love and to love a sibling as a separate object, the threat of sameness will not be too difficult to overcome. She or he will be enriched by making new identifications that include the differences of other group members. However, if the sibling is a narcissistic extension of oneself in one's inner world, that "other" may be a repository of undesirable aspects of the self rather than a separate person, and may become a dangerous other at the first moment when difference is felt. In some group structures, it is as if there is no difference between individuals, and the dangerous other is outside the group, perhaps in another group. By expanding the environment in which the child's first identifications take place from the vertical relationship with the parents to the horizontal relationship with the siblings, the diversity of identifications increases.

"Brotherly love" has not found a place in psychoanalytic theory. There are traces of it in Freud's *Group Psychology and the Analysis of the Ego*. Freud argues that group life begins in kindergartens and is essentially charged with aggression. The older child is jealous of his younger brother and wants to get rid of him. But as the older child sees his parents' love for the younger sibling, he feels forced to identify with the younger sibling. In other words, for Freud, the feelings of rivalry and affection between siblings are always a reversal, and this is what will later form the "group spirit" (*esprit de corps*). Feelings of envy and jealousy are transformed into feelings of socialization, sharing, and justice (Freud, 1921c).

Within the nuclear family, siblings as objects and the way they relate to each other are also internalized and become part of the identity. There is always some disappointment in the child's primary identifications with the parents. The boy wants to be as strong as the father but knows that he cannot be yet; the girl wants to give a child to the father like the mother but realizes that it is not possible. However, primary identifications with siblings are not so damaging; the child says, "I am both like my brother and different" and this positive identification leads to differentiation. This peer identification will be internalized in group identity as a whole or with differences in groups in the following years. It is not difficult to predict that the feelings of love, hate, jealousy, and envy experienced during the process of differentiation from and acceptance of the sibling will be reexperienced among the members/peers in the group.

The primitive defenses of splitting, projection, introjection, and projective identification are always present in the interaction of the group, especially in situations of regression. Both ego and object are divided into good and bad. One can divide and project onto the other the aspects of one's psyche that one cannot bear; just as in the past the sibling was the repository of negative parts of the self, so now another member of the group can serve this function. Klein (1928) talks about children's unconscious phantasies of destroying future babies in the mother's womb. The unconscious has no time, so these unconscious phantasies can be revived at any time and do not need real siblings for this. Peers, friends, coworkers, and group members can revive in the imago of the baby in the mother's womb that must be destroyed. Klein suggests that when these fantasies cannot be worked with, they can lead to great pressure and anxiety, and a fear of disintegration and loss of self (Klein, 1928, pp. 167–180). We can think that fears of disintegration and loss of self-identity, especially in unorganized groups, are related to destructive phantasies and fears of punishment that are revived in the inner world of each member of the group.

Here we can talk about group and gang formations with different levels of functionality. In the group structuring that can be defined as gangs, which overlaps with Freud's ordinary group and Bion's (1961) basic assumption of the fight–flight response, there is intense tension and anxiety in the group, an external enemy is sought, and all aggression within the group is projected outwards. A primitive, cruel, and deviant superego is dominant. When we think about a well-functioning group as a group with a goal, this group has certain objectives: the development of each group member, access to group culture, socialization of each member, and the ability to carry this experience to other groups. In this context, we can think of a well-functioning sibling group as Freud's organized group, and Bion's working group. These groups function better in terms of having a purpose, producing, enjoying togetherness and life. In a sense, the joyful and creative process of siblings growing up together seems to be revitalized in the group experience. At any time, however, positive or negative sibling dynamics may become dominant in the group and change the functioning of the group. In this sense, as Bion mentioned, all groups tend to regress and a study group can turn into a basic assumption group (ibid.).

Living with a sibling means finding a way to love and hate the same person. In adult life, siblings can be replaced by friends from peer groups, by people who are not like us, immigrants, enemies, and it is therefore important to understand the dynamics of sibling relationships in order to understand violence and power today. If we accept that the birth of a sibling is a trauma that displaces the child, we can expect this experience to be repeated in different relationships throughout life. If the sibling experience is not sufficiently psychically processed, every possibility of displacement or sharing can bring out underlying aggression. It is also possible to see traces of sibling dynamics in the social hatred of the other and even the desire to kill.

Siblings form a small group within the nuclear family. This group opens up new tensions but also new options for the development of the psyche. One of the typical characteristics of sibling–peer relationships is the ability to act altruistically within the group. Learning to function as a member of the group, learning to deal with issues such as leadership, equality of members, respect for the other, and acceptance of differences begins in the small group within the family. How we experience these difficult issues in the fraternity group can be decisive for our future friendships and peer relationships, our existence as a group member, and our perception of the other.

People tend to take on the roles in their nuclear family in their future relationships. In one way or another, we may unwittingly try to catch up with or surpass the representation of a sibling in the group, or we may unwittingly withdraw from the competition altogether, as in the past.

When one thinks of sibling relationships, thoughts of rivalry, envy, and possible murder run through everyone's mind. Positive feelings and love between siblings seem to be just a reversal. However, the relationship between siblings does not have to be defined solely in terms of the parent. J. Mitchell (2006) argues that the love between siblings is "the love of sameness." She argues that in brotherhood groups such as football teams, school groups, or sisterhood groups such as feminist groups, there can be a sense of ecstasy, an excessive enthusiasm.

The relationship with a sibling is like a journey taken together at a very young age. It is also a journey of growing up; siblings grow by connecting to each other, accepting their sameness and differences, and overcoming their destructive emotions. It is a never-ending journey that can begin time and again throughout our lives in relationships, friendships, and groups.

A view through the Turkish lens

Sibling relationships are shaped not only by one's individual history but also by the family, and the cultural and social structure in which one lives. In this section, I will discuss the plausible effects of the social dimension of sibling relationships on the psyche in Turkey and, through a case example, I will talk about a special sibling dynamic that has been common among siblings in Turkish culture until recently.

In traditional Turkish society, sibling relations are not between equals. The hierarchy among siblings is structured along two main axes: age and gender. The older sibling always has more say and can dominate the younger ones, and in traditional families the male child is more valuable. In our analysis rooms, we often hear the stories of women who are forced to give birth until they give birth to a boy, of girls who see themselves as a disappointment, of women who cannot embrace their feminine identity because they were raised as men. It is a common theme in Turkey that daughters have to cope with feelings of inadequacy and worthlessness within the family, which may exacerbate their feelings of competition and envy toward their brothers.

In the traditional Turkish family structure, the eldest son is a father figure in the eyes of the other siblings. This may sometimes mitigate the severity of the relationship with the father and facilitate constructive identifications. At the same time, the older son is an object for the brother to experience oedipal aggression and for the sister to experience incestuous desires toward more easily than for the father. The older brother can be both an idealized and envied object. He cannot be competed with, and the younger ones are left helplessly resigned to their fate. This situation becomes even more pronounced when it comes to the domination over sisters. During the neoliberalization process in Turkey after the 1980s, family dynamics gained particular importance within the increasingly inward-looking and conservative structure of society. Social movements and violence, which could not find a space for expression under authoritarian rule, caused the family to become an instrument of domination. In a society where domestic violence is on the rise, how should sibling relationships, which by their very nature involve competition, envy, destructiveness, but also solidarity and sharing, be handled?

Psychoanalytic literature on siblings frequently emphasizes competition, envy, and destructiveness in sibling relationships. In traditional Turkish society, the hierarchy based on age and gender makes it difficult to have a healthy competition between siblings. The pressure and domination of fathers and brothers over women is evident in conservative families. In our clinical practice, we often hear the stories of women who have not had a say in their lives or bodies since childhood, who could not stand up to their father or brother, who could not continue their education because their father or brother did not allow them, who were forced to marry not the person they wanted, but someone the family deemed appropriate. These stories are especially those of women from previous generations of conservative families. We often even hear news of young girls, especially in the most conservative parts of the country, who were murdered for defying the traditional values of the family. In some patriarchal, traditional families, it is still common to see the order to kill a sister given by the father and carried out by a brother. What role does being the enforcer of the father's law give to the brother? It is traumatic for one's psyche to deny the generational difference even for a moment, to become a "father," to realize an unconscious phantasy by murdering one's sister.

In traditional and conservative families, the solidarity of sisters against the violence and domination of the father and the older brothers who replace him is evident. This solidarity binds the female members of the family together, especially the sisters. Sometimes it is only through this sisterly bond that it is possible to protect oneself against violence and even survive. In this sense, the empathic relationship that develops between sisters in the face of domination and violence enables them to share their experiences and identify with each other more. This solidarity allows the sisters to share creativity, imagination, and humor in the third area, as Winnicott defines it, between psychic reality and violent external reality (Winnicott, 1971). Thus, they can soften the aggression against themselves in their psychic world. At the same time, this solidarity may lead to a greater suppression of feelings of competition, envy, and destructiveness toward each other.

The processes of separation from parents and individuation are particularly challenging in Turkish society. In traditional families, older sisters take care of newborns, and the maternal function is invested in or obliged from a very early age. Within the extended family, siblings play an important role as secondary objects helping to compensate for parental deprivations. Lindon points out that the older sibling is not only an object of distancing from the oedipal relationship, but also a substitute for the parent (Lindon, 1967). In traditional families in Turkish society, it is difficult to separate from siblings as well as parents. Even if they establish their own families, it is common for siblings to live in close proximity to each other, even for one member of the family to live with his or her nuclear family on each floor of an apartment building, for meals to be eaten at the parents' house, for joint business to be conducted, and for loans to be exchanged. These undifferentiated fraternal relations can continue as in the childhood home. In this living arrangement called "extended family," competition, envy, and destructiveness cannot change places, they are felt to be against their unique objects, the most envied but also the closest objects being siblings. Incestuous fantasies about the sibling may lead to conflictual relations with the spouse of the sibling within this extended family structure.

I would now like to talk about a special dynamic between siblings, especially between sisters, common in Turkish society until recently, and its impact on the psyche of the next generation through a case example.

Clinical vignette 1

When Ms. E. applied for therapy, she was thirty years old, single, the second of three siblings, with a sister two years older and a brother three years younger. She applied to therapy saying that she could no longer bear the feelings of emptiness, meaninglessness, and worthlessness that she constantly felt. She did not feel safe in her relationships. She had intense competitive feelings toward her siblings at home and coworkers at work.

Ms. E. had an interesting remark that I remember from her first session. While explaining why she came to therapy and what she expected from therapy, at one point she said with a very definite attitude that "the therapy will end in two years." She did not provide a reason and I could not make sense in the first session of Ms. E.'s conviction that her therapy would end in two years. After a short period of therapy, Ms. E. moved on to analysis. She was a very quiet analysand; sometimes she would not speak at all during the sessions, but at the end of these sessions she would leave smiling, with a satisfied expression on her face, saying that the session had been good for her. In one session I had an image of Ms. E. eating her fill by breathing deeply the air of the room. Sometime later, Ms. E. told me that she had spent hours in a department store trying on perfumes to find the one I was wearing. She finally found it. She also stored milk and dairy products of a brand bearing my name in her refrigerator and some days she ate only these. The early years of her life, the need to absorb the mother, to become one, was archaically alive between us. We communicated almost without words. She was very sensitive to smells, to all the sounds coming from my body, to her own sensory experiences.

My other patients occupied Ms. E.'s mind so much that she thought that if I grew tired of seeing so many patients, I would end my sessions with her first. She wanted to come to the

> first sessions in the morning so that I could give my mind completely to her. In the first years of the analysis, we worked with Ms. E. on her feelings of feeling understood with almost no words, her need for fusion with the mother/analyst, her feelings of competition toward her siblings and colleagues. In the second year of the analysis Ms. E. suddenly said that this work was enough, and that she wanted to finish her analysis. I reminded Ms. E. of what she had said in the first session and told her that now we needed to understand the meaning of this second year together. Ms. E. had no idea why she insisted on finishing the analysis; after a while she had a dream. She dreamt that she was in a foreign and cold country, wandering alone, digging in the frozen ground, pulling out pieces of cloth and stuffing them into her pockets. In the session in which she brought this dream, Ms. E. told a very important story from her childhood for the first time. Her mother had given her up for adoption to her aunt because her older sister had no children. When she was two years old, her aunt came and picked her up and took her to Germany. She saw her parents and siblings during summer vacations and lived with her aunt and uncle until she was eighteen. She always knew that they were not her real parents. She felt intense envy for her siblings who lived with their parents. It was this experience of abandonment that arose between Ms. E. and me. In her imagination there was an analyst mother who was going to send her away in the second year of analysis; until then it seemed to the mother that she had to stuff all her sensory experiences of the maternal body into her pockets, as in her dream. It was as if it was only the traces of these bodily contacts that remained in Ms. E.'s mind until she was two years old. She was almost sure that I was going to end the analysis; staying in the analysis and being able to study this earliest experience of abandonment in depth allowed her to see how she was repeating her traumatic experience in her dyadic relationships. Her mind was preoccupied with feelings of abandonment and worthlessness because she had been given up for adoption, and I was the analyst who would have given her up first, not my other patients. Being given up for adoption had organized her imagination, object relations, and defenses. There was no answer to the question of why she was the one of the three siblings to be given up. Her imaginative sadistic attacks out of frustration and jealousy turned into anxieties of persecution and rejection, extreme guilt, and attempts at reparation in fear of retaliation. Ms. E.'s mother had given her to her aunt, and after a while the relationship between the two sisters had broken down. Ms. E.'s relationship with her siblings was characterized by feelings of worthlessness and envy on her part and guilt on the part of her siblings.

The story of Ms. E. being given to a childless sister was a phenomenon that could be seen in all segments of Turkish society until recently; it was even possible to give birth to a child for a childless sibling and give the baby away shortly after birth. Of course, most of the children given away were girls; a girl could be given up, but a boy was too precious to be given away. On the other hand, the mother's refusal to give the baby away after the birth, even though she had promised to do so, could lead to years of resentment or broken relationships within the family. Although this practice is decreasing today, it can still be seen especially in traditional families.

It is possible to read this as a particular manifestation of sibling rivalry and envy. When it came to giving a sister her own child, a great price was being paid for the unconscious guilt of having the capacity to give birth that the sister lacked. It is clear that giving up a child that belonged to her had unique reasons specific to the mother's psyche. The social acceptance and normalization of this act may have increased expectations among the siblings. Giving birth or giving up a child for a childless sister can be seen as an extreme example of solidarity between sisters, but it also points to an intertwining and a difficulty in maintaining physical and psychological boundaries.

All in all, when sibling relations in Turkish society are reviewed in the context of the limited psychoanalytic literature on siblings, we can say that the basic dynamics of siblings are also valid in the Turkish family structure. However, it is possible to say that the distinctive feature in Turkish society is the overly hierarchical structure of sibling relations. It is possible that this structure leads to domination/submission dynamics and makes healthy competition in relationships difficult, but it is also likely to cause unconscious envy and destructiveness to grow stronger. The fact that the pressure and violence exerted by the family institution, however, underlining solidarity and cooperation, as another dimension of sisterhood especially among sisters, can be considered as a culturally specific feature in Turkish society.

Conclusion

Sibling relationships seem to have a much deeper impact on the psyche than has been discussed so far in the psychoanalytic literature. Developmentally, siblings play an important role in the structuring of the inner world, in the development of psychopathology, thus in transference–countertransference dynamics, peer relations, and group formations. The intense feelings of siblings toward each other are deeply influenced by their relationship with their parents, but independently of this, the sibling bond is a unique bond that contains many positive and negative emotions. As analysts, recognizing this bond more in ourselves, in the inner worlds of our patients, in the transference–countertransference dynamics will enrich our analytical understanding. Furthermore, reflecting on fraternity may provide us with new insights into racism, immigrant hostility, social cleavages, and wars, as peers who may or may not be able to live together in the world we live in. This overview of the psychic importance of sibling relationships has inevitably not included all aspects. Issues such as twinship, sibling death or illness, stepsiblings, half-siblings, adopted siblings, incest between siblings are not discussed in this chapter. It seems that the increased attention to siblings in psychoanalytic theory and practice may give us an opportunity to reflect on many related issues of siblings.

CHAPTER 7

The absence of *adolescent-like* traits in the adult psyche

Talat Parman

"I was tortured by CIA agents for weeks."

These were the first words spoken by my seventy-year-old female patient. In her youth, she had joined a left-wing organization and, like thousands of others, had endured severe torture at a facility known as Erenköy Mansion.[1]

She went on to describe her life, revealing that even half a century later, she had not fully recovered from this traumatic event in her early adulthood. She sought my help now because her husband, who had been her lifelong companion, had suddenly passed away from a heart attack.

"I never made decisions on my own. He made all the choices. For fifty years, we were inseparable at work and at home. I drew all my life's energy from him. We had two children because he wanted them. We built businesses and homes, always at his urging. I never thought about the future because he always did."

Could this be a case of old age depression? Or a melancholic clinical scenario triggered by the loss of a spouse? Possibly … However, what stands out is that following the profound trauma of torture, this woman had almost no personal ambitions or future plans. In the darkness of Erenköy Mansion, CIA agents stripped away something crucial from her. They robbed her of her drive for the future, her ability to sustain her youthful creativity, and her capacity to nurture a psychic intermediate space that fosters illusions—in essence, her *adolescent-like* spirit.

The importance of retaining childlike qualities

One of the most important aspects of Freudian psychology is the idea that earlier psychic arrangements influence current functioning of the psyche. Thus, the contributions of childhood to the psyche extend into adulthood. This concept applies equally to adolescence.

Philippe Jeammet, a French psychoanalyst, writes:

> adult functioning thus resides in the Ego's ability to be in contact with what remains childlike (infantile) in each of us (not necessarily childish (*enfantin*), but often felt as such by the Ego, which is ashamed of it and represses it), while adapting to external reality and above all to the presence of others, who may be our fellow human beings and with whom we can identify, but who are radically other, i.e. bearers of their own subjectivity and inalienable difference. (2000, pp. 426–427)

Philippe Jeammet defines the adult ego as follows:

> An adult Ego is not necessarily one that is a defensive or rigid Ego in its character defenses or fixed identifications, but one that is capable of allowing itself to be surprised by the emergences of the childlike, of welcoming internal impulses as well as novelties coming from the outside, without immediately feeling overwhelmed and threatened with overflow. (p. 427)

As can be seen, the childlike is not a threat to the adult; on the contrary, it revitalizes it. The real danger arises when an adult disconnects from their vibrant, impulsive roots, which are anchored in the childlike, resulting in a desiccated, joyless existence. Connecting to the childlike, the source of impulses, is crucial for maintaining vitality. In other words, the task of adolescence is to develop a psychic structure where these vital childlike impulses are not intimidating, and to carry this structure into adult life.

Then, it would not be incorrect to assert that an important component of the adult psyche is the childlike. I will now take this a step further and make the same assertion for the *adolescent-like*, and, just as the contributions of the childlike to the adult psyche are acknowledged, I will highlight the characteristics of the adolescent psyche that not only exist but should also persist in adult life.

Pubertaire and *adolescens*

Pubertaire and *adolescens* are two terms proposed by Philippe Gutton (1991), another important figure in French adolescent psychoanalysis, to describe what occurs during adolescence. Gutton, following a fairly common tradition in psychoanalysis of coining new words for new concepts, created the words *pubertaire* from the French word "puberté" and *adolescens* from "adolescence" (Gutton, 1996). Drawing on his work with infants, he views infantile sexuality and the fertile sexuality of adolescence as opposing, even conflicting, phenomena. According to him, a new instinctual current emerges that radically interferes with the infantile structures formed before and after the oedipal phase. Here, he aligns with the notion, long emphasized since Ferenczi, that puberty should not be seen as a repetition of trauma but as a brand-new and original trauma. In contrast, while infantile sexuality is a continuation of parental sexuality from the very beginning, the sexuality of adolescence represents an original experience, rooted in the reproductive instinct. It represents a need for self-creation. In this regard, Gutton particularly emphasizes the concept of "adolescent genius" (*génie adolescent*), highlighting the efforts of adolescents to engage in idealization and sublimation.

Philippe Gutton says that "the word puberty is to the body what *pubertaire* is to the psyche" (1991, p. 7). As for *adolescens*, "*Adolescens* is the present participle dealing with *pubertaire*" (1996, p. 7). The biological and psychophysiological constant that ensures the relative integrity of the *pubertaire*, as defined by its psychic effects, is the generative instinct. The sudden and genetically programmed emergence of this instinct marks the traumatic aspect of offspring sexuality and necessitates the domestication of what might be considered wild animalism. The adolescent metamorphosis results in the birth of a new pubertal being, achievable only through an adolescent struggle for subjectivation. During this process, the relationships among the three sections of the psyche—the id, the ego, and the superego—and their interactions with external reality undergo significant transformations. In this framework, the *pubertaire* and *adolescens* serve as two pillars supporting the dome of the adolescent structure.

Adolescent creativity and adolescent genius

Adolescence is fundamentally a period of creativity, perhaps even an act and experience of creativity in its entirety. The body's biological impulse for creativity naturally has a psychological counterpart. Furthermore, societal expectations prompt individuals to transition from childhood and forge a new adult existence. As a natural consequence, individuals also create themselves and their surroundings. This drive is motivated by the need for a superior talent (genius—*génie*). It is appropriate to speak of "genius" because adolescent creation involves not only projecting oneself into the future but also engaging in action, a state of motion, a psychic need, and a search for style. However, it is crucial to emphasize that what adolescents primarily create is their own identity. The internal imperative to shape oneself as an object is a fundamental need. Thus, this effort during adolescence essentially shapes the personality itself.

According to Philippe Gutton (2008),

> Creation presupposes the combination of an original, innovative impulse (sublimation) and an encounter with the (idealized) Other. The interaction between these two inhibitions of the drive's goal—sublimation and idealization—is as crucial as it is delicate. For sublimation to function effectively, it must be guided by idealistic cues.

> Sublimation entails the displacement of objects influenced by drive and aspiration. Within this creative complexity, a dialectic exists: ideals from the past (childhood) serve as triggers for pubertal sublimation, while new ideals are generated by sublimation itself. Thus, sublimation continuously innovates within the framework of idealizations. (p. 21)

On the other hand, to create is first to experience, to feel. The adolescent feels the transformation of his or her body. These profound and irreversible changes need to be interpreted and managed through childlike mechanisms to ensure the continuity of the personal story. Creating then becomes a matter of sharing these representations. Here, personal ideals, social and group dynamics, and of course, aesthetic elements come into play as value judgments. Finally, to create means to engage in identity formation through the pursuit of sublimation. The union of sublimation and idealization—this agreement, this meeting—is the source of the creative act. Sublimation enables us to produce, while idealization enables us to love. Of course, children are also creative, and play is a very creative act. However, there are no acts of production and reproduction in child's play. In adulthood, when both productive and reproductive abilities are developed, a sense of productive-reproductive creativity in the adult sense will emerge.

Adolescent-like (adolescentil)

If we are talking about production and reproduction, then adolescent creativity is, of course, about the future. It is the future that gnaws at the adolescent, caught in the dilemma of attraction and fear created by the return to childhood. The adolescent tries to capture the future through the window of the present. In discussing the future, I will attempt to define a new concept by borrowing from philosophy. Here, I will propose a theoretical idea and coin a new term in keeping with the tradition of psychoanalysis: *adolescent-like*. I define *adolescent-like* as the ability of adolescent creativity to blend elements of sublimation and idealization with "anticipation," continually pushing forward and allowing itself the opportunity to relinquish illusions and delusions. Additionally, I view *adolescent-like* as one of the foundational elements of the adult psyche, similar to the *childlike*.

French phenomenologist and psychiatrist Jean Sutter (1983) defines priming with an emphasis on anticipation: "Anticipation … is the movement by which a person carries themselves with all their being beyond the present into a future, whether near or distant, that is necessarily their own" (p. 19).

Anticipation involves experiencing the future in the present. We can differentiate between short and long anticipations. In short-ending anticipations, which are aimed at immediate psychomotor actions, the muscles tense, and sensory organs become alert, preparing the body for potential scenarios. Conversely, in long-ending anticipations, all individual activities are focused on preparing and creating the conditions necessary for the anticipated situation to occur.

However, it is necessary to distinguish anticipation from concepts closely related to it:

> Anticipation is not forecasting (*prévision*). Forecasting tries to imagine what the course of events might be, but it has no creative role. It is certainly used by anticipation, but by itself remains purely intellectual. You can foresee the future of others, or the probable course of less personal events, but you only anticipate your own future. Anticipation is not foresight (*prospective*), which is abstract reasoning, even further removed from the current of life. Expectation (*attente*) is in itself immobile and passive in the face of the hoped-for or feared event. Hope and despair share the same passivity, belonging entirely to affectivity. (Sutter & Berta, 1991, p. 6)

On the other hand, anticipation is also similar to volition (*will-volonté*); if anticipation is an attitude-behavior (*conduite*), it is unthinkable for it to occur outside of voluntary behavior. Of course, there is no magical thinking here, since magical thinking leaves all expectation to an external factor or coincidence.

Jean Sutter begins his book titled *L'anticipation* with Georges Bernanos' statement, "We don't suffer the future, we make it." Isn't one of the most important rebellions of adolescents the effort to take their future into their own hands? Anticipation cannot be reduced to advance preparation and detailed planning; it is like what Sutter calls "improvisational Italian comedies" (cited in Sutter & Berta, 1991, p. 20). On the other hand, in anticipation, the internal force and energy are the fundamental elements that enable movement toward the future, though not necessarily toward a specific goal. Sutter (Sutter & Berta, 1991) notes that there is constant movement in anticipation, where the goal can be continuously questioned and changed, achieving its objective only temporarily before immediately shifting focus. He states,

> For anticipation, while sometimes focused on one objective, always aims for several simultaneously. It has no truce, no end, no completion, no form, and can only be known by its movement. It is a powerful, continuous flow, like a mountain torrent. (p. 23)

In order to take control of their future, adolescents engage in self-anticipation by changing their ego ideals and integrating their creativity with the aid of sublimations and idealizations. The *adolescent-like* is shaped by the bodily, social, and legal pressures of the changes brought about by puberty; that is, by incorporating anticipation into the quest for new ego ideals based on identifications. This creative process, in Bernanos' words, is used "to make the future." However, it must also include the ability to create illusions and test them against reality.

Yes, there is also illusion! Donald Winnicott (1953) defines the word illusion as "an intermediate state between a baby's inability and growing ability to recognize and accept reality" (p. 90). Illusion is important because the transitional space, as defined by Winnicott, arises from the virtual bond formed between the child's illusion and that of the mother. The baby does not experience the reality test as a shock because he or she perceives this reality as part of the self. Initially, the mother fosters this illusion in the baby, but then she gradually helps the illusion fade, allowing the external reality to become independent from the baby.[2] But this is a process; accepting external reality takes a lifetime. In other words, there is always tension between external reality and internal reality—the psychic reality. What alleviates this tension is the creation of an intermediate space of experience, a direct continuation of the playground that the child has outgrown. Here, it is necessary to underline the difference between illusion and fantasy. An illusion is provided by another, whereas a fantasy is created by the individual. Winnicott (1953) states, "The mother's adaptation to the infant's needs, when good enough, gives the infant the illusion that there is an external reality that corresponds to the infant's own capacity to create" (p. 95).

In the case of adolescence, a "good enough parent" should provide the adolescent with the illusion that there is an external reality that corresponds to their own creative abilities. This is because adolescents require the presence of a "good enough parent" just as much as children need a "good enough mother." Similarly, just as a child's needs must be met by the mother, an adolescent's needs must be addressed by the parents. The child separates from the mother during the first individuation–separation period and from the parents during the second, which occurs in adolescence. At this point, a "good enough parent" facilitates the adolescent in realizing their illusions, which are based on their ego ideals, within a "playground."[3]

In fact, an illusion is often a mistake, and adolescence is fundamentally a period filled with illusions, mistakes, and errors. The harsh tests of reality are encountered most intensely either in the newborn period at the beginning of life or toward the end when death is imminent. Major changes in external reality compel the adolescent to create new illusions and to construct an intermediate, transitional space. It's important to remember that these illusions involve the faculties of the ego's ideal, serving the self. Just as a baby gradually becomes aware of the external world, the adolescent confronts the reality of the adult world—beyond the parental home. The process of forming these illusions and their eventual dissolution will liberate them, just as it liberates their parents and all adults. The path to freedom, which includes using one's abilities to love and work as an autonomous adult based on personal choices, hinges on the creation of a new transitional space. This space, a continuation of the childhood playground, allows the adolescent to project themselves into the future and anticipate it. These illusions not only help the adolescent adapt to life outside the family but also assist in gradually acclimating to and accepting external reality, much like a baby.

The *adolescent-like*, much like the childlike, must continue throughout adult life because the dynamics of existence do not end with the transition to adulthood. Considering that life is filled with constant changes, it becomes necessary to continually adjust identifications and ego ideals and, of course, to constantly engage in creativity. If we integrate the contributions of the *adolescent-like* with those of the childlike, they will facilitate the realization of the two elements that create happiness in adult life: production (work) and reproduction (love). Both reproduction and production are as vital as they are creative. While the childlike impulse is a source of vitality, the *adolescent-like* is at the root of the anticipation that shapes our ideas of the future. Moreover, the *adolescent-like* not only connects the childlike psyche to the adult psyche, but it also plays a crucial role in sustaining creativity and anticipation in the adult psyche. At nearly every stage of adult life, particularly at crucial junctures where creativity is demanded, the *adolescent-like* will be a core attribute that is invoked.

Of course, creativity exists in childhood. This is true, but childhood creativity, primarily exemplified by play, is a form of fiction, fantasy, or dream. During childhood, the pleasure principle dominates, and the reality principle is limited to the realm of play. In contrast, while a child may pretend to be a pilot using a toy airplane, an adolescent takes concrete steps toward becoming a pilot by enrolling in flight school and actively anticipating the realities of adult life. Thus, adolescents on the cusp of adulthood have a much clearer connection with reality.

On the other hand, the strength of the drives invested in sublimation increases with puberty. In other words, the power and effectiveness of adolescent sublimation have grown incomparably compared to that of child sublimation, due to the increase in the quantity of sexual and destructive drives attached to it. The pleasure principle has not been abandoned, but the compromise with the reality principle has become much more concrete and explicit. Therefore, the sublimations of adolescence allow for a greater investment in priorities that provide new beginnings. Moreover, the differences between the sublimations of adolescence and childhood are not only quantitative; the quality of sublimation has also changed. Now that reproduction and production have become possible, the adolescent has the opportunity to realize the two basic qualities of adulthood through anticipatory reproduction and production, that is, to "carry his or her existence beyond the present." The adolescent focuses on preparing and realizing the conditions for forming an anticipated future in adult life. This anticipated future replaces the image of a child holding a toy airplane with that of an adult holding the airplane controls in the cockpit.

If the ego ideal is a constantly renewing phenomenon, it will be the one that carries the psyche through life into the future. At various stages of adult life—such as starting or changing jobs, marriage, having children, making significant changes in living place or lifestyle, retirement, menopause, or andropause—old ego ideals will no longer be valid or sufficient, and new ones will need to be found. It is then to the *adolescent-like* that one must turn. By combining adolescent creativity and anticipation, the *adolescent-like* will enable new identifications to be reached with new ideals and sublimations at the moments of adult life when they are needed and will open the door to new illusions.

The consequences when *adolescent-like* traits are not constituent elements of the adult psyche

In the meantime, of course, there are those who cannot carry *adolescent-like* into adulthood. Here, akin to Philippe Jeammet distinction between *childlike* and *childish* (*enfantile-enfantin*), I will differentiate between *adolescent-like* and *adolescent-ish* (*adolescentil-adolescentin*). As much as *adolescent-like* contributes creativity and happiness of reproductive production to the adult psyche, *adolescent-ish* serves as an obstacle on that path. There are two scenarios to consider here. In the first scenario, as illustrated at the beginning of this chapter, there are adults who cannot utilize their *adolescent-like*. This woman, who was tortured for days by CIA agents as she transitioned from adolescence to adulthood, lost her *adolescent-like*. Consequently, she found someone to fulfill her anticipatory needs throughout her life, using her creativity, her illusions, and her renunciation of these illusions. In a sense, she relied on his *adolescent-like*. Thus, her *adolescent-like* could not become a constituent element of her adult psyche.

René Diatkine (1985), an important figure in French psychoanalysis, says,

> The impossibility of playing with mental representations is found to varying degrees in subjects with different structures. It is this particular disposition that results in some individuals never entering adolescence, while others never leave it. Some can never play; others can only play. (p. 61)

When the CIA agents did not allow her *adolescent-like* to last a lifetime, he became, as Diatkine notes, an adult who could not play with his psychic representations, who could not anticipate, and who lacked the courage for illusion. According to Diatkine,

> Adolescence begins for a human being when the time seems right to love and do what seems to justify its existence. It becomes tyrannical when the subject expects nothing more from others than limitless solicitude for the realization of his project. This is a regression to the previous organization, marked by a relentless search for numerous allies. (p. 66)

This is why this woman in her seventies felt completely bereft of a future after the loss of her husband, who had, to some extent, fulfilled her search for a parental figure for more than fifty years.

But there are also those who enter adolescence but cannot emerge from it; these are individuals who fail to integrate *adolescent-like* traits into their adult psyche and continue to exhibit adolescent behaviors, a phenomenon I refer to as *adolescent-ish*. Such people retain the traces of adolescent creativity but, unable to channel this into anticipation, they cannot transition to adult creativity and life. Their creativity, although somewhat closer to the principle of reality than childhood dreams, remains perpetually incomplete, manifesting as never-ending projects. These individuals are characterized by continually starting new schools, jobs, or relationships without ever advancing them to a level of productive maturity. They initiate many things but fail to complete them, leaving everything unfinished and in suspension. They do not allow their illusions to be tested by reality, maintaining them in a constant state of illusion, which paves the way for errors. I've mentioned that an illusion is a mistake, but a mistake is only recognized as such when it is acknowledged as a mistake. When an illusion is not recognized as a mistake, it becomes a constant error, trapping these individuals in a vicious cycle.

Time, of course, does not heed their reluctance; months and years pass, and they grow old. I am speaking of those who age without ever truly becoming adults. Indeed, some people possess a remarkable ability "to be old without being adults." I will conclude my article with the words from Jacques Brel's 1967 "Song of Old Lovers" (*La chanson des vieux amants*), which captures this sentiment precisely. In this song he was talking about an old couple who said: "We needed a lot of talent to be old without being adults."

Part III

Cultural studies

CHAPTER 8

The multilayered archeology of Turkish identity

M. Sağman Kayatekin and Z. Emel Kayatekin

As psychoanalysis is becoming more global, we are recognizing the fascinating richness of various cultures in ways that are pertinent to our theories and work. For example, in Chinese culture, a unitary sense of self, as it is defined in the Western world, doesn't exist (Chu, 2009). The family identity supersedes the individual identity. Thus, Chinese use the last name as their first name. A similar phenomenon is seen in Japan (Roland, 1988). In Arabic cultures a parent may be called after a son or a daughter with the terms "Abu" and "Ummu," the first referring to the father and second to the mother. Or a child can be named as "ibn" or "bint," as the son or the daughter, respectively (Rahman, 2003). In Korean, parents are addressed somewhat similarly: A umma (A's mom), B appa (B's dad)—even in family circles parents address each other this way, usually using the oldest child as a reference (Kang, 2020).

In Turkish villages the last name is an important signifier. One of the author's (MSK) family is known as the "Kayatekins" in his paternal village and there is a sense of pride as a central regulatory affect that guides the "Kayatekins" on how they should conduct themselves. Further, he would be called the "son of Kayatekins" when he was a young boy. Whereas, if he were to revisit the same village fifty years later, he would be addressed simply as Sağman. "Kayatekins" would no longer have a substantive meaning for current generations, who live in proper multiroom houses with running water, electricity, and TVs, and shepherds are using their own smart phones. Very different indeed from the village etched in the memory of Sağman forever; a small, closed-in economic and cultural unit with oil lamps, public wells for water, outhouses, and single room dwellings. A clear shift from identifying with the larger family to the nuclear family and defining an overarching, individual, self-identity as a central motivational concept.

Turkey has always been a busy geographic/cultural land bridge, at the intersection of three continents—Asia, Europe, and Northern Africa. For millennia, significant civilizations have flourished in these lands—including Persians Greek, Roman, and Turkic empires in the last two and a half millennia and many before them. Today, still, there are remnants of those civilizations in the daily customs, linguistics, religious beliefs, and many other aspects of social life. In the last century, the abolition of the Ottoman empire and gradual integration into the global economy have added additional dimensions to the identities in the region. Slowly, these became much more layered with internal immigration from villages and towns to larger urban areas. Thus, these lands are uniquely rich from the end of various shifting self/identity formations and can contribute to the psychoanalytic theory (Kayatekin, 2008, 2022, 2023).

We can expand this complexity endlessly—from the sense of identity around names, identity as a group, sense of morality, affect regulation patterns, developmental differences, and even the ego's decision-making styles. In this chapter we will give some clinical examples on the context-dependent variability of identity/self-formation (Erikson, 1959; Goldin, 2015; Weisel-Barth, 2015). As Akhtar (1995) so eruditely commented, we have ample evidence now that social variables indeed shape psychoanalytic theory and practice. With globalization, this is a field that has been gaining increasing interest and will help us to have a finer, more sophisticated, universal psychoanalytic theory of mind (Akhtar 2010; Kakar, 1990a, 1990b, 1993; Nayar-Akhtar, 2015; Roland, 1998).

Reporting from the field

We will look at this rich social-historical experiment through the lens of a psychoanalytically informed family work, an individual therapy, and an illustration of a prototypical young Turkish professional woman who immigrated to the USA. All portraits are seen from the angle of multiple identities in the rapidly shifting social and political contexts of Turkish people. These perennial identity shifts of the ancient cultural crossroad of Turkey pose interesting clinical dilemmas on the centrally important concept of identity as a contextually cohesive, adaptive, malleable construct. The first two vignettes are from MSK's practice and the third is from ZEK's practice.

Clinical vignette 1

> This is the story of S, who was in her early twenties when we worked, a student in a prestigious college, struggling with anorexia/bulimia. She started treatment as an outpatient and, a few times, needed hospitalization due to the deterioration of her eating disorder in the context of a budding love relationship that threatened the core aspects of the family structure. I worked with her and the family when I was the director of a psychodynamic open inpatient unit. In her treatment, I functioned as the team leader and the family therapist. A psychodynamic psychotherapist saw the patient three times a week for individual therapy. Another clinician contributed via cognitive behavioral approaches to address her severe

anorexic/bulimic rituals. She was also embedded in the complicated therapeutic structure of the inpatient unit.

It was a family of four going through multiple cultural transitions in both generations. The parents were from small towns and as young engineers were the first college graduates of their respective families. Both climbed up the ladder and became successful professionals in large corporations. S had a younger brother in a private high school and, as first-generation metropolis dwellers, they were learning how to navigate in the complicated culture of city life. The most striking aspect of the family was the parents' relationship. Despite being divorced, they were living as if they were still married. They didn't have any significant others in their lives, were on very good terms, having dinners, going to vacations together, making shared decisions on how to raise their kids. In sum, they had more than a friendly coexistence.

S and her father had a symbiotic relationship. Father was struggling with his boundaries—he was an endless source of patience with his daughter's illness, her symptomatic behavior, and was quite limitless in his giving—supplying her money, time, to the point of indulgence. In a striking contrast, the mother's intolerance of the anorexic/bulimic behavior was one of the reasons why she moved out to live alone. She was relegated to the role of a bystander/third in the complicated network of the oedipal triad; though in time it would become clear that her active removal of herself was mainly related to her immense sense of guilt over her daughter's illness, some aspects of which she recognized in her own self.

The treatment that lasted for a year and a half with weekly or biweekly ninety-minute sessions unfolded along the expected lines. After a period of family resistance, I was included into the family system as a participant observer through a group enactment. As treatment progressed, the patient became less symptomatic, more adapted; the parents became much less prone to project split aspects of themselves to the patient and started developing their complicated, conflicted, multilayered individual identities, their private spaces, and personal interests outside of the confining, smothering entanglement of the foursome that was functioning like an amalgamated unity.

Throughout the course of the treatment, however, with the recreation of the triadic mother–father–daughter generational differential and mother's active inclusion as a parent and (ex) wife to the father, the father managed to pull himself out of the symbiotic togetherness with his daughter, found his areas of personal interests, and started spending time with his friends. This differentiation initially infuriated the patient. The fact that her father would do things without letting S know meant he had a private/secret time, which was an enigma for her.

In parallel, the patient gradually liberated herself from this symbiotic relationship and started developing her own interests and friendships. Her spending less time with the father initially caused enormous jealousy, feelings of abandonment, and then relief in the father. Mother became more able to move inwards from the margins of this regressed dyad, and occupy more of a central role, spend separate time with her daughter. Father and

> mother were allowing each other to be simultaneous love objects of the daughter and son. The younger brother was freed from the constant worries he had about the rest of the family and felt free to pursue his interests and enjoy his youth. Finally, the patient's burgeoning new love relationship cemented the reorganization of the family. In certain ways, the treatment was centrally about restructuring the ordinary oedipal triads and transgenerational, developmentally necessary asymmetries. This in turn unblocked the stalling of the growth of all parties concerned.
>
> The development in treatment was wonderfully symbolized in food and eating-related rituals and relationships in the family. It became clear that the mother was quite restricting in her love relationship with her daughter; and it was condensed in eating patterns. When S was very young, mother was very meticulous in preparing her food, offering her plain, steamed carrots and other vegetables. They would get into endless food fights when S was young; now the mother had stopped insisting altogether. For example, she would go to a restaurant with her daughter, order a delicious dish of food and when her daughter refused, she would accept the refusal as final. One day, toward the end of the treatment, they came from a restaurant trip with a sense of victory. Mother ordered some expensive salmon and the patient, in her usual style, refused it. In contrast to her usual resigned acceptance, mother this time insisted that the patient give it a try. After a few requests the patient finally agreed to taste the oily salmon and managed to eat quite a bit and keep it in without throwing up. They both were pleasantly surprised. This was just like love: it was somewhat sticky, oily, and tasty. Love, the mother learned, clearly is not as bland as steamed carrots. That was one of the turning points as acted in and symbolized by food.
>
> Similarly, another symbolic turning point was when the father finally became exhausted from the anorexic and bulimic rituals of S, expressed this with anger, and sold the second fridge they had for the peculiar foods and drinks of the patient. He insisted that the patient share the same fridge and be respectful of others' foods and drinks in the space allowed by the family refrigerator and not invade that common space or the whole house with her rituals for that matter.
>
> Slowly, as we worked on the roots of the symbolism of anorexic and bulimic behavior, it became clear that the father was learning frugality, mother was learning generosity, and the patient was able to take both in, not gorge in food or purge it out but keep the identification/food inside of her mind and her body.

Here, for the purposes of this chapter, we will focus further on one of the last few sessions where some surprising aspects of the parents emerged. The parents, when they moved from small towns to İstanbul for college education, found themselves lost in the middle of a social chaos. At that time in Turkey there were intense armed conflicts between independent leftists and state-backed nationalists and Islamists. The cities were divided into subregions, local governance structures were erected under the control of these three groups, massacres occurred, and a Kurdish rebellion was on the rise. It was an unnamed civil war. Having lost their ways in the megalopolis, they found an adaptive solution by belonging to a political youth group with leftist tendencies that was rather peaceful in its political approaches. But a series of military coups crushed all leftist opposition with violence, swept them into torture chambers. They both were arrested as communists, accused of contemplating insurrection and severely tortured, most like any left-leaning youth. Typical of those days, to increase the impact, the couple were forced to witness each other being tortured, as they suffered electric shocks to the private parts of their bodies and endured severe beatings.

The mother heroically resisted the torture and didn't confess under pressure. Once, despite bleeding profusely from her vagina, the doctors evaluated her and said they could continue the torture because the bleeding was not that severe. This went on for weeks. After the torture was over, they were imprisoned in military facilities for some years, where brutality was rampant.

Once all fighting was subdued, political groups and the rebellion crushed, the leaders imprisoned or executed, there was an amnesty, and the couple were released. They went on with their lives, but this added another strong layer of bonding. The camaraderie through the torture chambers and their love as a couple now were intertwined inseparably.

Since the middle of the nineteenth century Ottomans had faced a question of who they were, whether they were pro-Western, pan-Turkic, or pan-Islamist. An interesting aspect of this quandary manifested itself in dress, hairstyle, and a sublanguage. The first sultan who lived through this was Mahmud the Second who famously got rid of the turban and ordered the fez to be worn. In the 1920s, with the establishment of the young republic, there was a new set of "revolutions," which again codified the looks of men and woman. The fez was banned, the Panama hat became the new symbol. Women were encouraged to avoid chadors and scarves; language was Turkified, cleared of Arabic and Farsi words. Following tradition, when the last quarter of the century brought the leftist rebellion to the country, it dictated a distinct dress code that included parkas and military style boots for men. There was a special way of wearing a moustache, whiskers were frowned upon. A beard was disapproved of, as well as long hair. No makeup in women was tolerated. Women should be casually dressed in below-the-knee skirts or jeans. High heels were unacceptable. Studying Marxist classics and citing them from memory was highly regarded. Very clear boundaries around sexuality existed, with disapproval of flirtatious behaviors or sexual liaisons; only marriage was tolerated. The leftist narrative had its own jargon, everyone called each other sister, friend, or comrade. It was a sublanguage with its euphemisms and vocabulary. An exemplary leftist gave the appearance of a serious person, avoiding jocularity and humor as much as possible. Probably the paranoid ghost of Stalin was floating in the background somewhere. This subculture was an important aspect of the youth of the parents of S. Parallel dress codes, stereotypical presentations, behavioral patterns, and narrative styles existed in Islamists and radical nationalists. So, one could decipher the political ideology of anyone through these visual and linguistic cues.

Neighborhoods were ghettoized; one would face the risk of a severe beating, torture, and murder if one entered the wrong neighborhood. Turkey had several subsocieties, ready to fight, and in fact killing each other on a daily basis (Massicard & Watts, 2012). Despite the fact that these things had happened many years before our treatment, the two parents were still carrying their political selves with them with a sense of pride, even though neither had been politically active for more than a decade.

Back to clinical vignette 1

At the end of our family sessions, the powerful remnants of the leftist political identities of the parents were dissolving, and the parents were reverting to their more ordinary selves, not in need of an adaptive/defensive layer of a political persona that was probably a necessity in the times of civil war. The civil war had subsided, thus the radical political cloak that was necessary in their youth and had stayed with them as an appendage to their young adult selves was now leaving its place for another set of social identity that was more in sympathy with how they had defined themselves prior to their political activism. It had contributions from the political selves but now it was a part of their own personal fabric, not as a social definer of the times of civil war.

In the penultimate session, as we all were saying goodbyes, reviewing our work, with a sense of gratitude and some sense of shame, father and mother made significant revelations. The father told his family that he now was reclaiming his religious beliefs—as a moderate Muslim, with progressivist, liberal political leanings. This was a courageous step for a self-proclaimed atheist of many decades. He also said he would not be interested in active politics but only in electoral party activities. Mother, on the other hand, was reverting to her tomboyish, rebellious, marginal self, bouncing around the progressivist feminist intellectual circles, a persona that was hitherto severely restrained due to what was expected of a proper left-wing rebel.

Within this liberation to redefine their identities, the children also became freer to find their own ways. The parents were finally actualizing the divorce, a finalized separation from one another, even though they would have a lifelong camaraderie and strong bonding because of the terrible trauma they had shared. In hindsight, it was an understandable aspect of what otherwise seemed pretty much ordinary family dynamics of a high-functioning borderline patient with an eating disorder. The layer of chronic, severe social trauma did clearly complicate the presentation, the organization of the pathology, and the characters.

Now we will move to an individual psychoanalytic psychotherapy that will highlight the well-established, centuries-old traditions of the intricate family relations that somehow osmotically infiltrate the professional lives of young Turkish people. There is an amalgamation of the new, professional relationships that are becoming more prevalent with the traditional roles of men and women in Turkey. The old is somehow symbolized in the stories of these lands in the mythic micropolitics of Byzantine and Ottoman palace intrigues, thus the concept of "Byzantine," from the millennia-old city of Byzantium, or current day İstanbul. These tell of an intriguing, complicated, mystifying level of complexity in the relationships that are narrated in the colorful, mythical, fanciful stories of a politically powerful harem under the protectorate and leadership of the chief eunuch, where ambitious and jealous concubines were living together, scheming their political plots and murderous political schemes. These fascinating complexities of the Orient have rightfully gained the evocative historical name of "Byzantine" and harem politics (Hathaway, 2018; Üre, 2014). As a side note, from these very old lands, besides "Byzantine" another universal phrase was born—the "Young Turk," which interestingly is related to the demolishing of these Byzantine relations in macropolitics, within social life, or in the micropolitics of marriages and love lives (Çalışlar, 2019).

Clinical vignette 2

D was a graduate student in her early twenties when she consulted me. The event that initiated the treatment was a breakup with a boyfriend who was also a postgraduate student in the same university. The patient was appalled by the abruptness of this split and developed a deep sense of confusion, and a painful mourning. She was impacted to a degree that was noticeable to her peers and interfered with her daily functioning and professional life. The chairperson of the department asked me to see D. He was worried about her depression and potential risk for suicide. D knew that the chairperson and I were in friendly terms; what I provided was seen as a favor. I was also known as a doctor coming from America, with an idealized halo around my name. I saw D for about two years, on an average about two to three times a week. There was one short-term hospitalization when her depression worsened, though overall she clinically did quite well. Her depression/mourning cleared, and she went back to functioning effectively as a resident. She was quite content with where her life was at the termination.

For a long while, her sole focus in therapy was on the intricacies of her relationship with her ex-boyfriend. There was a foursome in her stories; D, her ex, another young man, and his girlfriend, a young woman who had introduced D and her now ex to one another. At times, her presentation felt like painful ruminations for her to go through and for me to listen to. I felt bored and irritated by repeatedly hearing the same themes with almost the same text. Slowly I recognized that in between the lines of what sounded like a boring rumination to me, in fact in a fascinating "harem politics" way, D was intuitively evaluating and reviewing the micropolitics of the situation and devising plans to get her lover back. It dawned on me that the narrative was quite familiar in the history of Turkey—it was similar to the stories of Byzantine and Ottoman palace politics (Hathaway, 2018; Peirce, 1993).

What made it so unbearable for D was the fact that this was the first time she was ready to have a premarital sexual relationship. She had passionate masturbatory fantasies about this young man, talked about them openly with him, and was ready to surrender to her intense erotic passion for the first time in her young life. Especially coming from a small provincial town where women still had wedlock or arranged marriages, for an average young female, virginity was important, sometimes to the point where young couples would show bloodied linen to the relatives in the morning after the marriage ceremony, to prove the

> bride's virginity; and there still is a profitable sector of plastic surgery in Turkey, working on repairing the perforated hymen before marriage (Güzel, 2018). Even for this enlightened young student, sexual intimacy prior to marriage was unthinkable, but her love was so deep that she was ready to take a courageous step.
>
> At the beginning of their relationship, the ex-boyfriend responded to her affection, which raised her hopes. As they were developing a relationship, he broke up abruptly and unilaterally, without any discussion. Thus, a recurrent theme my patient talked about was her inability or reluctance to give up her love affair. In the sessions, D would come up with exhaustive palace intrigues on how to win him back. The reasoning she had was quite significant—she had a strong conviction that her ex-boyfriend's thinking and decision-making was influenced by others, and in reality, these were not his decisions; they couldn't be the decisions of the man whom she came to know and love. Perhaps he was impacted by the mutual girlfriend who had initially introduced them to one another. A significant number of sessions in the first six months or so were around the intrigues on how to change his mind and win him back. But the actions she initiated had no impact on him and she was not able to reawaken his interest in her, which intensified her internal searches.

The notion of being influenced, brainwashed, is a common theme in Turkish culture (Havlıoğlu & Uysal, 2023). We can see this attribute in politicians; the common narrative is, "Well, he was well-intentioned but the people around him didn't advise him properly." This is a way of absolving the leader, and in this instance the ex, from making decisions that were willful and voluntary, decisions that belonged to him. It's interesting that many people who make serious mistakes also explain it by their minds being impacted by others. For example, a famous politician who held high offices in the country told the public that he was deceived by a certain sect of religious movement: "I was just fooled," he said. It's of significance that this political leader, who tries to keep the image of a wise and intelligent person capable of making world-shattering decisions, was at the same time seeing himself as someone who can easily be fooled by others (Kıraç, 2022). This paradox in some ways is a standard and widespread Turkish philosophy of the mind (Abazov, 2009), and it was operative in how D, in the microcosm of her unconsummated love affair, was interpreting the events. She had a strongly held opinion that her ex-boyfriend's mind and free decision-making capacity was usurped by others.

In those within less educated circles, there is also a common religious explanation for disowning certain misdeeds of theirs by claiming them as down to the "devil" that has possessed their mind. For example, a prominent Turkish intellectual wrote about a real story of his youth. An esteemed and influential local religious leader (Imam) in his hometown in Eastern Anatolia, a relatively conservative part of the country, was caught molesting a preteen girl. The townsfolk were infuriated, and the imam was on the verge of being lynched. He was arrested. However, in a matter of a few weeks, as the heat of the event settled down, the story shifted to the imam being influenced by a devil hidden in the body of the young girl he molested, and thus he was forgiven by the populace and returned to his esteemed role in the local community (Laçiner, 2016).

While reviewing my notes on this patient, what really captured my attention was how women in Turkey, in certain ways, are quite powerful, albeit in "behind the scenes" ways. Without any interest in generalizing to patriarchy and matriarchy, I would like to state my observation that Turkish lore is replete with stories of women pulling powerful strings, though not within view, mostly through their sons. This is exemplified in the semi-mythical stories of the "sultan's mother." It's well known in Ottoman histories that certain sultans were heavily influenced and guided by their mothers or their beloved ones. Quite commonly they would inherit the throne at a young age, even as a teenager, and thus were developmentally open to the suggestions of their mothers. One of the most famous of Ottoman sultans, Mehmet the Conqueror, was a governor at the age of eleven and was a sultan at the age of twelve. Beginning with Suleiman the Magnificent in the seventeenth century, there is a period named the "Reign of Women" when wives and mothers had been actively involved in the meetings of the imperial court and impacted political decision making. This active presence gradually shifted to more domestic agendas like personal foundations and the building of mosques. Yet women never lost their importance in palace politics. Even though in the long history of the Ottomans and in the history of the Turkish Republic, there has been no woman as the sovereign who held political power directly (except for a female prime minister some years ago), it's also amply documented that the mothers and favorite wives of the sultans wielded enormous power (Altınay, 2005; Peirce, 1993). This is a common political phenomenon of Middle East history (Stenslie, 2011).

Beyond the confines of the imperial palace, there are plenty of similar stories of female feudal landlords. *Hanım ağa* (lady the landlord) syndrome is one such well-known theme. It is about powerful women who happens to own and run large estates due to the unexpected death of their husband at a young age. To use patriarchy and matriarchy in a simplistic way, these women would become typical patriarchs once they achieved positions of power. The eponym *Hanım ağa* summarizes this—*Hanım* means lady, *ağa* is the colloquialism for male landlords.

Clinical vignette 2 (continued)

Coming back to the sessions with D, let me expand on an atypical aspect of her treatment. My office had two entries. The front entrance was the primary one, which was through the waiting area, and the back door opened to a corridor, connecting to a different building of the hospital system. D asked to use the second entry because she felt deeply ashamed of coming through the waiting area, where her chances of meeting someone she may know were much greater. So, this, what seemed like an innocent request, and my acquiescence proved to be an important enactment. It gave a clear color of secretiveness to the treatment and furthered D's regression to the point of hospitalization. D was expected to live a life of a "good, successful, hardworking" young female doctoral student, as the source of pride of her family in her small town, whereas she had been deeply troubled by sadistic and traumatic aspects of her father and the ignorance of her mother. So, in time, when it became clear that she couldn't make it without a hospitalization, all this secrecy crumbled, and, to her deep sense of embarrassment and relief, this "goodness," that she needed to carry, was demolished and she was admitted to hospital. This perhaps played a role in the sudden death of her father, or at the very least had an impact in that direction. The loss of her father was going to be of monumental importance for D because it allowed her to mourn and internalize him as a person.

In hindsight, it appears as if the foundation for Byzantine/Ottoman intricacies in her therapy was laid down from day one. D was referred to me by the department chair, a colleague and friend of mine; she came without a search or action of will on her part, but just out of desperation. I had recently come from a prominent training in USA, and had a stellar presence in the hospital at that moment. I was seeing her for free and using the back door to the office, in what can be seen as "secret" sessions. Within this semi-secrecy, the transference vacillated between me being the victimizer because of my "insensitivity" and unwillingness to give advice, and being the victim of evoked painful countertransferences through the projective/introjective cycles. These emotional storms tormented me to a point where I, not infrequently, thought of resigning from the case that I had taken over as a favor. Part of this vacillation was embedded in the traumatic history of the patient. She told me a horrendous story of paternal aggression that at times led to violence, to the point of sadism and the brutal killing of animals. She had a constant fear of a tyrant at home, and I could sense her sadism in the countertransference through various subtle and overt ways. When her father suddenly died from a cerebral vascular accident D recognized how enamored she was with him and started a painful process of mourning the loss. She remembered how her father, in contrast to his sadistic presence at home, was also known for his benevolence, acts of kindness toward others, and was a deeply respected person in the community. We had sessions where she was in tears, wishing they could speak one more time and she could kiss him on his cheeks, hold his hands.

This shifted the transferences, where she moved from idealizing and passively and actively tormenting me to becoming more openly critical, and yet also identifying with me, wishing she could do similar things like going to the USA and furthering her training over there. She became more assertive in her professional life and managed finally to write the ex-boyfriend off by clearly telling me that she felt she was done with him. In the transference she became livelier, playful. It's probably fair to say that her capacity to hurt others increased dramatically once her father was dead and she located the sadism of the father as a harnessed aggression in her relationship with others, including myself in the transference. The good and victimized patient was gone; someone who is alive, who can exact revenge had come in full force by the time we ended after two years of intense work. The non-suppression of passionate sides of her had also tamed those down and she was now capable of holding herself and me ambivalently, freed from the yoke of a smothering love and vicious sadism.

Now we will move to another patient who demonstrates an important aspect of identity as it is becoming more of a central definer of self in Turkish modernity. Women moving out of the dark shadows of oppression as "wives of their men" and secret power holders of their children to becoming open equals, women as professionals; a feminist revolution one may say, from the banished Islamic dress code of women to universal suffrage, to women becoming professionally and politically active. A lengthy, complicated social process that has been occurring with increased intensity since the founding of the Turkish Republic in the 1920s, a century ago.

Stereotypes are important in human relationships. They organize the world in a fantasy construct that has significant capacity for being a major source of motivation. They provide a map for navigation through which one interprets the world and initiates action choices—in short, they may become a guiding philosophy of how we construct the human world and live in it.

As we saw in the case of the young doctoral student above, the place and definition of a woman's sexuality are centrally important in the constantly changing Turkish society. It is displayed in a wide range, from a woman in traditional Islamic marriages, as one of the wives of a man, strolling behind him in a row, in deep black chadors, covered from head to toe, hiding even her face, to a woman in a metropolis, living a liberated personal and sexual life, as depicted in some of the modern Turkish novels of Kulin (2000, 2014).

Centrally connected to their gender, an important common denominator of how women are stereotyped in Turkey, there is a widespread, almost universal perception of women (by self and others) as "the other" in comparison to men (Öztürk, 2022). In Turkey, definition of a woman's agency and will can be coined as a passively active "other," in contrast to a man in whom the will, decision making, and quality of an initiator of action are located. For over a century, many cultural wars have been fought in Turkey on the issue of women's rights: her external perception, how she should be dressed, what her role should be in society, whether education is helpful or harmful for her. These themes occupy the political arena, journal articles, TV shows, and religious sermons of preachers. For example, wearing a headscarf in a certain way has become a symbol of cultural wars for over a century in the unending polarization of the country. Like the parka uniform of the leftist rebels, the headscarf became the uniform of religious conservatism. And men claimed to be the protectors of their "sisters with headscarves," and got into serious legal and, occasionally murderous, mob fights over this theme. We see similar themes in the theocracies of various sorts—from Iran to Afghanistan.

In the ordinary lives of many citizens of Turkey, "working woman," as an identification, is still a relatively new concept, and probably most women still consider their primary roles as mothers and homemakers. In small towns, and slums, even though women work as much as men do—if not more—they still do not fully embrace their work as a centrally important definer. In recent decades, claiming their work identity, professional women of Turkey went through rapid changes. Only recently, though, there is a grassroots movement where women who have not been granted these freedoms, are now claiming them for themselves, forcefully, in the changing society.

Clinical vignette 3

Let me offer the profile of a woman whom I worked with, to serve as a symbol for the complicated transitions of the self-definitions of women as an element of the "we," not as a member of the perennial "other" in Turkey. The treatment was along the lines of simply listening to her journey of becoming a Turkish American with a deep sense of mourning and liberation. I had a sense of accompanying her during this phase where she reviewed and rewrote her history and used me like another woman who has been through a similar process who could understand her, someone who could hear her. Which was poignantly true.

When I first saw G, she was in her mid-thirties, married to a successful small-business owner and was an architect by training. She came to me a few years after immigrating to the United States and described intense difficulties in adapting to "American culture," which she perceived as amazingly different. There was a deep sense of confusion, mourning, and sadness over what was lost with immigration (Akhtar, 1995), yet she also felt rejuvenated in this interesting country. It felt like waking up—G was struck by how equality was a palpable social reality in USA.

G was born and raised in a big city in Turkey and considered herself the "equal" of men in many ways yet believed there should be different roles for women and men in the family and society. In her perception, gender didn't seem to play a major role in this new culture she had immigrated to. She noted women being as comfortable in having and expressing their own opinions, in any meetings; women and men sharing mundane responsibilities, from caregiving of a child to cleaning the house. Women might not be interested in knitting but there were some handsome, straight young men who would knit, even at professional meetings. Women could become cops, drive trucks, and dominate conversations in family gatherings. All of which was quite different from the role of a woman she was used to. It was a new world indeed, confusing and liberating.

Interestingly, the confusion of G intensified when their young adolescent daughter tried to integrate to the American life of her peers; this attempt awakened all the fault lines around the definition of woman and man in her Turkish conservative culture. The daughter had passionate fights with the father about what to wear, what to eat, occasional alcohol use, drugs, boyfriends, role of religion, among a long list of areas of active, heated conflicts. She was trying to be like her peers and was pushing all the boundaries, lines that were revered and considered as indisputable. G saw herself as more liberal-minded compared to her husband, yet she was also getting confused about what was right and what was wrong. The turbulent adolescence had hit all the decisions they as parents made, some clear-cut rules they established, making them question themselves with rekindled conflicts and ambivalence. It became clear that this in fact had precipitated G's search for therapy as her initial attempts to resolve these questions within the family failed miserably.

She told me about her parents, who had confusing opinions on how to be a "proper woman." As an example, she was expected to be an excellent student, graduate from a university, get a profession—"a golden bracelet" in Turkish colloquialism. That diploma would allow her to work anywhere in the world, yet she was also expected to get married, be a mother and a housewife, and hang her diploma on the wall, a visible yet useless witness to the fact that it was a guaranteed fallback if she failed in her projected life of a happy marriage with children.

G's parents had a strict code of morality which was not unusual in Turkish culture but perhaps more rigid; not only sexuality before marriage was a taboo, but any touch of a man would also be considered as a stain on her honor. "If honor is lost, nothing else would have any value," her parents thought. She was not allowed to go out with male friends; she was not even allowed to go to the houses of her female friends, as their brothers or fathers would pose a "danger."

No sexual education was given to G by her parents, not even about the ordinary issue of menses and how one takes care of oneself during these monthly ordeals. Sexual conversations were avoided "just in case her mind goes there," which caused unfounded fears and vulnerabilities. Sexual pressure was intense at her all-girls high school; skirts should be below the knee; hair would be combed in the most unattractive way to avoid any unnecessary attention. It was as if all men were ready to sexually attack the girls, and if there were no intense monitoring, girls would immediately submit and surrender. G remembered how, after school, young men would line up along the road and would show unsolicited interest with admiring whistles, giggles, and occasional bodily harassment. The role of the girl was to act as if she didn't see or hear anything. One of the surprising, disorienting yet freeing experiences she had in the USA was the inattentiveness of the American men, in striking contrast to the ways she was used to in Turkey. Not hearing admiring whistles while she walked on the street initially felt as if she was no longer attractive.

In Turkey, her life was expected to be restricted until she got married, and G was told she could do anything she wanted to or be anybody she wished to be after marriage, with the permission of her husband, of course. The only freedom she had before marriage was going to school. And perhaps out of boredom, and perhaps because of her outstanding intelligence, she excelled at the university and graduated with top honors. As she had limited chances to know her male peers, marriage was semi-arranged; the couple got engaged soon after they met and married in a year. She was ready to hang her diploma on the wall and assume the role of a mother and a housewife.

Male–female relationships were idealized, perhaps on both sides. The expectation from the husband was enormous yet the power was also his, which led to intense insecurity, again perhaps on both sides. She thought it would be very difficult to be a man as he needed to face all the challenges outside of the home while her role would be to maintain the interest of her husband which she also perceived as slippery. After marriage, she started feeling somewhat conflicted about her new identity. She felt she was losing her sense of self (successful, independent student) and was becoming someone whom she was not sure how to define. Though she pushed these thoughts and feelings aside.

They had their only daughter long before they moved to the USA, who kept her quite busy as a mother. She was defining herself as "the wife of a businessman" among other housewives, didn't even consider working in her profession, and tried to persuade herself that she was content being a housewife, taking care of her daughter and husband.

The husband was more religious and was close to a liberal Islamic sect. G was from a radical nationalist background, so they both clearly were anti-left in their leanings. They grew up in the same period as the parents of the patient with the eating disorder mentioned above, but were not as politically involved; they kept their beliefs as personal.

In the USA, not only my patient but her husband also was confused about how to raise their daughter and about how to define themselves. Her husband was ambitious and hardworking, trying to establish himself as a businessman in their new country. For G, being a housewife and wife of a businessman didn't seem as attractive anymore. G started looking for opportunities for herself. Her English was not great, which limited her opportunities. Yet getting any job was also unacceptable due to her narcissistic expectations. She was able to settle this dilemma by accepting an internship position, though integration was quite challenging. She struggled with feeling and acting as entitled, superior due to her superb education, and intensely inferior due to her insecurities. Her coworkers didn't seem to care if she was a female or male, whereas all her life her relations were defined by gender roles. It was confusing and freeing.

In Turkey she was always told by her mother that her intelligence and success could be threatening for men and no matter how smart and skillful she might be, she should look not too intelligent in order not to threaten men. She struggled about how assertive or submissive she needs to be; she felt like she was oscillating between the extremes on both ends, getting criticism either way.

G also faced some projections due to coming from a "Muslim country." Two highly educated professional colleagues originally from a military-Islamist country approached her and asked whether she could wear a headscarf. The patient was stunned with the response when she asked why she should wear one. "Because of your hair: an open head evokes sexual desires and passions in men," they replied. Her husband was also struggling; on the one hand he was now expecting her to contribute to the house equally, on the other hand expecting her to maintain her "duties as a woman." He seemed to be unhappy with being idealized, the unrealistic expectations put on him, yet he also didn't know how to be "equal" and was ambivalent about giving his so-called dominant status away.

All these years of work with this patient made me recognize a forgotten fact of humanity. In the evolution of human society, the nuclear family of father as a breadwinner and mother as a homemaker is too simplistic a paradigm. For many millennia, as the proverb "It takes a village to raise a child" wonderfully demonstrates, childrearing, after the first most fragile year of life, has been a shared occupation, and it happens beyond the confines of a nuclear or single parent family, sequestered in a home. In an interesting paradox, as women break out of their forced roles, new occupations have been created in the massive contemporary cities where infants attend daycare and kindergarten, where they are taken care of by professionals. It is quite clear that so far, we haven't seen any deleterious effects of this postmodern way built into the way of life of our megacities. In fact, they may be wonderful opportunities to rectify what parents are incapable of providing to the child. In certain ways, G was refinding the traditional role of women as professionals in the newly adopted but ever-changing culture she had transplanted herself into.

Conclusion

There is a widespread assumption about the universality of some core developmental social psychoanalytic constructs. This was challenged early on by prominent anthropologists, though it stayed as a marginal knowledge for many decades (Benedict, 2008; Boas, 2008; Malinowski, 2008; Mead, 2008). Nowadays, through technology, mass tourism, immigrations, and international training in psychoanalysis, there is an increased awareness of the globe as an interconnected unity. With so-called globalization the culturally determined aspects of our theory is moving to the center of our awareness and we are noticing that the assumed norms are rather culture specific as the distance between west and east, or, in the modern nomenclature, north and south, is becoming less by the year. This radical challenge confronting the social aspects of the foundations of theory can be seen as potentially expanding and enriching our understanding, which naturally goes with the questioning of assumptions and cultural norms that were taken as universal truths.

More specifically, through our psychoanalytic lens these considerations are perhaps best summarized eloquently in the "third individuation" paper of Akhtar (1995). Within the larger context of interpreting immigration as another process of individuation, Akhtar writes about the cultural shock as a catalyst of creativity and fecundity for the development of self. Building on the legacy of other psychoanalytic theoreticians (Grinberg & Grinberg, 1989), he talks about ongoing multiplicities of selves, subsets of selves, context-related domination of certain self-organizations and fragmented allegiances. These observations of Akhtar's we find are quite relevant to the patients we have discussed in this chapter. After all, during transitions within our cultures that seem to have lost their halting, staggered character and turned into an ongoing process, we become immigrants in our own lands and societies at all times.

CHAPTER 9

An exploration of hysteria through the Turkish movie *Nefret* (1984)

Elif Nisan İlkmen

In the 1980s, many movies dealing with women's sexuality were being released in Turkey. While the traditional understanding of the approach of Yeşilçam' (Turkish cinema) to women in mainstream Turkish cinema's commercially oriented movies continued, movies dealing with women with a realistic perspective began to be made. The extreme "good woman/bad woman" stereotypes in previous periods were broken (Lüleci, 2016).

When the fairy-tale universe of Yeşilçam began to crack during this period, all the identities and images that Turkey had censored and suppressed into the subconscious began to emerge. Women with cigarettes in their hands, wearing furs, elegant clothes, hats, and expensive jewelry often began to play leading roles and no longer represented pure evil. The explosion of words and images in the 1980s undoubtedly implies the recycling of repressed desire, exclusion, and deprivation (Deniz, 2017). In Yeşilçam's movies from the second half of the 1960s to the end of the 1970s, the path a woman must follow to attain sexual freedom was repeatedly presented to the audience as a simplified formula. This path requires her to be forgiving and sacrificial, as well as to persevere through all kinds of challenges. Her sacrifice is rewarded at the end of the movie when she reaches the only man she has ever loved. In the 1980s, on the other hand, the dissatisfaction of female desires arising from the lack of a savior and compassionate man was at the forefront.

In this new era, scenarios centered on women who could not be possessed, and the unsatisfied side of desire in both men and women was emphasized. The woman who does not surrender her soul to the man she makes love with and the man who perpetrates violence against the woman whose soul he cannot possess are the characters that symbolize unsatisfied desire. While the female characters of the 1960s and 1970s suffered because of their desire, the female characters of the 1980s symbolized dominance over desire.

Before the 1980s, when women's typologies in Turkish cinema underwent a radical change, women were mostly represented as objects of desire for men, and the narrative and form of movies were based on men's conquest of this object of desire (Yerlikaya, 2020). By the 1980s, the female body and desire were becoming increasingly prominent in the posters and credits of Yeşilçam movies. Women have needs and even have a strong sexual desire, but when we look at the meanings produced in the movies, we see that the responsibility of controlling this desire is delegated to traditional structures, and it is emphasized that women should remain within certain roles (Doğan, 2013).

In Yeşilçam's movies of the 1980s, women evolved from being sexual objects to being sexual subjects who began to experience their sexuality (Dorsay, 1995, p. 19). Henceforth, the female figure, who has had sexual intercourse and established physical and emotional relationships with her boyfriends without getting married, is presented to the audience with a realistic character structure that exists with its contradictions and complicated sides instead of as "pure evil." For these women, love was not the main factor shaping their lives. In Yeşilçam's narratives, when a woman is betrayed, she is expected to make all kinds of sacrifices and endure them; however, this attitude has changed since 1980. Now, the betrayed woman leaves her husband, and this situation is affirmed in the movie's narrative (Ekici, 2017).

The sociological content of the movies starring Hülya Avşar, who made her first movie in 1983, is in line with all these writings. As a person, Avşar is not only one of the best-known actresses of her generation and era but also the longest-running tabloid character in Turkish society. Her career, which began to take shape in the 1980s, continued throughout the 1990s, 2000s, and 2010s, and she has been engaged in many popular and media jobs, such as singer, television program presenter, columnist, theater actress, magazine editor, and advertisement actress (Uysal, 2021).

Hülya Avşar's characters stand in opposition to orthodox social values that became obsolete with the spread of neoliberal social values in the second half of the 1980s. In this context, Avşar's characters fulfill a specific task: they aspire to be a representation rather than a didactic role model (Uysal, 2021). In the 1984 movie *Nefret* (*Hatred*), although the character of Hülya, portrayed by Hülya Avşar using her own name, exemplifies exhibitionist attitudes and relationships that push the boundaries of social values, it also represents the delirium of a young woman crushed by the damage of her parents' dysfunctional marriage.

Synopsis and tagline of the *Hatred* (1984) movie

Release Date: 1984
Director: Osman F. Seden

Fatma and Metin are a married couple with a daughter, Hülya. Fatma is a successful businesswoman who has not found the love and attention she seeks in her husband and is devoted to her career. Metin, however, is a father who takes advantage of Fatma's financial resources, has cheated on his wife from the beginning of their marriage, and maintains estranged relationships with his wife and daughter. The couple's family life is full of problems despite living in luxury. Hülya is a young girl who uses drugs, disobeys the house rules, and openly expresses her hatred for her mother at every opportunity. Fatma is a mother who finances Hülya's expenses and condones her extravagant spending, but she struggles to bond emotionally with her daughter. Throughout the movie, Fatma repeatedly states that she has done everything to get close to Hülya but has been unsuccessful. These attempts at intimacy, however, are limited to Fatma taking Hülya shopping and purchasing her expensive gifts. Fatma accuses her husband, Metin, of being excessively tolerant toward her daughter and holds Metin responsible for Hülya's spoiled behavior.

Metin, on the other hand, is opposed to establishing any kind of authority at home or in his parenting style. He prefers to stay away from the realities of the domestic situation and ignore the gravity of the intrafamilial problems. Metin and Hülya have formed an alliance with each other. Metin does not speak out against Hülya's dangerous habits and friendships, nor does Hülya react to her father's detached life and cheating on her mother. In one scene in the movie, Metin wakes up to loud music from Hülya's room and goes to his daughter's room. However, instead of warning her to turn down the music, he prefers to admire Hülya's ecstatic dancing. Even if this scene does not prove the incestuous relationship between father and daughter, it indicates that this relationship is different from the usual father–daughter dynamics and that Hülya may find it confusing that her father displays this admiration that he does not convey to her mother. Rather than taking a protective fatherly approach toward Hülya, Metin adopts the approach of a friend who admires her beauty and encourages her to live her youth to the fullest by pushing all limits.

One day, the couple's marriage suffers a major setback. Metin's mistress confronts Fatma and Metin, exposing their affair, and tosses a suitcase full of Metin's clothes in front of her, telling her to wash and iron them. This time, Fatma refuses to accept being cheated on and divorces Metin. Following the divorce, Hülya starts living with Fatma, but she is unhappy with the situation. She blames her mother for the divorce and accuses her of separating herself from her father. Hülya also blames her mother for her father's infidelity and accuses her of being an inadequate woman, of not showing her father enough attention, love, and femininity, and of oppressing him with her money and using him as her servant.

As Fatma settles into her new life, she befriends a young businessman named Fikret. Fikret admires Fatma and calls her his queen. Fikret is someone who has not achieved the success he desired in his business and has fallen into debt because of his irregular business transactions. In a short period, this friendship quickly turns into a relationship. This development exacerbates Hülya's reaction to her mother. The mother and daughter's never-ending problems continue with arguments and fights, sometimes leading to physical violence. After Fikret enters their lives, Hülya informs her father that she wants to live with him and requests permission to move in with him. However, Metin refuses, claiming that it is not possible because he is a single man and that Hülya can live a more comfortable life with her mother.

Hülya, who resents her mother even more after being rejected by her father, sets out for revenge, prepares to seduce Fikret, and takes him away from her mother. Hülya believes that her mother divorced her father to be with Fikret and concludes that this is a betrayal that must be punished. Fikret adopts a policy of getting along with Hülya to gain Fatma's trust and convince her to marry him. Hülya and Fikret soon come close and begin spending time together. Fatma is happy that Fikret and Hülya are getting closer because she thinks that her daughter has become more harmonious and has moved away from her bad habits since Fikret entered their lives. At the same time, she believes that Fikret is like a father to Hülya.

Every day, Hülya's exhibitionist behavior to seduce Fikret increases. Hülya tells Fikret at every opportunity that she is very attracted to him, and soon the two start going out to dinner, going to the gym, and dancing in nightclubs. Wanting to fulfill her plan to spend a night alone with Fikret, Hülya convinces Fikret and Fatma to go on vacation to Bodrum. The scenes of the love triangle between Fikret, Fatma, and Hülya during the vacation are interesting. For example, Hülya secretly holds hands with Fikret while resting her head on her mother's knees. This scene may be considered to contain fragments of Hülya's oedipal fantasies. Hülya is a girl who grew up witnessing her father's illicit affairs and mistresses. In her relationship with her mother, she has always competed for her father's love.

During the vacation, Hülya invites Fikret to her room and has sex with him. After returning from vacation, the number of these assignations increases, and Hülya becomes pregnant. Hülya starts pressuring Fikret to reveal their relationship to her mother and gives him a deadline. However, when she realizes that Fikret is avoiding her, she tells her mother the whole truth herself. This confession sparks a heated argument between mother and daughter. Hülya leaves her mother and goes to Fikret, explaining that she has told her mother everything. Fikret then tells Hülya that he will deny that the child is his and that he will convince her mother that Hülya became pregnant with her marijuana-smoking friends, that Hülya is a fool, and that he never intended to have a serious relationship with her from the beginning. Hülya, influenced by feelings of betrayal and being caught in the middle, shoots Fikret several times and kills him. Immediately after the murder, Fatma arrives at Fikret's house and tells Hülya that she will take the blame for the crime, which brings her daughter out of her shock. As a result of these events, Hülya suffers a nervous breakdown and is hospitalized. (In a scene at the start of the movie, Hülya fainted and was hospitalized after a violent fight with her mother. This type of fainting is similar to the convulsive symptoms observed in patients with hysteria neurosis.) Metin visits Hülya in the hospital and tells his daughter that they have done her mother a great injustice and that she does not deserve this hatred. Metin explains in detail that Fatma has been working hard since she was young to achieve this rich life and that she devoted herself to her work to provide Hülya good opportunities. Metin also confesses that Hülya does not deserve the image of a perfect father that he has built up in her mind so far, that he himself has been gambling since his youth, that he has used her mother's resources extravagantly, and that he cheated on her in the first years of their marriage and fled abroad with his lover.

When Metin ran out of money overseas, he was abandoned by his lover and fell into misery. Fatma decided to continue their marriage because she loved little Hülya, who was constantly ill due to her weak psychology, and for her father, and called Metin back to İstanbul, saving their home life from destruction. The bond between Metin and Hülya grows stronger during Hülya's convalescence, and, in Metin's words, they were inextricably linked. Fatma's calling Metin back home makes her the character who ensures the continuity of this alliance. Influenced by these stories, Hülya realizes that she has wronged her mother. Finally, she realizes that her mother never wanted to separate herself from her father. In the finale, Hülya appears in court, confesses her guilt, and apologizes to her mother. Thus, Hülya's hatred toward her mother has ended.

Hülya: A post-modern Dora

Hysteria displays a clinical presentation with a dramatic course that results from an internal conflict that starts in childhood, manifests in the individual's impulsive system, and occurs after the suppression of an unsatisfied need (Kahya, 1975). In hysteria, symptoms manifest as a demonstrative tendency that patients are unaware of (Ebadi, 1988). It is as if the patient has an unconscious desire to inform someone about the conflicts and suppression in her inner world. She communicates using nonverbal symbolic language. She sends a message to those around her through physical symptoms. The hysteric exhibits abnormal reactions caused by repression mechanisms without realizing them and even against her will (ibid.).

At first, Freud viewed the etiology of hysteria as stemming from a single, physical seduction that was traumatic and repressed. Despite its limitations, the seduction theory was the first to provide insights into both interpersonal and intrapsychic factors in the evolution of a mental illness (Slipp, 1976). Preceding the celebrated Dora case, Freud had studied the functions of the unconscious and repression and the dynamics of infantile sexuality, which allowed him to engage in a more complex analysis of hysteria, emphasizing the inability to deal with the erotic drives on a conscious level.

Freud's treatment for hysteria necessitated that the hysteric speak. It was by putting words to the repressed desires that were dominating her body that her symptoms could be alleviated. Freud formulated:

> No one can undertake take the treatment a case of hysteria until he is convinced of the impossibility of avoiding mention of sexual subjects, or unless he is prepared to allow himself to be convinced by experience. The right attitude is: *pour faire une omelette il faut casser des oeufs* [to make an omelette, one has to break eggs]. (Freud, 1905e, p. 49)

During Dora's treatment, Freud observed how desire was split from consciousness and displaced, only to return in dreams and slips of the tongue. With the hysteric it was found that the symptoms were directed to another person and were related to identification; a way to displace desire. Again, unlike others, Freud listened for the metaphorical significance, and he settled upon the metaphor of "upstairs/downstairs"; that is, the displacement of unacceptable desires out of consciousness "down" to the unconscious (Breidenthal, 2010).

In "Fragment of an analysis of a case of hysteria" (1905e), Freud discussed how hysterical fantasies were deferred sexual actions, and were in fact ones any sexologist would have called not merely sexual, but perverse (Makari, 1997). The repression of perverse fantasies caused symptoms that serve as substitutes for the perverted longings. Dora did not perform fellatio, she coughed; she did not wheeze under her father's moving body, she suffered from dyspnea (ibid.). Through the study of hysteria Freud arrives at the idea of a *universal* human disposition, such that hysteria turns out to be, as it were, the "royal road" to the understanding of humankind as such (Haute, 2018). He concluded that hysteria and perversion are the opposite ends of the spectrum. While hysterics suffer at the level of fantasy, perverts act upon the level of reality.

In 1968, Zetzel wrote the eloquent article "The so-called good hysterics" introducing the categories good hysteric and bad hysteric, where she described the bad hysteric as something close to the personality disorders under Kernberg's borderline personality organization. Within this new description, Zetzel suggested four subgroups. The first group consisted of young women who are willing to commit to traditional psychoanalysis. The second group consisted of young women whose character structure, behavioral and emotional patterns promised analyzability but needed preparation to internally commit to treatment. Despite the lack of detail in her description of the subgroups, it is clear that the third and fourth represent the category of *bad hysteric*. In the third, women with an underlying depressive character structure frequently present manifest hysterical symptomatology to a degree that disguises their deeper pathology. In the fourth, there are women whose manifest hysterical symptomatology proves to be pseudo-oedipal and pseudo-genital. Such patients seldom meet the most important criteria for analyzability (Zetzel, 1968).

Throughout the last half century, Zetzel, Krohn, and many other scholars have suggested that the hysteric has endured an intense triangular conflict but was able to maintain significant object relationships with the caregivers. However, the post-oedipal relationship has been less satisfactory and more ambivalent than the relationship established in the pre-oedipal period. Hysterics, in brief, have paid too heavy a price in the attempted resolution of the oedipal triangle (ibid.).

Undoubtedly, dominating desire is one of the building blocks of hysterical personality organization. One of the main lines of the hysterical structure that the character Hülya displays in the movie is the need to dominate the desire of the Other. According to Lacan, it is very apparent that the structure of desire in hysteria is the desire of the Other. From this perspective, a hysteric is someone who identifies with others and appropriates their desires. However, it is important to note that the hysteric maintains the desire of the Other, provided that he or she does not become the object of the desire of others (Yorulmaz, 2020).

Hülya positions herself as the object of desire in her relationships with all the characters; however, she hesitates to satisfy these desires because hysteria keeps desire alive by leaving it unsatisfied. According to Lacan, hysteria is simultaneously an interrogation of desire that reveals the lack and dissatisfaction inherent in it. The hysteric seduces, provokes, and then escapes. Lacan states that desire can only be sustained through the dissatisfaction caused by removing oneself as its object (Cavasola, 2015).

In addition, hysterics claim that there is an oppressive force, structure, person, or thing that does not allow them to satisfy their desires. When there is no such oppression, the hysteric will fabricate things and somehow start to really feel this oppression. In fact, the less controlled they are in reality, the more frequent their hysteria symptoms will become (Krohn, 1978). For Hülya, her mother represents the movie's oppressive structure. For example, Hülya ignores her mother's rules about the time she enters and leaves the house, leading to an increase in her impulsive behaviors, such as drug use. Similarly, when she tries to get along with her mother, the reduction of the prescriptive pressure on her exacerbates her exhibitionist attitude toward Fikret. This exhibitionist attitude is clearly displayed in scenes where Hülya dances, sunbathes, and makes physical contact with Fikret. This exhibitionism can be defined as a kind of "enactment."

Performing is an attempt to escape a symbolic impasse (the impossibility of symbolizing or expressing) through an action, although the function of this action is to carry a coded message. With this act, the hysteric tries to pay a debt, invites a crime, and reproaches the Other (Žižek, 1989). According to Lacan, enactment is a field of display for the subject. For this reason, enactment is the same as a phantasm in terms of maintaining desire (Lacan, 1962–63, p. 963; 2014).

Prior to the use of the word "enactment" Freud first used "*agieren*" ("acting out") in the case of Dora. This contrasted with his previous use of the colloquial "*Handlung*" to describe symptoms and parapraxis (Freud, 1901b; Sandler et al., 1970). For the hysteric, the parapraxis serves the narrative function of transforming the self into an event. Through self-theatrical conduct, the hysteric materializes the lost parts of the mother and the father. These lost parts remain active players in the hysteric's theatrical conduct as ghost parents, helping her protect the images of a mother whom she loved intensely for her virginal presence and an omnipotent father whom she did not have to create a false self for. Thus, for the hysteric, the construct of an imaginary bisexuality emerges, as she endures a dual identification with the unprocessed fragments of both parents, often in high conflict with each other. Freud wrote that because these are auto-erotic scenes put into theatre, and because all auto-erotic fantasy involves the self in an imaginary bisexuality, such enactments are accomplished through multiple identification.

Dora, a teenager who is stuck in an emotionally overwhelming confidant relationship with her father and utterly disappointed by a compulsive mother who is withdrawn from family matters, is Freud's first extensively presented case in the psychoanalytic phase as opposed to the pre-analytic phase of his work. Dora's family was in close contact with another couple, the so-called Herr and Frau K. Dora's father and Frau K. were romantically involved; and, most importantly of all, Herr K. made sexual advances toward Dora, the first of which occurred when she was thirteen years old. Through examining the encounters between Herr K. and Dora, Freud began to develop his theory of the formation of Dora's conversion symptoms. The first was a "reversal of affect," where sexual excitement was turned into disgust, and the second "displacement of sensation," where a stimulus felt in one part of the body, and felt to be unacceptable, was repressed and relegated to another, unrelated area. Freud described the hysterical symptom as resulting from a path taken by the psychic conflict into the body: a somatic compliance (Menon, 2022).

Moreover, he coupled the concept of acting out with the notion of mastery of a passively experienced trauma by an identification in action with those felt to be the sources of the trauma (Segel, 1969). In his postscript to the Dora case, Freud stated:

> In this way the transference took me unawares, and, because of the unknown quantity in me which reminded Dora of Herr K., she took her revenge on me as she wanted to take her revenge on him and deserted me as she believed herself to have been deceived and deserted by him. Thus, she acted out an essential part of her recollections and phantasies instead of reproducing it in the treatment. (Freud, 1905e, p. 119)

Whether it is oversexualizing her relationships or embracing an intimidating demeanor in her dialogues, Hülya's acting out also stems from the deep-rooted distrust that the other will fail to gratify her needs. Just like Dora, through the dramatization of inflicting vengeance, Hülya is seeking to create an almighty, omnipotent object who will remain neutral under her never-ending tease; yet the blunt display of her superiority, by playing the man, is the utmost expression of a melodramatic femininity, which she secretly devalues.

According to Lacan, castration creates a void that can never be filled. Desire always leads to another desire, which is evident in hysterics. A suitable object to satisfy the desire, which keeps it moving, can never be found. The hysteric maintains his or her desire by remaining unsatisfied and leaving the Other unsatisfied (Soler, 1996). The hysteric assumes the role of the object in the relationship it establishes, and as an object, it slips away and cannot be caught (Lacan, 2006). For the hysteric, it is more important to complain about the other's inability to satisfy their desire than actually satisfying it (Krohn, 1978). This complaining attitude is evident in Hülya's relationship with her mother, father, and Fikret.

Throughout the movie, Fatma provides her daughter with opportunities and makes every effort to meet her every need. Unlike in other movies of the period, Hülya's needs are fulfilled by her mother, not her father. Her daughter's luxurious life is financed and supported by Fatma. However, Hülya is almost indifferent to this special attention. She feels no guilt for benefiting from these opportunities, nor does she feel any sense of gratitude. In scenes where the tension between mother and daughter increases, Hülya belittles and ignores her mother's efforts to satisfy her. "You can't buy me, mom; I won't feed myself to you." This line symbolizes the futility of her mother's efforts and Hülya's absolute dissatisfaction.

Hülya's anger toward her mother stayed constant in the post-childhood period because she did not give up her mother as an object of desire. The mother was punished for not meeting Hülya's pre-oedipal needs. Hülya found Fatma's plea to speak with her as mother and daughter insincere.

Fatma: I want to talk to you as a mother and a daughter.
Hülya: Aren't you a little late?
Fatma: What do you mean?
Hülya: Nothing at all. You've never thought of anything except that, until today, you've been meddling in my affairs and ordering me to do this or that.

Hülya felt that her mother did not feed her, did not raise her, but rather controlled her like an object. This led Hülya to cohabit with her mother, who was also a representative of the symbolic Other throughout her life, and to the development of her hysterical personality.

Even if Hülya's attitude toward her father is more tolerant, there is dissatisfaction with this relationship as well. However, this dissatisfaction is grounded in reality because the father does not really satisfy Hülya's needs. For example, when Hülya tells her father that she wants to live with him and not with her mother, her request is explicitly rejected. Hülya's response to this rejection is not anger but silent submission. The beginning of this submission is based on the explanations formulated by the hysteric in childhood: "I give up what I truly desire and conform to what is expected of me by giving you what you want" (Bollas, 2000). Bollas also formulates a theory of paternal narcissism that can be read as follows:

> You, who completely dominate my mother and me, want us to accept your image of absolute dominance. I accept it only because you are the strong one. We can never surpass you, so I will accept your laws to grow strong. (Ibid.)

An important point to note in these formulations is that the father's absolute dominance and power have nothing to do with the tendency toward aggression and cruelty. The father is supreme only because he owns the phallus. The glorification of the imaginary phallus is a phenomenon in which a child learns by watching the mother (ibid.). "My father has a great influence on my mother. He decides whether she is happy or unhappy. I don't have that kind of authority over my mom" (ibid.). Moreover, these formulations foreshadow the child's realization that the mother's desire is directed somewhere outside of him, and that the father's name will be involved in the duality between the baby and the mother.

Lacan conceptualizes the Oedipus complex as the "Name of the Father." This is and has always been the beginning of the official existence of the father, even when there is no living father, and therefore the beginning of the human signifier, the order, that is, the law of culture; it is the discourse that exists above every verbal discourse, that is, the discourse that does not exist in the depths. It is the discourse of the other, the discourse of the great third person who is this order itself; it is the discourse of the unconscious (Althusser, 1982). The father's name connects the imaginary, symbolic, and real orders. The impact of the father's name is referred to by Lacan as the phallic signifier (Ragland-Sullivan, 1989).

A hysterical subject oscillates between exalting and degrading fantasies (Bronfen, 1998). The sublimating fantasies of the hysteric serve to construct an infallible and capable Other that represents a protective function and seeks to develop these fantasies in accordance with the desires of the infallible and protective Other (Scheffer, 2016). The sublimating fantasy of the hysteric often entails the creation of an ideal father (or another father figure or authority), and at the center of these fantasies is the Name of the Father. The Father's name represents the function of the ideal father as an infallible, protective, and authoritative symbolic figure and replaces the fallible real father. In fantasies centered on the Name of the Father, the hysteric exhibits a high belief in the infallibility of the Other or its representative (ibid.). This belief can explain why Hülya idealizes a man like Fikret, who has an inconsistent profile. Hysterical fantasies and their enactment develop in an attempt to idealize the real father, who can provide the knowledge and identity she desires (ibid.).

The daughter will find a way to cope with her anguish over the unanswered question of what would satisfy her mother's desire by trying to understand the object of her mother's desire. As the construction of the subject depends on a loss, it does not have a structure that can be characterized as "normal." Each individual is faced with the trauma of a loss that cannot be replaced. However, a different basic defense mechanism emerges in each structure to cope with this loss. The neurotic copes with this loss through repression; the pervert copes using the disavowal mechanism; and the psychotic uses the foreclosure defense mechanism (Gessert, 2014). The subject's position within the neurotic structure is determined according to the strategy used to cope with the deficit felt by the subject at the stage at which it is separated from the mother. In the hysterical structure, the subject copes with the anxiety brought about by the separation by desiring to turn into an object that will fill the Other's deficiency (ibid.).

According to Lacan, the hysterical subject positions itself as the lack of the Other at the moment of separation from the mother (Fink, 1997). While the perverted subject does not recognize the lack of a mother, the hysterical subject aims to become the necessary object to complete the mother. In other words, in a hysteric's fantasy, the subject tries to struggle with the experience of separation by imagining himself as the other's loss. In the process of separation, the subject makes sense of her loss through the loss of her mother and becomes the "missing" object for her mother (ibid.). For example, the relationship between Fikret and Fatma causes Hülya to question what her mother loved in Fikret and what she endowed him with as a mature, bereaved mother. Traces of this questioning can be observed in the dialog between Fatma and Hülya.

Hülya: Will you get married?
Fatma: I hope you'll understand. It's every young woman's right.
Hülya: Stop with the literature. So that's the real reason you left my father. So the lady's been weaving her web in secret.
Fatma: I forbid you to talk like that. I'm your mother!
Hülya: And as soon as you left Dad, you found a handsome husband. Don't make me laugh. You sold my father so you could buy a better one.

A hysteric's mother is a woman who refuses to celebrate her child's sexuality. The mother experiences intense ambivalence toward the baby as a sexual being that cannot be celebrated. In reaction to this ambivalence, the hysteric will try to keep the mother's desire alive by leaving it unsatisfied (Krohn, 1978). This relationship dynamic established with the mother also shows its effects in adulthood. The hysteric takes the position of the object in the relationship that he or she establishes, and as an object, he or she slips away and cannot be caught (Lacan, 2006). This disappearance has a clear consequence: the emergence of a lack of a partner (Soler, 1996). Leaving his or her partner incomplete is his or her way of keeping the Other in a position of desire (Fink, 1997); this is how the hysteric consolidates his or her existence. Leaving desire unsatisfied is also a strategy used by the hysteric to avoid being the object of the Other's jouissance (Soler, 1996). Being the object of jouissance implies the annihilation of a hysterical subject. The hysteric's desire is about being an object of desire, not an object of jouissance (Gessert, 2014).

In *Hatred* (1984), the revelation of her husband's affair with his mistress is the reason for Fatma's divorce. Fatma puts this decision into practice without hesitation or delirium. Instead of suffering the pain of betrayal in bed, she clings to her professional life and soon begins a new relationship. However, Fatma brings into this new relationship the emotional baggage of her past relationships. Fatma is a woman who was not chosen by her husband. Hülya, on the other hand, is a figure who receives attention from both her father and Fikret; therefore, in a sense, she is in a position to fill the mother's lack of being chosen. In a sense, Hülya's presentation to Fikret can be interpreted as Fatma's attempt to fill her deficiency with Hülya. The hysterical subject is conditioned to become the necessary object for her mother. Throughout the movie, Fatma displays an attitude that supports the rapprochement between Fikret and Hülya. While Fikret and Hülya spend time alone together in sports, on the beach, and in nightclubs, Fatma's preference to remain a satisfied spectator can be explained by her ability to experience her desire through her daughter.

From the moment of birth, the female child provides a cover for the phallic lack in the mother, and the place of that child is, for a woman, the very measure of her emasculation. The phallic deficiency in the mother is the lack of the Other. The lack of the Other corresponds to the mother's lack as perceived by the child. The encounter with this lack worries the child because at this point the child is left alone with the question, "What does the Other want from me?" The child tries to answer this question by getting even with the mother's imaginary phallus (Hekimoğlu & Bilik, 2020). According to the Lacanian view, the hysterical subject is conditioned to complete the deficiency in the mother to cope with the deficiency in the mother but does not complete it. The phallus signifies the existence of the mother's deficiency and, therefore, the mother's desire (Korkmaz, 2021).

Hülya is a phallic symbol for her mother because she possesses what can keep a man's interests alive; therefore, Fatma needs Hülya to continue her relationship with Fikret. In this equation, because Hülya is in the position of completing her mother's deficiency, the mother's desire is fulfilled indirectly. This positioning allows Hülya to envision herself as her mother's hidden object of desire and then to eroticize herself by performing acts of objectification in her presence.

Lacan says that the answer to the questions "What is it that you desire?" and "What do you really want?" is fantasy. Fantasy functions as a symbolic script that fills the gap left by the Other's desire. Thus, the question of what the Other wants from us is answered by identifying it with a positive call, a task (Žižek, 1989). The figure of the vamp woman who offers her body to Fikret is a fantasy object that Hülya develops to cope with her inability to assume a symbolic task unconditionally. Hülya constructs herself as a savior figure who will make up for her mother's deficiency through the femme fatale, who sells her body and uses her femininity.

Alliances and chaotic borders

Because of the film's melodramatic narrative, parents are assigned the roles of absolute good and absolute evil. In the movie, the father takes a benevolent and more tolerant attitude toward his daughter, and this creates the "absolute good" parent image in Hülya's split. Therefore, the "evil" parent is the mother. Hysterical fantasies are based on passive relationships between the phallus and phallic figures (Krohn, 1978). Hysteria is a type of neurotic personality organization that does not involve severe division as a defense mechanism. However, the unanswered question, "Am I a woman or a man?" creates an identity split in the hysteric. Hülya's split is similar to the split of a body torn between activity, excitement, and beauty on the one hand and inactivity, pollution, weakness, and fragility on the other.

Taking a closer look at how Hülya's mother dealt with her unsatisfying marriage, we could better examine the roots of her split. Fatma distanced herself from her husband because she did not receive the attention and love she wanted from Metin. She overcame this resentment by holding on to her professional life. However, Hülya perceived the mother as rule-oriented and strict and concluded that her mother treats her father coldly because she despises him. The prominence of her mother's identity as a businesswoman contributed immensely to Hülya's experience of an unavailable mother. According to Hülya, both she and her father, Metin, share this lack of affection. Throughout the movie, the deprivation of the mother's affection is presented to the audience as the most prominent part of the alliance between Hülya and her father. Similar to Dora's conscious alienation from her mother and alliance with her father, the confidant relationship between Hülya and her father masks an unconscious longing for an available and nurturing mother and rivalry with a father who selfishly prioritized the pursuit of his own desires.

What Hülya shares with her mother—their inability to identify through their identity as women—is a painful process for Hülya. This pain, which probably started in early childhood, caused Hülya to turn to her father to understand being a woman. Hysteria identifies with her father or a very close copy of him in an equation of identity, knowledge, and sexuality (Ragland-Sullivan, 2004). This damaged identification points to the bisexual positioning of the hysteria, which was highlighted in Lacan's XIXth Seminar in 1971–72. However, hysterical bisexuality is quite different from lesbianism. The hysteric indeed identifies with the father but he does so to refuse to identify with the mother. Lesbians who experience minor identity conflict believe they have an imaginary phallus (Ragland-Sullivan, 2004). Hysterics, however, can never be sure whether they have a phallus. In this sense, the hysterical woman is an abandoned daughter who must act out the paradox of being in the middle (Restivo, 2013).

Lacan argues that the masculine is related to identification within the symbolic order of language, whereas the feminine is related to identification within the real order, which seems impossible to say or grasp. Therefore, masculine and feminine identifications cannot be equated with biological sex. In the Lacanian understanding, the bisexuality of hysterics does not refer to identification with anatomical organs. Rather, it refers to the masculine and feminine characteristics specific to the family and culture that determine the mother and father (Ragland-Sullivan, 2004).

In the movie *Hatred*, the parent–child relationship is full of damaged identifications and coalitions between an upper-class family in urban life. Identification is part of the developmental process through which gender roles are learned (Corey, 2008). Lacan states that the mirror phase is actually identification, and that identification constitutes the basic structure of psychic formation. A baby who sees himself or herself in a mirror recognizes his or her body for the first time and sees the identity as a whole. Using this approach, Lacan conveys to us the baby's first adventure on the way to becoming a self through identification (Haspolat, 2022).

Additionally, the characters in the movie face serious problems with boundaries and setting boundaries. Winnicott suggests that a psychological boundary is formed as soon as there is an awareness of something or someone that is the Other, that is "not me." As soon as there is an "I," there is a "not-self" and an "other," and there must be something that separates and unites them (Popp, 2015). The boundary defined here is itself a relationship and an interaction. For any two or more things or people to be in a relationship, there must be a psychological, physical, emotional, and intellectual space in which one stops and the other begins. Boundaries are a dynamic process of interaction that makes the relationship between the self and others possible and creates the relationships (ibid.). Both the boundaries between family members and the outside and their internal boundaries with each other are chaotic. Although chaotic boundaries and the pushing of all kinds of boundaries are common themes in the movie made after the coup on September 12, 1980, the effect of unlimited boundaries on Hülya in this movie is not liberating; rather, it is restrictive and causes a division in the perception of self.

How Hülya is caught in the middle is exemplified throughout the movie by the destructive effects of the chaotic boundaries. First, the challenges that the father has in resisting both his daughter and the other women are demonstrated very clearly in the movie. The father is a character who cannot control his daughter and, at the same time, cannot control his mistress, who is neutralized and silenced, in a sense.

However, the father's influence over women and his desirable identity glorified him. Hülya believed that her father had been silenced, neutralized, and stripped of his power. Hülya tolerates this uninhibited state of the father because it is caused by her mother's rigidity and despotism. Hülya is disgusted more by her mother's lack of compassion and femininity than by her father, who cannot react to take back his power. A hysterical woman finds herself in a triangular relationship, in which she competes with other women for the love of a man who is unattainable or who might forget her (Gabbard, 1993). "If I don't know how to keep my husband, that's my shortcoming." This statement explains the situation.

The boundaries can also be analyzed through other relationships in the movie. The scenes depicting the business life of Hülya's mother, Fatma, indicate her high rank and status only through her clothes. Fatma confidently wears the haute-couture clothes of a businesswoman of the 1980s. Fatma's clothes have masculine lines, and her constantly lit cigarettes emphasize that she is a woman in power, like a symbolic phallus. Simultaneously, it is just as easy to attempt a partnership with this woman in power. Fikret, who presented himself as a businessman, was able to get very close to Fatma. Fatma places no physical or emotional limits on Fikret.

The chaotic boundaries of the relationship between Fatma and Hülya become even more chaotic when Fatma needs Hülya to make her relationship with Fikret work. She seeks refuge in the importance of Fikret's father figure to Hülya, hoping that her second marriage will be more legitimate in the eyes of society and perhaps in her own eyes as well. The deficiency here is the lack of a boundary between Fatma and Hülya as well as the lack of a boundary that Hülya should have with the adult world. Fatma turns a blind eye to the fact that Hülya witnesses her relationship with Fikret and even allows her to have a relationship with Fikret alone, without her presence behind the scenes. The line "I'm taking your lover away from you; he's taking me to the Bosphorus for dinner" makes it clear that Hülya is openly challenging her mother, while at the same time, informing her mother of the situation, including her in the relationship, and expressing her need for triangulation; that is, she cannot have a desire for Fikret without her mother.

A hysterical personality usually successfully passes the pre-oedipal stages of libidinal and aggressive development. Unconscious desires that create neurotic conflict in this personality type involve triangular oedipal rivalries (Krohn, 1978). Conflicts revolve around forbidden or frightening desires for incestuous objects (specifically, desires for mental representations of parents). In female hysterics, unconscious desire involves a phallic-oedipal fantasy of replacing the mother, being penetrated by the phallic father, and obtaining a penis-child from him. This desire gives rise to the fear of losing the love of the rival parent and of being punished or killed by him. Unconscious guilt over competitive and matricidal desires leads to neurotic conflict.

Hülya's father is extremely selfish, using his child as a toy and a token ornament of parental responsibility rather than seeing her as a personality who needs to grow and develop. Hülya, who has been raised in this way, has also become selfish as she grows into adulthood, thinking of herself only in terms of superior attributes, disdaining and excluding those aspects of reality that do not support this superiority. Throughout the movie, despite her father's inadequate parenting, Hülya does not give up on getting along with him and defends his interests against her mother.

Furthermore, the severe incompatibility between Metin and Fatma and the irreconcilable differences in the parenting processes caused Hülya to suffer from an authority vacuum in the home and fail to complete a healthy personality development. According to Lacan, hysteria and obsessive neurosis are linked to the family environment and the role and function of parents. Disharmony between parents or an imbalance in the authority hierarchy can have detrimental effects on a child's normal development. Lacan states that this disharmony is paradoxically a long-term effect of the Oedipus complex, which is a female protest against male authority (Lacan & Gallagher, 2002).

The parents' roles in shaping Hülya's hysterical structure are closely related to the attitudes described above. Hülya declares war on her mother to cope with the fear of being punished by her. By ignoring the rules and acting impulsively, she condemned her mother to anxiety and worry, and, in a sense, she acted before her mother, that is, she chose to punish instead of being punished. Even if this behavior, which provokes the other side and creates a space for jouissance, is a positioning belonging to the perverted subject, Hülya's punishment of her mother stems from the hysteric's belief that jouissance can arise from the pain that leaving desire unsatisfied will cause in the Other. While the perverted subject rejects the lack in the mother through disavowal, the hysterical subject unconditionally accepts the lack in the mother. Hülya punishes her mother for her lack of being (Thomas, 2018).

Hülya's father, who only ostensibly takes responsibility for Hülya, demands that Hülya be content with this inadequate parenting and that she be positioned as his ally at home. While Metin tolerates Hülya's dangerous habits and maladaptive behaviors while convincing her mother to excuse Hülya, he asks his daughter to approve of his affairs with his mistress, his inadequate fatherhood, and his damaged treatment of her mother.

Hysterical denial and acting

The hysteric is so stubborn in maintaining illusions about the self and others that the factors that disrupt these illusions need to be limited. The hysterical ego needs to maintain an inner feeling that what it actually wants or feels should not be due to external factors or obstacles (Krohn, 1978). This attitude attempts to protect the father figure *that it should actually be.* Lacan emphasizes the hysteric's identification with the father's castration and his powerlessness in his efforts to prevent his father's deprivation from being seen by others (Ragland-Sullivan, 2004). For example, Hülya ignores her father's injustices toward her mother and herself and believes that her mother should also ignore them. Moreover, governed by feelings of guilt, Hülya clearly has an ambivalent attitude in regard to the paternal order. The reason is that, by transforming Metin's function into nothing but a source of nurture, Hülya castrated her father and turned him into a desexualized object who is kept around to be cuddled.

Although the audience has no information about Hülya's dreams, there are a few examples of situations where those in the audience position themselves by acting out under the influence of daydreams. A daydream is a visionary fantasy experienced while awake that can be constructive or destructive and is linked to repressed emotions (Oberoi, 2013). Hülya's fantasy of punishing her mother is brought into action by getting close to Fikret and showing her interest in him. One of the most famous scenes in the movie, when she walks into the living room wearing a fur coat and displays her bikini-clad body to her mother and Fikret, is Hülya's conscious daydreaming put into action.

Exhibitionism has been observed for both perversion and hysteria. Freud linked perversion and hysteria as both organizations resulted from repression. Throughout time, Freud's perspective on perversion evolved. In his case study on Dora, Freud writes:

> All psychoneurotics are persons with strongly marked perverse tendencies, which have been repressed in the course of their development and have become unconscious. (…) Psychoneuroses are, so to speak, the *negative* of perversions. (…) The motive forces leading to the formation of hysterical symptoms draw their strength not only from repressed *normal* sexuality but also from unconscious perverse activities. (Freud, 1905e, pp. 50–51, emphasis in the original)

Freud reserved the term "perversion" for the latter category of cases in which the sexual instinct tends to another act than genital intercourse. This category, in turn, falls apart in sexual activities which either (a) extend, in an anatomical sense, beyond the regions of the body that are designed for sexual union, or (b) linger over the intermediate relations to the sexual object that should normally be traversed rapidly on the path toward the final sexual aim (Hendrickx, 2017).

For Hülya, the tendency to linger over the preparatory activities with the objective of turning them into sexual aims was actualized through exhibitionistic fantasies and enactments, which I will explain in detail in the following paragraphs. Before going into decipherment of her enactments, it is important to distinguish between a hysteric's exhibitionism and a pervert's exhibitionism to contrast the overlapping features. What makes these enactments hysterical and not perverted lies under Hülya's repulsive regard toward an Other that enjoys or knows no lack. This repulsive regard stems from the hysteric's need to elude herself as object. By identifying with the other's lack, the hysteric maintains her arena to fantasize about becoming the other's desire. Henceforth, the much-appreciated lack, occupied by the hysteric, needs to be preserved as an unassailable enigma. While the hysteric never forgets that she is herself implicated in the deception of her interpolation, she continues acting her role in the play, choosing to self-sacrifice by renouncing her desire and consciously refusing to believe in the paternal truth.

The pervert subject offers herself—as *object a*—to the jouissance of the Other as an attempt to complete the Other; the hysteric aims to preserve the Other's stance as lacking. Unlike the pervert, the hysteric fundamentally believes that the Other already has access to grand amounts of jouissance, which is an utterly different reality from her own, as she lost her jouissance and her *object a* in her formative years. Hence, Hülya's exhibitionistic enactments are to ensure her special place in the Other. Throughout the movie, whether it's undressing in front of Fikret or dancing provocatively in her mother's presence, Hülya is attempting to recover this lost jouissance through reviving desire in both Fikret and her mother, always risking being used as an apparatus to the Other's jouissance.

Although the hysteric and the pervert occupy the role of object-cause in their relationship with the Other, the hysteric positions herself as the object-cause of the other's desire, whereas the pervert positions herself as the object-cause of the other's jouissance (Swales, 2012). Hülya's basic fantasy involves an Other who desires it at first sight, and this fantasy differs from the pervert's fantasy of an Other who experiences jouissance at first sight. Hülya fantasizes that she is being looked at by a desirous man, putting this into action by removing her fur coat and displaying her bikini-clad body to Fikret. Thus, under Fikret's gaze, Hülya is reduced to an object of desire.

In addition, Hülya exhibits her body to Fikret not when they are alone but in the presence of her mother. This can be attributed to the hysterical subject's fantasies that punish the mother's fundamental deficiencies. The hysterical woman experiences a masculinity complex and tries to find an ideal signifier to represent her sexuality. Consciously or unconsciously, the hysterical woman despises and wants to punish her mother for failing to provide her with a symbolic phallus (Daniel, 2009). The reasons for Hülya's daytime daydreams, especially in the presence of her mother, her unprotected sexual intercourse with her mother's lover, and making herself available to an older man, are listed below:

1. Fikret is a passive character who follows Fatma's rules and considers her superior. When Fatma refuses to adopt a passive attitude toward Fikret and sets rules for him, Fikret turns into a character who wants Fatma more. When Hülya sees Fikret as a passive follower of her mother without any valid reason, her mother's lack is again emphasized. In Hülya's subconscious, it is her mother who is both powerful and inadequate; Fikret is one whose jouissance is dangerous and whose jouissance must be restrained.
2. Hülya's fantasies of displaying her body and having sexual intercourse with a passive man with characteristics more commonly found in women, and their enactment throughout the movie are a reenactment of the oedipal fantasy of Hülya's childhood. Hülya's childhood memories, hearing her parents argue about sexuality and infidelity—her mother not being a woman to her father—and especially her father being criticized and belittled by her mother, played an important role in Hülya's construction of her fantasy. This fantasy can be explained as follows:
   - At the symbolic level, Hülya identifies with her father's masculine desire for Fatma.

- At the imaginary level, she identifies with the mistress who uses her father (Hülya thinks that her father should have sex with her instead of his mistress).
- Hülya thinks that the mistress partner is loved more by her father than she is and wants to take the place of the mistress.
- In her forbidden relationship with Fikret, Hülya returns to the idea that she was preferred by her father to her mother and mistress and that her father loved her more than her mother and mistress.
- On a real level, Hülya has become a used and abused *object a* by a man, and it is unclear whether she feels pleasure from this.

Hülya accuses her mother of "throwing her father away" to be with a younger and more handsome man. Throughout the movie, Hülya expresses her belief that her mother should experience the injustice that her father inflicted on her in the same way, which is why she is with Fikret. However, it can be assumed that the underlying fantasy was the influence of her father's mistress's life, which Hülya witnessed throughout her childhood. The father's mistress(es) functions as a solution to the mystery of womanhood. Hülya does not identify with her father but with her father's desire. At the beginning of the movie, Hülya seems to tolerate her father's relationship with his mistresses because they have a place in her father's life. After her father rejects Hülya's proposal to live with him, this fantasy is shattered. She sees that all women—her mother, the mistresses, and now herself—can be dishonored and discarded, and she is confronted with the reality of being a woman. The anxiety caused by this loss led to her desire for her father to regress, and her forbidden relationship with Fikret began. In other words, just like Dora, Hülya took a stance of revolt when confronted with the reality of being a woman, as it required embodying submissiveness. "She acknowledges the fact of her castration and with it too, the superiority of the male and her own inferiority; but she rebels against this unwelcome state of affairs" (Freud, 1931b, p. 229).

Lacan emphasizes the sexual impasse between men and women. This impasse is a structural asymmetry in the existence of both men and women in terms of language and culture. This stems from the fact that the lack (of desire) caused by separation can only be created by referring to the Name of the Father (Ragland-Sullivan, 1989). Using Lacan's distinction between the imaginary (pre-linguistic) and symbolic (linguistic) worlds, it is thought that women have a hard time finding their place in a foreign linguistic system that basically regulates the symbolic, the superego, and the law (Büken, 2016).

The boy enters the symbolic realm by realizing his separation from his mother. The mother is what he is not, and the boy is what she does not have. The emasculated woman, a sign of absence, is symbolic. In this conception of identity, women are excluded from language as subjects because they are always the Other of subjectivity (Ragland-Sullivan, 1989). In Lacan's view, hysterical suffering is the essence of neurosis because the hysterical structure depends on guaranteeing the continuing authority of the Other. Lacan realized that culture and language contain the inequality that feminists equate with patriarchy. He describes this resentment in hysteria as a restlessness arising from patriarchal oppression and revolving around the Name of the Father (ibid.).

Lacan defines hysteria as the desire to maintain the desire of the father. The hysterical subject is conditioned to make up for the lack of a father, something that should never be lacking. For this reason, he wants to know what a man wants while identifying with women (Ragland-Sullivan, 1982). Similar to Lacan's interpretation of the Dora case, it can be thought that Hülya tries to reach the position of a woman through imaginary narcissism by establishing an imaginary identification with her father's mistress. Presumably, Hülya inferred that women dominate men by using sexuality through the relationships she had with her father's mistresses. Metin is a character who cannot set limits for his mistresses, submits to their demands, and is discriminated against because he is afraid of his wife. Hülya approaches Fikret with an attitude similar to that of her father's mistresses; she pressures Fikret to tell her mother about their forbidden affair and mocks him for his fear of her mother. According to Lacan, even if the hysteric plays the role of a man in a relationship by identifying with the man and trying to avoid the feminine position, the femininity in his existence haunts the hysterical subject. The hysterical subject is always provoked by the question, "Am I a woman or a man?" (Monribot, 2013).

The hysteric's exhibitionism, flirtatiousness, and the need to mobilize attention are parts of one's self-esteem and are used to obtain the care one desires (Barnett, 1971). The longing to be the ideal object of desire that the hysteric carries in her identity shapes the "economy" of her desire. In this context, it is said that the phallic narcissism of the hysteric emerges at every opportunity, where the hysterical subject identifies with the ideal object of desire (phallus) of the Other and can establish an imaginary identification. Regarding gender differences, phallic narcissism emerges to avoid facing what is lacking. To ensure he or she does not face his or her deficiency, the hysteric puts on a "show" that he or she can be the ideal object of desire under the gaze of others (Dor, 2013).

Even if the hysteric clearly identifies with his narcissism, his fundamental problems lie in his deep dependency. Overwhelmed by the emotional overload of his childhood, he develops feelings of helplessness that he tries to resolve by depending on others for care, protection, and nourishment. While his addiction has become the most pervasive motivational force in his life, it remains largely implicit, hidden, rationalized, and denied in various ways. However, his narcissism was openly displayed. Moreover, this narcissism acts as a mask to cover his addiction; it is fake (Krohn, 1978).

Hülya's pseudo-naiveté toward Fikret is more of a façade covering the underlying intentionality. Pseudo-naiveté is the idealization and rationalization of motives, insisting that the hysteric's exaggerated and often aggressive behaviors be dismissed as loving and sincere intentions (ibid.). The hysterical subject, like many affect-oriented people, behaves as someone who believes that just because he or she feels something, it is right and must be right (ibid.). When Hülya starts flirting with him, Fikret tries to set boundaries, even if they are not clear. Hülya responds to Fikret, who emphasizes their age difference by saying, "For the first time in my life, I regret that I am not young," with the line, "What difference does it make? You are a god; I wouldn't trade you for any young man." Along these lines, there is a demand for tolerance of her mistakes through the use of pseudo-naiveté. Although she cognitively understands Fikret's attempt to set boundaries for her, she ignores them and wants to legitimize them, ignoring the age difference between them and the fact that he is already planning to marry her mother. She attributes this legitimization to her admiration for Fikret despite everything.

In seeking to impress the other, the hysteric plays up the touching image of the innocent victim of an unfavorable fate and satisfies the other by seducing him with boundless admiration. He is convinced that he is the only person who understands and can help him (Michel, 2022). Pseudo-naiveté enables hysterics to skillfully transfer their state of mind to others and for the people they associate with to identify with their state of mind (Bollas, 2000). Pseudo-naiveté refers to Hülya's deceptive masks. In fact, it is a cover of innocence that legitimizes her insistence on putting her fantasy into action, even though she knows that such admiration does not have a solid ground.

Conclusion

Hülya, who has the basic manifestations of a hysterical character structure, differs from the women of the 1980s, who dominated desire, because of the way she relates to her mother. Hülya's main conflict is with her mother, and the underlying conflict is the hysteric's complex bisexuality. Throughout the movie, Hülya resorts to various strategies to avoid the inner turmoil that she feels regarding her femininity. Playing the man in her relationship with Fikret with assertive and daring attitudes and getting involved with her mother's partner and trying to gather information about "being a woman" from her mother by including her in the love triangle are examples of these strategies.

In post-1980 movies, male–female relations are examined in a complex dimension, and women are identified with sexuality as a problem. These movies criticize the patriarchal system. In Turkish cinema, the female character who can live her sexual life as she wishes is punished or turned into a fetish and becomes an object of desire for the male audience (Çiçek, 2021). Turkish cinema also produces an anti-modernist discourse even when it shows the Western lifestyle as the backdrop of its stories; although it seems to imply a limited modernism through the representation of women in the Yeşilçam period, the social limitations or social relations in which women are positioned are traditional (Parlayandemir, 2022). The movie *Nefret* (1984) does not differ from other movies of this period. While Hülya's forbidden relationship with Fikret is punished, Metin's mistress's life goes unpunished; she is even forgiven by his wife and daughter at the end of the movie.

In *Hatred* (1984), patriarchy is criticized indirectly through the identity conflicts of the female characters. Fatma, who has achieved success in the public sphere and has a higher status than all the male characters in the movie, pays the price for this success by not being able to live her motherhood and becoming frustrated in her love life. The film's narrative focuses on the punitive effects of the female characters' appropriation of the phallus in certain ways. The narrative also highlights the inadequacies of the phallus: it does not take the two women where they want to go; it never provides the promised transportation. While it may be innovative and exciting for viewers to watch these women smoke, drive, and shoot, their adoption of masculine behavior does not liberate them.

Even if we do not have much information about Hülya's childhood, it is not difficult to guess that the desire she developed for her mother's unconditional love, while still imaginary, was suppressed when she entered the symbolic. The most important feature that makes the movie representative of hysteria neurosis is the centrality of Hülya's and Fatma's inability to identify within an identity equation. Hülya is a character trapped between the difficulty of creating her own identity beyond her mother's suffocating desire and the urge to identify with the symbolic father.

In post-1980 Turkish cinema, melodramatic movies conveyed the message that women's problems—one of the central issues in Turkish cinema—could only be solved by solving the country's general cultural and economic problems (Künüçen, 2001). This problem is linked to Lacan's definition of a woman's relationship with phallic terms as a disguise or as a mask. By becoming the phallus of the other, the woman actively acquires a passive purpose, becomes a picture of herself, and erects a facade. Behind this facade, there is no "real" woman to be discovered in the end (Kelly, 1998). The dilemma here is the impossibility of a woman being both the object and subject of desire.

Hülya struggles to find a place for herself in the foreign linguistic system that regulates symbolism and law. *Hatred* (1984) reveals that women's problems cannot be reduced to other problems and that this difficulty can only be solved by removing the limits of women's place in language and culture. With the audacity of her relationships, Hülya radically questions the status of women as objects and challenges the dominant expectations about masculinity, identity, and sexuality. Furthermore, Hülya's hysteria empowers her and her femininity to a certain extent. Her ability to comfortably embrace the emotional ecstasy and seductiveness caused by her hysteria and to challenge everyone, especially men, demonstrates this. Hülya depicts the struggle with the limitations of individual subjectivity and the difficulty with the lack of gender perception in our culture.

CHAPTER 10

Suffering and memory of Holocaust survivors in Eytan İpeker's *The Pageant* (2020)*

Bella Habip

The analysis of films often helps us to understand more thoroughly particular clinical facts and even revisit some analytic concepts or conceptions. Such is the case for the analysis of the documentary *The Pageant,* directed by Eytan Ipeker, presented to the public in 2020. The film reveals to us a reflection on memory and, in particular, on the trivialization of a memory marked by trauma.

Since the publication of *Studies on Hysteria*, written by Freud in collaboration with Breuer (Freud with Breuer, 1895d), we know that our memory is not satisfied with storing facts but that it distorts them, sometimes by erasing them, sometimes by modifying them, sometimes by simplifying them or by trivializing their affective content. Starting from the observation that hysterical individuals suffered from reminiscences, from memory without recollection, Freud and Breuer in their approach used talking therapy in order to find the recollections hidden behind the hysterical symptoms. Healing was possible by confronting the patient with their own psychic reality through the remembrance of repressed memories, and especially through the affect found through these memories.

At first these memories were supposed to have a direct origin in reality and the task of the therapist was to make the patient discover them, but this changed later, partly with the

* This chapter was originally published as Habip, B. (2023). Trivializing a traumatic memory of the Holocaust: The documentary *The Pageant. The International Journal of Psychoanalysis, 104*(2): 373–383. https://doi.org/10.1080/00207578.2022.2148530.

discovery of the fantasy world. Nevertheless, the element of reality in therapy was to have a decisive influence on all of Freud's work as well as on the concepts and practices of his successors. Freud would at first be particularly interested in the functioning of the unconscious with its own laws and defense mechanisms, which are largely unconscious, such as repression or splitting, that will be responsible for lost memories while maintaining a link with the historical reality of the patient.

Still following the same ideas, by studying closely the link between the laws of the unconscious and the distortions of memories, it is in *The Interpretation of Dreams* that Freud (1900a) demonstrates how affects help us to find the psychic reality of the dreamer, and, in this way, the meaning of the dream. The affects felt in the dream, or even the affect absent in the dream, are as valuable as the contents of the dream. Freud emphasizes the fact that the representative contents of the dream do not cause the resulting affect that we would necessarily have expected in conscious thinking. And, surprisingly, the opposite would be just as true in the dream, namely that an intense manifestation of affect occurs when there is content that does not lend itself to it: "In a dream I may be in a horrible, dangerous and disgusting situation, without feeling any fear or repulsion; while another time, on the contrary, I may be terrified at something harmless and delighted at something childish" (p. 460).

These facts relating to individual memory are equally valid with regard to collective memory. We note that the tricks of memory consisting of forgetting, ignoring, or distorting are staged in each society in accordance with its political and ideological aims at that moment in time. At a specific period in its history, each society will make use of memory according to its own objectives. There are many examples in contemporary history, and few countries obey the duty of remembering atrocities committed or injustices that have been ignored.

However, in our era we see the presence of a completely other memory, a different memory brought to light by all the means and tools of the mass media. It is a mass memory whose essential support is the spectacle. This memory is neither perpetuated in funeral odes, nor secured in museums at the whim of this or that painting, document, or narrative. It is a globalized memory, held universally, intended to display, to be captured and perceived, a memory centered on the visual. And it can be said that one of its characteristics is to simplify and trivialize everything it displays as in dreams. Does it not quite often happen that we watch a tragic event on television just after an entertaining movie, both in parallel with the news of the stock market scrolling at the bottom of the screen? We are ensnared on the perceptual level throughout the day, and what is most striking in all of this is that there is no hierarchy of values in all of this content that is paraded before our eyes. The news of the stock market is put on the same level as the repercussions of a bloody war in a corner of the globe. In this world, globalized and mediatized to the extreme, we are faced with a memory that lessens or distorts the emotional and affective substance of disturbing events, a memory purified of the weight of feelings.

The Pageant (2020) by Eytan İpeker

The documentary offers us an interesting demonstration of what a memory trivialized and stripped of all emotions and affects could be like. It also offers evidence of the complex relationship that individual and collective memory attaches to historical truths, and, finally, of how memory manages its dealings with feelings and affects.

The film takes as its subject a beauty contest organized annually since 2011 in the Israeli city of Haifa. But this contest is nothing like the ones we know. It is a contest featuring women survivors of the Holocaust, a contest that at first glance provokes a curious feeling of strangeness. It is organized by the administrators of a retirement home for men and women survivors of the Shoah. Sponsored by an evangelical Christian institution, the initiative is further enhanced by the presence of prominent figures of the Israeli right wing, such as Sara Netanyahu, who confers upon it a certain political aura, of which the political dimension becomes more and more evident toward the end of the film. Themes such as time and memory, the difference between individual memory and collective memory, the unbridgeable discrepancy between this unique memory and the memory of the Shoah solemnly exposed to the public, are all treated with great finesse. A finesse of analysis which, not depriving itself of mocking the trivialization of memory, bows on the contrary with respect before this tragic memory. In addition, the background music accompanies with respectful gravity the tragic images that succeed each other on the screen.

The film begins with a sequence revealing a large glittering theater scene lit by projectors. Immediately after the introductory sequence showing the illuminated scene where the contest is supposed to take place, the film takes us to a shop where the choice of fabrics for the competitors' scarves must be decided. The head of the retirement home says that the combination of purple and mustard tones could give a beautiful result on the stage and dazzle the spectators. She eventually convinces her colleague. We move on to the bargaining stage, when we understand that these fabrics will be used as part of a contest organized by the retirement home to host survivors of the Shoah, and which should provide funding thanks to its sponsors.

The following sequence focuses on Shoshana Kolmer, a nonagenarian with an aged appearance, fine features, and a deep gaze, who won this same competition in 2013. With her forehead pressed against her hand, she seems to be saying, "But what do you want me to tell you about the Shoah?" The silence that permeates this interview shows very cleverly that words are powerless to describe the horror. The camera pans slowly across the photos decorating her bedroom. The youthful photo on the wall, in which she poses in a fur coat, probably belongs to her pre-Shoah life. It seems that the steadfastness of her gaze denotes less the kind of impassiveness frequently shown by elderly individuals than her effort to concentrate on a specific moment, which she seeks to express in the best possible way. In fact, the elderly woman breaks this long silence and recounts the lies told by the Nazi soldiers of the camp in order to make the prisoners work: "If you work you can see your parents again!" they said. "But we all knew where they were," Shoshana continues. Also mentioning the working conditions, she explains how soldiers woke them up at one o'clock in the morning for a chore that was supposed to start only at four o'clock and recounts the long wait in the freezing cold. And we are transfixed with fear.

Following this overwhelming interview, we follow the choral rehearsal carried out by a group of elderly women on the podium of the forthcoming contest. Although tired, they participate in the choir with great energy and enthusiasm. "I managed to survive, hostility, enmity ..."

Immediately afterwards and in the same vein, we discover one of the phases of the organization of the beauty contest and attend a telephone conversation taking place in the offices of the retirement home. On the telephone is a survivor of a camp in Romania. The secretary explains to her that this is not a normal beauty contest and that the focus is on the inner beauty and strength it took them to stay alive. She encourages her to participate. At another stage of the preparations, we see the competitors in the hands of a hairdresser and practicing walking on the catwalk like models.

We then leave this atmosphere of lightness and superficiality to withdraw to the heart of the Shoah Museum where the motto "From the Shoah to the Renaissance" clearly stands out. Here we witness one of the moments when tragedy and lightness proceed in unison, not without triggering in us an uncanny feeling. A sense of revulsion accompanies us in the face of this seemingly absurd but equally violent tableau. The affects we experience are not represented in the film. The organizers work with zeal and conviction; the participants of the contest act as best they can, although there is something that saddens us in their involvement: they seem to fulfill their obligation to the organizers, but it seems that their spirit is no longer there. A kind of absence related more to their melancholia than to their age. An absence also perhaps related to their need to withdraw into themselves from any external excitement that does not touch their innermost being. In any case, as spectators, we are revolted, indignant, sad at the same time, while the film reflects an emotional panorama that is not of the same kind. Everything seems rational on the manifest level as in a dream where the dreamer feels disgust, fear, or even horror while the scene that takes place in the dream does not lend itself to it. But this show is not a dream, it is truly real.

A brief foray into theory

This confusion of levels, this reveling in the tragic and the superficial in the documentary, which makes us think of a dream when we are truly in reality, also makes us think of a perversion, of the ethics of perversion as Chasseguet-Smirgel (1984) so well described. It is about an undifferentiation of symbolic levels, a desymbolization and an attack on reason.

Freud's (1927c) discovery of the fetishism of perversion reveals where recourse to illusion and deception is one of the defense mechanisms in order to face denied reality. But Chasseguet-Smirgel goes further by arguing that the sphere of perversion cannot be limited only to the treatment of perverts, and therefore to psychopathology, and she includes in this the study of perversities or social deviations of the kind that subvert reason. According to her, perversion produces but does not create. What it produces is fake, a transmutation of the world. Fetish, idol, simulacrum, and illusion are the domain of perverse thought. It is through a study of Andersen's tale (1843), *Le Rossignol de l'Empereur de Chine*, that Chasseguet-Smirgel (1969) sheds light on the essence of truth and falsity. According to her, the tale suggests that falsity is identified with the inanimate and truth with the living. And, always in the same line of thought, if truth is identified with the living it is because it is always created according to natural laws and in turn generates the same laws while the false is outside any natural continuity: In short, the "true" obeys the principle of filiation, or, in other words, results from the union of the parents. Its origin lies in the primal scene, while the false is located outside any natural continuity while seeking to impose itself as an organic link in a chain, that is to say, as obeying the principle of filiation (Chasseguet-Smirgel, 1984, p. 179).

The fake produced in the tale would belong to the world of anality, which must be idealized through a glittering adornment to hide its excremental character. It is then that she hypothesizes a characteristic of the pervert, a compulsion to idealize, intended to make his ego and (pregenital) penis appear equal and even superior to those of his father. The pervert would imitate genitality in his sadistic-anal world. Is not the beauty contest of our documentary just an illustration of this glittering adornment that hides a horror?

Back to *The Pageant*

The director's gaze again returns to the disturbing memory. The interview with Sophie, resident of the house and competitor, reflects, with a gravity identical to the previous one, the same sensitivity to the inner world. Sophie talks about her sister Chava whom she lost two and a half months earlier. They were four sisters and Chava was the youngest. Sophie adds: "It has been said that there can be no beauty queen among the elderly but that's how we recall her when we talk about her." The need she feels to still talk about her sister seems part of the period of mourning. When asked if she wants to participate in the beauty contest, she says she does not like to talk in front of a camera but also adds that she agrees to it in memory of her sister and as a contribution to the financing of the retirement home. The camera follows the sorting of Chava's belongings into boxes. The grief and the accompanying feeling of separation, the heavily melancholic atmosphere, the camera slowly panning over the family photos, all this proceeds in harmony with the rhythm of the film. The duration of the eighty-three-minute film, quite long, successfully incorporates this slow and evocative rhythm.

Suddenly, the speeches by the representatives of the American evangelical institutions who are sponsoring the contest cause a sudden disruption in this emotional rhythm. Sophie continues her story: their parents succumb to typhus in the early years of the war, and, after four years in a Nazi camp in Romania, the two sisters arrived in Israel in 1944.

We return to the stage where the competition is to take place. Still during the preparations, each competitor tells the story of her life in front of the organizers and tells how she escaped the genocide. The organizers record these stories on a computer, supplemented by their photos. Later, each is given a summary of their own story, triggering protests in response by some of them. It seems that they would have so much liked to say more, to tell more, maybe to feel more! We are in fact witnessing a conflict between a narrative loaded with personal feelings and affects and another narrative, mediatized, staged for the public. The computer's memory emerges victorious from this conflict. Life stories and traumatic memories are abbreviated, shaped, purified of the feelings that were expressed in the telling. After all, the presenter of the contest cannot spare much time!

Another competitor, born in 1941, says she experienced the war through her parents' account of it. Yet another does not feel ready to bear witness to what she experienced. The simplification of these stories to a digital format and the assignment of a number to each competitor are similar to other elements that distance the film from the inner world and from the feelings and affects attached to it, in order to orient it toward the world of entertainment. Denying psychic reality and investing essentially in the visual and in embellishments, is that not part of the world of perversion?

And on the day of the competition, we see the women lined up on the podium, appearing in the spotlights and accompanied by powerful disco music, each one holding their number. Disrespectful music that is supposed to highlight the spectacle, and the equally disrespectful interruption of the president's wife and her followers, disrupt the story of the woman who is thus cut off. The show continues in all its splendor and ends with the Israeli national anthem. By dwelling on the employees who, even before the end of the anthem, are already starting to clear the tables and clean up, the camera seems to want to show the rush accompanying the end of the show, as if to emphasize the banal end of a day no less banal. Were we to say a few words about trivialization, then …

Enter Hannah Arendt

Although the term "banal" is not a concept specific to psychoanalytic theory, I think it can add something by the fact that it indicates a psychoanalytic perspective and a deeper understanding. The source of this concept is in the expression of "Banality of Evil" in the subtitle of Hannah Arendt's (1963a) book, *Eichmann in Jerusalem*. It can be said that this notion has been the subject of passionate debates and sometimes, detached from its context, sharp criticism, as if Arendt had said that evil was banal.[1] But Arendt describes how the monstrosities, which are committed by people unable to think outside the norms, clichés, and commands to which they submit in the performance of criminal acts, are made to seem normal.

Starting from the minutes of Eichmann's defense during his trial in Jerusalem, Arendt writes that the defendant's arguments were sometimes to be laughed at because they were so ludicrous; it is a bitter laugh, of course. When Eichmann declared, for example, that he had done no harm to the Jews and that, on the contrary, he had treated them very well, except once when, having been unable to keep his cool, he had slapped the president of the Jewish community of Vienna, a gesture that he much regretted, Arendt deplores the shallowness of his remarks, which testify to a pathological narcissism, of a narcissism that, at all costs, is concerned with the self-image he conveys to others. Clichés such as "I obeyed orders" or "I did not know what was happening in the camps" used by Eichmann, when he was in fact the head person in charge of the logistics of the deportations, served as an armor both against the truth and toward all those who came into contact with him. Eichmann's conformist and automatic manner of expression probably wearied the people in charge of questioning him, so boring and repetitive was he. Referring to the disturbing aspect of the contradiction between the mediocrity of a kind of human subordinate and the great misdeeds of which he is guilty, Arendt fundamentally speaks to us of a one-dimensional human type whose thought mechanisms are shallow. This type is so egocentric as to consider cause-and-effect relationships solely from the angle of his own subjectivity and so is incapable of thinking that he acts as if the difference between good and evil does not exist. This is a man who simply does not think.

What Arendt (ibid.) meant to say with this notion of "the banality of evil" deserves further consideration. Throughout the book the word "banality" is used only three times. The first use is in the subtitle "Report on the Banality of Evil." The second use is found at the end of the book where Arendt refers to Eichmann's euphoric and grotesque attitude, before climbing onto the scaffold. The latter had declared that, like any Nazi, he was not a Christian and that he did not believe in the afterlife: "After a short while gentlemen we shall all meet again. Such is the fate of all men. Long live Germany long live Argentina long live Austria. I shall not forget them" (p. 118). In the face of death, he had found the cliché used in funeral oratory. Under the gallows, his memory played him the last trick; he was "elated" and he forgot that this was his own funeral. And Arendt continues her thought: "It was as though in those last minutes he was summing up the lesson that this long course in human wickedness has taught us: the lesson of the fearsome word-and-thought-defying banality of evil" (p. 118).

A third use of the word "banality" is found in the postscript of the book, written in response to the strong reactions, especially those that detached the notion of "banality from evil" from the whole of her work. She writes:

> I also can well imagine that an authentic controversy might have arisen over the subtitle of the book; for when I speak of the banality of evil, I do so only on the strictly factual level, pointing to a phenomenon which stared one in the face at the trial. Eichmann was not Iago and not Macbeth, and nothing would have been farther from his mind than to determine with Richard III "to prove a villain." Except for an extraordinary diligence in looking out for his personal advancement, he had no motives at all … He was not stupid. It was sheer thoughtlessness—something by no means identical with stupidity—that predisposed him to become one of the greatest criminals of that period. And if this is "banal" and even funny, if with the best will in the world one cannot extract any diabolical or demonic profundity from Eichmann, that is still far from calling it commonplace … It surely cannot be so common that a man facing death, and, moreover, standing beneath the gallows, should be able to think of nothing but what he has heard at funerals all his life, and that these "lofty words" should completely becloud the reality—of his own death. (p. 134)

If the question of the banality of evil is relatively elliptical in *Eichmann in Jerusalem*, it is constantly to be found in *The Origins of Totalitarianism* (Arendt, 1951) with what she calls "radical evil" or "absolute evil"; here it is a question of a phenomenological description of the totalitarian world, an unprecedented world, especially after Auschwitz, characterized by the bleakness of humankind, by a humanity drained of its substance and by the appearance of the excesses of mankind. As Arendt explains, the epithet "radical" sets out to illustrate the total character of an evil that aims at "the transformation of human nature itself" (Arendt, 1951, p. 711) or even an eradication of man's humanity that destroys the faculty of experimentation and thinking.

The transition from radical evil to banal evil is more clearly defined in her letter to Gershom Scholem. In response to him, who had correctly pointed out this contradiction within "radical evil," a concept from Kant that is used in *The Origins of Totalitarianism* and displayed by *Eichmann in Jerusalem*, she replied:

> I have changed my mind and I no longer speak of "radical evil." At present, my opinion is that evil is never "radical," that it is only extreme and that it has neither depth nor demonic dimension. It can invade everything and ravage the whole world precisely because it spreads like a fungus. It "defies thought" because thought tries to reach depth, to touch the roots, and as long as it deals with evil, it is frustrated because it finds nothing. This is its "banality." Only the good has depth and can be radical. (Arendt, 1963b, pp. 250–251)

In this way Arendt clarifies that this new evil is more dangerous than radical evil because it can spread like a fungus over the surface of the earth and lay waste to the entire world. There would indeed be thousands like Eichmann, who, without being the prototype of the Nazi, that is, without being either perverse or sadistic, have committed the most terrifying crimes. Thus, Arendt discovers that the sources of evil are neither mysterious nor diabolical; rather, they are within the reach of all human beings. It is not necessary to invoke supernatural forces in order to understand totalitarian evil. The lesson that can be drawn from this observation will perhaps be to rethink human beings in a new light, with all that is involved in their ability to fight evil, thanks to their ability to think, to judge, and to reach inner depth.

This emphasis on superficiality, which gives to evil its banality, does it not tell us something about our mass culture which, on a planetary scale, promotes superficiality and embellishment and spreads like a fungus? Does not the spectacle of banality highlighted by our documentary provide a clear example of this social reality?

Moreover, Eichmann's superficiality, coupled with a lack of conscience, also reminds us of patients focused on the need to act, to always do something, to evacuate thought by the quickest means, in a certain way incapable of thinking, of dreaming, of imagining, and endowed with operational thinking deprived of affect and who come to us with organic concerns. These so-called "operational" patients, studied by the Psychosomatic School of Paris, are characterized by a flattening of thought and the same lack of depth specific to Eichmann.

Further explication

According to Marty and de M'Uzan (1963), operational thought has two essential characteristics: it is a conscious thought that (a) seems without organic link to a phantasmatic activity of appreciable level; and (b) doubles and illustrates action, sometimes precedes or follows it, but within a limited time frame. It is from listening to and treating patients who somatize that the authors have highlighted a type of mental functioning called "operational." These patients seem to have a linear and narrow-minded discourse, which does not open up to any other form of reality, other than tangible, factual reality. There is little or no room for phantasmatic and affective life. Associativity and elaboration are absent. The originality of this type of discourse "would consist in the fact that it does not tend to signify the action but to *double* it: the verb does nothing but repeat what the hand has done while working" (Marty & de M'Uzan, 1963, pp. 348–349, italics in the original).

The authors emphasize above all the fact that what is missing is a living inner object. The notion of judgment is replaced by that of assessment or standards, hence its dryness. Did Eichmann not say "Officialese [*Amtssprache*] is my only language" (Arendt, 1963, p. 27)?

This aspect of absence of inner life and of emptiness of thought is somewhat similar to that of the false and the non-living of the pervert who, studied by Chasseguet-Smirgel (1984), overinvests external reality to deny or manipulate it with certainty and who avoids internal life. In our documentary, the organizers work assiduously, they even appear sympathetic but seem careless about what their whole project could represent, like the operational patient cut off from his internal world and his unconscious. It is the viewer who makes the link between these two levels, the level of the spectacle, therefore of the banal and thus of the superficial, and the symbolic level of what it can represent; and it is the viewer who experiences the horror hidden behind. In this we can say that our documentary has a restorative character of the trauma denied and trivialized by the contest, thanks to the return of the affects in us, the spectators, and perhaps even through this essay. This is also what happens during an analytic treatment. The return of trauma is first symbolized in the psychoanalyst with their capacity for reverie (Bion, 1984), which in a second stage shapes and transforms (Bion, 1965) what is not thought or what is waiting to be thought in the patient.

Bion's theory of thinking assumes the existence of thoughts and an apparatus for thinking. The activity of thinking was originally a process intended to relieve the psyche of excess stimuli. Freud, in his article "Formulations on the two principles of mental functioning" (Freud, 1911b), emphasizes the liberating role of thought, and further indicates that thought provides the adequate means of restricting motor discharge and curbing the increase in tension produced by the postponement of this discharge.

According to Bion, thoughts preexist the ability to think. During the stages of their development, thoughts are nothing more than sense impressions and very primitive emotional experiences, proto-thoughts, related to the concrete experience of a thing-in-itself, and therefore of a thing waiting to be named. It is the lived experience of the infant inhabited by raw emotions, beta-elements, which are also a primitive form of thought and whose destiny will be to be got rid of because bad, and projected into the mother. These emotions will be transformed by the mother's ability to think and her capacity for reverie (Bion, 1984). The mother's reverie is a capacity for imagination not based on reasoning. In short, there is on one side the emotional life of the baby and on the other the imaginative life of the mother, who with her apparatus for thinking, a psychic apparatus more mature than that of the baby and its alpha function, welcomes the "bad" projections like a container. It is an encounter that is initially emotional and will promote psychic growth on both sides. It is this transformation that will give access to meaning and speech.

Thus, feelings and affects constitute from the very beginning the most fundamental element of our consciousness of existence, of our awareness that we are indeed living beings and that our memory is largely woven from them. "Feeling alive," an expression dear to Winnicott, is at the heart of the problem of existing, of being. According to him, feeling alive is above all feeling authentic, and the origins of this feeling authentic lie in the mother–child relationship. When a mother with her primary maternal concern responds almost one hundred percent to the needs of the child at the beginning of life, she promotes the creation of a space of illusion, in which the child will gradually recognize as his or her own all gestures, movements, in short, a personal creativity (Winnicott, 1958a). This corresponds also to recognizing in the child a desire, a will behind all gestures and movements, and therefore to making the child real, therefore authentic. This recognition of the "spontaneous gesture" in the child will open the way to creativity and this is how what he calls the true self can unfold. Winnicott (1960b) writes:

> Periodically the infant's gesture gives expression to a spontaneous impulse; the source of the gesture is the True Self, and the gesture indicates the existence of a potential True Self. We need to examine the way the mother meets this infantile omnipotence revealed in a gesture (or a sensori-motor grouping. (p. 145)

There is a need for the mother to favor the omnipotence of the child, making him or her believe that all this is the creation of the child, without submitting her own omnipotence to it, which would instead lead to the creation of a false self, resulting from the violation of the potential space of the child. The purpose of this false self would be to protect the True Self. If the true self is at the source of the continuity of being, of the true feeling of existing, its rupture will, on the contrary, install the false self, which is the beginning of psychic and somatic disorganizations. Winnicott was to write, "After being—doing and being done to. But first, being" (Winnicott, 1971, p. 85). According to Winnicott there is an intimate association between the psyche and the soma, and, according to him, "In these terms we can see that one of the aims of *psychosomatic illness* is to draw the psyche from the mind back to the original intimate association with the soma" (Winnicott, 1949, p. 254, italics in the original), and thus to regain a lost unity.

Which brings us back to the operational patients, who are cut off from their emotional life, and to their impoverished mental functioning in order to maintain at all costs a somatic equilibrium. The psychosomatic point of view of Winnicott and that of the psychosomaticians of Paris agree on a point that is relevant to our own point: both emphasize the presence of a functioning as false self with its affects cut off from their true root as soon as a dysfunction arises.

When a patient in analysis remembers the facts with the affects associated with it, a change in the psychoanalytic process is obvious. This too is the case when it is the psychoanalyst who takes the lead and proposes a construction to the patient. Similarly, when we listen to the narrative of an event comprising a trauma, and this through the feelings of the person who speaks, their memory becomes well engraved in our own memory. And this proves how much oral history has enriched collective memory in recent years, as to speak is to remember, and to remember is also to rediscover the affects related to these memories.

Some final thoughts

If we return to our documentary, we see that by putting before our eyes a memory devoid of affects, and therefore trivialized and devalued, *The Pageant* points to a particular secondary trauma, one that submits our psychic life to the preeminence of the visual and to the spectacle of our hyper-mediatized, hyper-rational, and so-called digitalized world, where the image occupies an important place. As in the so-called operational patient, the place for elaboration, for a second reflection, is set aside. In addition, is it not also a trauma in and of itself to strip the trauma of its affects, devalue it, and disavow it in order to make it an object of spectacle?

Ferenczi's (1949) observations on this subject are enlightening and equally relevant to our own era. The initiator of new techniques applied to trauma, Ferenczi argued that the denial of the reality of trauma by others constituted an additional trauma, and he showed this through his observations on dreams. The person who has forgotten their traumatic experience and who, nevertheless, frequently relives it in their dreams strives in reality to heal it, to make it understandable by means of repetition, and to symbolize it, as highlighted also by Roussillon (1999). Ferenczi argues that in the event that the "traumatolytic function of the dream" fails to heal the trauma, the dream turns into a nightmare (Ferenczi, 1949, p. 234). Our dreams give us back our life experiences with a different presentation and through images, sounds, language, and affects. This re-presentation includes also and to a large extent experiences related to childhood. Noting that some traumas have been fixed in our psyche without our knowledge, that they continue their existence unconsciously and remind us repeatedly of them in our dreams, Ferenczi explains that these repetitive dreams actually indicate that the dreamer works psychically on the trauma in different ways. When the dream fails to accomplish this task, in other words, when the subject fails to work on their feelings and sensations, the dream turns into a nightmare and they wake up terrified.

Now at last, it seems possible for us to establish the same analogy with the spectacle of the contest in our documentary; and it is perhaps possible to make the same analogy to our current cultural world, especially our surrounding media world relying essentially on the visual, and therefore on the superficial, on the surface. While our mental life strives to live and experience life in close connection with in-depth affective life, our current cultural environment tends to evacuate, devalue, and remove everything related to the internal world and in particular to the world of affects and emotions in order to put forward the visible and the perceived.

Is this not also a nightmare? Could we not from now onwards consider the spectacle of the contest examined by our documentary as a horror film? In the same vein, could we not make another analogy, one between the director of *The Pageant* who works meticulously with his silent camera and without judgment, and the psychoanalyst who works with neutrality in their procedures, but is anxious to link, in their reverie and in their interpretations, the different levels of our mental and emotional life?

Part IV

Clinical reports

CHAPTER 11

Incest and the role of silent mothers

Ülkü Elif Gürışık

One of the most disquieting stories in Greek mythology is the tale of Myrrha, the beautiful twelve-year-old daughter of Cinyras, king of Cyprus. Myrrha angers Aphrodite, the goddess of love and beauty, by failing to worship her sufficiently. Aphrodite's narcissism is injured by Myrrha's apparent insolence and she puts a curse on the girl, condemning her to fall in love with her own father and seek to sleep with him. Driven almost mad with longing for Cinyras, Myrrha attempts to hang herself. Her nurse, Hippolyte, saves her and comes up with a plan to help Myrrha achieve her desires.

An important, twelve-night festival is about to take place, in celebration of Demeter, during which married women are forbidden to sleep with their husbands. Cinyras could not therefore be with his wife, Myrrha's mother, Cenchreis. The nurse goes to the king and tells him there is a beautiful young noblewoman in the court who wants to sleep with him, but, to save her reputation, she will only do so if the bedroom is in total darkness. Cinyras agrees, and sleeps with his daughter for twelve consecutive nights, not consciously knowing her true identity. The king only realizes his crime after his curiosity overpowers him, and he holds a lamp up to the face of his sleeping lover. He takes his sword up in horror and attempts to slay his daughter in order to atone for his sin. She flees, with her father in pursuit. A god, perhaps Zeus, takes pity on her and transforms her into a myrrh tree.

It was said that a son later came forth from the transformed tree: Adonis, son of Myrrha and Cinyras, the issue of their incestuous coupling. Unfortunately, real-life incestuous relationships have other outcomes and consequences, all of them damaging, and in every case it is the victim who suffers most. In the Myrrha myth, however, as in real-life incestuous family stories, the mother and mother-figures—vengeful Aphrodite who instigates the abuse, the absent Queen Cenchreis, who remains oblivious to it, the scheming nurse, Hippolyte, who enables and facilitates it—as well as the father, in the form of the unconsciously collusive king (who in some versions of the story is drunk throughout the festival and incestuous liaison)—take no responsibility for the incestuous relations in which all have played a vital part. It is the twelve-year-old daughter, Myrrha, who is made to carry the burden of guilt and to receive the punishment: by being turned into a tree she loses her future, her freedom, and her humanity. However, in this chapter, I will focus on the mothers—so often the silent players in incestuous relationships: their psychopathology, their role, their input, and their impact.

Preamble

I first became interested in the subject of incest in 1965 when all the Turkish newspapers were splashing the story of a fourteen-year-old girl over their front pages. The young teenager was accused of shooting her father. She claimed she had killed him because she could no longer tolerate his sexual abuse of her. Her trial was followed by media and public with a heady mix of excitement, disbelief, and revulsion, and there was enormous relief at the outcome. The girl's plea of manslaughter in self-defense was accepted by the court and she was acquitted.

Soon after the trial ended, a twenty-year-old male conscript was admitted to the Department of Psychiatry at Ankara University Teaching Hospital suffering from an acute schizophrenic breakdown. On arrival, he was incoherent and delusional. He repeatedly claimed he had been sleeping with his mother and that he was carrying the stamp of this evil affiliation in the form of a highly visible mole on his forehead. He believed anyone who so much as glanced at his face would immediately know of his incestuous relationship. Obsessively rubbing his forehead, as if trying to erase the "mole," he demanded that we remove it, and threatened that if we did not do so according to his specific instructions, he would cut it out himself with a knife. Our first thought was that, in his psychotic state, his unconscious oedipal fantasies had broken into consciousness and were being expressed through delusions. However, to my great dismay, his widowed mother subsequently confirmed his account. She claimed he had come home drunk one night and made sexual advances toward her and that, finding this totally abhorrent, she had violently resisted him. During the ensuing struggle, she went on, she had fainted and he had made love to her as she lay unconscious. Unfortunately, it transpired, as she continued with her story, that she had then gone on to make a habit of fainting whenever her son wanted to have sex with her. As an inexperienced young physician, I found it hard to believe her claims. Conflicting questions were rushing through my mind: could I accept her assertion that she was raped on every occasion and did not in any way actively participate in the incestuous relationship? Had she not been giving her tacit permission to her son by fainting? Could the blame really all lie with son? Like King Cinyras, was this mother keeping herself in the dark as a way of evading all responsibility.

I later published a paper based on this case titled "The mother and son incest." This was the first paper on the subject of mother–son incest to be published in Turkey. Indeed, in 1965

I could find only two published papers on the subject in the entire world literature; both were in American publications (Wahl, 1960; Yorukoglu & Kemph, 1964).

It seems it was not just the main adult players in incestuous situations who were trying to keep themselves in the dark; the world at large wanted to keep its eyes firmly shut to the disturbing subject of incest, too.

Theoretical perspectives

In *Totem and Taboo*, Freud (1912–13) discusses the function of incest taboo at length. He originally believed his patients' seduction stories but, so great was the general resistance to the existence of actual incest, that he later stated (1914d, pp. 15–18, 1925d, pp. 33–34) he had made an error of overestimating the importance of seduction as a route for the formation of neurotic symptoms. He said that he now believed these stories were wishful fantasies and asserted that, as far as the neurosis was concerned, psychical reality outweighed material reality. However, he did continue, until the end of his life, to regard childhood sexual abuse as one among the many determinants of adult psychopathology (Laplanche & Pontalis, 1973).

In fact, the incest barrier is broken in reality more often than is generally thought or believed. Incest occurs among every socioeconomic class, regardless of people's religious beliefs, cultural background, and level of educational attainment. The most common form is father–daughter incest, followed by sister–brother incest. Mother–son incest and mother–daughter incest are less often reported. Nevertheless, as we shall see, the mother can play a vital role in all forms of incest, whether as an active participant or not.

Except among some obscure sects and primitive groups, incest is regarded as taboo by every society, whether civilized or uncivilized, and the violation of this taboo is met almost everywhere with abhorrence. It arises in a certain pathological family dynamic, created by the individual psychopathology of both parents and their distorted patterns of interaction with each other and their children. Any mother who claims to be ignorant of an incestuous relationship between her husband and daughter is, to my mind, as instrumental as the father in the occurrence of that transgression. As the mother of the family she is always a key player in its interactions, including the pathogenic ones.

I consider that incestuous parents express their perverted wishes and, either directly or vicariously, satisfy their pregenital or genital needs—which could be pedophilic, exhibitionistic, voyeuristic, or sadomasochistic—through the incestuous relationship. On the surface, both parents appear to have achieved genital primacy; however, their hold on this attainment is rather tenuous and shaky. When they face marital and parental responsibility or excessive external or internal conflicts, they easily regress to a pregenital position. They then express and enact their infantile fears, conflicts, and fantasies through the medium of the family. Though overtly heterosexual, such marital partners also carry unconscious homosexual tendencies. Each partner resents the other for not understanding his or her needs and wants, and these needs and wants are then transferred onto the children. The inactive partner uses the actively involved partner as a vehicle for his or her unconscious homosexual, voyeuristic, and aggressive impulses through projective identification. She or he then derives vicarious sexual gratification from observing and facilitating the incestuous relationship.

During an incestuous experience, probably the most significant change produced in the child's mind is the introjection of guilt feelings, originating in the abusing adult "partner," through the child's fear-ridden identification with the adult (Ferenczi, 1933). What began as an apparently harmless game has become a shameful, punishable offense. Following such an assault, the child feels confused, owing to a psychical split arising from simultaneous feelings of innocence and guilt, and loses confidence in his or her own sense of reality.

Even now, there continues to be a widespread, erroneous assumption that mothers do not directly sexually abuse their children, an assumption challenged in Welldon's seminal work *Mother, Madonna, Whore: The Idealization and Denigration of Motherhood* (Welldon, 1988). Here she writes in detail about the often less obvious manifestations of women's, and, in particular, mothers' sexual abuse of children. Nevertheless, the sexual arousal and gratification of incestuous mothers continues to be unrecognized, resisted, and even denied, so incongruous is it with the universal desire to preserve the idealization of motherhood. Despite a growing body of information identifying mothers as sexual abusers (Kramer, 1983; Marvasti, 1986; Welldon, 1988), public resistance persists.

Anna Freud (1965) states that incestuous abuse ranks higher than abandonment, neglect, physical maltreatment, or indeed any other form of abuse in terms of its potential to harm a child's normal developmental growth. In her view, it is a betrayal of children to underestimate either the seriousness or the frequency of its actual occurrence. It is also a betrayal of children to deny the occurrence of seduction by the mother, or the frequency and degree of mothers' complicity in incestuous situations. In my own clinical experience, I have observed that sexually abusive mothers present across a broad spectrum of psychopathology, with differing degrees of severity. However, I have observed that such disturbed mothers fall broadly into three distinctive groups.

Three types of silent mothers

The first group operates on a perverse level. These mothers have an organized perverse psychic structure. They either abuse their children alone, collude with their partner's sexually abusive acts, or instigate and foster abuse without taking an active part in it. In all these mothers, sexual gratification is obtained at a conscious as well as an unconscious, fantasy level.

The second group suffers from neurotic or narcissistic character disorders. Such mothers are never actively involved in the abuse; however, they know an incestuous relationship is taking place between their partner and their child, and they participate in the ongoing abuse from a distance. They willingly play the passive role of voyeur, gaining their own gratification vicariously. The allure of voyeuristic power is strongly evident in these women, who share many characteristics with the perverse mothers of the first group. This second group includes mothers who minimally register the abuse, but who neither incorporate it into full awareness nor act upon it. They can become mute, paralyzed, even almost "imprisoned" by their ongoing, unexpressed suspicions. Such manifestations of apparent ignorance and inability to act are psychically necessary to protect them from painful experiences that might otherwise threaten the self with fragmentation. In destroying perceptual and intuitive knowledge, these mothers guard themselves against being psychically destroyed (McDougall, 1990) while Bion (1965) attributes the attacks on the linking function to the hatred of both external and internal reality, as well as to ensure a struggle against the awfulness of awareness. Some mothers in this group can employ an unconscious strategy that enables them to avoid any conscious inquiry into what they at some level "know" to be going on. Such strategies can include huge denial, repression, and splitting. They may feel compelled to resist full awareness of their intuitive knowledge, or resist making use of it: a position that defends them heavily against the likely guilt, shame, and horror of facing reality. These mothers' denial and repression of the incestuous relationship between their husband and their child leads to an intense sexualization of knowledge. Johnson (1992) attributes these mothers' immobility to their confusion and lack of confidence in their feelings about incest and their lack of judgment about what to do. Some mothers also lack confidence in their own perception of reality.

In the third group, even stronger repudiation of reality is evident as they strive to unconsciously preserve the cause of their own and their child's suffering. According to Sandler (1987), the motive for such repression stems not from the traumatic experience itself, but from the fear of punishment, reflected in internal feelings of guilt as well as the equally powerful feelings of shame or humiliation.

The psychic origins of silent mothers

Some of the mothers in these three broad groups might have experienced sexual abuse themselves during their childhood. For example, a mother who has herself been sexually abused, perhaps repeatedly over many years, can have her sense of identity and her coping strategies permanently reshaped by the experience. Sexually abused mothers not only identify with the father who abused them, but can also identify with their own silent, apparently oblivious mothers. Throughout their childhood years, they have come to believe they cannot turn to their mothers for protection or emotional nurturance. Consequently, they come to identify instead with their mothers' perceived cruelty, hostility, and passivity, which will, in turn, compound the passivity and helplessness they learned as a child victim of incest. Or, as Kernberg (1992) puts it, a mother with such a childhood experience can transform her hatred of her parents as victimizers into an identification with them as cruel, sadistic, and destructive objects.

I have noted that such women have often consciously promised themselves that if they ever became a parent, they would never allow their children to be abused and would never be as deaf or blind to their children's plight as their mothers were to theirs. However, as Anna Freud (1946) suggests, parents treat their children exactly as they themselves were treated.

When they become parents, they inevitably assume their own parents' role toward their own children. As a result of this double identification, with two parental aggressors—the sadistic father and the passive aggressive mother—they attempt to turn the passive, painful experiences of the past into active, gratifying ones in the present. They do so by reenacting the same drama that destroyed their own childhood but now in a different role—that of the parent, through which they unconsciously attempt to master the original, overwhelming, unrememberable yet unforgettable trauma.

Anna Freud and Greenacre (1960) suggest that no traumatic experience can be assimilated without leaving a scar, visible or invisible, and there is no scar in mental life that cannot revert to being a wound under specific conditions. Children, with their undeveloped ego identities, cannot wholly digest their traumatic experiences. This invariably leads to their becoming vulnerable adults with an increased predisposition to repetition compulsion, itself a pre-ego process. In other words, the turning of a past, passive experience into a present, active one is a belated attempt to assimilate the experience. The mother becomes a voyeur, a silent accomplice to the abuse of her child, in her attempt to seek an escape from the pain and passivity of her own early victim experiences. Through her silence, immobility, and lack of differentiating boundaries, a nightmarish repetition of these early experiences takes place. From the safe vantage point of the spectator, she can now convince herself that she will never again be the victim. As Stoller (1976) argues, "The child believes that it can prevent further trauma by reenacting the original trauma. Then as a master of the script he is no longer a victim" (pp. 6–7). The silent mother perpetuates her original trauma by reliving it vicariously through her child's present-day experience, while blocking out its actual existence and her involvement in it. By presenting herself as an onlooker, she can effectively separate herself from her sadistic and voyeuristic wishes. However, there is a mixture of pleasure and pain in the "spectacle." In her role as a sadistic voyeur, she masochistically manages her own suffering as well as that of her child. As Freud in his *Three Essays on the Theory of Sexuality* stated, "A sadist is always at the same time a masochist" (1905d, p. 158).

The silent mother's psychic strategy is that of a survivor. She may have come to believe that the maintenance of her fragile ego boundaries is possible only on the evidence and within the constraints of an abusive situation. Consequently, she allows her children to be subjected to the same painful experiences she went through herself. The mother's shifting identification between abuser and abused enables her to maintain her silent role as "spectator". Ferenczi (1933) suggests that

> these children feel physically and morally helpless, their personalities are not sufficiently consolidated to be able to protest, even if only in thought. The overpowering force and authority of the adult makes them dumb and can rob them of their senses. The same anxiety, however, if it reaches a certain maximum, compels them to subordinate themselves like automatons to the will of the aggressor, to divine each one of his desires and to gratify these; completely oblivious of themselves they identify themselves with the aggressor. (p. 201)

Kernberg (1992) describes these mothers' experience in this way: "Once identification with the cruel object is achieved, an exhilarating sense of power and enjoyment, of freedom from fear, pain and dread [ensues], and the feeling that gratification of aggression is the only significant mode of relating" (p. 95). Thus, their psychic equilibrium is achieved through the use of projective identification, splitting, denial, turning passive experience into active experience, and identification with the aggressor.

Observations from my practice

Cognitive distortions can enable some mothers to rationalize their abusive sexual acts by seeing them as an expression of love, or an act of kindness, toward their child or their partner. Sexual arousal may be associated with fantasizing that the child is an adult or that they themselves are an adolescent or child. Another source of sexual arousal is the sense of having power in the relationship, when this is usually absent from their interaction with fellow adults. Some of these mothers, having been brutalized by their male partners, can end up turning to their adolescent sons for a sexual relationship and behaving with them as if they were adolescent themselves. They hope to be loved and for their sons to be kind to them in ways that their adult male partners were not. Moreover, the majority of silent mothers claim they were initially coerced or forced to participate in the abuse. However, a number of them join in willingly and some even initiate their husbands into abusing their children. Another subgroup may abuse their children indirectly in a non-touching, exhibitionistic way, obtaining sexual gratification from turning their children into voyeurs.

One mother attempted to justify her sucking of her toddler son's penis by saying she was trying to pacify him to sleep. Another said she was teaching her son the facts of life in vivo in order to spare him from traumatic sexual experiences. Both such mothers are, through these actions, expressing their unconscious hostile and envious wishes. A need for acceptance, attention, closeness, a sense of isolation, low self-esteem, or a fear of rejection are all given as pretexts for sexual abuse, as are anger, jealousy, a wish to gain power, or a wish for revenge. The desire, conscious or unconscious, to inflict pain on the child, dominate, overpower, and cause suffering are central themes for these mothers. The child's submissiveness reinstates, albeit temporarily, the mother's sense of power, freedom, and autonomy. She consciously or unconsciously enjoys her child's suffering and humiliation.

Some brief illustrations

A few examples from my clinical experience with perverse mothers can shed significant light upon the severity of their psychopathology.

- A father claimed during his assessment that while he and his friends were taking it in turns to rape his ten-year-old daughter, his "helpful" wife held her struggling daughter's hands and head, rather like the enabling and facilitating nurse, Hippolyte, in the myth of Myrrha.

- A male patient of mine not only sexually abused his two underage daughters but also persuaded his wife, daughter, and son to stage sexual acts for him.
- Another male patient's wife suggested he fantasize making love to their ten-year-old daughter to spice up their fading, passionless sexual relationship. She then turned a blind eye when her husband began sexually abusing their daughter in reality. Even though she did not directly abuse her daughter, she had perverse fantasies about her daughter and was instrumental in the occurrence of the abuse. Interestingly, it was her husband who initially sought treatment. When the treatment offer was extended to include her, she refused. The couple continued living together and claimed to be very happy when their daughter was fostered out.
- A female patient I saw initiated incestuous relationships with her children in order to feel whole. "I wasn't a whole person unless there was someone with me," she said. "Otherwise, I would think I was nobody." Incest was initiated in this case by the mother's need for a form of parasitic symbiosis (Mahler, 1965). She had neither established a secure sense of identity (Greenacre, 1958; Mahler, 1958) nor had she developed a capacity to be alone (Winnicott, 1958b). Structurally, her capacity to differentiate between the self and the object was blurred. She tended to invade her children's boundaries to avoid the pain of feeling her separateness. Her constant need for identity confirmation compelled her to seek a symbiotic fusion with her children. Through these incestuous unions, she attempted to stem the panic she experienced whenever she felt empty or incomplete. She also found expression for her terror and rage, which were aroused by the threatened experience of separateness and its accompanying sense of loss. The inner realization of her need for the object led to fear of the loss of the object.
- Another mother I saw told me, "I didn't try to stop myself. He was lying there helplessly, unaware of the sexual or physical abuse. Despite the boundary breaking and justification, I was still able to say to myself what was wrong with this activity. In any case I did think it was really wrong. I was repeating something that was done to me. There was so much denial in the family, and I continued that denial. I treated him as a man, not as a little boy and I set him up as my lover. I was oblivious of his needs and feelings. I believed I was invincible while I was sexually abusing him." This mother became aware of her denial, justification, and the dehumanization of her son. As long as she was sexually abusing her son, she felt powerful and in control. Such feelings of omnipotence and invincibility reversed the helplessness and vulnerability she had experienced as an abused child. By turning her son into the vulnerable, helpless one, perhaps she temporarily erased her own vulnerability and helplessness. I would suggest that the role reversal from victim to victimizer, as well as the reversal of her associated feelings from helplessness, defenselessness, and vulnerability to omnipotence, invincibility, and strength, was an essential component of the maternal seduction. She seemingly protected herself from being destroyed by dominating her son erotically and, thereby, destroying him.

Longer vignettes

Welldon (1988) states that motherhood is sometimes chosen for unconscious perverse reasons. The woman would know that in achieving motherhood she is automatically achieving the role of master, in control of another being who has to submit himself or herself not only emotionally, but also biologically, to her demands, however inappropriate these may be.

Clinical vignette 1

> A who was a forty-three-year-old, bisexual male sought treatment and presented in an acute state of severe anxiety shortly after he nearly killed his girlfriend in a frenzied attack while they were making love. He suddenly felt overwhelmed by intense hatred and murderous rage. He ripped out her uterus with an animal horn. He had been aware of his cruelty and violence toward women, having a history of beating and raping his girlfriends and, on occasions, inserting knives into their vaginas. However, even he was shocked and appalled by the ferocity of this latest attack.
>
> During the initial assessment interview, A almost casually questioned whether there might be a link between his violent behavior toward women and the ongoing incestuous relationship he had with his mother. He believed that his mother took him as a lover because he reminded her of his father, who had left her shortly after he was born. "I was a complete substitute for her lost man," he told me. She kept telling him his laughter and voice were exactly like his father's. He described the sexual relationship they had as very enjoyable for him and very precious to his mother. She repeatedly told him that she experienced orgasm for the first time with him and only with him. Though his sexual relationships with other women were characterized by extreme violence and sadistic torture, overt violence had never played a role in his sexual relationship with his mother.
>
> A recalled that when he was twelve years old, his mother had rhetorically asked him, "Who could teach you the facts of life better than me?" She had promptly taken him into her bed and given him his first practical sex lesson. She remained his sex "tutor" until he left home at the age of eighteen, but the sexual relationship continued. Whenever they met up over subsequent years, sexual intercourse was always involved.
>
> For A there were no other escape routes from the pathological state of primary fusion with his abusing mother than the temporary relief he achieved through violence inflicted on women or by running toward men. Bisexuality and violence were his adaptations to get away from a demanding, terrifying, and devouring mother. Ultimately, to kill may have become the only way to finally free himself of her, once bisexuality and violence as attempts to manage the severe core complex anxieties (Glasser, 1992) no longer sufficed.

Freud (1931b) wrote, "Where seduction intervenes it invariably disturbs the natural course of the developmental processes and it often leaves behind extensive and lasting consequences" (p. 232). Steve's mother encouraged her son to believe that he was the perfect partner for her and easily surpassed his father. Chasseguet-Smirgel (1985) stresses that if such narcissistic confirmation is coupled with sexual seduction it may result in perverting the child's development by preventing the ego ideal from being cathected in the genital father. The sexual seduction itself constitutes the narcissistic confirmation the child is so desperate for: it is confirmation that he is, after all, a suitable, even superior partner for his mother. Steve had no chance to cathect his genital father, something he was desperately and unconsciously seeking through his sexual liaisons with men.

Such children are robbed of their childhood when they are subjected to overwhelming and premature genital stimulation. Greenacre (1952) emphasizes that early, repeated overstimulation of the infant increases primary narcissism, prolongs and intensifies the tendency toward primary identification, and impairs the child's developing sense of reality. During the first year of life, when the differentiation of the infant from the mother is incomplete, the genitalization or even erotization of the relationship deforms and degrades the later oedipal relationship to the mother. Such premature stimulation of the penis could be said to turn the penis almost into an umbilical stump.

Clinical vignette 2

B, an exhibitionist, was seemingly destined for an exhibitionistic career from his childhood, when he was forced to be a voyeur to his mother's exhibitionism as she had sex with her various boyfriends in front of him and her other children. She was at these times not only inattentive to her children's physical and emotional needs, but also totally oblivious to her children's inevitable sense of shock, shame, and confusion. B was not directly sexually abused by his mother but rather, as her captive spectator, he was coerced to watch her sexual activities at a distance. This is relevant in that he also exposed himself from a distance to unsuspecting women in his adolescent and adult life. He moved from a passive voyeur position to an active exhibitionistic position. By doing so he took revenge for his own passively experienced trauma (see Arlow, 1980, for further details of such dynamics). Hence, he successfully projected his pain, shock, and vulnerability onto his victims. He enjoyed his "promotion" from victim to victimizer. In his unconscious eyes, every woman became a substitute mother who must pay for what was done to him. His identification with the aggressor is all too evident.

Mothers may also confuse love and care with sex and sexual relationships. Another patient I saw claimed she wanted to show her son she really cared for him. She insisted that sexual molestation was not her intention. She fondled his genitals and asked him to do this for her too. She knew at the time it was wrong but felt there was no other way to show him that she cared for him. As far as she was concerned "sex is love and love is sex." She did not know the difference because of the sexual abuse she had experienced from her own father while her silent mother watched.

Clinical vignette 3

C and D were both voyeuristic mothers living under similar circumstances and each had a childhood history of paternal sexual abuse. They both knew their husbands were abusing their daughters, but they sanctioned the incestuous relationships and remained silent until their husbands left them. Both men left their wives for other women and rejected their pleas to return home. It was only at this time that they informed the police about what their husbands had done to their daughters. These women, as uninvolved partners, may have used their abusive husbands as a vehicle for their unconscious, voyeuristic, and aggressive impulses through projective identification and identification with the aggressor. Both C and D not only reduced their daughters to part-objects, using them in the service of their own perverse wishes, but they also channeled their sexualized hostility by seeing them as a substitute child-wife for their husbands' sexual gratification.

More detailed cases

The following examples illustrate how abusive mothers maintain the dual position of wishing to know and wishing not to know.

Clinical vignette 4

Mr. and Mrs. E came from a middle-class background with no history of child abuse in their respective families. They met at school and married soon afterwards. Mrs. E, though brilliant and a high achiever, dropped out of her university degree course to be with her husband. Their first child, Jane, was born after a difficult pregnancy. Becoming a mother was a great shock to Mrs. E, who initially greeted her daughter's birth with "amazement." Soon after, she became altogether disenchanted with motherhood. A year later she was feeling depressed, was unable to sleep, and started drinking. Her alcohol intake increased, and she began self-harming in the form of tranquilizer overdoses and cutting herself. She was admitted several times to the local psychiatric hospital and became known to social services. Despite offers of outpatient psychiatric care and social worker support, she did not take up appointments and there was no improvement in her emotional state or self-harming behavior. A son was born four years later, following a pregnancy that was uncomplicated despite her alcohol abuse. During the following years, a pattern became established, in which Mrs. E descended into gross alcohol abuse, sometimes lying unconscious in her own vomit with her starving children crawling around her in a pitiful state. She also neglected her relationship with her husband. Though working full time, Mr. E had to take on the running of the household. He too become depressed. Gradually, he recruited and trained his daughter, now aged eight, to help him out. One night, when Jane found her father in tears, she put her arms around him to comfort him. He found solace in the arms of his young daughter, who was by then managing many of the household tasks. Soon after this incident, he initiated sexual abuse with her.

Mrs. E's feeling that she was sexually unwanted coincided with the start of the abuse. Prior to the start of the incestuous relationship, there was some suggestion of a rivalry between Mrs. E and her daughter. Two years later, when their daughter was ten years old, Mrs. E reduced her drinking and the family moved house. Responsibility for the running of the new home was once again shared by her husband and daughter. One day her son, now aged six, told his mother that his sister and father were having a bath together. Mrs. E froze and could not bring herself to go upstairs and see what was going on. She kept trying to convince herself that what her son had told her could not be true. A few days later her daughter handed her a note on which she had written "Me and daddy do sex together." Mrs. E was shocked but not surprised. She had felt for some time that there was something wrong about the atmosphere at home and her daughter's claim fitted in with her unnamed anxiety. She was dumbfounded at how far things had gone between her husband and daughter. She admonished her daughter for not informing her earlier. As one of the silent mothers, she conveniently ignored the fact that she had been neither physically nor emotionally available to her daughter over a number of years. After some initial recriminations, Mr. and Mrs. E hoped to resolve the situation between themselves. Mrs. E, however, found the sense of betrayal and hurt too much to deal with. She began drinking heavily again. A few months later, she confided in her mother that her husband had been sexually interfering with her daughter. Her mother responded by telling her that she did not want to hear about this and changed the subject. Mrs. E was left feeling isolated and deeply troubled, unable to deal with her own feelings or her husband's now manifest depression and their daughter's distress. Mr. E, feeling he could no longer cope with his own guilt or his wife's alcohol abuse, attempted suicide. He was picked up by the police in the early hours one morning in a confused state. At the police station, and subsequently in hospital, he said repeatedly that he could not carry on living with the knowledge and shame of what he had done to his daughter. The following day, the police visited Mrs. E. She denied any knowledge of the incestuous liaison. Consequently, the police did not investigate the matter any further. The situation between the couple stabilized somewhat as a new dynamic developed between them: she had become agoraphobic and utterly dependent on her husband and there was no more sexual abuse. One year after the abuse stopped, Mrs. E telephoned the police in an intoxicated state and reported the incest. The children were taken into care three years after the start of the sexual abuse.

The development of an incestuous relationship with his daughter seems to have mitigated Mr. E's overwhelming anxiety about his masculine identity, which he may have felt was under threat as a result of performing tasks traditionally assigned as "wifely" or "maternal." His young daughter's apparent compliance and submission may have boosted his self-esteem and made him feel potent. His use of "double denial" permitted him to obliterate the differences between wife/daughter and woman/child. In other words, the transgenerational boundary was eroded and breached. By psychically rendering his wife and daughter interchangeable, he could avoid the experience of humiliation and rejection as well as overlook his wife's desperate state and consequent neglect of him and their children.

For their daughter, the incestuous relationship came to represent a way of obtaining nurture and care. A perverse sense of mutual support developed between her and her father. Despite his sexual exploitation of her, their liaison meant he was at least physically and psychologically available to her. In contrast, her mother had been unavailable for any kind

> of interaction or care since she had been born. The incestuous relationship with her father mitigated her mother's neglect. From the age of three, she had witnessed day after day her mother's slow but almost total disintegration. She somehow knew that the whole family's survival was solely dependent on her father's well-being, and she may have felt obliged to support her father in any way he needed or wished. So, the responsibility for the preservation of her family unit was placed entirely on her little shoulders—an enormous and inappropriate burden. The incestuous relationship not only contributed to the family's precarious homeostasis, but it was experienced as an "antidepressant" by Mr. E, and perhaps his daughter, too. Once it was established as an effective solution, it became self-perpetuating. Mr. E developed the idea, not fully conscious, that incest with his daughter was preferable to overt family disintegration, and perhaps most importantly to fragmentation of his self.

Kernberg (1991) suggests that "In identifying himself with both suffering self and sadistic object, the subject is himself 'swallowed up' by the all-encompassing aggression in the relationship." The abused child does not identify simply with her mother, but also with the relationship to her, so she experiences the hatred of the mother as victimizer, as a cruel, destructive object along with its painful, impotent, paralyzing implications. Mrs. E belonged into this category of mother. She had neither confidence in her feelings about incest nor in her own perception of reality. She lacked the capacity to make any judgments or decisions about the situation, until she finally felt prompted to telephone the police. The actual trigger for this action remains unknown.

Clinical vignette 5

> I assessed a twenty-three-year-old young man, F, who had been publicly self-harming on underground trains by cutting his wrist before going on to expose himself and masturbate. He always selected underground carriages that held a large number of female passengers. Some of the women screamed in shock, others tried to stop him, and, on a few occasions, he was arrested and sent to see a psychiatrist.
>
> During his assessment, I noticed F was very restless and seemed to be constantly glancing at my legs. After a while, he said "Hey, Doc, I'm trying to see what color your knickers are." I replied in a calm voice that I thought he was testing me to see whether I would respond in the same way as the women he had been exposing himself to. I asked him to make up his mind whether he wanted to seek help from me as a doctor, in which case I was ready to help him. He appeared surprised by my calmness. After a pause, he replied that he wanted my help.
>
> When he was around six or seven years old, his mother, lying back on a couch, had called to him, and asked him to suck her breasts. After a while she began slowly pushing his head down between her legs and asked him to lick her genitals. This routine was repeated almost every day until he reached puberty at the age of thirteen. Now it was his turn to state his wishes and needs. He demanded full sexual intercourse with his mother. She, however,

refused and complained about him to his father, who threw him out of the house. For two or three weeks he slept on the streets, before being discovered by social services and taken to a children's home.

During the lengthy interview, F stated that he wanted to kill the two male psychiatrists who had examined him before. He complained bitterly that everyone he had seen up until now had treated him like a pervert, and he said I was the only person who had tried to find out what was motivating his behavior. I offered him weekly psychotherapy, but he didn't attend any of his scheduled sessions. Several weeks later, I learned he had been admitted to a high security psychiatric hospital after threatening to kill one of the psychiatrists who had previously assessed him.

His silent mother had exploited him in secret, from an age when he was helpless, dependent, and powerless, for her own sexual gratification. She did not speak up until she felt she was losing control of the situation, at which point she denied all responsibility, placing all the blame on the shoulders of her thirteen-year-old son, even though this ended with him living on the streets.

His later public self-exposure and self-harm on underground trains was an illustration of his identification with the aggressor. It seems he was attempting to turn the tables on his mother, represented by anonymous women travelers, by enacting the drama of sexual wounding he had experienced at her hands. Like himself as a child, these women, behind the locked doors of the train, had no escape. In threatening to kill the dismissive male psychiatrists who had previously interviewed him, it seems he was expressing his rage toward the silent father who had dismissed him from the family home. This case is a powerful illustration of the lasting and damaging effects of child incest.

Clinical vignette 6

Some years ago, I assessed Mr. and Mrs. G and their twin daughters Marie and Carol at a specialist London clinic. Both parents gave an account of being rather naive about sexual matters when they first met. This changed when Mr. G served a short prison sentence for a driving offense. His repertoire of sexual fantasies vastly increased from the stories he heard in prison. Upon his release and return home, he wanted Mrs. G to submit to a number of sexual acts that she regarded as humiliating and degrading. She refused to succumb to his demands until Mr. G used violence. This led to their relationship becoming conflictual and fraught. Mr. G felt increasingly sexually frustrated and tense. It was then that he turned to Carol, eighteen months old at the time, to satisfy his sexual urges. When Mr. G started masturbating the toddler regularly, Mrs. G became suspicious that sexual abuse was taking place but remained silent. It was only when she actually caught him in the act six months later that she immediately left with her daughters. Mr. G made a solemn promise not to interfere again and she returned to the family home. Nevertheless, a few years later, Mrs. G caught him again and, on this occasion, she insisted he see a psychiatrist and they were seen by a registrar at a leading psychiatric hospital. However, both Mr. and Mrs. G claimed to be dissatisfied with the registrar, saying he did not take their claims of incest seriously, and they attended only one session. In the following years, Carol's obedience allowed Mr. G to become much bolder. He committed assaults including mutual masturbation and oral genital contact. On a number of occasions, he also attempted to penetrate her. Three weeks before they attended our clinic, Mrs. G heard Carol saying, "It hurts daddy." She walked into the bedroom and witnessed Mr. G trying to penetrate their daughter. This third discovery brought new strain and discord to the family. A social worker friend she confided in dismissed Mrs. G's concerns saying, "There is nothing to worry about, it will pass." However, Mrs. G knew better. After all she had first-hand experience herself. Her father had also tried to put her at ease when he sexually abused her by saying "there was nothing wrong with it" and "everybody else did it." She recalled her own painful helplessness and confusion when her father had started sexually abusing her, from the age of six. She only became free of her father's abuse when she was fourteen, as a result of his death.

Although Mrs. G sought our help and appeared to be genuinely concerned, her conscious refusal to accept what she had known over such a long period of time was striking. During the joint interview, Mr. G talked in a matter-of-fact way about how he had made use of every opportunity to abuse Carol since she was eighteen months old. Mrs. G repeatedly insisted, "I know it only happened three times and I caught him on each occasion."

Mrs. G used the defense mechanisms of projective identification and denial to preserve her self-image as a concerned and protective mother. By conscious sanctioning of the incestuous relationship, she was not only venting her hostile feelings toward Carol but was also taking revenge on her own mother, who had similarly turned a blind eye to her own suffering. She convinced herself that she was a better mother than her own mother. Her mother had found out that her husband, Mrs. G's father, initiated continuous, incestuous abuse of both their two daughters, Mrs. G and her sister. When, following his death, one of the girls disclosed what had been going on, their mother's only gesture was an impotent protest: she burned everything that had belonged to her husband. Mrs. G's treatment of Carol as an extension of her own helpless, narcissistic self could explain her failure to stop the incestuous relationship. A few weeks after attending the consultation at the clinic with her husband, Mrs. G left the family home to begin life with a new partner, who was a fellow alcoholic. She left the now-seven-year-old twins Carol and Marie behind in what must have been the certain knowledge that the incest would continue. Perhaps, with her awareness becoming fully conscious, she could no longer use denial as an effective defense. The conscious recognition of the incest was experienced as a threat to her insecure identity and fragile self-esteem. She had made this one last cursory attempt to repair the fissures that had appeared in the facade of an apparently functioning family, but then felt she had no alternative but to run away with another man. Simultaneously, she gave ultimate expression to her markedly ambivalent and hostile feelings toward her daughters, just as her own mother had done with her two daughters. Nevertheless, perhaps in a final bid to acknowledge reality, Mrs. G did not run away before placing the responsibility for her daughters' safety with the clinic's staff. Each girl had

> been assigned her own child psychoanalyst, but in the event we saw them only once. After Mrs. G had left the scene, Mr. G, who himself had only attended a handful of sessions with us, made no attempt to continue the girls' treatment. In those days, confidentiality laws meant that no third parties could be informed. Proof of the long-lasting damage incest inflicts on child victims came when, several decades later, I was contacted by the police, who informed me that one of the girls, now in advanced middle age, was seeking to press charges against her father.

Anna Freud (1963) reminds us that "infantile and adult sexuality are not on the same wavelength." While Mr. A satisfied his phallic and genital needs, an eighteen-month-old baby was abhorrently exposed to stimuli for which she was developmentally—both physically and psychologically—completely unprepared. Nevertheless, as is often reported by children who have been sexually abused—and as contributes further to their confusion—Carol could not avoid being physically aroused by the incestuous encounters. At later stages of her childhood, she sexualized her fear and anxieties, trying to overcome them through sexual activities, her disturbed mind having managed to find only this conduit for the perverse, premature stimuli she had been subjected to since infancy.

It may be difficult to imagine or voice, but the inevitable regression caused by the abusive situation can be a painful and frightening experience for the silent mother. By using her daughter, Mrs. A may have hoped to escape her own painful feelings: the sense of loss and confused rage evoked by her own childhood abuse. But inevitably her perverse fantasies about herself as the abused child were reactivated by her narcissistic identification with her abused daughter. Mrs. A not only identified with her cruel, sadistic, victimizing mother but also with her abusive father, while projecting her own attacked and denigrated self onto her daughter.

Conclusion

In *Three Essays on the Theory of Sexuality* Freud (1905d) writes:

> At the same time as these plainly incestuous fantasies are overcome and repudiated, one of the most significant, but also one of the most painful, psychical achievements of the pubertal period is completed; detachment from parental authority, a process that alone makes possible the opposition, which is so important for the progress of civilization, between the new generation and the old. (p. 227)

In incestuous families, due to the parental failures of the father and mother, the boundaries between the younger and older generations become blurred or even disintegrate entirely. The normal generational differentiations and roles become confused and sometimes reversed. Projective identification, coupled with denial, facilitates such role reversals for the parents. Because both parents' identification with their own fathers and mothers is so disturbed through the abuse they experienced themselves, their marital and parental tasks become daunting, if not completely unmanageable.

A mother who has been unable to identify with her own mother may feel she is not a good enough wife and mother but she can, for example, try to actualize her failed ambitions unconsciously through her daughter. She may abdicate her role as a wife or sexual partner and even, in some cases, as a mother. She may no longer be able to provide affection and nurture. On the other hand, she might then treat her daughter as an extension of her narcissistic self. Such mothers often adopt a rejecting attitude toward their male partners and denigrate them and their masculinity. They then consciously or unconsciously facilitate or collude with incestuous relationships in which their daughters are sacrificed to act as a surrogate wife or mother.

The fathers may equally treat their daughters as an extension of their adult partner/coparent. Incest allows them to restore their fragile masculine self-image and preserve a facade of themselves as a potent man. These individuals temporarily repair their self-esteem and pride, which has been shattered by their partner's denigration of them as men.

The children may be cast in the role of need-satisfying objects. Instead of being protected and provided for by their parents, they become protectors and providers to their parents. In the absence of caring and protective parents, they learn to sexualize their childhood anxieties and fears through the incestuous relationship.

Incestuous families and their interactions are too complex to be described in a single uniform way, but each family member plays a contributory role in the formation of an incestuous relationship. A continuous sense of insecurity and alienation from society at large is omnipresent, which then finds its way into the family dynamics. As a result of parental insecurity and confusion, each member becomes insecure and confused about their role and identity. The family bonds between members are fragile and constantly under threat of disintegration. Because of this strife, all family interactions are primarily designed to preserve the integrity and survival of the family unit. Since the threat of family disintegration is seen as the ultimate catastrophe for all its individual members, the family is prepared to pay any price, including incest, to maintain its apparent integrity. Any threat to family integrity may trigger powerful fears of fragmentation and annihilation within individual members. The shifting of identifications between abuser and abused enables the silent mother to maintain her spectator role. The intrusive relationship with her children is necessary to her sense of wholeness.

In this contribution, I have illustrated the use of incest as a perversion and a perverse act, using a number of extreme cases as examples. Not all incestuous families are as severely disturbed as those I have discussed. However, I have not come across any incestuous family that has not contained the nuclear disturbances in both parents, who regress to pregenital levels of relating when they face external or internal stressors. These disturbed parents are terrified of losing their fragile identities, which are the consequence of their own traumatic early histories. Through incestuous acts, either directly (mostly by fathers), or indirectly (mostly by mothers), they are desperately seeking ways to prevent their narcissistic self-image from disintegrating. They experience profound anxieties, particularly around separation and merging and in that, these epitomize core complex anxieties (Glasser, 1986). They seek fusion with the object but equally fear merging with the object.

All the anxieties and conflicts described here are experienced and enacted within the context of the family. Each adult partner resents the other for not understanding his or her needs. They then use each other as a vehicle for discharging their own unconscious conflicts. They use one another abominably, but they also use their children as a channel for their now sexualized hostility. In many respects, the children of such families are dehumanized by both parents. Just as in the story of Myrrha, her inebriated and irresponsible father, King Cinyras, her proud, absent mother, Cenchreis, the conspiring and enabling nurse, and the vengeful, narcissistic Aphrodite, almost no concern is shown for the child's physical or psychological well-being.

Let me conclude with the following words of Sigmund Freud (1931b):

> Actual seduction, too, is common enough; it is initiated either by other children or by someone in the charge of the child who wants to soothe it, send it asleep, or make it dependent on them. Where seduction intervenes it invariably disturbs the natural courses of the developmental processes, and it often leaves behind extensive and lasting consequences. (p. 232)

CHAPTER 12

Art as a way of coping with the psychotic self

Ayla Yazıcı

The most fundamental problematic of human existence is the duality of sanity and madness. The duality of sanity and madness has been of interest to psychoanalysis from the beginning. In this contribution, I will give a clinical example of a case of an artist trying to cope with his psychotic self as an actor. Artists of all kinds enter therapy for a variety of apparent reasons. They may want to deal with an obstacle to their creative work; they may be in a personal crisis, or they may be so confused that they want to explore the roots of their misery. Their art may not always be at the forefront of their therapy, but in this case I will describe a patient whose art was a matter of life and death.

The technical issue for the therapist is when and how to engage with the writing, painting, composing, or other creative acts of their clients. Art exists in a third space, separate from both creator and audience, offered by one, and received by the other, but existing beyond any individual dialog and open to various interpretations across time and culture. Winnicott's assertion that for all artists there is an ongoing struggle between the desire to communicate and the need to remain hidden, suggests that the most productive therapy should involve exploring what is expressed and what lies just beyond expression, the space of the absent, the silent. While the analysis of repressed material will later include some valuable work that will unleash more creativity, in my experience attention must also be paid to the balance between what is already expressed in the artist's work and what is only partially conceived. Therapy can provide a large container to expand into the space just beyond the edge known as artistic (Winnicott, 1974).

If I may mention the theories of psychosis, Freud uses psychotic terminology when he describes unconscious functions and explains dream formation. In *An Outline of Psychoanalysis* (1940a) he goes on to say that every evening there is a small psychosis: a dream is a psychosis with all its strangeness, delusions, and illusions.

Klein (1946, 1957) greatly expanded our understanding of psychosis by defining the first developmental stages of the infant. Her description of the paranoid–schizoid and depressive stages and her work on this subject formed the basis of the theoretical background of the following generations. Klein's demonstration of the importance of projection and projective identification in the formation of the self helped us to understand the basic pathologies of psychotic disorders. She believed that sadism and the death drive formed the basis of the impulses and anxieties that constitute schizophrenic persecution. According to her, the predisposition to psychosis depended on primitive drives and anxieties that normally develop and transform during infantile development.

Klein also stated that people who later function psychotically were partially withdrawn in their childhood experiences. They may have a delusional world of their own, but it may not be apparent from the outside. Her concept of psychic withdrawal was later defined by John Steiner as a psychic retreat. Klein developed the importance of primitive destructiveness and projective identification in the psychotic state. The main feature that distinguishes psychosis from neurosis is the overused mechanisms of splitting and projective identification, which have replaced repression.

Bion's (1957) concept of the psychotic part of the personality is very important. It requires us to consider that there is a gradient between the normal states of hallucinosis and the most severe manifestations of psychotic disorders, even those on the schizophrenia spectrum, where these processes are most markedly manifested. Bion argues that psychosis is not a return to primitive stages of development and introduces us to a separate model in which it is the expression of an impaired capacity to think. In this model, the disorder concerns the functions that transform sensory perceptions into thoughts, and the patient is unable to work out the events of his mental life on a symbolic level. His articles on this subject, "Attacks on linking" (1959) and "Distinguishing psychotic from non-psychotic personalities" (1957), which are the mainstays of this chapter, have opened new windows on the functioning of the psychotic mind.

A detailed clinical illustration

Berna, a forty-year-old actress, came to therapy with complaints of not enjoying life, suicidal thoughts, extreme anxiousness, and inability to do her job. Acting was very important to her. She described it as the purpose of her life, and the reason for her existence. She felt very anxious when she was not performing a play or working on a character. This painful passion for acting caught my attention. And she had been unable to do her job with that passion for some time. In her own words, "The dresses were covering my emptiness, my filth. I was an empty dress and I couldn't wear a dress anymore. I lost my dress."

In the theater where she worked, she had fallen in love with a male actor who was quite a bit older than her. Her mind was constantly occupied with this man. She was constantly seeing him, following him, and daydreaming about him. She imagined living in the same house, having dinner together, watching movies, walking side by side, and shopping.

She sought psychic treatment because this man was having an affair with another woman, also from the theater, and she was suffering from severe anxiety attacks and depression. She "wanted to die"; she said her life had no meaning. She did not want to take medication and wanted to apply for therapy. During the sessions, she wanted to talk about the theater and this man. The woman with whom this man was having an affair was the director of the theater, who did translations in the theater, and whom Berna described as a very strong woman with very large breasts. The words are Berna's: "I am not worthy of anything. Maybe he will be happier with someone else. I cannot give him what this woman gives him. It is like she keeps him alive. She is his everything, his mother, his lover, his sister, his friend. I am not even a woman compared to her. Sometimes I feel like their child ... Suffering and sadness. This pain has made me distance myself from everything, from my husband, from my brother. I want to be someone else, someone else even for a very short moment. Ahmet's [the name of the man she fell in love with] girlfriend's breast is so beautiful that I could sleep there. This woman can feed everyone." About her relationship with her partner, she said that she was dependent on him, and that she clung to him to avoid falling into emptiness. But she did not accept his marriage proposal.

We know that different defense mechanisms affect our contact with reality in different ways. Repression, for example, maintains a symbolic connection to reality even when the actual material causing the conflict is unconscious. With projective identification, contact with reality can be completely lost or indirectly maintained through another person's sense of reality. In some cases, knowledge of reality can be fragmented through pathological splitting, while in other cases, perception is completely attacked and distorted by ignoring it all through denial (Bion, 1957). Berna seemed to be trying to create a family for herself that was not a hallucination but a projection of what was inside her: a mother with large breasts and a father she was in love with. She imagined scenes of daily life and more scenes of eating with this man she was in love with. There was no sexuality in her daydreams.

Herbert Rosenfeld showed us the confusion in psychotic organizations due to the failure of the concepts of projection, externalization, and internalization. Rosenfeld called the defense structure that protects from psychic pain in consideration of obedience to an "inner narcissistic gang." Berna was in serious confusion (Rosenfeld, 1965).

During her sessions, when I interrupted her discourse with a question, she did not respond and instead talked about theater, her love for Ahmet, or the director woman's breasts. Her body movements were also peculiar. I felt helpless and intrusive as if I had entered her stage and was about to ruin her play. One of the first dreams I remember is like this; she and her partner were in a house in a foreign country. The house is made of glass. They throw Molotov cocktails outside, people throw them, and it's very dangerous. They go inside, everything is made of glass. She goes into the bathroom and will look in the mirror. There is a landscape in the mirror. A field, a still life. Her inner world was like hell. She had to talk about this world that she was constantly fictionalizing. Only there could she stay alive. The other sides were like a war zone.

We could never talk about Berna's inner world. She was always talking about the characters she played. When I wanted to bring the conversation back to her real life, her anxiety would increase, she would get confused, change the subject, and state that she did not want to talk openly.

Once I asked her bluntly and then she said that she did not understand why I wanted to talk about it, that her life was not attractive at all. When she was talking about her life, she would make nervous gestures, and make sudden limb movements as if her limbs were not under her control. She would turn her head nervously from side to side, huffing and puffing, wanting to close the subject quickly.

At first I struggled, but then I realized that it was pointless, and I began to listen carefully to the characters she was describing. She described some stage scenes. I would feel like something was missing in the story, like I was incomplete, and I would find myself trying to fill in the blanks. The very flamboyant theater character she was describing—I would often feel like she was acting in front of me—she would describe very vividly: how she dressed, what this woman thought about, how she talked to this man. I would often think of theater scenes. It was like I was watching a female character on the stage, but I did not know how she slept at night. I did not know what her relationship with her partner was like. I had an idea of what happened in between. For example, at home, her partner did the dishes. He did the cooking. She never cooked. "I don't know how to cook," she once said. I realized that this man she lived with treated her like a baby, taking care of her and meeting her needs.

Segal's description of the symbolic equation in psychotic minds has helped us a great deal in understanding psychotic functioning. In the infant, the sadistic impulses toward the objects inside the mother's body and the fear they generate become the basic relationship to the external world and reality at the moment of bonding with objects in the external world. In this sense, the formation of symbols and the richness of the imaginary life depend on a certain amount of anxiety and the ability of the self to cope with this anxiety (Segal, 1957).

Psychotic patients usually communicate their psychological problems through "concrete thinking" or "concrete actions." There is no room for the "like" quality, associations, or imagination necessary for symbolic thought. This kind of communication is stripped of its psychological meaning and does not convey emotional meaning in an accessible way. The symbolic equations used by adult psychotic patients in analytical work reveal the pathology of symbol formation because they correspond to the initial stages of symbol formation. The transition from symbolic equations to symbols was not complete. It was as if Berna had created a semi-concrete world for herself and was able to establish a game within this semi-concrete world. By using this concrete family, she was able to "as if" and keep her psyche intact by dreaming. Only in this way could she abstract and fantasize. And that kept her from falling apart, so she was able to maintain her ego integrity.

Winnicott's (1953) concept of the transitional field indicates the existence of a field of illusion created by the child and accepted by the mother. It is a creative space in which subjective experience and the experience of external reality coexist. Without the transitional field, no contact between the infant's psyche and environment is possible. This is a necessary stage of development. If there is a failure, there can be a split between the child's hidden inner life and the external reality. As a result, there is a danger of entering a psychotic state (Winnicott, 1953). Berna was able to relate to reality in her concrete mother's dress right in the transitional space. Winnicott's (1960b) concepts of the false self and true self and issues of feeling alive are the possible accompaniments of psychotic anxiety. Madness is associated with falsities in one's existence.

Winnicott is concerned with the struggle of most individuals with a sense of the real, as opposed to those who struggle with a sense of unreality. The problems of discontinuity associated with the loss of a sense of continuity and the involvement in a non-integrative state in which one "falls forever," loses a sense of reality, and cannot relate to objects or to oneself, are discussed.

Berna had been living with her partner for ten years. He wanted to get married and have children, but she refused. Because she thought she would never have anything. She was like a ghost in her real life.

Her partner took care of the housework. She could not drive a car. She said she did not like sexual intercourse. They argued about it sometimes. Her partner was an engineer and worked in a corporate firm. Economically, Berna did not contribute much to the household.

I couldn't visualize either the man or the woman in this house. I could only visualize stage images during her sessions. For example, when she was describing a fight at the dinner table with her partner, I was visualizing a husband and wife fighting at a table on a theater stage. It was like watching a theater play, not real characters. After a while, I realized that this was how the patient experienced life and could only communicate it to me in this way. I would not feel this way with my other patients. I feel their lives and understand my patients through that feeling. But with this patient, even the sessions felt like a theater stage to me.

It was as if the therapist and the patient had written a play and we were putting it on. I could not perceive the patient as real. After a while, I realized that she did not have original words to express herself. She was picking words from the characters that she was playing and saying the same lines over and over. She was projecting her inner world to me. It was only from my own experience that I realized how helpless and wordless she was.

How did this woman deal with reality? I feel like answering: by wearing costumes. Her character was not clear. That is exactly why she needed the characters on the stage, the dresses, and the costumes. She found such a way. The moments when she was alive were when she was talking about her character. Other times I would see a mass of mush in front of me, as if the light was fading from her eyes and she was dying in the session.

I think that Segal's concept of the symbolic equation is decisive in the subject's relationship to reality, in the distinction between the psychotic and non-psychotic sides that Bion uses. Assuming that the quantity and quality of the subject's symbolizing function is decisive in the interaction between the two sides, can we say that Berna has a kind of symbolic equation?

It is possible to say that she was able to do a kind of sublimation with a little bit of concrete reenactment (by getting into character roles and wearing costumes) on this stage she set up herself. She could not come up with a work that was entirely fiction. She wanted to write a drama, but she could not do it. She could not complete a work of fiction. But she was able to perform the role she was given very successfully. At the end of her analysis, she was able to write scripts.

Berna was trying to repress the paranoid–schizoid material or the inner gang in the primary processes; maybe she was able to repress some of it and sublimate it in the secondary processes as an actor. But the other parts and this side were much larger, it was as if she was imprisoned in some rooms. These rooms were made of glass, very fragile, breaking and shattering with little blows, just like in her dream. What could the glass walls do with so many Molotov cocktails? Her defenses were collapsing and she was so afraid of going crazy that she wanted to die, to destroy herself.

When we look at her life story briefly, Berna grew up in a city in Eastern Anatolia. Her mother was a housewife, and her father was a civil servant. Her father died in a traffic accident when she was aged four. She had a stepbrother who was eight years younger. She had no contact with her mother or any of her relatives. She entered university, where she discovered theater and decided to drop out and become an actress. She came to İstanbul and started acting in theater plays.

She went to acting training courses. She said that acting was the only thing she wanted to pursue in her life. She was a very beautiful and elegant woman. She also had a long-term relationship with a man who had come to one of her performances on the stage. She then started this relationship, living in the same house with him.

Her mother is an alcoholic, married three more times after Berna's father. Berna's stepbrother is from her last husband. Berna's mother fell apart after her father's death, her alcohol abuse increased, and since she was a beautiful woman, she had many lovers. These lovers met their economic needs, otherwise they would have suffered a lot of poverty. Berna had only good words for her stepbrother; she spoke badly about everyone else. She hated her mother, describing her as manipulative, incompetent, selfish, and man-loving. She remembered her childhood home as very dirty. She said that her mother and the house were very filthy. One of her tragic memories is as follows in her own words: "I would come home from school and the door would not open. The thing I was most afraid of was when I pushed the doorbell and it did not open. When the door did not open, it meant my mother was not at home, it meant we could not get in the apartment. We used to go to the old neighbor's apartment. My mother would take us home whenever she wanted. Sometimes she would not come home for two or three days. We would stay with the old woman next door. I hated this old neighbor. I never complained or made a noise to my mother during my childhood."

When Berna was angry with her partner, she would hit, throw things, and be physically violent. She had temper tantrums since childhood. She was very afraid of becoming like her mother. She used to say that her mother was jealous of her, jealous of her partner, she couldn't stand it when she was good. Berna did not speak well of her father either. She described him as an alcoholic and irresponsible man, although she did not remember much about him.

In her own words, "My brother and I were a burden to my mother. My mother was unhappy with my father, she wanted to be with another man, even the times he was still alive. I wanted to sleep in that disgusting smelly house to make my mother happy. I wanted to get out of the house, and I did not care about my brother. When my father died my mother became like him, the same alcoholism, the same smell, the same vomiting, the same alcoholic look. I used to be afraid of my father; when he died I got rid of him, but when I looked at my mother I saw my father as if the dead had come back to life. The same smell, the same vomit. My father used to beat my mother." After a while, about the sessions, she said that she was obliged to come here, but when she left she felt like she had been raped.

She used to say that owning was not for her, that she could not go and get what she wanted, and that there was nothing in life that was hers. Berna was not given the leading role, but rather the second- or third-level roles in the theater. In her own words, "I can't stand out in the theater either, but when they come to me, they are surprised, that's my strength. That I am different from others, that I am not like everyone else, that I arouse curiosity. So I am in control. To appear to be in control, to be fascinating, to impress people."

I could not reach the patient. It was as if she was wearing a dress but it was empty, and some voices and lines were coming out of it. What she called her power became one of the biggest resistances between us. She would come and go to the sessions, but did we have a connection, or what kind of connection was it? She wouldn't even let me close to a point inside her. I couldn't find my own words in the sessions either. It was like trying to hold an object with my hand, but just when I thought I was going to hold it, it was flowing out of my hand like a liquid, and I could not hold it. I was disappointed every time.

At first, I worked with her once a week for a year and then twice a week. It took a long time to increase the session hours. I think, contrary to what happened in her childhood memory, opening the door every time she knocked on it allowed her psychotic sides to be covered in the process and we began to be able to talk and work on these areas that she had always avoided and closed off in rooms.

Klein (1957) describes the child's pleasure in destruction and states that the child uses several weapons against the united parents, in the attacks on the mother's body and, within it, the father's penis. Sadism, which develops very early in the child, develops before the anal stage and it is also the stage where the Oedipus tendencies begin. That is, the Oedipus conflict begins under the complete domination of sadism. Klein has shown us that the formation of the superego closely follows the onset of oedipal tendencies and that the ego is therefore dominated by the superego even at this early stage. When objects are projected inward, attacking them with all the weapons of sadism revives the subject's fear of a similar attack on him or her from external and internalized objects. The oral frustration which turns the indulgent "good mother" into the "bad mother" stimulates the infant's sadism. Berna couldn't seem to hold anything but the beautiful clothes of her mother inside her.

In "Infantile anxiety-situations reflected in a work of art and in the creative impulse," Klein (1929) gives a case example of empty space. Ruth Kjar, a woman interested in painting who has never painted before, is receiving psychological help for depression and anxiety attacks. Her wall is full of paintings by her brother-in-law who is a painter and one day one of the paintings leaves the house and that part of the wall remains empty. It is such an unbearable emptiness that Kjar does not know what to do with it or how to fill this emptiness. According to Klein, this space on the wall is a space in which she reflects the emptiness within herself, as if a part of her body were missing. And at someone's suggestion, she takes paints and makes a painting on that empty part of the wall. She feels better and after that she continues to paint and becomes a very good painter. It is like a fairy tale, but in my patient, as an actress, she was combining her psychotic self with her unintegrated self, as if she was putting all her fragmented parts into a costume and having a whole body. So, she was creating a woman in these costumes. She was thinking about the finest details of her possible character and shaping herself into that form as if she was creating both a mother she could control and herself. So, she was creating a kind of fusion with the mother.

She would describe these scenes with such admiration that I would listen with equal admiration, and these were the moments when I merged with the patient. The theater group became an imaginary family: a mother who has all the milk, a father figure with whom she thinks she is in love, and who takes most of milk. When the relationship between these two parental figures began, life became unbearable for my patient. She was unable to control her destructiveness. She was thinking of leaving the theater and ending her life. The mother would no longer feed her, she would give her milk to that man, and the father did not prefer her anyway. She thought she had lost all her charm. While she was very seductive on the stage with her mystery, she was suddenly thrown off the stage. She could no longer maintain her ego integrity. It was as if the costume had been taken away from her.

The object had abandoned her again and she was alone. Once again, the door she had knocked on did not open. She could not control the destructiveness inside her. Once again, she had fallen into the hell of her real world, which she had destroyed, which was always bad, and there was no way she could live, she wanted to die. There was hope in ringing the doorbell and waiting for her mother to open the door: maybe her mother would open it and she could enter the house, she could maintain the illusion, but now the hope was gone, and it was proved once again that the door that her mother did not open was closed and could not be opened anymore, there was no hope left to maintain the illusion.

This theater and the characters of the performed plays were like her moment of ringing that bell. The moment when she can create an illusion, in the transitional space. But she was in a situation where she could no longer create the illusion.

The good enough mother who could have nurtured her had once again turned into the mother who deprived her. The father was dead once again. There was even the mother who had retaliated by kicking her out of the theater and destroying her. Berna and I worked face-to-face for a long time. She did not want to be on the couch, so I left that option to her. It was as if she wanted to recreate this world by describing it to me. By talking to me she was able to return to the stage again. By keeping me and the sessions under control, she was able to function in the outside world and was protected from falling apart. As the reparative function increased in the process, the mother in her became more reparative and the ego function of the patient became integrated. At some point in the process, she took a break from the psychoanalysis, during which time her attachment to me and her need for me increased greatly. One year later we started to meet again. It was a long work.

Freud (1926d) said that the loss of a beloved object or the threat of its disappearance is the biggest cause of anxiety in girls. Klein also points to early dangerous situations as the greatest source of anxiety in the little girl. In the later years of development, the content of the terror changes from that of an attacking mother to the fear that the real, loving mother may be lost and that the girl will be alone and abandoned.

For Winnicott (1945), the development of a sense of reality requires the presence of the environmental mother. The infant can develop a creative function through this reciprocity with the mother. A failure here creates a problem for the subject's symbolic function and sense of reality. Berna seemed to have created a kind of concrete environmental mother from the dresses.

Berna's desire to repair herself, to compensate for the psychological damage she had done to her mother, and to find her again, was recreated in these female characters. By doing this, Berna was able to soothe her anxiety to some extent, and she was able to do it over and over again, to try to restore her mother and to renew her by integrating with her. Creating these characters was a painful process for her, a very detailed and passionate one. The process of creating each new character was like the process of recreating the mother, destroying the character at the end of the game, and creating it all over again in the new game. In this way, she was able to realize the illusion that she could control the destructiveness inside her.

Return to theory

In the analysis of children, when the representation of destructive desires is replaced by the expression of reactive tendencies, we constantly see drawing and painting being used as a means of recreating people. In a way, my patient, in a playful way, creates a character and gets into her mother's dress. She created a family in the theater and by this means she created her playground and sublimates it. But when she was out of her parents' bed, that is, when she lost Ahmet concretely and became very angry and her sadism increased, she was afraid of this very nourishing but at the same time very frightening mother's revenge and could not continue this sublimation and the integrity of herself was jeopardized.

In the very first stage of development, Winnicott (1945) points out that the subject and object are in a primary merged state and the object is a subjective object. This had prevented the psychotic self from disintegrating, but now Berna could not maintain it, and she was so afraid that the psychotic self would overtake her that she could see no other solution but death.

According to Winnicott (1963), in artists of all kinds, there is an inner dilemma of the coexistence of two tendencies: the urgent need to have contact and the even more urgent need not to be found. In the theater, she could both show everyone what a good actress she was and attract them and keep their curiosity alive by being able to hide.

In his essay "On communication," Winnicott (1963) argues that at the center of the healthy personality is a silent, non-communicating, non-findable structure, like the true self of the split personality. The paradox of the human relationship is our simultaneous desire to communicate and relate as fully as possible, to be recognized and known, while at the same time needing to remain hidden, to live in our central and unique self. Winnicott sees this not as defensive but as a healthy knowledge of the unique. Berna could be visible on stage in these dresses, and when she took them off and left the stage, she became a ghost again.

Steiner (1993) argues that psychic pain consists of a nonverbal feeling of self-destruction, longing, and psychic helplessness that is vague and difficult to convey to others. It usually follows the loss of an important object or a sudden refusal to meet one's anaclitic needs. This results in a rupture of the unconscious, fused self-object core of the self. Sudden discrepancies between the actual and desired states of the self contribute to the formation of psychic pain. Hatred, guilt, moral masochism, and fantasies of being beaten can also be included in the experience of psychic pain. This feeling is extremely disturbing and is avoided through psychic withdrawal, manic defense, inflicting pain on others, and changing the form and function of the pain. Art is used to make mental pain bearable by empathizing with the rejected parts of oneself. Berna, too, had creatively found a way to deal with the great psychic pain within her through art, which had imprisoned the psychotic parts of her psyche in rooms of fragile glass.

Because of the false self she had developed, Berna had a sense of emptiness and could never feel like a real person. In other words, she had to use the costumes of the characters in the staged play because she didn't have a real dress of her own. This kind of contact with the world made up of the false self does not feel real; it is not a real contact because it does not contain the essential essence of the self, what can be called the true self.

An individual can succeed in the world, but success based on the false self leads to an intensification of the sense of emptiness and hopelessness. This is related to the intellectual false self that Winnicott talked about in 1960. I think Berna's state of feeling unreal finds a very striking expression in the metaphor of the empty dress. Winnicott suggested something quite new: the split or dissociation that is evident in pathology (withdrawal) has a corresponding parallel in the healthy individual—indeed, it is part of health.

It is easy to see that in milder cases of illness, with some pathology and some health, one should expect an active miscommunication (clinical withdrawal) because communication becomes so easily linked to some degree of false or congruent object relation; silent or hidden communication with subjective objects, bearing a sense of truth, must periodically take over to restore equilibrium. It is this silent communication, especially with subjective objects, that Winnicott (1945) associates with the establishment of feeling real. And this is all part of creative perception and the ability to be. The fragile stability that Berna had established completely collapsed when she was disengaged from the parental figures.

With the focus on unconscious communication, Winnicott considers that the ability to communicate does not rely, initially, on language acquisition, but on a preverbal interaction through mutuality. Therefore, the infant's ability to play and symbolize precedes the time he begins to use words. Winnicott is interested in the individual's approach to external reality, that creativity is universal and part of being alive.

Conclusion

Forty years after the paper "Creative writers and day-dreaming" (Freud, 1908e), with *Playing and Reality* (1971), Winnicott elaborates on Freud's contributions and observes that the relationship between playing and creating "stretches beyond the whole intermediate field between the internal psychic activity and the external world." That is, it encloses the whole cultural field: "To study the play and then the cultural life of the individual one must study the fate of the potential space between any one baby and his mother who is essentially adaptive because of love." In this way, Winnicott emphasized the vital dialectical relationship between what the world offers and what the individual creates. According to him, in normality, the mother makes it possible for the child to have the illusion that the breast he is imagining is the same breast she is offering to him: the paradox lies in the fact that the created object is, at the same time, the found object.

The concept of illusion, as a non-pathological process, is different from delusion because it does not give way to the problem of what is believed, it never becomes a dogma, and it is also different from hallucination, which is intended as a false interpretation of real experience. Milner (1949) says that transference is also a creative illusion.

Except when Berna was playing or practicing a character on stage, she was full of badness, she felt so worthless that she was lifeless, dead. When she was able to talk about her crazy sides in her third year in the course of the analysis, we were able to talk about how she was denigrating everyone, to stay strong, that her mind was very scattered and she didn't know what to do. Only the characters knew what to do and what to say; she didn't know herself. In the process, as Berna's sense of being real grew, the characters on the stage stayed on the stage and she began to take control of her own life. The illusion created in the analysis room increased Berna's ego's capacity to move in the direction of symbolization.

She accepted her partner's marriage proposal, she wanted to have children but could not because of her advanced age, but she got a foster child. She was able to finish a script and the movie was made of it. She felt more real and complete when the analysis was finished, she was able to control her creative space, and she was able to control both her real life and her stage life. She had her own real clothes apart from the clothes of her characters.

Throughout the ages, artists and their works have been a source of curiosity. The mysterious alchemy that produces original creations, wonders of imagination, inspiration, talent, and genius, has aroused envy, admiration, and awe. Whatever the image, story, drama, music, medium, or genre, a creative work emanating from a singular mind has the power to deeply affect many.

In this chapter, I have tried to explain with a case example that the creative act can be used to cope with the psychotic self. Every human being creates him- or herself. And feels that the person he or she creates is real.

Berna could not create herself, but, with the help of a concrete animation, she pretended to do so with a mother who could never be internalized. Berna lived a life of confusion with her psychotic self. Her acting was the only tangible thing she could hold in her hand that saved her from this emptiness. She was also able to establish a relationship with others through the creative path she found. As she was able to bring her own real life into the analysis, the stage and the theater became a joy instead of a painful compulsion.

CHAPTER 13

Some reflections on the psychoanalytic understanding of smells and sundry amorphous clinical material

Cemile Serin Gürdal

The baby begins to settle and starts to get rooted in his mother's mind before he is conceived in the womb. This process is full of complex emotions, sensations, and representations. The relationship that the mother begins to establish with her unborn baby is textured with both her projections about the future and her early story which is an "unthought known" (Bollas, 1987). After delivery, the mother and the baby become a couple, and both literally and symbolically, they settle in a room, in a corner and the cohabitation starts (Bolognini, 2008). The first phase is filled with amorphous feelings and states of mind. In this process, the structures that come from the baby and whose form is not clear, find meaning and form by passing through the mother's mind. They are given back to the baby in a transformed way. These steps, which are passed in the first moments of development, are also to appear on the scene of the psychoanalytic work in the following years.

Sigmund Freud was the first to address the undefined and amorphous layers of the psyche. In his paper "Repression" (1915d), Freud stated that the essence of this defense is to turn away from something that is avoided, to keep a distance from it and thus to prevent it from reaching the level of consciousness. He mentioned that the psychic representation of the instinct is prevented from entering the level of consciousness in the phase he defined as "primary repression" (p. 148). Working with such unmentalized, preverbal, and amorphous material forms the basis of this contribution. Such clinical work rests upon certain fundamental theoretical and technical concepts in psychoanalysis.

Four essential concepts

In order to delineate, decipher, and technically utilize the material mentioned above, one must rely upon four important concepts in our theory. These include: (i) the unspeakable, (ii) projective identification, (iii) metapsychology of the analyst, (iv) analytic instrument and field theory. Brief comments on each of these concepts now follow.

The unspeakable

Laplanche and Pontalis (1973) stated that the origin of primary repression lies in very deep archaic experiences and that excessive excitement and the breaking of the protective shield when faced with stimuli prepare primary repression. Kinston and Cohen (1986), who examined the concept of primary repression in detail, stated in their article that primary repression is the hole in the mind that Freud defined as the mysterious core of mental illnesses. Frank (1969) defined primary repression as masking the "unrememberable and unforgettable" residues of trauma. Based on Frank's definition, Kinston and Cohen (1986) stated that primary repression refers to the lack of psychic structure that provides emotional meaning. They associated primary repression with the unrepressed unconscious considering that it is in a place where there is no consciousness in the mind. The unrepressed unconscious is different from complete repression, which keeps various desires and thus conflicts away from conscious awareness. The repressed unconscious is a representable experience, it manifests itself in dreams, slips of the tongue, symptoms, and can be brought to consciousness through interpretation. In contrast, the trauma that constitutes primary repression cannot simply be observed or experienced by the analysand. Nor can the analysand's attention be drawn to it through interpretation. With the reappearance of the traumatic situation in the analysis, these experiential elements begin to come into the room. These elements appear through sensory impressions, stereotypical reactions, or isolated images or feelings. All these elements are loosely connected with each other and do not form a schematic structure in the analyst's mind that will lead to interpretation.

Following Freud, both Winnicott (1974) and Bion (1957) turned their attention to this area. Winnicott proposed the concept of "fear of breakdown" and Bion the concept of "catastrophic change." Both of them examined regression and primary communication in the treatment of more severe patients and observed how the initial forms would turn into an emotional experience (Eshel, 2019, p. 239). They focused on how unmentalized material threatens the mind through a psychotic dimension (Bergstein, 2013, 2018).

In his article on the fear of breakdown, Winnicott (1974) referred to the fear that has already happened and is encapsulated in the unconscious in an unthinkable way. The unconscious mentioned here is not the repressed unconscious of psychoneurosis. It refers to the fact that the ego integrity is not sufficiently developed and cannot be held together. It is not possible to handle and define the traumatic experience psychically (Botella & Botella, 2005). Abram (2013) suggested that the concept of amorphousness is related to the concept of "non-integration" proposed by Winnicott in his earlier studies. The primary nonintegration phase refers to the baby's earliest sensory experience. At the earliest stage, the mother identifies with the baby in her arms and his or her helplessness. This is where "primary maternal preoccupation" takes its origin. In the beginning both mother and analyst offer a space for the infant to be in the analysis. True form and true integration can only be possible by coming out of the formless and nonintegrated. Winnicott (1971) stated that formlessness is an important experience in early infancy and that the absence of this experience will create a void in the core of the self. Abram stated that amorphousness itself has a place in the analytical field. The early experience of the self is fragmented and at the same time is (with the help of the mother) "gathered" in a way that allows the infant's experience of self, now and again, to come together in one place (Ogden, 2012, p. 134). Here, it is very important that the mother, as well as the analyst, does not push the patient "into an insufficiently mature and defensive mindset that causes him/her to disconnect from his/her own bodily experience." Ogden's point brings to mind Bion's concept of negative capability. Keats was the first to use the concept of negative capability. It refers to the person's ability to tolerate uncertainties, mystery, and doubt. Bion, on the other hand, considered this concept as a feature of the analyst's mind. In each session, the patient focuses on one of the many associations. In order for other stories to emerge, it is very important that the analyst's mind is open and permeable (Ferro, 2005; Vermote, 2018).

In his 1957 paper "Differentiating psychotic personalities from non-psychotic personalities," Bion mentions a specific area of personality. This area has a more primitive structure, is not sufficiently developed, and lacks important psychic faculties. It has no language and no expression. Thought is largely distorted, so experiences are not mentalized (Bergstein, 2018). Bion (1962), hypothetically proposed beta elements and called the most primitive manifestations of the psyche beta elements. The mother receives and accepts these mostly primitive manifestations from the baby and transforms and returns this content to him or her. If the mother cannot tolerate projections, the infant is obliged to carry on the more primitive projections with increasing strength and frequency. Bion then hypothetically proposed the alpha function. In the transformation of beta elements, the function he defines as the alpha function comes onto the scene. The alpha function transforms the unthinkable into a thinkable and digestible form. Thus, emotions begin to be thought about. According to Bion (1963), if beta elements cannot be transformed and cannot gain a thinkable form, then they may be evacuated out through projective processes in an emptying nature or may cause somatic symptoms. The first relationship is between the mind of the mother and the mind of the infant. The infant vigorously discharges sensory experiences that he does not know how to metabolize, nameless dread. At this point, if the mother's mind is capable of receiving them, then it not only transforms those sensory elements, the beta elements, into alpha elements, but also gradually communicates to the infant how to do this. Projective identification is the main tool here.

Projective identification

Melanie Klein (1946) introduced the concept of projective identification in her paper "Notes on some schizoid mechanisms" and placed it in the paranoid–schizoid phase of development. In the paranoid–schizoid phase, the "bad" parts of the self are split and projected into the other person to get rid of them. Bion (1959) made a more detailed evaluation on projective identification. He considered projective identification as the most important form of interaction-communication between the patient and the therapist. Bion did not see projective identification only as a phantasy, but as the manipulation of one person by another. In this context, it is an interpersonal interaction (Ogden, 1982).

Projective identification allows the infant to explore his or her own emotions in a personality which is strong enough. The mother's refusal to serve as the depository of her baby's emotions, or the analyst's refusal for the patient's hatred and envy, leads to the denial of the use of this mechanism. This causes the breakdown of the bond between the infant and the breast and, as a consequence, to a severe impairment of the urge for curiosity on which learning depends (Bion, 1959).

One of the most important aspects of normal development is that of the child's parents becoming a reliable container for his or her projective identifications and the child's ability to utilize this function (Ogden, 1982). In projective identification, there is a mutual interaction between the projector and the receiver. Projective identification allows the receiver to create an experience which is different for him- or herself and enables them to have an experience which is other than the one experienced before. The receiver does not simply identify with the other, but becomes the other and experiences what it is like to be the other through this new field of experience (Gaddini, 2004).

O'Shaughnessy (1983) mentioned that projective identification is a very important process, especially in communicating the unspeakable experiences. Rosenfeld (1971) made an important distinction between the use of projective identification for evacuative purposes and for communicative purposes. When it is used for evacuative purposes, any attempt of interpretation will be pushed back by the patient and will not be successful. The patient will feel that something he or she does not want is forced upon them. Ogden (1982) also emphasized the importance of silence and waiting at this point. Rosenfeld (1971) stated that when the patient uses projective identification as a primitive means of communication, understanding what is projected can help the patient. In this way, the analyst can help the patient to get in touch with that element which he or she could not get in touch with before, by reexperiencing this situation with them (as cited in Feldman, 1992).

The metapsychology of the analyst

Robert Fliess (1942) elucidated the metapsychology of the psychoanalyst and noted that he or she is bound to become hopelessly caught in the ambiguities of interpretation and would never convince anyone because he would never have convinced himself of the "true nature" of what he sees. What the analyst or the observer sees is related essentially to his ability to put himself in the latter's place, to step into his shoes, and to obtain in this way an inside knowledge that is almost firsthand. The common name for such an achievement is "empathy." A correct metapsychological description of this process would be as follows. We know that the nuclear process in identification is introjection. The analyst's identifying with the patient, however, cannot possibly mean—as the idiom "stepping into somebody's shoes" would suggest—that he introjects himself into the patient's mind, for it is in the analyst's mind that everything has to occur. It can only mean that he introjects the patient's mind, the patient's ego as the hypothetical subject of the utterances to which the empathy is to be directed. A person who uses empathy on an object introjects this object transiently, and projects the introject again onto the object. This alone enables him in the end to square a perception from without with one from within; it is a trick that one can see operated by anyone who attempts anywhere a psychological evaluation.

According to Fliess, as we apply our concept of empathy to the transference, we shall be laying the first theoretical hold on a sequence of intrapsychic events in the analyst during the analytic session. For the formula that we obtain by such application informs us that the patient's transference conflicts, while passing through what might be called the psychic "working metabolism" of the analyst, have temporarily become intrapsychic conflicts in the latter. The four phases in this metabolic process are the following: (1) the analyst is the object of striving; (2) he identifies with its subject, the patient, (3) he becomes this subject itself, (4) he projects the striving, after he has "tasted" it, back onto the patient and so finds himself in possession of the inside knowledge of its nature, having thereby acquired the emotional basis for his interpretation.

The psychoanalyst has to proffer toward the patient's utterances what Freud calls "free-floating attention." His activity when he complies with this technical requirement seems to be correctly covered by the term "conditioned daydreaming." The foremost metapsychological characteristic of the dreamer's personality is its topographical re-differentiation: the dreamer's ego is reduced to a sort of perceptive surface of the id, whose unconscious contents appear as hallucinations restricted only by the superego whose activity is reduced to that of the dream censor. In daydreaming, reality testing is not lost but is temporarily renounced, and the ego obtains, at the price of this renunciation, free access at least to the whole range of the preconscious psychic content. This state of affairs is commonly reflected in the relative coherence of a daydream compared to a dream; for the primary process has only a limited influence on its formation. By availing ourselves of our preconscious psychic content and of the help of primary processes in elaborating, by means of conditioned daydreaming, upon our analytic perceptions, that is, the patient's material, we supplement most efficiently our rational elaboration upon this material, both in transference and elsewhere.

From the "analytic instrument" to the current "field theory"

The concept of the analytic instrument was originated by Otto Isakower (1963a, 1963b). In an elegant summary of Isakower's postulates Jacobs provides the essence of this concept. According to Jacobs (2007), "analytic instrument" refers to:

> a joint creation of patient and analyst. Assembled in, and existing only, during the analytic hour, it might concretely be imagined as a brain containing two halves. One half

> belongs to the patient, the other half to the analyst. In the analytic session as both analyst and patient loosen their ties to the external world and enter into a slightly altered state of consciousness—essentially a condition of daydreaming—those two halves come together in a temporary union, a bridge is built, and unconscious messages can flow between them. In this state of mind, which the analyst must consciously employ—and arguably due in large measure to this state of mind—it is highly likely that the analyst's subjective experiences will be meaningfully and importantly related to communications from the patient. (p. 100)

The echo of Isakower's concept can be readily discerned in the contemporary notion of field theory which was developed by Madeleine and Willy Baranger (2008). The Barangers mentioned that the analytical dyad and their inevitable contact with each other creates a dynamic field. They stated that we observe this created field moment by moment and in a particular way. The analyst observes himself as well as his patient in this field. When we think in terms of a perceptual definition, we know, in the analytical environment, there is a room where sessions are conducted and two flesh-and-blood people. Beyond this, there are always other people who enter the room through the patient's dreams and narratives, and sometimes even delusions. The coexistence of present, past, and future in the temporality in this space not only helps the patients to realize their past but also offers the possibility to transform them by reexperiencing them. Until it appears in the analytical field, the past historically includes severe traumas and damaging situations. When patients come to the analysis they have some knowledge of their past, but through the analysis these experiences can be brought back into the room, experienced, and integrated through deep processing. The environment created by the analytical dyad has a fantasy, and it is not only the patient who creates this fantasy, but also how the analyst structures the session has an effect on this fantasy. The important point here is not the sum of the patient and the analyst dyad, but a new unit that they form together moment by moment in every session.

In analytical work, the analyst belongs both to the patient's inner world through projective identification and to reality. Insight in the analytical environment begins with the understanding of the structures that appear in the field at that moment by bringing them together with the countertransference of the analyst. The situation in the field is interpreted by the analyst and shared by the patient. Interpretations that are not shared fall into the void and insight is not developed on this situation. Through this kind of interaction, a new communication emerges between the patient and the analyst: not only seeing the same thing, but also constructing something together or sharing a reparative process (Baranger & Baranger, 2008).

Neri (2009) suggested that the Barangers' concepts of the unconscious imagination shared by two people (patient and analyst) come together with Kleinian concepts. He considered it as an area where the projective identification processes specific to the analytical dyad overlap. The paralysis of the processes of projection and absorption that come to life in this field is painful, so it is aimed to mobilize these processes. The perceptions in the analyst's mind about the flow of the session can be used as helpful observations for the further sessions. Sometimes they may not be recognized as observations but then may turn into images, dreams, and stories that can be shared with the patient when appropriate.

Baruzzi (1981) emphasized the importance of "emotions integrated with stories" and underlined the expression of a specific emotion or experience. According to his approach, the importance of expressing in this way is equivalent to understanding and making sense. "Emotion integrated with stories" is the expression of lived experiences in a very concentrated form through words, scenes, or stories (Neri, 2009).

In the following passages, I will attempt to forge links between a sequence from an infant observation and a sequence from a psychotherapeutic work with a patient. The intersecting point will be the particular amorphous and formless content of the field and how it is transformed into emotions integrated with the stories.

An experience in mother–baby observation

This observation was carried out according to the method that Esther Bick (1964) has developed, by visiting the mother and the baby at home at the same time and on the same day of the week. Defne Hanım and I first met a few days before the delivery. She was thirty-eight weeks pregnant. When I visited them, Defne Hanım was there with her husband and her mother. Although the due date was so close, there was a calm atmosphere in their home. After the delivery, I phoned to congratulate her and to ask when it would be appropriate for me to come, and we agreed to talk again in a few days. Two days passed and the mother called and said that they were ready and were waiting for me. She also added that they were worried when I didn't call. So I went for the first observation. The calm atmosphere of the prenatal period was there at home after the birth. The grandmother was in the house and with swift movements she did not let anything fall on the floor. From time to time she appeared with a boiling teapot she took from the stove and disappeared. The most frequently repeated phrases of the first observation were "Did he hold it? Did he take the nipple? Don't let him fall! What will happen if he falls and can't take it again? It has settled, no, not completely …" The mother turned to me and told me to sit comfortably, and I had not yet found my corner … The baby and I were looking for our suitable corner. Toward the end of that observation, we clarified our day and time. According to Bolognini (2008), the baby's first relationship with the nipple is the first essential step in the cohabitation of mother and baby. This first step of the baby taking the nipple involves a benign and necessary physiological fusion.

During the first four observations, the grandmother was also at home, the house was tidy, the mother's rigidity increased as her tiredness increased. For example, when Ali pulled his feet to his stomach, she immediately tried to straighten them. She was trying to breastfeed for twenty minutes, and when Ali vomited in the fifteenth minute, she would stop for a while and continue again. At such times, the grandmother would step in the room with a blanket in her hand and wrap Ali in the blanket, preventing him from entering the sucking–vomiting cycle.

When the grandmother wrapped Ali in the blanket and she took him in her arms, she started talking to the mother. In this way, she also ensured that the baby heard his mother's voice, thus soothing and encompassing both the baby and the mother in a way. This process was like a period of time in which everyone in this nuclear family tried to understand each other's boundaries. The father occasionally complained, "He is always sleeping, dreaming, he must be dreaming about breast!" The grandmother came and sat cross-legged on the floor in front of me with a boiling teapot in her hand, poured tea for me and asked, "What are you looking at?" When I started to explain about baby observation and said Tavistock, Bick, etc., she said, "I'm not asking about that, what are you looking at?" While I was stunned, she said, "to the newborn." And she continued, "I observed a lot, every year … sensitive and quiet and natural …". She said that she had animals in the village where she came from and that she watched all of them from delivery with great pleasure and enthusiasm. As she told this brief story she stood up in one move with the teapot in her hand, and went to the kitchen. In that one month, the grandmother contained all the boiling and burning and destructive emotions of the atmosphere by symbolically putting them into the teapot in her hand, until she reached the end of the month when she said she would return back to her village.

When I came to the next observation, the mother was in the living room and the baby was sleeping. There was a mess, some things had fallen on the floor. Ali woke up after a while and the mother started breastfeeding him. At that time, the news was on the television. There was a news report about mass graves found in a village. The mother was engrossed in the news. The baby stopped breastfeeding after a short while. The mother tried to give the breast without looking at the baby, but the baby did not take it. We know from studies with babies that starting from the womb, babies seek interaction and are able to interact. Reciprocity is a very important dimension for the regulation of affect from birth. Ed Tronick's (Tronick et al., 1978) "still face experiment" proves this. We know from Gallese's (2009) work that the baby shows the precursors of interaction from birth and even from the fourteenth week in the womb, and from birth he is able to identify his own body and emotions separately from others, and has the capacity for empathy. At this moment of the observation, the mother was both watching and commenting on the news and trying to breastfeed the baby. A sense of horror began to spread in the atmosphere over the news of the mass grave. The mother had her hand on her breast but her eyes were on the television. The feeling of horror spreading through the atmosphere had also spread to the baby; he did not want to suckle. The baby started to resist to take the nipple in. He was grabbing the nipple, holding it and letting go. After a short while the mother gave it again and after suckling for a while the baby vomited it all up. The mother cleaned the baby, and she wanted to breastfeed again, but the baby resisted. The mother was puzzled, she said, "He just started to suck, shouldn't he be hungry?" And she turned to me and said "This milk is heavy." "He can't digest it, he's uncomfortable." Defne Hanım had encountered mass graves. With her mother's leaving, she had been shaken by encountering unknown feelings, affects, and sensations about herself through the skeletons of people who had been buried long before, and who knew why they had died or had been killed? This bitter taste had spread to the atmosphere and the baby was resisting: that milk was bitter and hard to digest.

When I went for the next observation, the baby was forty-five days old and although it was spring, the stove was burning inside and the curtains were closed. The room was dark. I had reached the end of the seat, I thought I had settled in, the symbolic smell of the atmosphere in the room had displaced me. The baby was sleeping, the mother looked very tired. She said she had a headache. I didn't say anything, thinking that it might be related to the stuffiness inside. She said in a desperate way, that Ali threw up very frequently this week. After a while the baby woke up and the mother picked him up, talked to him for a while and asked "Do you want that breast?" She started breastfeeding, while her face occasionally showed an expression of pain. She turned to me and said, "He is pulling my nipple, it hurts, I used to think it was because he didn't want it, now I think this milk is making his stomach ache and that's how he tells me about his pain." After breastfeeding, she hugged him. The baby pulled his feet to his tummy and the mother tried several times to straighten them by pulling them and then gave up. "Let it stay curled," she said. At that moment the baby threw up all the breast milk. He wasn't crying, but he was restless. He made noises like "uummm." The mother calmed him down a little. She took him on her lap and started to walk around the room, then she said that he had pooped. "It's been a while but I haven't changed it, is it okay? It's probably warm," she said. She said, "Do you know salt water? They say applying salt water makes the smell goes away." The smell of stool was added to the bitter milk of the atmosphere. She couldn't open his diaper, but she was looking for an additional mixture to put on it and prevent the smell.

The next observation started again in a dark and hot room with no air. On the one hand, I noticed that the mother was gradually regressing and depressed; on the other hand, she was trying not to lose contact with me and the baby during the observation. A few observations were that the suckling-vomiting cycle increased, the air in the room became heavier, and the question of what was mixed into the milk so that he could not suck so much was both in my mind and in her mind. She was postponing changing his diaper and could not get away from all the smells surrounding the baby. However, she started to ask me about the weather outside every time by looking at the thin clothes I was wearing. The window was closed tightly, the curtains were drawn over it. I started to give answers like "Actually it is nice, spring came, we're taking the jackets off, etc." I didn't have a corner anymore, I was trying to observe the baby from a corner that I could find but I couldn't settle down. And at the same time, I was trying to endure all the suffocating feelings. I felt stuck in a corner, the baby was stuck in his mother's lap, and the mother was stuck in a certain discourse. When she was talking to her baby, she was saying the same things one after the other, but she was having difficulty making authentic contact.

After a month of this difficult period, the baby was two and a half months old. When I came for the next observation, the curtains were slightly open. It was a bit more fresh inside. After breastfeeding the baby, the mother helped the baby burp. Then she tried to place the baby on her lap, saying, "I tried every position, you couldn't settle, are you hungry, should I breastfeed again?" She breastfed and the baby vomited. The mother then tried a few more times and gave up each time when the baby threw the milk out. And while she was trying to place her baby on her lap, she looked at me and said, "You know, after the caesarean section, they showed Ali to me and he did not turn out to be blond as I expected, but dark and hairy,

I felt that this is not my baby. I couldn't believe it, is this my baby? It felt so aloof and alienated for a second. When the operation was almost over, I saw his feet and it seemed like there was a missing toe." The mother was tired but smiling. By this time the baby had calmed down and had found a place in her lap where he stopped squirming restlessly. Lebovici (1983) made a distinction between the phantasized baby and the imaginary baby. While the phantasized baby is an expression of the unconscious world of the mother, the imaginary baby is an image created and shared by the parents together. All these dreams and fantasies will interact with the reality of the baby after he is born (Ammaniti & Gallese, 2014).

In the next observation session, the grandmother came. The mother said that the baby who could not cry, had started to cry. The baby was in the mother's lap and I was in front of her. The grandmother started to turn around in the room with all her quickness and flexibility. The window was open, it was airy inside. The mother looked at me and said, "I am very tired." The mother went inside. The grandmother put the baby to sleep and with a boiling teapot in her hand, she sat cross-legged on the floor in one move, showed me a seat opposite her and said in a very direct way, "Sit down." She poured tea for both of us and started to explain: "When Defne was born, I had to go to work in the fields. Starting from her being forty days old, I had to leave very early in the morning and come back at noon to breastfeed her. My sisters-in-law were taking care of her. However, I was not getting along well with them. Every time I came, I would find her in her crib, very hungry, dirty and crying. These periods are very difficult and painful, you feel very sad, you cannot do anything. After she was four or five months old, I put Defne on me and started to take her with me when I had to go for work." By telling this story, the grandmother helped me to create a ground on which I could build the previous experiences in the room, and also a corner in which I could place my thoughts during the past one month and five observations. In his book *The Birth of a Mother*, Stern (1998), writes about the meaningful impact on a new mother of a few sentences spoken by a cleaning lady who came to his house every day and how he waited for her arrival every day. Stern calls this woman a craftswoman, who is more experienced than the mother and knows the *story*. He mentions that motherhood is a craft and that new mothers need to be together with a master, a craftswoman who has been there before. This guide is not there to give information, but to surround the mother with a psychological environment that will make her feel safe. The craftsman of my observation was the grandmother; sometimes she came with a blanket in her hand and swaddled the baby quickly, sometimes she carried the boiling emotions in a container-teapot safely and without spilling a drop on the floor. And the last story she told me served as an inclusive cover, a swaddle for my mind to wrap those forty days we spent together—cohabited together.

In mother–infant psychotherapy, Salo (2018) has underscored how the past history of the parents impairs their functioning and thus the infant's functioning, as well as stressing the influence of reality-related factors on the infant's subjectivity and self-regulation. This is not a mother–infant psychotherapy, but it shows us how powerful the influence of the nonverbal and archaic is. The observer observes the process as it should be, without any comment or intervention. During the whole observation process, the observer lives in the room and in the atmosphere with the mother and her baby and other members of the family for a while. As Bianca Lechevalier (2004) states, for a while the observer's eye is internalized by the other members of the house and, as time passes, by the baby as well. In this part of the observation, I was a person through whom some untold stories were told, the weather outside was asked about, and bonds were established. Lechevalier also said that the observer is also a family observer. Sanchez (1986) emphasized that the term infant observer is inadequate. What is really observed is the family into which an infant is born. Bick (1964) stated that in order for the observer to feel the emotional impact, it is indispensable for him or her to feel sufficiently in the family without feeling obliged to take action. The observer must also accept the anguish of seeing a mother who cannot function properly without intervention. In line with all these principles, I tried to observe and make sense of all kinds of sounds and smells in the atmosphere during the time we were together in the room, in parallel with the baby's cycle. My position changed several times until the observation was over, but I was never on the edge of the sofa again during that two-year period. Although the places where I sat changed from time to time due to my following the baby as he grew up, my corner in my mind became more and more prominent and I continued to observe by settling there gradually.

The case of Seda Hanım

Seda Hanım was in her early thirties when she came for the first interview. She had received psychiatric treatment since mid-adolescence. She had been hospitalized once due to a suicide attempt. After that process, she was referred to me by the psychiatrist who was working with her.

I was surprised to learn that Seda Hanım, who seemed to have mental incapacity, graduated from one of the top ranking schools of Turkey. She had dropped out of school despite being very successful in the university exam, which she took several times. When Seda Hanım, who was quite overweight, first entered my room, she headed toward the armchair and as she was sitting, my first thought was "the armchair will break." She was always sleepy in the sessions after we decided to work together twice a week. She mentioned that she had difficulty waking up in the morning. She showed no signs of any vitality in the sessions. She was interested in strategy plays, and this was the only place where I could see the sparkle in her eyes, but then the darkness came back again in the room. At times, her very loud laughter made me jump out of my seat. Simultaneously, she started to bring her childhood story. Her way of speaking was very superficial and rather isolated. She slowly started to talk about the history of violence in her childhood. She told that her father had beaten her from a very early age. These were very severe beatings, she felt very humiliated and left alone. Her mother was the silent witness of the beatings that followed a very sadistic pattern. Her mother was "watching helplessly, not knowing what to do." From time to time, she "seemed" to see a vague smile on her face. The psychiatrist who referred Seda Hanım to me told me that in one of the interviews they had with her mother during her hospitalization, her mother had commented on her suicidal thoughts as "Let her die." These stories were weighing down the atmosphere with all their gravity. I was sometimes a silent witness to the stories; for her I was a patient listener and she was the reporter, but the contact part was missing. She was asleep between all these stories. A heavy, suffocating air was filling the room. Simultaneously, a smell began to spread into the room. This smell first started as the smell of sweat. She was in a sleepy state. Sometimes the smell of sweat was replaced by the smell of urine. We had entered a very difficult period where I did not know what to do. I realized that I was leaving the window ajar on the days she was coming. At times it became too much to bear and I felt disgust, nausea, I felt as if I was going to vomit in the middle of the room. The smell changed form. When we were approaching the summer break, she had asked her mother for help with a situation involving her son. Her mother had refused and left her alone. She started to fall asleep while telling how her mother had left her alone all her life. She was very angry that I was leaving too, blaming me for leaving her at such a difficult time. When we returned from the break, she had a dream: "I am with a woman. We are in a place like a glass room, there is a fire outside, everything is on fire, the flames are all around. I'm very angry and I'm shouting that either we stay here and drown here or we go out and get burned. Either way we're going to die. Do you dare to say anything? I shout at that woman." She said the dream described the feeling of her being stuck. "That's exactly how I feel, I feel very stuck and I feel like I'm going to burn up." I said: "Just like here, you and I have been trying to survive with this smell in the room for a while. I think you are telling us, that is, me and yourself, how suffocating things are, through the smell, how difficult it is to breathe sometimes. If I don't, we will suffocate, and if I do, we will have opened the doors and windows instead of the fire outside." When I said this, she was startled: "I am very embarrassed … I am also aware that I smell, sometimes I smell sweat, sometimes urine, and sometimes menstrual blood. I have recently been unable to bathe. I can hardly enter the bathroom … It is as if that smell is a part of me … it must be here too …"

A: It has to be so we can trace it.
Q: Yeah, it's like I'm chasing something, and maybe nothing is that far apart.
A: Actually, the glass between you and that fire is not so separating anymore.
Q: I'm burning too, I'm hurting … I'm scared … I feel terrible … I can't speak.
A: You have a mother who doesn't dare to speak out, who doesn't speak out when all this is going on. It took time for me to say it too. The one who doesn't speak will suffocate to death inside, and the one who speaks will burn outside. Either way, it will be a fatal move. It took me a while to say that it smelled, because at first I wasn't sure if it really smelled, and then I didn't know how to say it. Maybe I was scared … and angry, and I had to think about how we could build a platform where we could work all these feelings through without erasing them.

The inside of the glass room in her dream and the place of the fire outside were the parts of Seda Hanım's psyche that were not in contact with each other. She was drowning in that chamber and falling asleep, or she was both creating and staying in the fire outside. Death was inevitable.

During this time of our work she started to visit her aunt more often. She started to hear her story from her aunt. Her aunt told her that her mother did not want her and that she had a lot of difficulty with her as a baby. She told her that she was a baby who could not be heard or cared for, even though she cried and shouted a lot. She said that her mother had left her in her cradle for a long time without touching her and had closed the door on her so that she would not hear her voice. Her grandmother had chosen her aunt among her two daughters, the aunt was the special child and she had educated her, and she didn't send the mother to school and wanted her to have a profession quickly and to take care of her. The baby left in the cradle by her grandmother was her mother. Her mother had left her in her crib for hours without touching her or changing her diaper. Later on, her mother did not make a sound when she was beaten by her father. Her mother and aunt became two children growing up in two different rooms of the same house. One was that beautiful and capable baby and the other was the baby that was avoided and feared. That fear-inducing baby later gave birth to another fear-, horror-, and disgust-inducing baby. These babies, locked in different rooms of the same house, also symbolized the parts which were locked in different rooms of the psyche and remained closed there, unable to come into contact with each other. As Seda Hanım said, everyone knew that the inside of the room was suffocating and the outside was on fire. Being stuck between this duality was one of the biggest obstacles to thinking and transformation. It was necessary to maintain flexibility against the collapsing weight, that is, to resist to survive.

All the untransformed aggression of Seda Hanım was coming out as a bad smell at that time. That weird baby that could not be touched had also come among us. What made these smells bad was that they stuck to the body for a while. Whether it was urine, blood, or sweat, the longer you couldn't wash them or touch them, the heavier they became. It brought the untouchable, untransformed parts of her body through smells and secretions. These parts seemed to cover her potential. As the smells became thinner, I began to see her intellect and comprehension capacity, and her "pseudo-stupidity" (Mahler, 1942), which was another texture that covered her, become diluted.

Back to theory

I would like to discuss this intersection point in these two examples in terms of transgenerational issues, smell, and the feelings of suffocation I felt in the countertransference. I would like to build the background of my discussion on how these nonverbal expressions find a form and language in relation and interaction with each other.

Transgenerational knots

A common theme in the section I presented of both the infant observation and my work with Seda Hanım was the untold but known stories that pass from one generation to the other. Faimberg (2005), talks about the parents' narcissistic adaptation of the child, which is the first moment of narcissistic love, and their intrusiveness, which is the result of the narcissistic hatred that immediately follows. The internalized parents put the unacceptable for them into the child and define it as a negative identity. Thus this child is hated. This child is not only hated because he or she is different, but paradoxically also because he or she has been a part of the story that is compatible with the narcissistically unacceptable personal history of his or her parents. Here there is not enough physical space for the child to develop his (or her) own identity, he cannot free himself from the alienating power of his parents' narcissism. This function of alienation is also the cause of the split in the ego, which makes the child feel alienated. What Faimberg means by alienation is both the alienation of the child from himself and the alienated organization of the other. Faimberg notes that the parents in these stories are not only the protagonists of the relationship but also form the unconscious family structure. Three generations are involved in such families. Just like in the story of Seda Hanım and the story of Ali. That weird, incomplete, disgusting, and frightening baby, which was passed down from generation to generation, was looking for a place for himself not through people but through an unconscious structure. Defne Hanım couldn't believe when she first saw Ali and her question was important in this context: Who is this baby? Was it a ghost from the past? Or was it a possible ghost to be sent to the future? Faimberg argued that as the hidden history of the family is revealed, its effects on the ego can be transformed, and thus the alienating parts of the split can also be transformed. It is through the transformation of these identifications that the desire and structure of the future can be liberated.

Smell in the clinical situation

Smell was one of the main sensations in the stories of the babies that I presented here. Today, studies in neuroscience and biology further elaborate on smell. In addition to recent contributions from different scientific fields (Khamsi, 2022; Poo et al., 2022), the relationship between smell and early memories and traumatic experiences has also been mentioned in psychoanalytic literature. Freud (1895d) stated that smell and memories are often interrelated. Akhtar (2009) stated that the psychological meaning of smell can be handled in different ways. One of them is that smell is an important part of the bond between mother and baby. Bucci (1997) talked about the forms in which nonverbal systems are represented in many ways and mentioned new areas of experience created through these forms. The transformation of the not-yet-symbolized or beta element is possible in these new spaces. This space is bidirectional, the listener can translate what is communicated verbally into nonverbal, and the new expressions that come from it can lead to new nonverbal connections. This interaction cannot be controlled by the subject because it takes place on the affective level (Boccara et al., 2009). Such a sensory-affective flow can be accessed through regression within the analytical process, in fact this raw material continues to operate on a psychic or somatic level and is waiting to be recognized by the other's mind (Bion, 1962; Ferro, 2002).

Both in the infant observation with Ali and Defne Hanım and in the psychotherapy with Seda Hanım, I tried to address the somnolence of the emotions, sensations, and imaginations that spread into the room and how they transform as they come into contact with this residue, even if partially. At this point, Antonino Ferro's "bi-personal field" theory formed the background of my thinking. Ferro developed the bi-personal field theory by combining Winnicott and Bion's theory with the Barangers' field theory. Although the psychoanalytic origins of his theory can be traced back to the Barangers' field theory, its earlier origins can be traced to Freud's (1912e) view that the unconscious of two people can be in direct interaction and, in the technical realm, to Isaak Hoover's concept analyzing instrument. It focuses on the dyad in the psychoanalytic encounter through Bion's (1961) observations on groups and his formulation (1962, 1970) of projective identification, the alpha function, and the container–contained. Seda Hanım, on the other hand, brought disgust through smell emanating from her core, which she camouflaged in a way with her sleepy-state depression for a long period of time, and the associated aggression and desire for rejection. Ferro (2006) says the following:

> In my view, the game of analysis is to be able to come into contact with the world that is completely unthinkable and unrepresentable, which is crashing left and right in an unpredictable way. It is to be able to create a representation through a story. Only then can the unconscious composition, although repressed, become narratable. (p. 108)

According to Levine (2022), the field is the name of the hypothesis on the emotional dimension created by the conscious and unconscious affective interaction of the patient and the analyst in the analytic process. This dimension is special, unique to that dyad, unconsciously reconstructed, and reappears in the analysis within the patient's needs for emotion regulation, growth and development, improvement of symptoms, satisfaction, and wholeness. In analytical work, the analyst works with anxiety that cannot be seen or touched, that has no shape, sound, or smell (Bion, 1970).

In the observation process of the mother–baby dyad I mentioned above and in my work with Ms. Seda, the anxiety gradually appeared through a smell. Through this, the split structures became more visible. This process of transforming the undefined into a structure that has splits and is relatively more distinct was made possible by entering the same room and allowing two psyches to cohabit. The undefined sensations and the state of not knowing, which I dealt with in two sequences, first took me out of my corner both as an observer and as a therapist. The process of crystallization of the raw material enabled me to settle down and get rooted in my corner, in a corner of my analytical mind. Settling into the nonverbal space full of sensations was possible through interactions that developed in cohabitation and reciprocity. When Defne Hanım asked me how the weather was, she was partly aware that there was an outside, but contact with "that outside" was frightening. It took time to open that window, the baby could get cold, but other than the baby, a part of her that was very sensitive and not swaddled could be damaged. As she asked me the weather my reply starting with "in fact" showed that there was a "fact," but that access to there was limited for both of us. I was looking for a symbolic corner for myself through this fact, and the grandmother's last move helped me find it and start to take root in that observation. In Seda Hanım's case, my feeling uncomfortable might have had something to do with my being less experienced, as I felt that my words, what I was trying to interpret, remained on the surface. As soon as she started to smell, my emotions began to take their most real form. We cohabited in that environment for a while and she could feel from my facial expressions or from the way I slowly closed my shawl as it was difficult to breathe in the room, besides my attempts to give a name to the atmosphere. At the end of this period, she was able to have a dream and then she brought me to the house where the outside was a place of fire and there was a danger of suffocation and death inside, the split-off parts of her inner home. Seda Hanım also presented that part of hers through the smell.

Both Ali and Seda Hanım were "weird" babies who had to be kept in the other room as they first met with their mother. Neither of them was "that baby." Ali was not blond as expected, he did not get the nipple easily in, he vomited, and he did not stand in the posture his mother desired. Seda Hanım's mother did not know what to do with her and locked her in a room. The longer she stayed in the room, the more she smelled. Her mother never knew where to place her. She had not been able to cope with her since she was a baby and had openly stated in consultations with other specialists in the psychiatric inpatient unit that she wanted her to die. Many authors have stated that the child's mind needs a thinking mind in the course of development (Bion, 1962; Fonagy & Target, 1996; Fonagy et al., 2004; Schore, 1994; Winnicott, 1967). Ferro and Basile (2004) stated that when there are blind spots in the mother's mind, unbearable content is passed from mother to child. These blind spots that cannot be thought are passed from one generation to another. Both Seda Hanım's mother and Ali's mother could not escape from the blind spots of their own stories and, in Faimberg's words, from their ghosts. Both Seda Hanım and Ali did not have a mind to think together in a particular part of their infancy. Ferro and Basile (ibid.) said that if the mother cannot digest what comes from her baby and instead feels overwhelmed, the infant experiences the undefined elements in himself as an experience which he either throws out or encapsulates and closes. Thus, it is not only the inevitable blind spots that are passed on from the mother to the baby, but also the "solutions" that the mother found to them.

Feelings of suffocation

In these two sequences, one of the obstacles to settling into a corner and getting rooted through reflection was the sense of suffocation felt in the countertransference. De Cortinas (2011) mentioned that when emotions are not sufficiently digested, space and time can be occupied by projective identifications and things could be disguised as ghosts, turning it into a claustrophobic or agoraphobic space. At that time of the observation, both Ali and I were suffocating; he was vomiting and I was suffocating from the heat. This feeling came between me and

Seda Hanım through the smell, which had been ambiguous from the beginning. De Cortinas stated that for the development of the human mind, the organization of psychic pain in the context of the container–contained relationship is essential. In order for the emotional experience to be recognized and given meaning, the baby needs the dreams that appear in the mother. In the session room, it is about how we can cover what appears there at that moment, how we can transform emotional experiences that are difficult to digest, and how we can create the space for psychic reality in our clinical practice. The corner in my title refers to the space in which we can root this psychic reality. In the archaic situations I presented, it was of course difficult to find a place in the fog and to be able to endure in it despite not knowing what was happening. It is part of psychic growth that pain goes through a process of authentic symbolization. Perhaps an original and authentic symbolization can only take root on a ground where thinking and feeling can be free and sometimes weird, through "being not that baby," resisting to be "that baby," which is the process that Faimberg calls disidentification. A corner built on this ground can form the corner where we do our work and observations.

There are windows in both Seda Hanım's and Ali's stories, and in both experiences my position was directly opposite the window. Window comes to our language from Persian and means air hole. Its English equivalent, window, contains the eye in its etymology, *Wind-auge*. Pontalis (2001) wrote about the windows that contain the meaning of both the flow of air and the clarity of vision and symbolically the clarity of thought.

In his essay on "Windows," Pontalis begins as follows:

> My analyst's chair by the window: tree leaves, birdsong. The desk where I write: always by the window; the summer house overlooking the heath, the forest and the sea beyond. It happens that an excited and bewildered stork comes to visit me, even hops and flies around the room for a moment …

The last paragraph says: "Of doors, I insist that they be closed properly: but each room must have its own particular good use. My subjective space is both open windows and authentic rooms."

Coda

Preverbal, nonverbal, and otherwise psychically deferred material continues to linger in the analytic field. It is generally conveyed via psychosomatic gestures such as postural changes, thermal sensitivity, granting awkward silences, eye-gaze peculiarities, a furtive pain around the mouth, and, in the material cited above, smell. Under these circumstances, unconscious communication, uncanny empathy, and discernment of projective identification through meticulous countertransference scrutiny become the main allies of the working psychoanalyst. This is what I have tried to demonstrate in my contribution here.

CHAPTER 14

Transforming the "enslaving mother" image to "liberating mother" image through the "analyst's womb" in transference

Gülgün Alptekin

Many analysts have written about patients perceiving the analysis room like a womb (Silver, 2007). Beyond this perspective, the "analyst womb" may function as a representational space onto which many feelings, conflicts, and images are projected during the analytical process. This chapter will focus on the analytic work of two female patients working through the analyst womb as a transforming space in many aspects, especially transforming the enslaving mother image to the liberating mother.

Womb fantasies, the womb, and the intrauterine life, which were initially hot topics (Freud, 1918b; Horney, 1923; Rank, 1924) for psychoanalysis, were later on neglected. In recent years, however, especially female authors have been giving these subjects their due credit (Mariotti, 2012; Pines, 1993; Raphael-Leff, 2014; Silver, 2007). Every person begins life in the body of a woman. The mother and the fetus in her womb live a life of mutual physical and emotional exchange for nine months. The therapy-analysis room, which may represent an unconscious womb, provides us a tremendous opportunity for investigating intrauterine experiences. This is especially true for female-to-female analyses.

Clinical vignette 1

In our session following a two-month-long birth leave, Ms. K told me about a dream she had during this period. In her dream, Ms. K, her mother, I, and my baby were together. Her mother was telling me how cute the baby was. First herself, then her mother were cuddling the baby. The mother began to play with and kiss the baby. She was deeply disturbed by this. Since I am her analyst, she felt such a close relationship would be inappropriate, and was angry at her mother. "Don't exaggerate, mom. She is my analyst. We have to be serious," she said. Simultaneously, during her dream, she was thinking "Ms. Gülgün will no longer think I am jealous of the baby because she saw that I like it." After she told me about these dreams, Ms. K laughed and said, "Turns out, according to dreams, I was jealous of your baby." This dream was the first time she told me something warm and affectionate about her mother. She was always angry at and distant toward her. The positive mother object of Ms. K, who grew up in a large family, was her grandmother (her father's mother). Her mother, unhappy due to problems within the crowded family, was unloading a significant burden on Ms. K. It was because of her that she was putting up with this miserable life. Without a doubt, Ms. K's preference over the grandmother, with whom she was in conflict, was yet another source of unhappiness for her mother. However, it was not until Ms. K was seventeen that her mother became a true burden for her. After a domestic argument among the adults of the house, her mother had attempted suicide, which had paralyzed the entire household. Ms. K had to carry her mother out of the house, and stay with her in the hospital for two weeks. Yes, her mother was just an awful burden for her—until today. It was a burden she had to carry on her shoulders, in the form of a half-alive body, when she was seventeen. Now, through me and my baby, she had made an affectionate connection with her mother for the first time. It was as if when I and my baby became a new couple, she and her mother were able to become a new couple as well. After this, it became possible to work on her anger toward her mother. Previously, she used to describe her anger by saying, "You know how you fill the bathtub, and then the water pulls away swirling when you empty it? My anger is exactly the same—I pull away like a whirlpool." These were difficult sessions for me, during which I would only endure her anger. The dream she had following my pregnancy and birth, and the fact that we were able to talk about her anger toward her mother, could be about the resemblance between a bathtub filled with water and the womb. The full bathtub with water swirling away reminded me of Raphael-Leff's (2014) placental paradigm. Until that day, the mutual exchange she made with the baby inside the mother's womb through the placenta metaphor had not been possible for Ms. K. If the bathtub is representative of the womb, the amniotic fluid was drained in the blink of an eye. Through my womb, Ms. K was able to experience the placental paradigm. The anger she was not able to process so far, probably because it was not capable of being represented, and the idea that she will turn into a slave if she were to be involved in a relationship where the mother is just a burden, began to be represented with the bathtub metaphor. Here, I endured and contained her aggression. Afterwards, the placental paradigm took the stage through my pregnancy, and she was able to both talk about her anger and process it. Interestingly enough, during the further periods of the analysis, there were some developments regarding the womb representations.

I would like to speak about a session that took place within the fourth year of analysis. She had missed the session due to being stuck in traffic for an hour. In the next session, she told me how she imagined a session as she waited in traffic. In that session, she was telling me: "I remember my ex-husband being uncomfortable about psychoanalysis. I have never questioned you or psychoanalysis. I agreed to four times a week right away. Maybe I was one of your first patients." During this daydream, I was replying to her as such: "Yes, this is a possibility. You may be my first patient, but you also see how much you have progressed." And then she responds: "Yes, many things have changed, but there are also some things yet to be fixed."

After Ms. K told me about her imaginary session, she continued: "So I made a session in the car. Why did I do that? Did I want to say this was not only your success, but mine also? I don't know why I daydreamed such a dialog in the car."

"How nice," I replied, "that we are both here now. We can be curious about it together."

Ms. K responded by saying: "Perhaps I ask myself how many patients Ms. Gülgün has analyzed so far. You would not tell me even if I asked. My only criterion is Ms. Gülgün's success in my analysis. Maybe it is one of her first analyses, but she is successful, I tell myself. Perhaps all these are about my desire to get to know you better, and my curiosity about you. Maybe I want to be an important party in our relationship. Us, two women! We did this good job together. I have improved, progressed. Maybe you have improved as well. So this way, my money was not wasted since I made the imaginary analysis. You always say the analysis continues even if I don't come to the session. I understand that very clearly now. I did not come to my session yesterday, but the analysis continued. In the past, I used to get very angry when I was late to a session, or missed one. It felt like a waste of my money. My aggression became a step in my analysis, serving me to move forward."

Ms. K's thoughts about completing the analysis were first verbalized in this session. Curiously enough, she was alone in a car, and was talking to me in her daydream. Again, like a baby in the womb, but mutually interacting with her mother through the placenta. After these thoughts, three months passed with steps forward and backward. This process helped her integrate the good and bad mother representations in the form of myself.

Three months later, she told me about a dream. This was the dream she had after her boyfriend of two years, with whom she was in a satisfactory relationship, proposed to her in a lovely setting in the X mansion.

Dream: You, too, were staying in the X mansion. You were staying there with a big crowd. I don't know whether they are your family or friends. You and I are chatting in the garden. You are so pleased to tell me about your plans for that day. I will go to the bazaar, I will go to the cinema, to the bookstore, and then I will make a stop in Kadıköy, you say. I realize how you talk about these plans as if you were retired. Then, we go to Kadıköy together. We continue our conversation. In Kadıköy, before we go on our separate ways, we give each other some bags and packages. There is also a large tray with delicious food on it. I ask to take some of the food, unless you want to take it all with you. I take some really good items and we say goodbye to each other.

Her associations were as follows: My first reaction was: "Oh! I had a dream about Ms. Gülgün again!" I've had dreams before in which I had turned you into my mother or my friend. This time, as I was thinking about why I had turned you into a mother again, I felt like this dream was different from the others. You were going somewhere, talking about your travel plans. I feel like you have retired. You give me nice food—food to feed me in your absence.

The place we go together, Kadıköy, is where I have spent my childhood. I guess it is meaningful that we visit Kadıköy. I feel like I was preparing to separate from you. I have taken everything I can from you. I also have the back-up food for your absence. So you are free to go to the cinema, take a vacation etc.

After this session, we worked for a little longer and determined a termination date. The mutual exchange within the womb continued as the mother that was in my form got her daughter married. As a female analyst preparing to terminate her female analysand, I also represented the mother who was preparing to marry her daughter. Ms. K was now nourished enough through the mutual exchange in her mother's womb; as a fetus that had taken what was good for her, and had discharged what was not, she had progressed into a mentally healthy woman during her analytic journey, and was now preparing to be a mother herself in the future by getting married. This session with the dream was emotional for both of us.

Clinical vignette 2

The other patient I would like to discuss is Ms. D. She came to analysis when she was thirty-five years old, saying, "I want to get rid of my mother, for the fact that she never leaves my life alone." Up to that point, her mother had made all the decisions regarding her life, and she had complied with them. In the second month of the therapy, she brought a dream in which a baby falls into a pit. After reciting the dream, she told me about an event in tears. In the beginning of the therapy when she was telling me her story, she had failed to mention this event. In fact, she had avoided talking about it throughout her entire life, as if she had simply erased it. When Ms. D was six years old, her mother was in the house with a few guests, and they had put her six-months-old brother in Ms. D's arms. As she walked, Ms. D had tripped and dropped her brother to the floor. This event that she had not dealt with so far began to be mentally represented thanks to this dream. It was a turning point for us as well. We moved on to a deeper working through.

In the beginning of the analysis, there was a period of reciprocal humming. Whenever I said "um-hum," she made the same sound or she herself ended her every sentence with "um-hum." Silver (2007) argues that bodily stimulants resembling intrauterine experiences, such as touch, voice, rhythm, smell, resonance, and vibration, which are recorded into bodily memories, are neglected in psychoanalysis. According to Kristeva (1984), intrauterine space can be approached by transferring from colloquial language to poetic intuitions. Intrauterine life is a floating space free of weight—a space where physical sensations are filtered, and felt through the membrane of the mother's body. Now, I equate our "um-hum" phase to the intrauterine period. "Um-hum" was not just a sound. It was a deep communication with all senses—just like the intrauterine conditions. I, too, was intuitively stayed in the intrauterine condition. Now, as I look back on those moments, I imagine myself as a pregnant mother; touching her naked belly with both hands, making voices in different tones, smiling, having fun … After Ms. D finished her sentence, she would say "um-hum" and wait. She seemed to wait for an "um-hum" directly from me. If I did not make that sound, she would repeat it, this time in a questioning tone: Um-hum? This was just like how the fetus waits for the mother's reaction after moving, kicking her belly. Mothers usually respond to the moves their baby makes. They talk to, touch and love the baby over their belly. The "um-hum" period never disturbed me. I did not experience it as if something was being demanded of me. I did not question it consciously. I only let myself be present in this situation, be present with her there. I think this intrauterine-like experience enabled a transformation for Ms. D, from a killing womb image to a sustaining one. Afterwards, the slave-like girl turned into a lively girl who is capable of getting into a relationship with her mother. Following this period, Ms. D was able to talk about a lot of things, and stay with many of the things I said. She no longer waited for an approval for everything she said, at least not with an "um-hum."

Further into her analysis, she brought this dream:

I'm pregnant, I'm shopping with my mother. I feel the baby sliding downwards. I turn to my mother and say that I am about to give birth. My mother continues shopping. The contractions become more and more frequent. I hold the baby from down below, so it won't slip away. I ask for help. My husband is unable to get the car out of its parking space. I hop into a cab. I am alone. I can feel the baby's head in my hand. Right at the moment when baby is about to be born, I poop on the taxi seat. Oh no, I say, I am mortified. But it is normal to poop during labor, I say. I've messed up the man's car but I am happy that he has plastic covers on the seats.

Her associations were as follows:

It was like salvation. I was happy that I had pooped. It was like getting rid of the evil in me, which made me happy. I was happy to have completed all the tasks by myself. It was so difficult until I got into the cab. I was unable to receive the help I much needed—first from my mother, then from my husband. My mother carried on with her shopping. My husband tried, but there was an obstacle. I wonder if the back seat of the taxi was the couch?

Around the time she was thinking about completing her analysis, Ms. D regressed intensely. She went back to the beginning of the analysis. All her pre-oedipal, oedipal, and adolescence conflicts were revived. The dreams she had around this period were as follows: "You had forced me into a straightjacket and made me sit down. You were shaving my head. 'Why do you do this to me?' I ask." Her associations were: "After all, my mother did not chain me. So how did I get this persecutory mother image in my mind? My mother used to say, 'Kids don't get angry.' She did not give me the right to be angry—*that* was persecutory."

The bad mother image she had turned me into with this dream and the hopeless self-image that yields to the bad mother had dominated the entire life of Ms. D. Being so much under the rule of the mother was like being in a dead womb. Not having any thoughts or feelings about herself and others could be thought of as symbolically being in a dead womb. Maybe this dream, in which I tie her up and make her motionless, showed how still she was in the womb.

This regressive period initiated by the idea of terminating the analysis was like adolescence; and it was perhaps the phase before the transition into adulthood, into independency—the second separation–individuation period (Blos, 1967). Luckily, this time she was facing a new mother figure who approves her sexuality and the desires of her body, respects, liberates, and encourages her.

Shortly after this intense period, Ms. D told me another dream of hers: "I am bathing a baby. It looks like the infancy of my brother. I cover the rough corners of the sink with pieces of carpet. As I wash the baby in my hands, all of a sudden its waist slips away. It hits its head on the sink. Nothing happens. I am relieved." Her associations were as follows: "In this dream, there is the situation when I drop the baby, the anxiety of whether I've hurt it or not, and the theme of it slipping away. There is this feeling that I am unable to get a hold of it completely. This time I am aware of the possibility so I cover the floor with carpet, I make it soft."

A sink covered with soft towels may resemble a containing womb. It is possible neither to die in a containing womb nor to kill the rival baby in a protective one. She and her rivals can safely live within the womb as well as in the world after birth. A new mother figure, containing her in her womb, was now formed. This new mother image would continue to contain her after her birth and separation.

Discussion

Raphael-Leff coined the term "placental paradigm" in 1996. The bidirectional placental system was argued to provide not only a biological exchange, but also an emotional exchange, between the mother and the baby through the umbilical cord. It has been a common wisdom in many societies that whatever the mother eats, drinks, and feels is passed on to the baby. The pregnancy experience, the condition of being merged with another creature inside, revives any unconscious merger fantasies, depending on the psychic situation of the pregnant woman. Sometimes this blur in boundaries becomes a magnificent ecstatic experience, while at other times it may be experienced to be overwhelming or dangerous. Therefore, the placental paradigm is about the woman's representations on different affective conditions, regarding herself as a mother and the baby in her fantasy. These representations may be highly positive or negative, and usually tend to oscillate on a wide spectrum spread between the two poles. A benevolent relationship between the mother and the fetus only becomes possible when the pregnant woman can tolerate this ambivalence. Even after birth, the mother's ability to tolerate her ambivalence toward her child and, later on, the child's ability to process his or her ambivalence toward the mother are, without a doubt, important topics. This ambivalence, through the transference–countertransference relationship, is also a valuable material in the analysis process. As we talk about the placental paradigm, the representations in the pregnant woman's fantasy toward the baby, her ambivalence, and the impact these make on the fetus, we are in some way trying to make sense of proto-emotions and proto-thoughts—things outside the capacity of representation and verbalization.

We were not able to work through Ms. K's anger toward her mother for two and a half years, until I gave birth. Interestingly enough, it was only after the fantasies about my womb and the baby inside my belly took the stage that she was able to share a positive experience about her mother for the first time. The pathetic, helpless, unhappy mother image was perhaps installed in her by the mother, during the intrauterine life. One can imagine that a pregnant woman who lives with her in-laws and is persecuted by them may have difficulties in handling her ambivalent emotions toward her baby. She may even have expected this baby to save her. Yet, Ms. K had also called her grandmother (father's mother) mom, and had been extremely angry toward her mother for as long as she could remember. After she began to form a positive bond with her mother through my pregnancy, she began to appreciate her point of view as well. Until then, she was only able to deal with her mother through anger—her mother who, perhaps since the intrauterine life, had imprisoned her with her own desperateness and misery. During and after my pregnancy, she was able to work through her both negative and positive emotions toward her mother, using our transference–countertransference relationship. In these working-through processes, womb and placental exchange representations frequently took the stage.

Ms. D, too, was also unconsciously enslaved by her mother, but in a rather different way. She had coped by complying, and had paid many prices just like Ms. K. Ms. D's mother got married when she was fifteen, and was pregnant afterwards. The father was very keen on her young wife, and would pamper her a lot. It is plausible to assume that a pregnant woman, who herself is a child, should have ambivalent feelings toward the baby she carries. Especially while she was being so pampered by her husband, and with a rival who took her worth away from her on the way, Ms. D's difference was her decision to apply for therapy in order to get rid of her mother's impact upon her. Ms. K, on the other hand, had not sought therapy with a conscious desire to get rid of her anger toward her mother. This topic was out of discussion for her. Ms. D was a step forward on this matter. Yet, on a more similar note, Ms. D was also able to begin working through the enslavement by her mother using the womb and the representations of the intrauterine experiences. After the dream with the baby falling into a pit, she was able to talk about her memory of dropping her sibling, which she had previously never talked or thought about, and was able to verbalize her emotions as well. However, this was not enough. Ms. D was unable to define her thoughts and feelings. She seemed confused and timid. It was not easy, of course. After all, she had spent her whole life under her mother's rule. Her mother had thought, felt, talked, and decided for her. The "um-hum" period that started later on was, in a way, a chance to reexperience the mutual emotional exchange phase, following which Ms. D was reborn as a baby who has reciprocal and lively relations with her mother. After the first space, as a sustaining womb, the new and original mother–baby relationship provided a second space enabling the mutual working through of emotions.

Freud (1926d) argued that between the intrauterine life and early infancy, the effective *caesura* (pause) caused by birth is actually a big continuance. Bion (1989) expanded Freud's concept of a caesura between the prenatal and the postnatal life. He argued that the caesura provides an example of the continuance between dissimilar yet closely related mental states and events, such as past/now, memory/desire, sleep/wakefulness, transference/countertransference, affective experience/interpretation, psyche/soma, and conscious/unconscious. According to Bion (ibid.), there is another mental state beyond the conscious and the unconscious, which includes inaccessible states of mind. These may be the prenatal parts of the personality that were not mentally represented during the birth pause. They are inaccessible because the fetus gets rid of them immediately. The fetus, too, has primordial thoughts and feelings from the beginning, such as its awareness of the heartbeat and different sounds. It tries to cope with them by evacuating them to the amniotic fluid, discharging them from the body.

I have previously discussed the mutual affective interaction between the pregnant mother and the imaginary baby in her womb using Raphael-Leff's (2014) concept of the placental paradigm. I believe that the caesura (pause) notion complements this concept of the placental paradigm. Both stress a state where two opposing conditions are handled together. It is only by looking at the mutual emotional exchange between the mother and the imaginary baby and the pause during birth that we can try to conceive those mental states that cannot even be represented unconsciously, that are inaccessible. Bergstein (2013) talks about our capacity to touch primordial parts of the personality that cannot be represented. If the patient's dream or daydream come to or are met with a pause, we can do what the patient cannot and dream for her (Ferro, 2009; Grotstein, 2009; Ogden, 2004). This initiates a movement between different parts of the psyche. The pause also makes a connection between mature thoughts and feelings and the intrauterine life. It serves as a bridge model for inapproachable mental states. For Ms. K, it was my pregnancy, and for Ms. D, it was our interaction in which I was like a pregnant mother and she was like a fetus in the womb, that made it possible for us to contact mental conditions that were inaccessible and incapable of being represented. The analyst's capacity to dream for the patient and his or her intuitions are perhaps the residues of the intrauterine life. Bion (1970) presents intuition by paralleling it to physicians' use of their sight, touch, smell, and auditory senses, further adding to this mix the embryological intuition. The intuition Bion talks about is an element next to scientific thought; it is the ability to reach to a process-centered thought from a content/subject-centered thought. We listen to what is in the cleft, beyond the spoken, and hear more than the sounds words make (Parsons, 2007).

CHAPTER 15

Technical challenges with bereavement in the course of an ongoing analysis*

Işıl Vahip

As Freud (1917e) stated long ago in "Mourning and melancholia," adult mourning involves a slow process of revisiting, reviewing, and transforming the mourner's emotional investment in the images of the lost object. The work of mourning refers to an internal encounter between the images of the lost object and the corresponding self-images of the mourner. Freud differentiated melancholia, a pathological form, from normal mourning.

> Melancholia … borrows some of its features from mourning, and the others from the process of regression from narcissistic object-choice to narcissism. It is on the one hand, like mourning, a reaction to the real loss of a loved object; but over and above this, it is marked by a determinant which is absent in normal mourning or which, if it is present, transforms the latter into pathological mourning. (p. 250)

Guilt and self-reproach are prominent features of melancholia. The melancholic is convinced that some aspect of his or her self is worthless or defective. Self-critical thoughts can extend to suicidal ideation or acts. In essence, it is the inability to selectively identify with enriching aspects of the representation of the deceased due to excessive ambivalence in the relationship, which leads to melancholia. A total identification occurs and aggression is turned toward the assimilated object representation within the self-representation.

---

* This chapter was originally published as Vahip, I. (2020). Between diagnosis and death. In: S. Akhtar (Ed.), *Loss: Developmental, Cultural, and Clinical Realms* (pp. 206–223). Abingdon, UK: Routledge.

Since Freud's seminal paper, the topic of mourning has taken its place in psychoanalytic papers extensively. Lindemann (1944), Pollock (1961, 1987), Bowlby (1960, 1980), Volkan (1981, 1984), and Horowitz (1990) delineated recognizable stages of mourning and examined the complications that lead to pathology in the mourning process. Klein's work (1940, 1946) contributed to the illumination of the processes of normal mourning. Parkes (1972) described normal grief in adult life in detail. In more recent years, Kernberg (2010) derived conclusions about the normal mourning process from a set of in-depth interviews with widows and widowers, one of the latter a past patient who had lost his spouse and undergone mourning during psychoanalysis, and his own personal experience. He assigned a special role to guilt over lost opportunities (not necessarily over aggression) in the stimulation of reparative impulses.

These writers are among many who have made valuable contributions to the area. I will not dwell on the literature on mourning in general since the focus of this chapter will be the anticipation of loss and the processes it triggers. But before giving a brief summary of the relatively limited number of papers on anticipatory mourning, a note on terminology is needed.

Anticipatory mourning

Mourning and grief are used interchangeably in the literature by some writers, whereas some others conceptualize grief as a "stage" in the beginning of the mourning process. Volkan (1981) uses the word "grief" to name the initial reactions to loss in the process of mourning. Itzkowitz (2001) points at the transitory nature of grief and views mourning as the entire process before letting the deceased go. Similarly, Malawista (2017) differentiates grief, as a state, from mourning, as a process:

> Grief is ... chaotic overwhelming *raw* [emphasis added] state that can include shock, numbness, weeping, longing, irritability, anger, and trouble sleeping and eating .... Mourning, in contrast, is a more complicated ongoing process that is set in motion after a loss, requiring a higher level of abstract thinking to truly comprehend death. (p. 37)

Loss is the trigger for the initiation of mourning. *Anticipatory* mourning, first described by Lindemann (1944), is a complicated concept in this respect. Lindemann introduced the term anticipatory grief to describe the process of mourning triggered by a significant other's placement in a potentially fatal situation such as severe illness or war. When looked at from the "stage" perspective, the mourner goes through some or all phases of grief and some mourning.

S. Levin (1966) noted that a number of patients enter therapy "in what can be called an anticipatory grief reaction," evoked by the anticipation of loss. One patient, a forty-year-old man, started analysis when his eighty-four-year-old father developed heart failure. Anticipatory grief persisted until the father died two years later. Another patient, a thirty-eight-year-old man who had a stormy marriage entered therapy in a state of depression that arose when he learned that his wife had a metastatic malignancy. He used therapy largely as a means of achieving reconciliation with his wife in anticipation of her death.

There are a few more cases of anticipatory mourning that are only mentioned briefly in some papers focusing on other topics. I am not aware of any extensive reports. Horowitz (1990), in an article where he described "schematic change" in self and other during mourning, reported a male patient whose mother was diagnosed with cancer in the second year of his analysis and died a few months later. He explained at length the patient's mourning process after death occurred. Hagman (1995a) presented the case of a thirty-year-old woman whose mother was diagnosed with cancer when she was sixteen years old and died after a seventeen-year course of illness. The patient was one and a half years into the analysis when her mother died. Hagman used this case as an example to his proposition that beyond problems in the resolution of their relationship with the deceased, bereaved persons may suffer from conflicts and deficits that are structurally, genetically, and dynamically similar to other neurotic conditions amenable to analysis. In another article, Hagman (1995b) mentioned another case, a thirty-four-year-old woman who lost her mother during her eighth year in analysis. As the patient had resolved much of her infantile attachment and conflict regarding individuation, her grief did not seem to be complicated. However, when the first anniversary arrived, the residue of her conflicts surfaced and worked through in her ongoing psychoanalysis. Neither Horowitz nor Hagman gave much detail about the period of anticipation before the impending loss.

Schlesinger (2001) wrote on technical handling of the mourning patient but he mentioned anticipatory mourning only once in his paper. He stated that the context of the eventual loss of the analyst and the analysis can be considered as anticipatory mourning in one sense. He pointed at the "immediacy of the feeling and the necessity to deal with it now, not to put it off until the someday when actual separation will occur." However, he did not include the anticipated loss of a significant other to death (p. 123).

Clulow (1991), on the other hand, does not accept a real possibility of anticipatory mourning and states that "fighting for life, it is neither possible nor productive to anticipate death." However, a more commonly shared view seems to be that anticipatory mourning has a protective function of preparing the mourner for the shock of loss. The wide acceptance of this understanding is implicitly present in the literature on mourning even where the term is not used. For example, sudden death, as opposed to an expected loss, is accepted as one of the factors that may complicate mourning. Evoked by the anticipation of loss, anticipatory mourning precedes and paves the way for the anticipated separation and mourning.

I feel I need to note once again that the term anticipatory mourning is a problematic one. As Kernberg (2010) states, "during the struggle for survival, the immediate tasks, keeping hope alive for the dying person and the person who loves him/her, leave little time or mental space for mourning. The working through of these experiences comes later with long-term grieving" (p. 606).

Even so, there is a part of the mourning process which takes place before the actual loss when death is inevitable, although it varies according to the age of the sick person, generation of the sick person (from the previous generation, from the same generation, or from the next generation), nature of the sickness, and the individual psychological factors related to the mourner.

Concerning fatally ill individuals, most of us have ourselves experienced, or observed in significant others, anxiety, denial, anger, guilt, explicit or implicit waves of intense sadness. Denial generally serves as a buffer for the anticipatory mourner more than it does for the usual mourner. He or she is mostly the same person who is functioning as the primary caregiver of the ill person. Mostly, this buffer eases, to some extent, carrying out the hard realistic and psychological duties of caregiving. A severely angry, anxious, or sorrowful caregiver is also burdening for the fatally sick person who is already burdened with symptoms, impairment, and is probably in anticipatory mourning of his or her own death.

In cases of death due to natural causes, anticipatory mourning is becoming the rule rather than the exception, as a result of the sophisticated medical procedures of the twenty-first century that prolong the interval between diagnosis and death. Illness brings the necessity of adaptation to both the sick individual and the significant other(s). Declining health conditions require adjustments to fight the consequences of the illness, and psychological challenges initiate intrapsychic processes, which lead to adaptive or maladaptive outcomes.

The reason that anticipatory mourning did not attract much attention in psychoanalytic literature is perhaps because no distinctive feature seems to differentiate it from the mourning process per se. However, its preparation for the reality of death puts anticipatory mourning in a separate time interval. Whether the significant other is still alive or has been already lost makes a real difference in respect to having or not having the possibility of realization of reparative efforts. I will refer to a case example, which I will name Belgin, to point at the internal and external reparative phenomena. I will first give some background information about the analytic work with the patient from the perspective of resistances against mourning and reflect on one function of mourning, namely the enhancement of psychological growth. I will also try to discuss briefly the technical aspect of the analytic stance during anticipatory mourning. My main aim is to draw attention and evoke questions pertaining to this neglected area in human experience.

A detailed clinical presentation

Background

Belgin was an attractive and clever woman in her mid-forties with a successful career when she sought analysis with me. She was married and had a teenage daughter. She was born and named after a female sibling who had died shortly before. She was assigned the task of saving her parents from depression through keeping the dead child alive in her. This was one of the major factors that disrupted her development of a total self-concept. She experienced two previous sudden losses. In her oedipal years, her grandmother who substantially took part in her care died. In adulthood, her father died in an accident.

Belgin was mentioning about her mother as emotionally and, many times, physically unavailable. In the beginning of her analysis, she was totally denying any role or contribution of her mother in her development. She was strongly holding the idea that she received all the nurturance from her father, whom she idealized. Later, she came to understand him as a depressive and irritable man who could verbally become very abusive toward family members. He had died ten years earlier. Belgin never visited his grave. Indeed, she avoided cemeteries and funerals because she was afraid of dead people.

In short, Belgin came to analysis with a disrupted capacity to mourn and a very restricted ability to tolerate painful affects.

Mother's diagnosis of cancer

Belgin reported the fatal illness of her mother at the end of the first month of her analysis when she heard that a metastatic tumor was detected in her mother. Actually, the diagnosis of cancer had been announced two years earlier. In a short while, I understood that Belgin had regressed to defensive splitting after her mother was diagnosed with cancer and started displaying signs of manic defense to ward off the reality of the impending death of her mother. With omnipotent control, she abandoned her before she was abandoned: She argued with her over a minor issue and then ceased contact despite her mother's efforts. She thought, "I have no mother, no father. I am completely free. I can do as I wish." She even announced to some friends that "Mother is dead for me from now on." She spent the next two years constantly engaging in animating actions. For example, she entertained herself by going to this or that party; she made a lot of new friends but never got close to any of them; she went to concerts, took long trips, etc. It was the complications of this state that brought her to psychoanalysis. Even though she denied any regret or feeling of loss, stating she was "very happy with the way she lived these past two years," she was seeking protection from more destructive complications of her acts.

Learning about the metastasis

When Belgin learned about the metastasis at the end of the first month of analysis, she mentioned her "fear of loss" in the next session and brought a dream. In her dream, she was hosted at a friend's house and there was a conversation about money. She was considering leaving earlier than she planned "without taking the rest of the money." Noting her perception of psychoanalysis as equivalent to being a guest and realizing her strong urge to act out on manic defense, I was warned to keep an eye on a therapeutic alliance.

By that time, I had noticed that she had been sometimes giving me a slightly excessive amount of money. My pointing this out had not changed her attitude and I had been continuing to be careful to sort it out whenever she repeated it. I pointed at the similarity between the dream and this pattern. This intervention initiated her talking about her pattern in close relationships. She experienced anger that she was always the giver of money, attention, care, etc. and others were the receptive side. Soon her mother became the main target of her verbal attacks in the sessions in this respect. She believed that her mother was weak and in need of Belgin but she did not need anyone herself. She was projecting her hungry, needy self to her mother in order to maintain her grandiose self.

Manic defense in reaction to separation from the analyst

Developmentally, manic defense (Klein, 1935) protects the infant in the depressive position from the danger of the loss of the object along with other defenses such as splitting, reparation, and regression to the paranoid–schizoid position. Later in life, usually together with a group of defenses including denial and omnipotent control, it emerges to ward off the reality of loss.

Manic defense formed resistance in Belgin's analytic process in reaction to separations from the analyst and this provided the opportunity for interpretation and understanding, to pave the way for mourning of the losses of earlier idealized and devalued self and object images.

The first separation occurred during the third month of analysis. I announced in advance that we would have to skip our sessions for a week. Belgin reacted indifferently on the surface. At the very end of the last session before my departure, she informed me briefly that she would be on vacation for ten days starting on the date of my return to the sessions. Not surprisingly, Belgin's reaction to separation was to deny her need for the analyst and escape to manic defense.

When Belgin came back, she brought two dreams. In the first one, she was coming to my office and finding out I was not present. She reported the second dream in hypomanic-like excitement. She was inside a ball, searching for something, opening one door after another with quick movements. The analyst was outside the ball. She gave Belgin a duty to perform inside. Belgin was tied to her with a rope. In case of danger, the analyst would pull her.

Belgin was projecting onto me the split object and the corresponding fearful, dependent, and controlling self-representation. What fascinated me was the rope in the dream connecting her to me like an umbilical cord reflecting her yet-to-be completed psychological birth (Mahler et al., 1975) in her analysis. To endure separation and loss without regression to splitting of self and object representations and to mourn like an adult, Belgin needed the fostering of the separation–individuation process and attainment of a higher degree of object constancy.

Optimal distance and object constancy

Akhtar (1991, 1992) described fantasy of a tether pertaining to object constancy. The main issue is distance vs. safety in the "tether fantasy" as it is in Belgin's dream after our first separation, where both the anxiety and the pleasure in her wish to distance from me are revealed. The rope in the dream, like "[T]he imagined tether ... clearly served a defensive purpose insofar as it minimized the anxiety of separation while permitting [her] autonomous function" (Akhtar, 1991, p. 271). Her elation and grandiosity while reporting the dream and her associations were also typical of a tether fantasy.

Tethering images appeared in Belgin's later dreams and fantasies giving clues about her relationship with her mother's representation and also with the analyst's representation. One example is a dream that she brought in the session following that of the rope dream. Belgin was standing on a pier (wharf). She was going to go on a trip by sea. A storm erupted and as the ship was sinking, an expert approached from behind saying, "If you rush, you cannot do it. There is a technique for it," and applied a technique on the *cordage*.

Zeavin (2016) views dreams "as a statement about the relationship of the analytic dyad" and thinks "more of the dreams as a reflection and commentary on the ongoing psychoanalytic process, representing the patient's internal world as it plays out in the workings of the transference and counter-transference" (p. 85). This dream also reflected the emergence of the analyst as a new object helping Belgin and also giving her the opportunity to identify, showing her the technique to apply on the tether that represented Belgin's optimal distance issue. The compromise in the dream was that the ship was saved but the procedure was a slow one and winter came, so Belgin could not go on the wished-for trip. At one level, the wished-for trip represents manic defense and the ship with its promised joy represents the libidinal mother. Belgin's wish was to recapture the bond with the blissful symbiotic mother. She aggressively defended against merger by sinking the boat in her dream. The second part of the dream, where the analyst appears as an expert, offers a solution. From a developmental point of view, the libidinal mother is needed to neutralize Belgin's aggression.

In the dream, Belgin was not fully engaging in the gradual work but watching carefully with hope and also disappointment with the slowness. Slowness was contrary to her usual flurry of action-taking behavior. In her analysis, she was struggling to find an optimal distance with her analyst. Nevertheless, her bond with the analyst as a new object was developing, and simultaneously time was taking her to the point of confronting nature's order, dark days of winter—grief. I will discuss later the themes of death in these and other dreams.

Tether phantasy was reactivated again later (quite some time after Belgin's mother's death) as a metaphor of the rope of a kite: "When one winds the rope in a hurry, it gets tangled. You cannot fly the kite with ease next time. Psychoanalysis helps to sort it out and teaches you to wind and unwind the rope properly. I am much better with it now but I need more work. I want to fly my kite with pleasure, without killing or getting killed." Again, this expression is condensed with many meanings, one of which is her conflictual relationship with the representation of her mother. What I find worth noting here is Belgin's utilization of the ongoing intrapsychic process pertaining to identification with the functions of the analyst.

Toward mending

Toward the end of her first year in analysis, Belgin repeated in transference her escape to manic defense, her subsequent rage and primitive guilt. She displayed her need for omnipotent, magical control of the analyst.

I went away for three weeks and although she was in town and went on with her daily routine, Belgin did not make herself present in her sessions for three weeks following my vacation. When she came, she asked with a slight tone of anger in her voice "Why didn't you call me?" Our exploration brought to light her disappointment over "being forgotten." When she could experience her rage toward her unavailable, rejecting childhood mother in transference, she howled to me, "How come you did not care and say to yourself, 'What happened to Belgin? Is she *dead* or something?'" (This Turkish phrase of reproach is commonly used in daily language not for actual death, but for lack of curiosity and caring about someone and his or her whereabouts.)

With interpretation and some working through, this became a "crucial juncture" (Klein, 1946) experience in her analysis, bringing together Belgin's opposite self and object images so that she could mend her internal world. She could experience and express genuine guilt feelings over her grandiose, unempathic attitudes: "I used to accuse my family members for not being able to accomplish what I did accomplish. Now I can understand them and I have a bad conscience because of what I did to them." It also enabled the initiation of grief over the impending death of her mother.

In Klein's sense, Belgin's process of mourning was enabled with the relinquishment of manic defense and the working through of the depressive position. In Mahler's sense, it was enabled with the attainment of a higher degree of object constancy and a more stable sense of self.

Bergman (1996) states that:

> Seeing object constancy as a process rather than an end point makes it comparable to reaching the depressive position in the Kleinian sense … reaching the depressive position implies a process of mourning, which Mahler has also described a characteristic of the rapprochement subphase … In the thinking of Kleinians, reaching the depressive position is like object constancy in Mahler's sense, a life task. In Kleinian thinking there is always a danger of regression into the paranoid position, which is similar to the rapprochement crisis. (p. 63)

Helen Meyers (1996), on the other hand, views object constancy as a capacity to maintain constant objects, which does not get lost once obtained, rather than a specific object relationship. Regardless of each perspective, the key point in Belgin's case was the growing libidinal aspect of the relationship with the object representation. Settlage (1993) and Settlage et al. (1990) see object constancy as essential for empathy and working through of object loss. Attainment of a higher degree of object constancy was a prerequisite for Belgin to mourn.

After accomplishing the above psychological tasks, Belgin could relinquish excess denial and could proceed to get better prepared for the forthcoming reality of loss. She was going to have approximately half a year before her mother passed away. During these six months, she would spend more quality time with her mother in contrast to her attitude during the first year of her analysis. With this I do not say that denial was gone completely. Belgin's analysis proceeded with regressive and progressive movements as expected. Piecemeal, the mourning process also progressed with its symptoms, denial, and waves of painful feelings. Now I will try to explain some elements of Belgin's anticipatory mourning, referring to clinical material from the whole one and a half years of her analysis prior to her mother's death.

Themes of death

Belgin did not openly mention the topic during the first year of her analysis. However, symbols such as winter, ice age, tsunami, disturbing images of white sheets (when Muslims die, they are wrapped and buried in white winding sheets) appeared in Belgin's dreams, and past or current deaths of people other than her mother appeared in her associations.

For example, the rope and the cordage dreams that came consecutively include, in addition to her optimal distance issue, evidence of her unresolved past losses. Associating to the immobilization and winter themes in the cordage dream, Belgin expressed her fear of death, her previous object losses, and childhood and adulthood memories of white-sheeted bodies (of her grandmother and her father). Giovacchini (1967) and Volkan (1981) reported dreams with frozen elements addressing complicated mourning. The winter element, when added to the previous session's rope dream where Belgin was inside a ball opening the doors and searching for something, is similar to the dream of Giovacchini's (1967) patient who was seeing frozen bodies in the rooms of a castle. Giovacchini described how the neither dead nor alive introject led to a specific ego state. Belgin's unconscious was populated with such introjects (of her grandmother, her father, and also the induced introject of the previous dead sibling).

When later Belgin's mother's health deteriorated further, closed spaces such as rooms with earth floors started appearing in Belgin's dreams that reminded her of graves, nonetheless without associations including her mother's impending death. She also brought dreams of being left by her spouse and feeling very sad and a little anxious.

Putting death into words

Loss and mourning are not exceptional during psychoanalysis, mostly as consequences of the intrapsychic change in the patient. Although not a usual occurrence, the death of a significant other may also take place during analysis. Reports of such cases are scarce when compared to the number of cases with past losses. There is much to learn from Volkan's work (1981, 1984) on normal and complicated mourning and his beautifully handled rich clinical examples. However, it is curious that not many psychoanalytic writers have addressed directly the technical handling of mourning. Schlesinger (2001) wrote a paper addressing this issue. He highlighted common technical problems, which may impede the spontaneous flow of mourning in three clinical contexts (loss of a significant other, loss of part of self, and eventual loss of analyst and analysis). He stressed the analyst's responsibility to protect the mourning process and the technical considerations derived from this responsibility. He warned against defensiveness in the analyst against mourning in the patient.

The mourning process may need protection both against the patient's efforts to minimize pain by denying loss, thus seeming to make mourning superfluous, and protection also from problems the analyst may have in dealing with loss (Schlesinger, 2001, p. 119).

Among the forces that may interfere with the analyst's ability to discriminate whether to intervene technically or allow the mourning process to continue unimpeded, of course, are the transference and countertransference of the analyst. The intrusions may take several forms. Some clinicians have difficulty tolerating the seeming passivity of remaining in a posture of witnessing; they feel impelled to intervene, to "do something." More common, perhaps, is the wish to spare our loved ones, including our patients and ourselves, pain of any kind, and in particular, prolonged pain, and we may feel impelled to alleviate our distress by intervening to ameliorate their suffering. It takes great discipline to allow a patient (or a loved one) to experience the process of grieving and mourning fully and to appreciate, and help them appreciate, the importance of doing so. The tendency to interpret inappropriately at such times, or even to offer unneeded support, perhaps better called by its right name, "meddling," may be almost irresistible for the analyst who has also become attached to the patient and for whom empathy has drifted too close to identification (Schlesinger, 2001, p. 124).

Nonetheless, while working with a patient during the anticipatory period, there is not much to refer to for drawing implications except the above-mentioned studies, and maybe a few more that I am not aware of. One has to lean on one's general knowledge of psychoanalytic technique and of mourning.

I will now give more detailed vignettes from the clinical material to provoke questions in the mind of the reader. The first example is from the first year of analysis while Belgin's emotions were still restricted. The second example is from the beginning of the second year. The third one is when eventually I addressed her mother's death openly.

Example 1

During the seventh month, Belgin brought a dream in which she was very tired and lying in a bed under white sheets. Mother was colorfully dressed and having fun at a party, behaving inappropriately. As to the manifest dream content, I did not express the aspect of my understanding about the projection of the manic defense in response to the fatal illness of her mother and the reversal of roles in her dream. I restricted myself to suggest Belgin's identification with her childhood "dead mother" (A. Green, 1980) who was void of maternal functions such as devotion, selflessness, survival, soothing, nourishment, etc. due to her own inner world of grief, anhedonia, and deadness; and to refer to the induced introject of the dead child in Belgin's internal world. The main helpful device during this period in her analysis was to concentrate on the transference manifestations of manic defense. Besides, Belgin was not ready to deal with the forthcoming loss of her mother.

Example 2

Associations of accusatory women reappeared at the beginning of the second year. Belgin was also expressing irrational guilt over issues around her mother's illness. Soon she started bringing dreams of vital tasks that she had neglected and therefore could not fully accomplish. Sometimes a child, but more frequently a mother figure, was in danger because of Belgin's neglect in her dreams. The compromise at the end was that both mother and child survived, but a defect in the child was the sequel. Together with oedipal connotations that I will not dwell on, the issue of saving or not being able to save a mother and a baby from a dangerous position was evident. The object of her concern was not one person but a mother–baby dyad. Belgin's separation guilt (Modell, 1965) was reactivated. She could not accomplish fully her separation–individuation from her psychologically needy parental figures in her childhood. Now attempting to complete the developmental task in her analysis, she was again facing similar conflict realized by her mother's unavoidable needy position. Linking these two situations was not enough because the intensified survival guilt due to the forthcoming death of her mother was producing resistance against deeper work on the dynamics of being the beneficiary of the death of the previous child. Another deep root of guilt was excessive aggression derived from frustration of childhood developmental needs.

During this period, I made my empathic presence audible through touching on how her mother's illness burdened her emotionally and made it difficult to work through her separation guilt and survival guilt. I felt I had a dilemma with two dead ends: Without touching the issue of mother's impending death, my explanations were inadequate. She was defecting/sacrificing part of her self (as evident in the defected baby dreams) in order to save her mother in fantasy. Was I colluding with the patient and sacrificing part of her analysis? On the other hand, interpretation of her denial would put me in a position of a fortuneteller, moreover a heartless one. Most importantly, what good would it do for the psychoanalytic work? My subjective sense was it would make rigid her defenses.

Etezady (2001), reviewing Schlesinger's paper, agrees with him that sometimes resistances provide important protection and we need to appreciate and respect them; in such instances, understanding what this protection is guarding against is more essential. For an individual who is faced with a real threat of losing a significant other to death, the more crucial thing is the experience of being an as-good-as possible caregiver and also the experience of trying to increase the mutually gratifying moments while there is still time. During the course of psychoanalysis, there will always be other chances for interpretations, which will release the repressed aggression whatever its origins are.

Example 3

Toward the middle of the second year of analysis, Belgin reported that her mother had severe aches and called, "I'm dying." Gripped by pain of grief and anxiety, Belgin had rushed to her. The next-door neighbor, a nurse with a baby, had arrived before she did and had already eased her mother's pain with medication. Belgin had felt relief and thought to herself, "Good. The baby will raise my mother's morale." This association implied Belgin's core conflict over being born as a replacement child.

She continued with deeply felt grief, "How will I and my mother say goodbye to each other? It's very difficult for both of us." This was the first time she openly talked about bidding farewell.

Then she brought another story of a woman who was threatened with death when she was delivering her baby but somehow survived, which again implied her intertwined survival and separation guilt but now this issue was used defensively against affective experiences of mourning.

At that point, I said, "And there is the impending death of your mother." After a short silence, she echoed my words with a very sad but relieved tone of voice, "My mother's death ..."

Schlesinger (1995) stresses that it is important

> to diagnose the ways in which the patient attempts to restore stability ... The analyst's immediate aim should be to prolong this period of instability by ... interfering with ... the efforts of the patient to seal over the incident and restore the status quo ante. (p. 663)

My interfering with her efforts to seal over her grief helped to prolong the affective intensity of Belgin's fear that she would be devastated. My intervention was effectual because she was now ready to hear the word "death." Hearing that her analyst was not denying the reality had a soothing effect and helped her to see that talking openly about her mother's death is not a shameful crime. In cases of fatal illness, almost everybody, kindly (and in magical thinking), refrains from touching the harsh reality.

Theoretically, the analyst must be free, as in other socially taboo topics such as sexuality, aggression, etc., of social restraints and put into words at some point when she feels it is necessary. But how can we be sure that it is the right time? In the above example, the result proved good my decision to verbalize. I understood that it was not too early. But how do I know that it was not somewhat late? Such questions are always relevant and, I believe, must be kept in mind in order to free space for alternative ways of looking at clinical material.

Kanwal (2017) reflects on "sounds and silence" (p. 174):

> The role of speaking as well as sharing silence is obviously important from a therapeutic perspective. Ours is a listening and talking cure. When it comes to bereavement, the nuances of our patients' need for silence as well as for things to be spoken about are what we try to be attuned toward ... silence may represent being alone, and speaking represents a relational context, the capacity to be able to speak (to someone) about one's grief can be an important signal of the progression of the mourning process. (pp. 175, 176)

Displacement of anger

Later, as her mother got worse, I started hearing in the sessions that Belgin became intolerant and mildly irritable in her daily life. The displacement of anger in transference is not an unusual phenomenon for a patient in analysis and needs the attention of the analyst, but I was convinced that Belgin's displacement was much more related with the upcoming death of her mother.

Soon she could verbalize her frustration and anger as well as her fading of hope and intensifying feelings of despair and grief in sentences such as, "Perhaps I will get used to death. We will have to accept it. So much effort for my mother … Still she is not well." She reported that she attended a funeral. She realized that the floor lamp in my room was removed to another corner and a new lamp now occupied its place. She said, "The old are replaced by the new. We will all die one day."

Readjusting the relationship

When someone close falls seriously ill or is diagnosed with cancer, one is forced to readjust to the realistic needs such as taking him or her to the doctor, supplying medications, providing physical care, etc. It is possible that this can take place somewhat mechanically, avoiding grief and mourning, as in Belgin's case during the first year of her analysis. A second possibility is its taking place together with affective experiences of alternating hope and despair. An oscillation between the two ends of this spectrum is a more expected consequence. Some features of this period consist of efforts to help fight the illness (magical thoughts are not infrequent, leading to alternative methods to rescue the person from death when medical science reaches its limits), and devoted caring not only for the well-feeling and comfort but also for the concerns and wishes of the fatally ill person.

Early in her analysis, after hearing the metastasis and mentioning "fear of loss," Belgin had a dream in which her mother was accusing her of not calling and caring. Her guilt lacked the affective component of a deeper concern for the object and carried a rather primitive quality leading to fears of punishment. Still, she acted on the manifest content of the dream next day and went to visit her mother and restored contact. This "day precipitate" (Kelman, 1975) can be understood as submission to the orders coming from a not-depersonified superego with accusatory, punishing features. But it was also a sign that Belgin had a capacity at least for material attempts at reparation. After one month, her mother had some symptoms and Belgin expressed verbally "devastating sadness." Again, the emphasis was on her devastation. But her anticipation of and her fear from sadness were sincere.

Starting with the second year of analysis, Belgin could make her move toward deeper affective experiences in parallel to the changes in her internal world. She engaged in long conversations with her mother. With her expanded capacity for empathy, she realized that her mother was mourning over the years that she could have spent better. She observed and accompanied the old woman in this endeavor. I sensed that her mother was also in an anticipatory mourning process with her life coming to an end.

When death became imminent, her mother's symptoms got severe and Belgin suspended the sessions in order to devote her time. She came back after two weeks and made a detailed chronological summary for me. Her summary consisted mostly of her mother's fluctuating health condition and the medical procedures applied accordingly. Additionally, it included the exacerbations of the long-term tensions between family members. Scattered in her reporting, I also heard the mutual verbal exchange of love and gratitude between the old woman and Belgin. I sensed that Belgin was able to receive her mother's approval and appreciation, an effective ingredient for her to deepen her sense of goodness, of womanhood, of motherhood. The following sessions were also filled with emotions.

After a short while, worsening of her mother's health accelerated and Belgin suspended her sessions once again to engage in the care of her mother. She came back after three weeks and I learned that her mother had died one week earlier. She said she felt the need for her sessions but she also felt that coming to her sessions was a luxury under these conditions, hence she did not come sooner.

She reported the events chronologically and in detail. On one level, I considered it as part of her mourning over her loss of mother. This type of talking, that is, repeating with every visitor what had happened to the deceased just before death or the victim of severe illness, accident, etc., is common. It functions to keep the other "alive" and at the same time as a reminder of the loss. Additionally, a need to restore continuity of the mind after the rupture—created by loss and separation—may play a role. For Belgin, who had to experience ruptures due to some childhood traumas, maintaining continuity was especially important.

Belgin's reviewing of events, tensions in the family, and her own approach to all that had happened was mixed with her accompanying perceptions and feelings. Her detailed review with me served for her not only to ensure continuity of her relationship with her mother's and her analyst's representation but also to show me her newly developed functions and her wish to get my approval while she was dwelling more deeply in the big task of grief and mourning.

Photographs and looking at the past

Soon after Belgin had started to experience feelings of grief upon the alleviation of denial, at the end of the first year of her analysis, she started to look through old photographs. She brought some childhood memories to her sessions. Some were good memories with her mother. Some were about very disturbing events in the family; Belgin understood that she was deeply traumatized by them. At the same time she considered, now being an adult woman, how her mother must have been traumatized, too. However, this attitude of hers at first lacked depth in the affective component. It was more on the cognitive level; she was trying to find the possible rationales underneath her mother's incapacities. It functioned as a defense against intense negative feelings toward her dying mother.

Later Belgin started to examine the photographs, searching for signs about how her mother was feeling at the time the photograph was taken and also how Belgin herself was feeling in the same time period. She examined the faces in the childhood photographs of her mother, too. She looked closely at the child face of her mother and the adults' faces in the surroundings.

Belgin's interest in photographs surpassed a mourner's hypercathexis of the lost object's representation and efforts to keep the memories "alive" with the deceased. She was curious about her own past which affected her personality makeup, and she was curious about her mother's past experiences that affected her mothering. This curiosity was hand in hand with her visual incorporation of her mother. In short, there was surely a dialectic relationship between her anticipatory mourning process over her mother's impending death and her analytic process that inevitably included the piecemeal work of mourning over what she had missed during her traumatic childhood years.

Gradually, the affective component deepened. Belgin collected further information about her mother, this time directly talking with relatives, neighbors, etc. Some told her that they enjoyed exchanging ideas with her mother and benefited from the old woman's advice. She remembered with regret that her mother had given some wise words of advice to adult Belgin about practical life situations, but instead of assigning them value, she kept her ear open to some "idealized" others who often led her to act in ways that brought negative consequences. This time, her love and appreciation of the old woman dominated and her guilt feelings carried the quality of the depressive position. She was also mourning over her lost opportunities of deeper human contact and genuine closeness not only with her mother, but also in general.

Belgin attempted to turn to her mother as an identification object from whom she tried to "learn" how to mourn a maternal figure. She grew curious about her mother's relationship and conflicts with her own mother, that is, Belgin's grandmother. Her mother shared her hurtful feelings and anger but at the same time verbally expressed gratitude toward her own mother upon Belgin's inquiries.

Fulfilling the last wishes

Kernberg (2010) writes, "Grief creates a powerful reparative impulse, strengthening the internalized object relation with the lost object as an aspect of preconscious experience, and fosters the development of new value systems, a part of superego, and particularly ego ideal structures" (p. 612). He states that, as a consequence, fulfilling the wishes and hopes of the deceased becomes a moral obligation as part of the mourner's superego, not as an impersonal aspect of superego demands and prohibitions, but, rather, preserved as highly personalized relations with the lost object.

I wonder if the precursors can be traced back to the anticipatory mourning period. On two different occasions, Belgin sent messages to some relatives who were dear to her mother. She was not on speaking terms with them and she did not attend the meetings herself. Her conscious aim was to provide her mother (and the invited persons) pleasure and a symbolic bidding farewell between the two parties. It was also her own bidding farewell to her mother.

During her last hospitalization, Belgin's mother desperately wanted to go home and drink Turkish coffee at her small table as she used to do in her daily routine. Belgin was aware that there was nothing more to be done at the hospital. She took the initiative and asked the opinion of the doctors if it would be OK to externalize her under the condition that the same palliative care would be provided. She made the decision-making a shared responsibility by including two other members of the family.

Belgin was left behind at the hospital to take care of the paperwork while others transported her mother. When Belgin arrived at her mother's home, she found her sitting at the small table, exhausted. She sipped a few drops from her coffee and then went to bed, never to rise again. The relatives told that she had postponed her coffee saying, "I want Belgin to see me sitting here, drinking my coffee."

Belgin's tearful reporting of their mutuality of love and gratitude was a sign of the developing representation of a good enough mother, which was replacing gradually the split idealized and devalued object images.

We know that such memories are remembered and sometimes told and retold by mourners with much emotion during the acute stage of mourning and over the years. The availability of libidinal investment in the object, as well as in the self, supports healthy narcissism. This availability is important for the mourning process but not enough to ensure protection from complications of mourning especially when the libidinal aspect was short of adequately neutralizing the aggressive aspect during the early years of life.

Belgin's early self and object representations were contaminated with excessive aggression and they were not successfully mended with the libidinally invested self and object representations leaving her prone to splitting. When she came to analysis, she was projecting "all good" to her idealized father and "all bad" to her devalued mother. In her relationships and in transference, her omnipotence and her denial of aggression were dominating. Gradually she gained a more realistic view of her parents. Her continuing coming to terms with her aggression enabled her to some extent to understand and tolerate the ongoing frustrating external events in the family without acting on them. These real events evoked the memories of her mother's past failures repetitively. Attempting to maintain her libidinal investment, she rationalized her mother's attitude and "understood" her. She was far from forgiveness; this was rather an attempt at protecting the good mother representation. More importantly, her newly developing self-concept as a "good person" was becoming a source of gratification and received approval and reassurance from her mother.

As her mother's symptoms got more and more severe, Belgin's grandiose self was activated, but this time in a rather adaptive way. She gratified her narcissistic needs through placing herself in a "higher" and understanding position toward the "selfishness and thoughtlessness" of others. This kept her from engaging in emotionally intense fights as she did before. Instead, she was in the role of peacemaking in many instances. She utilized her analyst as a witness to her frustrations and pain, but also the course of her development. Shortly after her mother's death, narcissistic rage toward her was poured into the sessions with accompanying grandiose fantasies. Narcissistic rage and intense feelings of grief alternated. However, she did not regress altogether to denial of her need for her mother's love. She did not disown her love of her mother.

Concluding remarks

The psychological makeup of the mourner profoundly affects the course and outcome of the mourning process. Every analyst deals with resistances against mourning in everyday practice according to his or her theoretical background. When an anticipated death is hanging in the air as a harsh reality, how will it come to the floor and be worked through? As I tried to demonstrate in Examples 2 and 3, Belgin was bringing tempting material about her deeply rooted conflicts but utilized this in the service of denial of the impending loss. This way, patient and analyst may collude in denial and so-called "psychoanalytic work" may be used as a defense against mourning. This point needs attention and tact.

The dynamics of the relationship between the deceased and the mourner are another important factor. The more conflictual the relationship, the more aggression is present. Management of anger is sometimes one of the key issues for the anticipatory mourner. Anger, when directed verbally or behaviorally at the dying person, has realistic consequences for the ill and this will intensify conscious or unconscious guilt feelings of the mourner sooner or later. When disruptive behavior is directed at others, such as family members, the mourner's sources of social support are restricted. If the mourner is one of the primary caregivers, he or she will be either burdened with more practical responsibilities and duties or will be excluded from at least some of them and left in isolation to some extent. The sick person may also get deprived of the care which might be of a higher quality from a "team" formed by a larger number of people in cooperation. (Although I did not address directly the cultural aspect of mourning/anticipatory mourning and care of the elderly and the ill, this chapter is clearly written in a cultural context.)

On the other hand, reparation is not possible without owning and working through aggression. A useful guide here is the sincerity of the reparative efforts of the patient. For example, in Belgin's case, who engaged herself in sincere acts, I believe that attempts on the analyst's part to interpret or confront her with her lack of feelings of anger toward mother during the anticipatory mourning would deprive her of the affective experience of libidinal aspect of her object relationship with the representation of her mother in the presence of her analyst. I would be attacking the goodness in her. Working through of the depressive position, which is activated during mourning, is not possible without the libidinal aspect. Interpretations of aggressive aspects are definitely required when they block the way. However, silent respect for even the slightest reparative effort is as valuable.

CHAPTER 16

Spiritual elements in psychotherapy and psychoanalysis*

T. Byram Karasu

There is no organized and structured school of spiritual psychotherapy; that would be anti-spiritual by definition. Spiritual therapy may frame other therapies but is itself frameless. This means that it cannot be contained by the human mind, just as the mind may comprehend something about itself but does not reach the ineffable depths of self (i.e., the soul). As the philosopher Karl Jaspers observed in his *Way to Wisdom* (1954), man is fundamentally more than he can know about himself, because the way to self-knowledge is twofold: the person "as object of inquiry, and as existence endowed with a freedom that is inaccessible to inquiry" (p. 63). It is the latter that is both the subject and the object of spiritual psychotherapy. As such, this type of therapy does have its own tenets, not as principles of treatment but as principles of *existence*. Moreover, although certain nonspecific therapeutic practices may emanate from its precepts, spiritual therapy at best becomes not what the spiritual therapist does, but what he is, in Lasch's (1978) words, a virtuous man who has little to repent of or apologize for at the end of his life.

How does one arrive at this exalted state of virtue? According to the fourth of Chopra's (1994) seven spiritual laws of success—the Law of Least Effort—such an individual tries to do nothing; he just is. He accepts people, situations, circumstances, and events as they occur, life as it unfolds. He does not struggle against the moment, in the same way that "Grass doesn't try to grow, it just grows. Fish don't try to swim, they just swim. Flowers don't try to bloom,

*This chapter was originally published as Karasu, T. B. (1999). Spiritual psychotherapy. *American Journal of Psychotherapy, 53*(2): 143–282. https://doi.org/10.1176/appi.psychotherapy.1999.53.2.143. It is reprinted with permission.

they bloom. Birds don't try to sing, they just sing" (p. 53). For the therapist who aspires to such a soulful and spiritual existence, it reflects a natural and quiescent state, a union with nature characterized by the principles of fewest words (i.e., profound silence) and least actions (i.e., inner harmony).

Venturing beyond the boundaries of science and medicine, life of the spirit and soul is directed toward devotional belief in the influence of the ethereal, incorporeal, and immaterial aspects of beings, as distinguished from the influence of one's physical, concrete, and evidential existence. Comparing the essence of both these perspectives, the sacred and the non-sacred, it can be said the spirit is to the soul what blood is to the body. More specifically, spiritual psychotherapy conceptualizes care and compassion within the dual contexts of love and belief beyond oneself—love of others, love of work, love of belonging, belief in the sacred, belief in unity, and belief in transformation. In this context, a clinician who belongs to any school of psychotherapy or profession can become a spiritual therapist, *if* regardless of his own ardent allegiances, he conducts his practice according to these six tenets of transcendence.

An overview of the vast variety of psychotherapies of the last century reveals their attempts to resolve the individual's past and present conflicts and remedy his or her deficits by three major change agents: cognitive mastery, affective experience, and behavioral modification (Karasu, 1977). Yet even when this entire armamentarium is applied, psychological conflicts are relatively resolved, deficits filled, and defects corrected, ultimately patients still experience post-therapeutic dysphoria, a loss of meaning or sense of emptiness, a non-luminous hollow. These diverse strategies have shed limited light and left patients bereft, because in the process of treatment (if not the psychopathology itself) the person's soul has been neglected and spiritual connections severed.

Of course, all therapies may provide at least transitory relief simply by the presence of someone who is interested in the patient, provides an explanation for his or her condition, offers some semblance of comfort and support, and even expressly teaches coping mechanisms in the form of alternative modes of thinking and behavior. However, traditional approaches eventually reach an impasse, a place where the therapist himself resides and in which he and his patients can become irretrievably trapped. This invariably occurs when confident clinicians, regardless of their respective schools, present themselves as prototypes of health and salvation for their recipients to emulate. Alas, they are limited by an inherent constraint: they can take their patients only as far as they themselves have come. Then the question—and the quest—remain: How does the therapist get beyond this barrier; more aptly, how does he venture toward, and eventually attain, soulful and spiritual existence?

A soulful and spiritual existence

The soul and the spirit are frequently used interchangeably as equally rarified concepts. Although they reside neither in consciousness nor unconsciousness, they may be "found" (i.e., infused) in objects and events from the sacred to the secular, from the divine to the ordinary. They are related as the sacred to the secular, from the divine to the ordinary. They are related as transpersonal abstractions but are also quite different. According to Hillman (1992), the soul calls one "down and in" whereas the spirit calls one "up and out" (p. 26). The soul immerses itself within the world through intimacy, relationships, pleasure, and pain, and aspires to egoless attachment and engagement. It views human suffering and illness with reverence, by "honoring symptoms as a voice of the soul" (Moore, 1992, p. 3). It is personal as much as transpersonal to the extent that it cultivates depth and sacredness in everyday life. Alternatively, the spirit aims for the impersonal and toward detachment. As Kovel (1991) has pointed out, "*Spirit* is the more general term, connotating a relation between the person and the universe; while *soul* is the more self-referential term" (p. 33).

Moreover, the soul is the seat of human emotions and sentiments with all its lowly limitations and descents, whereas the spirit is the repository of the moral and religious; it has the highest inspirations and can soar. In addition, the spirit's road can be straight and well paved, while the soul's road is more rough and roundabout. Moore (1992) refers to the latter as meandering, likened to "the odd path of Tristan, who travels on the sea without oar or rudder making his way by playing his harp" (p. 259). Based on the myths of the ages, Campbell (1949) suggests a more difficult and demanding route, referring to "a dangerous journey of the soul, with obstacles to be passed" (p. 366). Moore (1994) clearly contrasts their dual courses:

> In spiritual literature the path to God or to perfection is often depicted as an ascent. It may be done in stages, but the goal is apparent, the direction fixed, and the way direct. Images of the soul's path are quite different. It may be a labyrinth, full of dead-ends ... or an odyssey, in which the goal is clear but the way is much longer and more twisted. (p. 259)

In sum, they are both archetypally distinct entities from the physical body and physical world. They are immaterial in nature but can make their appearance in all earthly matter. The soul gazes at life inwardly, while spirit gazes beyond it. The discovery of our true self is only possible by allowing our souls to wander and wend its way, and however circuitous, bring us closer to our spiritual selves. Whereas the soulful and the spiritual each may be pursued separately, one opens the door for the other. In tandem, they form a divine union.

At the same time, the therapist must tend to the patient's soul as well as his own. In early Christianity, tending needs of people was known as *cura animarum*, the cure of the soul, and the role of the curate was to maintain the individual in a religious and spiritual context, to sustain him for the inevitabilities of fate. The care of the psyche and soul thus began as a sacred act by its practitioners and priests. Then medicine and psychology as secular science started to differentiate the two. In fact, these sciences removed the soul from their vocabulary by objectifying subjective experiences. They even went one step further, emphasizing the individuation of the person at the expense of belonging and believing. Thus modern man was subjected to the demise of his soul-making connections. As a result, not only did the original illnesses not disappear, but they were compounded by the individual's lack of spirituality and faith. The colloquial cure was worse than the disease itself. In ancient Greece, "therapy" meant service to the gods. In modern psychology, however, it has more often meant coming to terms with the death of God—and its success has brought with it the impoverishment of the soul. Indeed Moore (1992) refers to "loss of soul" as the great malady of the twentieth century (p. xi).

The ways to soulfulness and spiritually inhere in our basic ontological disposition. Yet these fundamental capacities tend to get overlooked, if not destroyed, in contemporary living. Thus they need to be cultivated if they are to be preserved, bearing in mind that they are separate, albeit often overlapping, and at times, even contradictory roads. More specifically, the way to soulfulness is achieved by transformation of the extraordinary to the ordinary—and its only required ingredient is *love*. Comparably, the way to spiritually is achieved by transformation of the ordinary to the extraordinary—and its only required ingredient is *belief*. Taken together, they respectively comprise six tenets of transcendence:

Three on the way to soulfulness—love of others, love of work, love of belonging, and three on the way to spiritually—belief in the sacred, belief in unity, belief in transformation.

The way of soulfulness

Love of others

The love of others is, first, a matter of self-differentiation. Love demands attachment, yet requires a healthy distance. Here the subject is separate from the object, heading toward subjective selflessness. For such love to occur, one must make sure that the other's separateness is secured independent of one's own. As the poet Rainer Maria Rilke so eloquently advised, each person has to protect the solitude of the other. As explorations of intimacy inevitably reveal, it is only by being separate that one can truly be together with another; enmeshment is not intimacy. Love that strips the other person from his or her sense of self, in which privacy is invaded and boundaries are blurred, is not real love. Indeed, getting to know and love someone deeply may require not seeing too clearly or being too close.

Love also means forgiving. The soul soars when one concedes to one's loved ones their freedom and cherishes what they are willing to give without asking more. There is no categorical goodness or badness, and one must expect failings, betrayals, and also (if one is fortunate) expressions of contrition. Then one must forgive. After any ethical transgressions, the slate must be wiped clean and the relationship permitted to continue as if the wronging never existed. Humanness, we know, is always imperfect, relative, and tainted by sin and folly. This view might help us to tolerate our own shortcomings and many uncertainties, including interpersonal, moral, or religious waywardness. Forgiving would free us from the corrosive effects of anger, hate, humiliation, and embarrassment. It would allow us to save otherwise unsalvageable relationships among spouses, parents and children, and friends. At bottom, love means totally accepting the other. As Adam was formed out of the mud of the earth, so are the rest of us. Any attempt to destroy the impurities of nature also removes the fertile soil that can be nourished to grow.

Love of work

Work is *liber mundi*, monks said, a life literacy, whereby their religious duties were highly intertwined with daily labors. Both activities could be paths to divinity, provided that they were carried out with the same profound regard. Although contemporary secular work is far from early monastic life, it could be equally sacred if we were to accept its special calling. Every act of labor, no matter how seemingly commonplace and trivial, if attended to with a depth of devotion, can open the path to soulfulness. In this sense, God is not only in the details of prayers, but also in details of everyday chores. Not only through the rituals of the temple, but through the hard work of ordinary tasks, does one enter a higher plane. Rituals of the church (liturgy literally means "the labor of laity") and the divine acts of the worshiper need to be transported to the commonplace. The ultimate purpose is not to differentiate between the sacred and the secular, but to bring a reverence to everyday living.

One cannot search for soul only from within; it cannot be divorced from one's relations in the outside world. In the quest for coherence of the self, Storr (1988) has suggested that work in the form of creative acts, such as making art, music, or literature, or other human interests and labors that may be more mundane, can also serve as substitute for good objects. They may function as reparation for early losses or later difficulties in fruitful interactions with others, in Eagle's (1981) words, "interests as object relations" (p. 527). One of the indispensable ingredients of the transmutation into soulfulness is the sheer love of work, through which the self and other can be unified. In cultivating depth and sacredness in everyday life, "The love that goes out into our work," says Moore in his *Care of the Soul*, "come back as love of self" (1992, p. 187).

Love of belonging

Belonging is living together; it is outer communion—*convivium*, celebration of "the sweet communion of life—the demonstration of love and splendor, the food of good will, the seasoning of friendship, the leavening of grace" (Moore, 1994, p. 104). Conviviality requires some degree of sacrifice of one's self-centeredness and being part of communal life. It means not focusing on one's own success, but that of the society at large; not striving to possess things individually, but viewing all of life's riches as shared. It means appreciating the simple life, honoring basic virtues, and above all, promoting selflessness. One does not lose one's self by such conviviality; in fact, it is the only way that one can truly find one's self. As Kovel (1991) has pointed out,

> the group is the larger being from which individual being emanates and to which it returns ... the group, be it family, clan, tribe, class, nation, or church, becomes the intermediary representation of being to the self, a way station between the isolated particle of consciousness and the universe. (p. 78)

Belonging means believing together. It provides communal meanings and finds faith through kinship and mutual accord. Expressions of faith, however, need not always be strictly religious.

In his book *Gods and Games*, which aspires toward a theology of play, David Miller (1973) describes faith as "being gripped by a story, by a vision, by a ritual … It is being seized, being gripped by a pattern of meaning that affects one's life pattern, that becomes a paradigm for the way one sees the world" (p. 144). It is difficult for every individual to formulate such a personal paradigm, and religion provides a ready-made one. Such a shared worldview is likely to facilitate an identity of universal being, embodying the spiritual power of belonging to the group.

Kovel (1991) further suggests that religions always engage spirit, but to differing degrees; they are particular historical ways of binding spirit and socially expressing it. But to the extent that they are an institutionalization or regimentation of spirit, they ipso facto become less than fully liberating. Although religious institutions, at least superficially, serve the process of belonging by believing, at bottom spirituality has the capacity to transcend religion in that "the quality of spirituality, religious or not … depends … on the social relations it advances" (p. 4). Thus religious congregations can perform the role of communal cement, a shared belief system serving to establish and reinforce cohesiveness relationships. As the rabbi Harold Kushner (1981) concluded,

> One goes to a religious service, one recites the traditional prayers, not in order to find God (there are plenty of other places where He can be found), but to find congregation, to find people with whom you can share that which means the most to you. (pp. 121–122)

The way of spiritually

Believing in the sacred

This refers to believing in the sanctity of everything around us, whereby ordinary things are experienced as truly extraordinary. Seeing the luminosity of nature transports all of our experiences, including health and illness, pleasure and pain, joy and sadness, gain and loss, success and failure, birth and death. They become life events that are not dualistic, but reflect a dialectic of the ineffable, equally worthy of veneration. Such a sense of sacredness demands detachment from worldly possessions, yet endows them with the wonder of life. As in the poet Pablo Neruda's (1994) famed exaltation, *Odes to Common Things*, one looks at everyday objects as one might at a star in the sky. It is a beholding of the universe in all its majesty. It is an epiphany that may come as a form of revelation, not as a matter of logic, just as God surpasses logos and is exempt from proof or disproof, in Jaspers' (1954) words, "distant, … hidden …, and indemonstrable" (p. 50). Rather, "God is accessible not through thought, but through faith" (p. 41).

The sacred experience demands some detachment from others. As soulful as belonging is, it does not mean never being alone. Man also needs solitude for his spiritual growth. Being with people for long periods of time, no matter how loving, wonderful, or interesting they might be, interferes with one's biopsychological rhythm, with one's synchrony with nature, with one's own authenticity. Solitude synchronizes the body with nature and reinforces man's belonging to a larger presence. Private religious devotion provides similar harmony, in that the person who prays in private feels himself to be alone in the presence of God.

According to Storr (1988), who posits a return to self through solitude, this is a way of putting the individual in touch with his deepest feelings. In a reciprocal process, the more one is in contact with one's own inner world, the more one will establish connections with the sacredness of the outer world. It is only by becoming a part of the sacredness of that world that one may unearth one's spirituality. It is there waiting for transformation. In his attempt to transform the everyday into the sacred, the visible into the invisible, the poet Rainer Maria Rilke said in an early letter, that our task is to "stamp [the] earth into ourselves … deeply … so that its being may rise again invisibly in us." T. Miller (1995), who presents a program for achieving balance and contentment in a demanding world, offers Albert Camus' wise words on the road to discovering the magic of ordinary existence: "If there is a sin against life, it consists perhaps not so much in despairing of life as in hoping for another life and eluding the implacable grandeur of this life."

Believing in unity

Believing in unity means a sense of being undifferentiated from the outside world—natural and supernatural—in Buddhist words, "a feeling of oneness" (Kawai, 1996, p. 4). This unity brings meaning and serenity to the self, as life's burdens become too heavy to bear if one can find no universal meaning. Universal meaning, of course, is not a quantifiable and measurable entity. As Jaspers (1954) noted, "Unity cannot be achieved through any rational, scientific universal. Nor does unity reside in a universal religion … Unity can be gained only … in boundless communication" (p. 106). It is a sense of responsibility for all, a sense of total commitment, a selfless way of relating to the world around us. Moreover, believing in unity ultimately reflects the seamlessness of mind, body, and spirit. As Kovel (1991) put it, "If mind-body is a unity, then spirit can be read as the coming-to-be of that unity. And this coming-to-be depends on the way we act and on our relationship to the world" (p. 20).

Rinpoche (1994) refers to an "unfolding vision of wholeness" (p. 352), a sense of a living—and implicitly loving—interconnection with humanity. The glue for that mysterious unity is a kind of love that dedifferentiates ourselves from other persons, other things, and finally, from the universe, extending our limits, a stretching of our boundaries. According Peck (1978), "In this way the more and longer we extend ourselves, … the more blurred becomes the distinction between the self and the world" (p. 95). We become identified with the transpersonal and we begin more and more to experience the same sort of feelings of ecstasy that we have when we fall in love, but instead of having merged temporarily with a single beloved object, we have merged more permanently with the universe—a primordial unity.

Such transpersonal love is praised by the religions and exalted as the ultimate goal to be attained, surpassing one's knowledge, skills, power, and all worldly possessions. "I may understand all mysteries and have all knowledge. I may even have enough faith to move mountains. But if I don't have love, I am nothing" (God's word: *The Bible*, 1995 edition). Variations of love, be they passionate love, maternal love, affectionate love, or spiritual love, are at times differentiated and even mutually exclusive, but if you don't love others, you cannot love God or vice versa, you don't love animals, you couldn't possibly love humans and all of nature. There is an undifferentiated base of faith and love from which other variations spring. This love is not possessing, not capturing, it isn't *doing* something. Love is a way of existing, a way of being with people, animals, nature, and God.

Such unity brings compassion. This compassionate unity is inculcated by all religions. Jesus' crucifixion is to awaken our heart to compassion and turn our minds toward shared suffering. Such is the Hindu story of Menon:

> When Menon arrived in Delhi to seek a job ... all his possessions ... were stolen at the railroad station. He would have to return home on foot, defeated. In desperation he turned to an elderly Sikh, explained his troubles, and asked for a temporary loan of fifteen rupees to tide him over until he could get a job. The Sikh gave him the money. When Menon asked for his address so that he could repay the man, the Sikh said that Menon owed the debt to any stranger who came to him in need .... The help came from a stranger and was to be repaid to a stranger. (Fulghum, 1988, p. 152)

Believing in transformation

Believing in transformation is believing in spiritual continuity and rebirth. We may be finite in our presently expressed form, but eternal in our true nature. As Rinpoche (1994) concludes in *The Tibetan Book of Living and Dying*:

> In death all the components of our body and mind are stripped away and disintegrate. As the body dies, the senses and subtle elements dissolve, and this is followed by the death of the ordinary aspect of our mind, with all its negative emotions of anger, desire, and ignorance. Finally, nothing remains to obscure our true nature, as everything that has clouded the enlightened mind has fallen away. And what is revealed is the primordial ground of our absolute nature, which is like a pure and cloudless sky. (p. 259)

For Campbell (1949), transformation is a brave "reconciliation with the grave" (p. 356), akin to the departure of the hero.

We inherit spiritual as well as physical and psychological elements from our parents as well as from the previous generations. Similarly, each generation is endowed by the experience and knowledge of all the prior ones. Whereas our physical and psychological qualities carry the assimilated elements of past lives, wherever and with whomever they have been, they are relatively limited to genetics and familial life. When these are embodied in us, they give us our unique physical and psychological essence. Our spiritual essence, on the other hand, possesses the assimilated elements of past lives of the community, history, arts, cosmic world, and beyond. When these spiritual elements are embodied within us for the duration of our corporeal life, they give us our soul.

The soul evolves in a particular existence. After the death of the person the soul fragments again to its spiritual elements and coalesces again in someone else. Every culture is rich with the telling of this process of transmutation. Their mythology, their songs, their religion, their rituals gravitate toward that spiritual realization. The Chinese tell of a crossing of the Fairy Bridge under the guidance of the Jade Maiden and the Golden Youth. The Hindus picture a towering firmament of heavens and a many-leveled underworld of hells. The soul gravitates after death to a story that assimilates the whole meaning of its past life. When the lesson has been learned, it returns to the world, to prepare itself for the next degree of experience. Thus gradually it makes its way through all the levels of life-value until it has broken past the confines of the cosmic egg. Dante's *Divina Commedia* is an exhaustive review of the stages: "Inferno," a misery of the spirit bound to the prides and actions of the flesh; "Purgatorio," the process of transmuting fleshly into spiritual experience; and finally, "Paradiso," the degrees of spiritual realization (Campbell, 1949, p. 368).

Transformation starts by coming to terms with one's ending. Coming to terms with one's beginnings is difficult and ambiguous; it may occur in different ways (regression, analysis, self-reflection) and mean different things (forgiveness, charity, or simply the end of an addictive litany against the past). Coming to terms with one's ending, one's finiteness, is clearer but even harder. Socrates said, "Practice dying" to youngsters asking for wisdom of life. On a less lofty level, Rinpoche (1994) speaks of the necessity of "letting go of attachment" (p. 224). In fact, Moore (1994) paradoxically views loss of love and intimacy as a form of initiation, suggesting that although initiation means beginning, the most powerful initiations always involve some sort of death.

At bottom, all endings are potential beginnings, and all beginnings have an end. To the soul, death is the ultimate beginning, for all the particulars of precious ordinary living creatures, famous or not, human or not, are still transformed into another form. As Chopra (1993) says, in nature "death is part of the larger cycle of birth and renewal .... Our atoms are billions of years old and have billions of years more life left in them. In the remote future, when they are broken down into smaller particles, atoms do not die but just get transformed into another configuration" (p. 303). Similarly, our body is programmed to cease as a specific functional unit, but its elements are capable of taking quite different physiological forms: animals, flowers, ice, salt. Substances that make up living and nonliving things are one and the same. We are not diverse from things, from space, from light, from time, but one product. This ultimately reflects the reanimation of life, finding the soul in everything, *anima mundi*.

Our most cherished thoughts of eternity are the bright side of our ending in this world and are often associated with beauty and light. Its realm and its nature change from one culture to another, from one religion to another, but it is typically a transporting destination. It is being forever and can hold the promise of a state of ecstasy or grace, an intrinsic radiance, or a hidden fellowship with other immortals and even rebirth. Death, on the other hand, is often construed as the dark side of our ending, an oblivion, nothingness.

Full joyful living now and in eternity nonetheless requires understanding of this nothingness, in Rinpoche's (1994) phase, "living in the mirror of death" (p. 3). In fact, only "nothingness" can become everything. And one cannot enter into this nothingness without giving up everything. The spiritual self is obtained by the negation of the ordinary self, letting go of the subjective sense of being. This subjective selflessness is not an absolute state of nonbeing or nonexistence. Rather, it is a state of non-differentiation from overall existence and reflecting deeply on impermanence. It is giving up differentiation, self-awareness from the universe. It is living everywhere and in everything. It sees our own flesh in continual exchange with the whole of nature.

To reconcile *being* and *nonbeing* simultaneously, to live within the external world while striving for inner transformation, and to search for the grail while not grasping its nature, provides a transcending state. Salvation for ordinary mortals is not radical negation of living; nor is it waiting for a better life. Rather, it is an embodiment of the contradictions of life and death as transformative harmony. Believing in transformation also applies to our selfhood. More specifically, Christensen (1999) talks of the "dialectical self," borrowed from Buddhism. It does not deny that the self exists, but rather has diametrically opposed qualities, in sum, (i) has no structure (form) and is impermanent (empty), (ii) is unsatisfactory (associated with suffering) and also liberated (joyful), and (iii) has no separate essence (interdependent), and is also separate. In the harmonious words of Shobogenzo Genkoan, Zen Master Eiheri Dogen: "To study the self is to forget the self. To forget the self is to be at one with ten thousand phenomena. To be at one with ten thousand phenomena is to free one's body and mind and those of others."

The making of a spiritual therapist

The healer status is bestowed upon the individual by his or her society. As such, professional degrees for the patients of psychotherapy, including their credentialing and academic requirements, are forms of social sanction. However, too much attention is often paid to the professional training of therapists and not enough to their personal formation. Maybe this is because there are so many teachers eager to teach. As one supervisor sardonically said, "Psychotherapy cannot be learned, but thank God it can be taught."

The formation of the therapist encompasses personal growth, a broad education that goes beyond psychotherapy per se, and a life philosophy. It is for the therapist—as it is for everyone else—the issue of being and becoming, insofar as the therapist can help a patient grow only as much as he, himself, has grown. That is why what really matters is not schools of therapy, but the psychotherapists themselves. Although one's theory is generally reflected in the particular modality he or she chooses to practice, "the person" of the therapist overrides both theory and school to which he or she is attached. In fact, the therapist's technical skills are contextually tailored manifestations of his or her personality, although the therapist's self is frequently lost in the quagmire of polarized theories and allegiances. Indeed, these theories have often replaced philosophy, and even religion, in extreme cases. For example, those who believed in Freud, "where ego was, there shall id be," themselves behave like an alter-superego to their patients, whereas those who believe in Fritz Perls', "where id was, there shall ego be," become an "alter-id" to their patients. Similarly, the traditionalists value the mind over the senses, while the experientialists say that you should lose your mind and come to your senses.

Either way, both the traditionalists and the experientialists set man against himself (i.e., neurotic), or for himself (i.e., narcissistic), because they compartmentalize man and do not view him as part of a whole. Instead of "where ego was, there shall id be," or vice versa, the spiritual therapist in effect replaces these with, "where *it* was, there shall I be." *It* is that whole, the collective us, comprising nature and the supernatural. Unfortunately, psychotherapists of the past have frequently thought of religion as a mass neurosis, if not a communal delusion. A single exception was Jung, who embraced spirituality, but considered religion a defense against the experience of God. Religion, however, will always remain a common ground toward spirituality; religion is also part of the *it*.

Those therapists who become overcommitted to the sciences of psychology, biology, or sociology, invariably end up underplaying man's ethical and spiritual dimensions. Other therapists, overemphasizing specific techniques, whether analyzed or behaviorally manipulated, also make man impersonalized, compartmentalized, calculated (and most recently, "managed"), thereby diminished. The contemporary therapist needs to regain his innocence by not being too scientific or too regimented about people, love, and pathology. He must maintain a certain free margin, an openness, credulity, and even ignorance.

The spiritual therapist is one who is concerned with man's anguish of isolation and alienation, sense of meaninglessness, and existential guilt over forfeiting one's potential. Real pathology is "human diminution," says Maslow (1970), and this is especially the case regarding one's spiritual diminution. Thus the spiritual therapist is one who must himself transcend into a universal consciousness, in order to practice psychotherapy that itself opts for such a higher state of consciousness and growth and that targets the spiritual center of man. That target is approached by fertilizing one's self with broad curiosity and engagement, by expanding interest while seeking informed simplicity, by anchoring the self within through solitude and without through intimacy, by belonging and believing, and finally, by grounding one's soul in the serenity of spirituality.

The spiritual psychotherapist is also someone who identifies past and present conflicts and deficits, not in order to resolve, but to *transcend* them. He accepts the person with all his limitations, at the same time he does not settle for that as an end in itself. Moreover, the spiritual therapist doesn't just apply various techniques toward the resigned acceptance of human dilemmas, but helps the person toward harmonious emancipation from them.

Spiritual existence is a spectrum state. At the near end (earthly and accessible), it is a theology of secular man; here the therapist is a minister of everyday life. At the far end (celestial and inaccessible), it is a theology of cosmic man; here the therapist is a knight of sacred faith. He is at one with the numinous, a part of the incorporeal continuum. At both ends of the spiritual spectrum, the therapist cultivates a set of values, beliefs, and practices in veneration of the divine in life. He relates to the world with ethics of conviction, and like the advice given to physicians by Paracelsus, shall have the courage to "speak of which is invisible, unnamed and immaterial" (Moore, 1992, p. 165).

The patient

For the spiritual therapist, there is no "patient" or "client," but rather, an uninitiated human being. The spiritual therapist rejects dualistic terms and discriminatory labels, like normal–abnormal, sane–insane, and all other diagnostic attributes in the form of binary categories. When such duality is transcended, its form disappears. This is the wisdom of non-duality, which is the foundation of the spiritual therapist's philosophy. He or she thus opens all unrecognized directions and sees the person not with psychopathology, but with human frailty. Implicit here is a predisposition for growth and strength, wherein our best potential resides not at the pinnacles of our accomplishments, but at our breaking points. These are the fractured places at which we may begin to mend.

Moreover, the spiritual therapist exemplifies two overall orientations or attitudes toward the patient that reach beyond diagnostic limitations. This refers to a

> dual search for the *unique* (selective) and *universal* (shared). The former looks for what makes the person singularly special, at his or her worst and best; it seeks those individual qualities that define and distinguish the person from all others. The latter orientation takes a seemingly quantum leap in the other direction to locate what he or she has in common with others, not … within the framework of psychopathology, but on the larger level of what fundamentally binds or connects him or her to all humanity with similar struggles. (Karasu, 1992, p. 16)

Beyond this, the clinician's knowledge is independent of his own experience of reality; it is Kantian "*a priori* knowledge" not supplied immediately by the senses (Pirsig, 1974, p. 116). For the spiritual therapist, the person is as he is because the "whole universe is as it is" (Chopra, 1993, p. 157). Beyond this, the uninitiated is a person who is becoming. He or she is not only to be analyzed, interpreted, desensitized, confronted, explained, or managed. Ultimately, spiritual therapy is a stepping-stone to the larger universe—the spiritual therapist only points the way.

Theory of mind and its psychopathology

Spiritual psychotherapy considers all theories about the human mind as temporary attempts of filling the gaps of knowledge and, at times, justification of their therapeutic techniques. Nevertheless, even contradictory techniques, that is, the resolution of past and present conflicts (when there is no before and after), or the remedying of deficits and strengthening the individual's capacity to cope, are all potentially useful—provided that one recognizes their relativity. The spiritual therapist thereby sees no contradictions among various schools. In fact, such conflictual polarities invite an offering of faith. Then psychopathology, as defined by all these schools, becomes merely the surface reading of the human condition; similarly, symptoms of conflicts and deficits thus become manifestations of problems at the deeper levels of the soul—*spiritual* arrests, conflicts, and deficits.

Similarly, for the spiritual therapist, the mind does not comprise only conscious and unconscious forces (the prohibitive superego, the impulsive id, or the executive ego), but also collective spiritual forces that are pre-structured to love and to believe. This makes our mind not a simple mechanical mind, but a spiritual one. It carries with it a remembered oneness, a sacred belonging. There is no royal road to it, simply a sacred one.

The therapeutic relationship

The therapist's relationship to the individual in spiritual psychotherapy at times carries some elements of that doctor to patient (or client), teacher to student, friend to friend, parent to child, or lover to lover, but most of the time it has none of these. The spiritual therapist's therapeutic role is not that of transference figure, cognitive structurer, behavioral trainer, supportive counselor, or empathic self-object, although at times it may resemble any or all these alliances.

Rather, the spiritual therapist's type of relatedness is primarily a redemptive one and superordinates all other forms of relationship, that is, two persons mutually confirming each other's underlying sense of common destiny without blame or debt. Such redemption is not geared to common sin and guilt, but to a more benevolent restitution and liberation. There is no finding of fault, no punishment, and in effect, no need for forgiveness. It is the rescue of self and other, an emancipation from the confinement of ordinary human attachments and entanglements, and deliverance from the imprisonment of mind and body without soul. It is a peaceful and restorative union.

The role of technique

The spiritual therapist has no technique of his or her own. Instead, as Moore (1992) depicted it, "Its rituals are effective *ex opere operato*—from the things done—rather than because of the intentions of the performing the rite" (p. 227). He or she considers the application of specific strategies to another person, especially engaging in deliberate measures to change the other, as an exercise of bad faith, an inauthentic act. Nonetheless, under that spiritual umbrella, he may borrow from any or all other schools of therapy as a basis for "technique," because they are equivocal. That is, utilizing interpretation, confrontation, cognitive training, hypnosis, catharsis, role playing, encounter, free association, dream analysis, regression, mediation, or praying, within the context of a working alliance, erotic transference, and self-object relationship, makes no difference—because spiritual therapy is a way of *being with* someone in a soulful manner that targets the spiritual center of man.

The spiritual therapist does not treat an illness, or try to cure a person who has an ailment; instead he remains with a person who is in the process of becoming. The spiritual therapist and the uninitiated person are a contextual unit—a single entity, and although this single entity can have external and internal dialogues, it relies primarily on what is not said. This is consistent with Jaspers' (1954) two paths of philosophical life: the path of solitary meditation and the path of communication with men, a "mutual understanding through keeping silence together" (p. 122). If words are also deeds, as the philosopher Wittgenstein (1951) proposed, then by plumbing the depths of spiritual solitude, silences are also words.

What spiritual therapy is *not*

Spiritual therapy is not religious counseling. The Church and its religious counselings typically represent a structured and organized form of spirituality with highly specific traditions, proscriptions, and rites; they impose God as a separate and superior theological conception, accompanied by required rituals of seeking His hand. By contrast, spiritual psychotherapy rejects strict formality and substitutes flexibility and freedom. It embodies a contemporary religious view that is universal and nonsectarian, best portrayed as perennial wisdom or philosophy (Huxley, 1944) or the transcendent unity of religions (Schuon, 1975). Accordingly, it warrants no piety, no worshiping. Rather, in Campbell's (1949) words, "The contemplation of life thus is undertaken as a meditation on one's own immanent divinity" (p. 319). In short, the divine being is viewed as a revelation of the omnipotent self that dwells within everyone. Sheikh and Sheikh (1989) put it as follows:

> All of us have the potential for transcendent experiences. The great saints and sages of human history are said to differ from the rest of us by virtue of attainment and realization, not by some unsurpassable God-given ontological divide that forever sets them off from us as a separate order of being. (p. 546)

Similarly, spiritual psychotherapy makes no godly claims beyond man's won human realization. Spirituality is a path of quiet contemplation, in which we find the divine in the given world and within ourselves. Spiritual existence—and spiritual therapy—is a journey; one makes the way by going.

Spiritual therapy is not existential psychotherapy. Existential therapy negates the spiritual to the extent that its fundamental negativity, anguish, doom, and sense of man's finitude are diametrically opposed to an emphasis on beauty, rebirth, and reanimation of life. In addition, with its phenomenological reduction to immediate experience as the only valid data, it deliberately doubts all notions that are inferred, invisible, or carried over from the past—those that are easily embraced by spirit. Since it believes that "human living is torn from the un-self-consciousness of objects or plants and animal existence" (Gurman & Messer, 1995, p. 233), it construes consciousness as making human life qualitatively different from that of any other species, thus setting man apart from the unity of nature. And although its method of doubt is intended to create freedom from existential isolation, instead it can generate freedom from faith. In contrast, the spiritual therapist is a perpetual beginner, whose uninitiated positivity generates hope, creates harmony with one's self, and continuity with the universe.

Spiritual therapy is not like analytic psychotherapy. Analytic psychotherapy is founded on the model of sickness. It is pathomorphic; it makes diagnoses; it seeks a cure of the patient's illness. In addition, it is deterministic (if not overdetermined) and is concerned with etiology and cause. In particular it has a mission; it seeks to crack personal unconscious codes in linear time. In its most orthodox form, analytic psychotherapy is an artificial induction of therapeutic illness by transforming form (the transference) into content. It aims at knowing, that is, insight, and such self-knowledge is its end point. Thus any puzzlement or obscurity must be undone. Furthermore, as the analyst makes transference-driven demands on the patient, he paradoxically creates an iatrogenic hothouse that itself cultivates psychopathology.

By contrast, spiritual psychotherapy is founded on a model of health; it is normative; it eliminates (if not transcends) diagnoses. It is interested in salvation and healing (not cure). It is undetermined, transformative, and non-causal, a transpersonal journey in omnidirectional time. In its most ardent form, spiritual psychotherapy is the induction of stillness, the cultivation of quiescence and harmony between mind, body, and soul. Spiritual psychotherapy aims not at "knowing" but at enlightenment, whereby self-knowledge is not the culmination, but the starting point. In so doing, it seeks the regaining of lost innocence in order to experience—not *answer*—the eternal riddles of life. In fact, the spiritual therapist stays observant, until things gradually become obscure. He knows that puzzlement is a necessary state that precedes enlightenment.

Spiritual therapy is not like academic psychotherapies. Spiritual psychotherapy cannot be standardized in operational manuals that homogenize all treatment. It is not based on large-scale bureaucratic research requirements, efficacy, efficiency, or cost-effectiveness. It does not steer in shallow water, is not superficial or strictly short-term; it does not prescribe and predict. Rather, it is highly improvisational and fully accepts (if not promotes) heterogeneity. Its N equals one and is by definition immeasurable. It is *not* a matter of science and proof, but belief and faith. It steers in deep waters.

Spiritual therapy is not like New Age therapy. New Age psychotherapies promote search for the self—but never get beyond it. They are geared toward self-actualization, self-protection, and self-love (in the smallest sense of the word). They primarily offer quick-and-easy answers and derive from pleasure, not insight or enlightenment. In fact, they don't ask questions or look beneath the surface—of one's own myopic life. In this sense they are selfish—never selfless. In seeking instant gratification, they are indulgent, excessive, and exalt only the immediate moment—never eternity. They reject the simple life and instead urge their recipients to indulge hedonistic desires and pleasures, to seek narcissistic gains. In short, you can only get there by riding others.

In contrast, spiritual therapy seeks the self beyond itself, in order *not* to be self-preoccupied; in short, it is ego-less. It is geared toward self-transcendence, the love of others in a universal, timeless, and spaceless field. Spiritual therapists help their recipients to relinquish self-serving actions, to express compassion and forgiveness. And you get there by carrying others.

Conclusion

In the consolidation of a soulful and spiritual existence, the therapist continues to come to an authentic self. Only such authenticity contains really meaningful therapeutic tools, because what endures ultimately emanates from within. Finally, alas, the therapist must recognize that this is not a field for spectacular successes (if any field is); as Freud early on warned us, every therapy is a relative failure. The tranquility of the therapist thus largely depends on his or her ability to live with optimum disillusionment and still maintain profound faith in all persons, with all their vulnerabilities and strengths. Then spiritual psychotherapy becomes not so much a profession as a way of being in a harmonious relationship to man and infinite nature. In Kovel's (1991) words, "We do not *have* a spirit; rather, we *are* spirit" (p. 20). This does not mean, however, that we reside in a realm that is lofty and elusive, unable to be touched. Instead, it is a unified quality of mind and heart and soul, a commitment to a spiritual existence.

CHAPTER 17

Some thoughts on tele-analysis in Turkey

Mine Özgüroğlu Çukurçeşme

About four years ago, with the pandemic, we found ourselves in a new life reminiscent of fictional movies. Our bodies had become dangerous for both the target and the carrier of the virus. In a world where closeness was considered dangerous and distant, relationships were considered safe, we had locked ourselves in our homes, had become isolated and lonely. We tried to stay away from our loved ones in order to protect both ourselves and them. Technology moved to the center of our lives, and the internet became a very important need and communication tool that enabled our contact with the outside world.

Of course, not only our daily lives but also our psychoanalytic practices were affected by this change. In the early days, when we did not yet know about the contagiousness of the virus and how to protect ourselves, we found ourselves very quickly in "remote practices." Realizing that we would not be able to return to our usual work setting, that we were in a process without a foreseeable end, was a situation difficult to tolerate. As we left behind more than a year of dealing with the pandemic, it seemed that we had no choice but to accept this reality and discover new adaptive ways in our private, social, and professional lives. To be able to discover such ways, we first had to observe and evaluate what was happening. This need was one of the reasons that pushed me to prepare this contribution.

Due to the multidimensional nature of the topic, I could not address every aspect of it, so I limited myself, focusing on my patients' reactions to the loss of the physical component of the analytic environment, which is one of the results of working in electronic settings. How did the inability to share the same physical environment and the lack of bodily interaction affect the psychoanalytic work? Based on my experiences with my patients, I aimed to look for an answer to this question, sharing my thoughts and hoping to think together.

A lot of time has passed since I presented this text as an article toward the end of the first year of the pandemic. Now, the World Health Organization has announced that the pandemic is over. And most of us have gone back to our daily lives, back to our work routines in our offices. As I revisited this article, I thought while some observations were still relevant, I had to reconsider some of my ideas. Furthermore, I wanted to add some thoughts about remote working, which has perhaps been, paradoxically, one of the professional benefits of the pandemic.

First encounters on the electronic setting

Shortly after the announcement of the first cases in Turkey, I had heard about my colleagues quickly switching to online practice. I, on the other hand, seemed to have not yet fully grasped the reality. I was puzzled. My patients had begun to voice murmurs of concern. The anxious voice inside me was still muted, but my patients who coughed, blew their nose, and sneezed for several days in a row woke me up. The virus was no longer solely in China, nor was it just some news on TV. It was very close, perhaps right outside the door. Through this invisible danger, ghosts or soul-suckers could get inside our bodies. The possibility of our bodies being potential carriers of the disease had rendered consulting rooms, and thus physical intimacy, unsafe. I was now facing a reality very different from most situations I had ever experienced as an analyst. I was one of the victims of this catastrophe, and I had patients to protect and help in the face of a similar threat. How would I protect both myself and my patients? We had to continue the treatments using a method that did not involve physical interactions. For now, the only way was the telephone and any kind of electronic communication. The virus was spreading so fast that I felt like I didn't have enough time to think too much, or work through this, to process the situation. Either I was going to take a break from my job, which was not possible, or I was going to continue, assume a "better than nothing" approach. And so, it was …

As soon as I made the decision, I started to greet my patients with masks and disinfectant, which created a kind of bewilderment and concern as well as some sort of relief. They were worried because I was worried, but also relieved because I was trying to protect them and myself. Later on, I would realize that these initial concerns were quite useful as material to work with for some of my patients. Some took a further step before I did, informing me that they were scared and wanted to continue the work through online methods. Within a week we discussed the situation and started working from our homes.

Before we started working remotely, the first thing I thought about was how we could build the analytical setting in an electronic environment. One of the components of the analytic environment is, of course, the frame. An analytical framework is needed in order for a space to turn into an analytical room and a duo into an analytical relationship.

Maintaining the frame allows the processes of transference and countertransference processes to develop and be examined. Roussillon (2006) mentions three main functions of the frame:

1. The carrying function. It involves Winnicott's "holding" and Bion's "containment" concepts.
2. Its role in symbolization. It represents the necessary conditions and laws necessary for the working-through process for both the analyst and the analysand. Thus, a ground for symbolization is provided.
3. Metaphorical function (Displacement game). The analysand's past enters the analytic setting through transfer into the frame.

We know that the analytical frame is not just a set of rules but includes many physical and psychical components. Winnicott (1962) talks about the importance of the mother's or caregiver's ability to provide a physical and psychical space for the newborn during the journey toward developing a sense of self and object. Similarly, the analyst, too, creates a psychical and physical space for patients through his or her body, inner world, consulting room, and the organization of the room—the furniture, the armchairs, and the couch. This place offers the patient a space in which he or she can analytically settle and develop. To use an analogy, we can liken this to the fetus settling in the uterus. With this perspective, it becomes clearer how the analyst's room, how it is furnished, the objects used, the way they are arranged, become important as physical extensions of the framework. Beyond the concrete rules and the physical environment, another important component of the frame is undoubtedly the analyst's internal frame. The analyst's ethical stance, the theory he or she feels close to, and his or her personality traits are the cornerstones of the inner frame, and thus the analyst can stretch and protect the physical frame according to the needs of the patients. This physical and psychical framework also creates a space for the analyst to do his or her work freely. In other words, it serves both a holding/carrying (Winnicott, 1960a) and a containing (Bion, 1970) function for the analyst as well as the analysand.

When we had to move to online practice, I thought that the analyst's internal framework would be needed more than ever because of the difficulties in setting up the concrete components of the framework. There would be no room for analyst and patient to coexist. How could we build this highly important component of the holding/containing environment within an electronic setting? Together, my patients and I tried to figure out how we could build the most suitable analytic setting, minding our psychical and physical conditions and needs, without neglecting the basis of reality. Our workplaces would be our homes. We had to come up with solutions in our homes to various issues, including a comfortable room with a closed door, a couch, silence, isolation, as well as payment. While sharing the same space, it was solely the analyst's responsibility to prepare and protect the consulting room. But now, my patients would have to take responsibility for the preparation and maintenance of the analytical room. From our homes, through a screen or a phone, we would enter our patients' space and they would enter ours. How would it be possible to clarify the boundaries? And who knows what transference issues this would lead to? Would we be able to create spaces to carry out the analytical work safely?

Beyond the framework, how would not being physically able to share the same room affect the analytical process? Working in the same room enables interacting with all our senses and renders the contact with the analysand a multidimensional experience. Russell (2020) states that in an interpersonal interaction, 65 percent of the interaction is nonverbal. In the electronic setting, with the use of a screen, only two of our senses would be actively engaged. Thus, the analytic relationship would inevitably be dominated by visual and auditory perception. How would sensations and affects arising from the bodily interactions of the analyst and the analysand enter the online work? In other words, how would the vividness of being in the same room with someone, being close enough to kiss and kick (ibid.) be achieved in this setting? How could a disembodied analyst, without an inside (hollow), be able to carry the deeply regressed patients?

Another major difference of online work from sharing the same physical space was that both the analyst and the patient would be able to reach the analytic work through just one click and would also be able to end it in a similar simple fashion. There would be no arrival to the room, which can be considered as a preparatory process before contact with the inner world, and similarly, there would be no leaving the office after the end of the session, which allows a progressive reconnection with daily life beyond. Russell (2020) states that many patients experience visits to the consulting room as a journey, and this plays an important role in recollection of the sessions. She further adds that online work is not perceived as a journey in this sense, so much so that one patient resembled the one-click end of sessions to cesarian section, rather than vaginal birth. The author also underlines the connection between the three-dimensional qualities of coexistence and the connection of movement learning, mentalization, and memory. How would my patients experience this seemingly easy way of reaching and separating, and how would it affect the transference processes?

I started working with a thousand similar questions in my mind. The transition process was so fast that it was practically nonexistent. The very first day, through the absence of patients in person, I experienced the extent to which the room in my office provided a holding environment not only for my patients, but for myself as well. I had tried to prepare an isolated, quiet, and comfortable environment for myself at home. My study room was very suitable for this. Unfortunately, by the first day, I realized that the WiFi connection to that room was weak. As a result, I had to move to the living room to be as close to the modem as possible. The living room was isolated and quiet, and the connection was strong. Yet it was too large a room, and the furniture was distracting for me. I was looking for a room like the one I had in the office … the one I had lost … small and with only what I needed to work … Fortunately, the internet problem was soon solved, and I was able to settle into my study room.

My patients too, soon after their confusion was alleviated, tried their best to adapt to this new way of working. In the analytic work over the phone, we only saw each other at the beginning and the end of the sessions. Aside from the occasional connection issue, at first there seemed to be no major problems. It was a bit more difficult to adapt to face-to-face work via the screen. The distance between us was now different than what would be expected of a normal communication. We were also unable to see each other's bodies as a whole, with our visual field limited to our faces. Being too close this way could narrow the private personal space down, and even be experienced as a violation. It could also affect the processes of free thinking, free association, and evaluation. Another issue was the feeling of being stuck in a two-dimensional space. Bodily interactions were now replaced by the limited interaction through a lifeless screen.

The first reactions in the electronic setting

In the first months, both my patients and I spent a kind of honeymoon period in our own homes, in a space where we were free from the worry of our bodies harming each other. Interruptions in internet connections, images that appeared and disappeared, sometimes blurred, or gaps that could not be determined whether it was silence or disconnection, were not so much of a concern at first. The expectation that this situation would not continue for long made it easier to tolerate. There was a smell of death on the outside, and it was as if we were in the bunkers, trying to continue and keep analytic work alive. Our therapeutic endeavor was part of our effort to survive, trying to find creative possibilities for reparation and development. Even though our losses were highly obvious, the excitement of having discovered a way to stay alive helped us to stay above the water and push these losses into the background. However, Scharff (2010) emphasized two important criteria necessary for adaptation to the online work. The first was the mourning of what had been lost, and the second was the ability to use technology as a third element.

This period, which I characterize as a honeymoon, did not last long. Soon, each of my patients began to react differently to this radical change in the way of working, in relation to their own psychological structure. The severity of these reactions varied according to both their personality organizations and the duration and quality of our work in the room. As much as I try to avoid generalizations, for the purpose of clarifying my observations, I will attempt to categorize my patients into two main groups according to their adaptation difficulties: those who had serious adaptation difficulties and those who were able to continue their analytical work even though they had difficulties. Among those with serious adaptation difficulties, I tried to pay particular attention to a subgroup of a few people who were very resistant to returning to the room.

The most visible issue that was often reacted to was the one of analytical space. Communicating from two separate spaces instead of a shared physical space caused serious difficulties. Unlike before, my patients were forced to assume an additional responsibility. While some people did not have much difficulty adapting to this situation, others were beginning to have a hard time carrying this new responsibility. Especially when it became clear that this process was not short-lived at all, they began to react, first with murmurs, then with grunts, and then sometimes with words, sometimes with actions. I was gradually realizing that it was becoming difficult to maintain and sustain spaces, and it was not a good sign when they started calling sometimes from a bedroom, sometimes from a car. Similarly, the rooms they tried to transform into an analytic space were sometimes violated by a pet, a doorbell, a child, or a spouse, interrupting the integrity of the session. Through the screen, I was trying to watch and understand what was being staged. Some of them seemed to be staging to me, through the actors at home, how they were out of place, in the void, some of them how their boundaries were violated, and of course, the reason for this was the work in the electronic setting. The stage was adorned with both external reality and the materials they brought from their stories. The frame had become fragile, there were holes on it. Furthermore, physically, our communication was limited to voice and image which was also occasionally interrupted. For some people, it became very difficult to maintain a relationship with an analyst who was disembodied, who was just image and voice, perhaps even two-dimensional, without an inside.

The group which I thought adapted relatively more easily consisted of patients with whom I had been working for a long time. Although their personality organization contained some degree of primitive pathology, they had enough ego strength to maintain their connection with reality without difficulty. In addition, before the pandemic, we had worked with most of them on the couch at least three times a week and we were able to create a sufficiently safe ground. We agreed that continuing by phone was the most reasonable decision under these circumstances. They could talk about how voice-only communication increased intimacy on the one hand, and how they were affected by the lack of physical interaction on the other. The deprivation and losses were knee-deep. Despite my physical absence, hearing my voice repeatedly had allowed for the phone communication to function as a transitional space (Bassen, 2007). They had begun to develop a new psychic representation of me as the analyst. The phone gradually became an object of transference. One of my patients told me how he worried in his dreams when he couldn't find his phone, another how he wanted to break his phone, another how he panicked when his phone battery died. Sometimes the phone cable would get thin and break. Sometimes the earphones would malfunction for some reason and the voices would seem to come from far away. In our new working method, we were able to work on our losses and move on with the facilitating effect of the fact that they had internalized my analytical functions to a certain extent while in the room.

However, it was not as easy with some of my patients with whom I had recently started and/or who were in a dependent transference. These patients had serious difficulties with their earliest object relationships, resulting in not only acting-out, but also serious anxieties. These anxieties were similar to the ones that Winnicott (1974) discusses under the heading of "primitive agonies," such as a feeling of emptiness, fear of being homeless, fears of annihilation. There were some patients who were showing signs of disintegration. This rapid transition created a feeling of almost "falling off the lap" and revived the deepest fears and anxieties in their stories. They felt like they were in a limitless void, blind holes, just as they had once been in their childhood stories. Many in this group could not relax until they returned to the office. I noticed that those who could not relax were those who had settled in the room before the pandemic and had developed dependent transference.

A few of my patients in this group, although it took a long time before their anxiety calmed down, were able to settle into the electronic setting and adapt to the new arrangements. I must add that I was surprised to see that our work had become more efficient and gotten deeper, compared to the one we carried out in the consulting room. They were people who could not settle into the office and analytical work. Before the pandemic, going back and forth to the office was almost a burden for them. In each session, they would discuss the efforts they make to reach me with a fed-up and angry attitude, emphasizing the difficulties in maintaining this arrangement. Attacks against the physical components of the frame were also significant. They were imagining a limitless work and considered every limit unnecessary. It was difficult for them to settle within the boundaries of the office space which they had reached by overcoming the unbearable conditions of the external reality. Similarly, when I resumed working in the room, this time they did not want to go back and were very insistent to continue online. I must state that I had to work on this issue for a long time. These people had personality organizations that I would almost call psychotic organizations. In fact, they showed some clinical signs that might be described as psychotic as well. I was observing that these symptoms disappeared in the online work. Was this seeming improvement a false, temporary improvement? If not, what was the mechanism of this improvement due to and how could it be explained? What did working online mean to them?

Discussion

The patient group that, in my experience, had the most difficulty in online work had some common developmental and transferential elements. The most important common feature in their stories was that they had serious difficulties in their earliest object relations, especially in the first relationship with the mother. They felt neglected, unheard, unseen, and even unnoticed. Another common feature was, shortly after we started working, they regressed to develop a dependent transference. Winnicott (1954) talks about two kinds of regression. One is a return to a relatively more gratifying stage in situations of distress, which is a kind of rest. The other is to return to the problematic stage in order to continue to develop, which is a kind of need. It is the second type of regression that is in question here.

Winnicott (ibid.) thinks that a baby is born with a potential originating from the evolutionary biological structure in the form of a tendency to grow and develop, and bases his theory of development on how the unintegrated primitive structure gradually moves toward integration. He mentions that throughout the life course, the individual "goes back and forth" between integrated and unintegrated conditions in order to integrate parts of the self that were left outside. He considers this "capacity to go back and forth" as a criterion of development. He underlines that the attainment of such a capacity is only possible with the existence of a good enough environment/mother in the earliest object relations. From this point of view, we can easily infer that for those who have serious difficulties in the first contact with the mother/caregiver, this round trip will not be easy. In fact, we might also expect the regression to be experienced as a necessity while raising serious anxieties. Winnicott (ibid.) discusses the need to regress to this most primordial period, despite the fact that it is anxiety-provoking, in his article on regression. He states that some people who have developed a false self in order to protect their true self, need to regress and pick up where they left off in order to continue their development. He mentions what was once characterized as "failure/inadequacy" in relation to the environment being frozen until favorable conditions arise, and when these conditions arise, what was frozen is unfrozen and re-experienced in order to continue development. As clearly seen, the regression here is a need for the purpose of healing, and it contains hope. It is the hope of achieving, albeit belatedly, a mutual harmony with the environment that is good enough under the current conditions. In other words, the aim of regression to dependency is to become independent, it is an effort to integrate.

The reassuring quality of the analytic work can, for these people, create the favorable conditions I have mentioned above, which could facilitate the regression toward the early or earliest object relations. Sometimes after the work has begun, or at the beginning, they may quickly develop a dependent transference with their analyst. Thanks to this transference, they have a chance to make contact with their previous unexperienced painful experiences, this time in the presence of the analyst. Primary narcissistic needs, issues of oneness and differentiation with the analyst, and the deprivations that accompany them come to the surface. It is at this stage that the need for holding, not only on a psychical but also on a physical level, comes to the fore. The bodily interaction with the analyst surpasses the verbal communication. The couch, the cushions, and the room become very important as representations of the analyst's body parts (breasts, arms, hands, etc. …) (Winnicott, 1954). Sometimes, in extreme cases, the couch and the room almost become the analyst himself, rather than a representation. Changes, such as session breaks, weekends, summer vacations, become intolerable experiences.

During this process, the task of the analyst is to mediate the experience and understanding of the inevitable inadequacies that will be experienced in a state of absolute dependence. Ogden (2014) describes the work of the analyst as follows:

> Paradoxically, the analyst must simultaneously fail the patient in a significant way that breaks the tie between patient and analyst during a period of dependence, and not fail the patient by living the experience of the current breakdown with the patient and helping the patient to understand his experience of the breakdown. (p. 215)

This two-way experience allows the patient to gradually move from where he or she left off on the path of creating a sense of self and object.

At this most primitive stage of transference, the task of the analyst that I am trying to describe is akin to the motherhood dynamics discussed by Winnicott (1956) as "primary maternal preoccupation." The analyst, just as the mother/caregiver does, moves around the essence of the patient's personality, must avoid approaches that might be perceived as interfering or threatening, must try to open the suitable holding space for the core to develop, and must be very cautious against neglect and violation. Sometimes there is no room for words or comments. In some extreme cases, the comment may even be perceived as a kind of harassment or violation, as it may point to the existence of the other and may become a stimulus that disrupts the state of unity. Ogden (1995) talks about the importance of listening to the differences between the silences during the sessions and sensing the vitality of the transference. Sometimes the most effective help is the presence of a consulting room as a representation of the analyst's body, and waiting for the patient to prepare for the existence of the other.

After this short theoretical introduction for providing a basis for discussion, let us now return to the work in the electronic setting. I hope it is now clearer how the sudden separation from the room was a traumatic experience for individuals who were in a such sensitive dependent transference prior to the pandemic. Just as the omnipotent illusion (Winnicott, 1945) experienced in the earliest relationship with the mother is suddenly shattered. While sharing the same room, on my couch or on the armchair, they had to separate from me very quickly at a time when they felt as if I was part of them. Some of them had an experience that corresponded to physical pain, such as the rupture of a body part or being left in a void. An increase in bodily complaints might have been an expression of this. One patient has actually said, "I feel a pain as if my leg had been severed." They were very angry and had serious anxieties reminding them of fears of annihilation. In their dreams, fear of hurting me was a dominant theme. Although talking about these concerns provided some relief, their minds were still focused on the order they had lost. When would we return to the office? When would we be reunited? Not only had the omnipotent illusion been disrupted, but also, we had to move into a space that was inherently insufficient to carry this regression. Furthermore, it was uncertain how long we would reside in this new place. Displacement was added to the traumatic effect of the pandemic. With a two-dimensional screen, an inside-less platform, as my patients put it, it was not possible for me to offer the holding environment they needed. Some of them were left in complete "desolation" as their destructive emotions destroyed me internally as well. In this case, it would not be wrong to assert that "primary trauma" (Abram, 2021) was repeated, but this time in an electronic analytic setting. Furthermore, I had expected from them, who were in such an infantile regression, to create an analytic environment for themselves. How realistic was this, and what meaning did such an expectation have in their minds? Either they would maintain their false selves as if nothing had happened in order to reassure me/the analyst, or they would cling to psychotic defenses such as the manic defense, or be terrified with the fear of annihilation, just like in their early childhoods.

I have encountered all of these options at various levels. The first thing I did was to try to switch to a face-to-face method with a few patients having serious difficulties on the couch. Even though my face was just a body part, it worked as a proof that I was alive, and it calmed their anxiety a little bit. The facial expressions, my hair, my jewelry had all become very important. In every session, I felt that my face and the background were being scrutinized. One patient, noticing my necklace, which I almost always wear, was able to make a connection between the analyst in the office and the person on the screen. Every session she would check to see if the necklace was still on my neck. At times they tried to guess my whereabouts, using outside sounds as clues. All these were indicators of us not being in the same room anymore; in other words, that we had a lot of loss. However, mourning our losses required a certain level of differentiation between the self and the object. At this level of regression, the sense of loss would lead to being terrified, reviving the fear of annihilation. It was a matter of survival, life and death.

Over time, I noticed that for some patients especially my eyes, my gaze, and my voice gradually gained importance. In the absence of the body-room, eyes and voice were apparently trying to assume an important function. Just as in childhood, the baby looked for him- or herself in the eyes of the mother. As is well known, during the earliest developmental periods, the mirroring function of the mother plays an important role as the holding environment. The baby needs to be seen by the mother in order to feel alive (Abram, 1996). However, this process between the mother and the baby is not only the product of an audiovisual exchange. It is rather a psychic and physical interaction containing all sensory perceptions. The baby is seen-seeing, heard-sensing, smelled-smelling, felt-feeling, touched-touching, and, of course, moving. Over time, this relationship paves the way for the development of the perception that the other and oneself occupy a place with their presence.

Although I observed that the gaze, the voice, and being heard gained special importance, these were not enough for the symbolization and integration of early experiences. It was partly soothing, but not therapeutic, especially for those who looked forward to returning to the room and whose survival anxieties were more pronounced. As Winnicott (1969) wrote in his article "The use of an object," for an object to be used, it had to be real, as part of a shared reality. The mother had to be able to survive against the baby's destructive fantasies (Winnicott, 1945). From this point of view, it is of vital importance for the patient that the analyst is able to survive despite everything; in other words, the analyst has to maintain his or her analytic functions. It was important to help my patients perceive the fact that I survived as an analyst and that my office lived on, too. I started to think about the conditions for returning to the office. For sure, working at the office would help not only my patients but myself as well, in terms of feeling more secure. For this reason, when the weather warmed up and the threat of the pandemic relatively decreased, I began to see those patients, the ones having serious difficulties and could never adequately calm down, in the office once a month. Although we were wearing masks, the excitement of meeting in the same room brought some vitality to the process, enabling new dynamics to stir up between us. Being able to meet again in the room, as a proof of our survival, provided some relief to their fears of annihilation and destruction, contributing to the progress of the analytic process. However, it was not easy to synchronize office sessions with online sessions. It had some disadvantages regarding both transference and the protection of the frame. I think it worked partly, but with a few people who found it very difficult, we switched to working entirely in the room as soon as possible.

Over time, I was able to meet most of my patients at the office. Although masks and other hygienic precautions brought other difficulties, the carrying and holding power of being in the same room was comforting. On the other hand, the precautions for hygiene and protection were all signs indicating we would not be able to carry on as if nothing had happened. Those patients who reacted to these were probably trying to deny the heavy load of the loss and deprivation. Nothing was ever the same as before.

Despite various conflicting situations, only a few patients objected to the return to the office. Those who objected, as I mentioned in more detail above, were a few people who had serious difficulties with online work in the beginning, but later adapted to it. A different situation developed with them over time. These people, who had not been able to settle in the room before the pandemic, were surprisingly settled in the electronic setting. And we were even able to find an efficient way to work. They seemed comfortable in the new order. There was a palpable harmony between us. They were happy to reach me with just a click, without showing any special effort. But, when I told them that we could go back to the room, I received responses that they were happy with the arrangement and did not want to change it again. I sensed that behind this resistance was a reluctance to let go of the harmony achieved in the online work, an experience that was almost equivalent to the experience of being one with the analyst. Reaching the analyst with just a click was almost like a blessing for these individuals who needed a "nonexistence" experience. They had the opportunity to experience, at least for a while, the illusion of omnipotence that perhaps they had once been unable to experience in the mother–infant relationship. They were far from perceiving the reality of two separate individuals, two separate spaces, as if the environment didn't matter to them; they had serious difficulties with reality testing. I thought, going back to the room, taking a step toward the outside world was equivalent to forcing them through a psychic birth they were not ready for. Even when I did feel they were ready, I could observe how reluctant they were to move from an omnipotent world into a world of realities that they would not be able to control.

Many authors agree that electronic space paves the way for dependent transference and omnipotent experience. Russell (2019) argues that with instant access to a therapist, there is no real tension regarding the kicking or kissing potential, so that the movement toward otherness is insufficient. The author further adds that "in mediated therapy, as well as in technologically mediated relating in the wider world, there is little opportunity to experience the reality of the object as outside the subject's omnipotent control, to find externality itself." Lemma (2015) argues that electronic media can blur the boundaries between the inner and outer worlds and as a result the two may be perceived as almost identical. She mentions that people can get lost in an omnipotent experience, as if there is no limit to what can be imagined and realized. And yet, based on my experience with the patients I mentioned above, I can say that this situation, which can sometimes be quite dangerous in everyday life, can sometimes be turned into an opportunity and have a healing effect in the presence of a therapist/analyst.

This is what I observed in the few people who were much more primitive, with almost psychotic personality organizations. The virtual nature of the electronic setting perhaps opened a space that corresponded to their need to "become one with the analyst" and to experience omnipotence associated with this. I assume that these experiences contribute to the reparation of the basic trust or "the capacity to believe in life (mother–analyst)." Of course, they also needed disillusionment in order to continue their development and to be able to differentiate. Otherwise, it would be possible to continue this way, without any progress or development, in a dependent transference for years. I tried to keep up with their paces without rushing or pushing them, inviting them to understand this resistance, in order to prepare them for the work in the room. One of the questions that puzzled me was whether the disappearance of their clinical symptoms was related to structural changes. If there were no structural changes, the previous symptoms could easily reappear when we returned to the room.

Especially when working with patients with severe psychopathology, I relied on the guidance of my countertransference feelings. I guess the fact that I didn't feel anxious was a sign that things were going well. So, it was. When they were finally able to return to the room, I was surprised to see that the change was not limited to the clinical picture, there were significant transformations in their mental functions. The way we communicated had changed. Actions and bodily complaints were replaced by more verbal expressions. There were significant developments in the integration of the self and object perceptions. Especially, one of these patients had been almost unable to take care of himself; his psychotic core was very evident. When he was able to return to the room, his self-care had improved, and he was able to make observations about himself and others. His capacity to cope with disappointments and deprivations had changed. But, of course, we still had a lot of work to do to achieve enough self–object differentiation. In order to differentiate they first needed to become one. And I think online work had enabled them to experience this unity more easily in adequate levels. This, in turn, may have made differentiation easier as well.

Conclusion

Even before the pandemic, technology was being used for remote analytical work and there were debates on the effectiveness of online work (Brainsky, 2003; Merchant, 2016; Neumann, 2013; Scharff, 2013; Yamin Habib, 2003). In the twenty-first century, with the impact of rapid globalization and technological developments, there were significant changes in social and personal lifestyles, and these changes began to change the direction of needs. Some psychoanalysts were looking for new ways to adapt their treatment approaches to the dynamics of the twenty-first century (Scharff, 2012, 2010). This search for new methods was criticized as much as supported. However, with the pandemic, these methods have necessarily entered the agenda of even those of us who had never thought about them before or even rejected them. This forced introduction led us to question our prejudices about the effectiveness of technology in analytical processes and to think more about it. After the pandemic, it was impossible for us to continue from where we had left off. Nothing was the same, and this was true for psychoanalytic practices. Nowadays, although the worst of the pandemic is behind us and the need for remote analysis has decreased, the demand for online work persists. This interest comes not only from our patients, but the analysts themselves as well. And compared to before the pandemic, we have significantly more experience to evaluate the effectiveness, indications, possible advantages, and disadvantages of online studies. Sharing, discussing, and trying to evaluate these experiences may help us discover how, when, and how much technology can be used in psychoanalytic practices in the new, sometimes chaotic world of the twenty-first century.

In this context, when I evaluate my own experiences, I cannot speak of a clear conclusion about the effectiveness of my remote work. I think that such clarity would be a superficial and forced approach. For now, I would like to state that I cannot go beyond a few observations which require further elaboration. I will try to summarize these observations in a few sentences.

As I mentioned in detail above, I tried to categorize my patients in two main groups according to their adaptation skills. All of them had difficulties in the beginning, but some had adapted relatively easily, so that we could continue with our work. However, there were also those who had serious difficulties in adaptation and for whom it was very difficult to carry on with the online work. Among these, a subgroup of a few people, with whom I was able to work quite efficiently after adaptation, was both surprising and promising.

Those who were able to adapt relatively easily were the ones who had internalized my analytic functions during our work in the room. It is known that an important element of the analytic work is related to the activation of the symbolization process. In the process of symbolization, the absence of the analyst is of particular importance (A. Green, 1975). Winnicott (1958b) states that we can only talk about the absence of another if that other was once present. From this point of view, it is expected to be more productive to work online with patients who have felt the confirmation of their existence in the first mother–infant relationship, in other words, who has achieved some measure of differentiation between me and not-me, and therefore who have enough ego strength. In this context, my patients who were more capable of the distinction between self and others more easily carried me as an analyst within them, even though we did not physically share the same environment, and thus we were able to continue our work.

However, the situation was different for the patients I had difficulty with in the electronic space. Those, who switched to online work at a stage when they were developing dependent transference, were the most difficult. These patients, due to their level of regression, had serious difficulties with self–object differentiations. And our analytic work had not yet come to a point where they could internalize me as an analyst. For them, sharing the same physical space with the analyst was as important as needing the physical presence of the mother in the earliest stages of infancy. Unfortunately, online sessions only managed to keep them alive until we went back to the office.

Jan Abram (Zurich, June 2020 Zoom study) considers that online work has made or can make the analyst unable to survive. From this perspective, she asks how differentiation, as the structuring process of subjectivity, can occur without the physical presence of two bodies. I would like to further elaborate this topic by adding one more question: "Despite the inability to share the same physical space, could eyes, mimics, and perhaps the voice play a holding role, or could the gaze be sufficient for the confirmation of existence?"

While searching for an answer to this question, my mind turned to the work we did with a few patients in the subgroup who had perhaps the most primitive pathologies compared to my other patients. I think the success of working with them must have been due to the online process being able to create a sufficiently good holding environment after a certain stage. At the very least, I assume that with the help of my eyes, my voice, and my analytical stance, all elements of the online practice functioned as a sufficiently good holding environment, and therefore opened a space for the experience of becoming one with the analyst. And this experience may have provided a facilitating basis for the self–object differentiation. However, I would like to point out that these were not enough to symbolize and integrate the early experiences, and that we needed to physically share the same space in order to continue to develop.

To summarize, for now I tend to see online studies as a supplement to the main work we do, using the possibilities of technology when the circumstances require it, rather than treating it as an alternative model to in-room studies. Although technological methods offer valuable opportunities to continue our analytical work, to keep doing our work, and although it has been observed by many clinicians that it works for some patients (Scharff, 2013), and although what we do is to some extent sufficient as many of us have experienced during the pandemic, we should not forget that human beings need physical contact, just like breathing.

True presence is irreplaceable, even though it is unpredictable, spontaneous, and dispersed.

Notes

Chapter 1

1. This hospital is known today as *Bakırköy (Prof. Dr. Mazhar Osman)*, and it is still the major psychiatric institution in the country.
2. For a general review of psychiatry with a specific focus on the history of descriptive and dynamic approaches, see Lunbeck, "Psychiatry" (2003). For the increasing popularity of psychoanalysis from the 1920s to 1960s, see Shorter, who addresses it as a hiatus or interruption in the "evolution of biological approaches to brain and mind" (Shorter, *A History of Psychiatry*, 1997, p. 145). In contrast, Andrew Scull sees it as a meaningful interlude, bringing an "emphasis on psychic conflict, trauma and repression as the source of mental turmoil" (Scull, *Madness in Civilization*, 2015, p. 324). It should also be noted that there were cases, such as in France, where the psychoanalytic approach could not take a strong hold simultaneously with the Anglo-Saxon or Central European examples. See Goldstein, "Neutralizing Freud" (2013). For the resistance of eminent German psychiatrists such as Emil Kraepelin, Alfred Hoche, and Oswald Bumke to psychoanalysis in Germany, see Shorter, *A History of Psychiatry* (1997, p. 15), and Scull, *Madness in Civilization* (2015, p. 326).
3. On the dominance and authority of the descriptive psychiatric approach, and particularly of German (Kraepelinian) descriptive psychiatry in Turkey, see Volkan, "Turkey" (1975, p. 393), and Kılıç, *Deliler ve Doktorları* (2013, p. 42).
4. For the history of İstanbul Psychoanalytical Group, which later became the İstanbul Psychoanalytical Association and was recognized as a "provisional society" by the International Psychoanalytical Association (IPA) in 2012, see "About Us—History," İstanbul Psikanaliz Derneği website, www.İstanbulpsikanalizdernegi.com/en/about-us/history (last accessed August 17, 2017).

5. For an anthology of the earliest texts on psychoanalysis in Turkish, see Taştan, *Türkiye'de Psikanaliz Hakkında En Eski Metinler* (2011).
6. For a history of Turkish psychiatry that follows the emergence of its two branches, namely descriptive psychiatry and dynamic psychiatry, and their major Turkish representatives, Mazhar Osman [Uzman] (1884–1951) and İzzettin Şadan, see Yalçıner and Hanoğlu, *İç Bahçe* (2001).
7. For more on the issue, see MacIntyre, "Tradition and translation" (1988) and Asad, "The concept of cultural translation" (1986).
8. Liu, *Translingual Practice* (1995, p. 15). Also see Benjamin, "The task of the translator" (1968). For recent historical studies on science and translation theoretically informed by such views, see Elshakry, *Reading Darwin in Arabic* (2013), and Yalçınkaya, *Learned Patriots* (2015, pp. 11–14).
9. Şadan, "Hatırat" (1968, p. 79). On Toptaşı and its transformation into Bakırköy Mental Hospital, see Artvinli, *Delilik* (2013).
10. Yalçıner and Hanoğlu, *İç Bahçe* (2001, p. 44).
11. Holmes, "Subject of Focus" (2010, p. 12). Also see Uşak-Şahin, "Another dimension of the émigré experience" (2012, pp. 135–136), and Volkan and Itzkowitz, *The Immortal Atatürk* (1984, p. 294).
12. For contemporary depictions of Şadan in the popular press, see Cündioğlu, "Freud'un Türk Talebesinden İlginç (Psiko) Analizler" (2007); Atsız, "İzzeddin Şadan ve Fetullah Gulen" (2008); Özdemir, "İzzettin Şadan' ın Dünya Görüşü" (2017); and Belge, "Ana Düşünce Akımı Irkçılık" (2003).
13. Şadan, *Birsam-ı Saadet* (1943, pp. 3–4). Unless otherwise noted, all translations are mine.
14. Şadan, "Freudizmin Sırr-ı Muvaffakiyeti" (1925).
15. Şadan, "Psikopatoloji" (1936e, p. 10).
16. Şadan, "Akıl Hastalıkları" (1937a, p. 6).
17. Ibid. There is a huge and often conflicting secondary literature on the issue of Freud's determinism and reliance on causality. It is possible to claim that Şadan's interpretation of Freud's determinism and causal methodology is directly parallel to Freud's biographer Frank Sulloway, who depicted Freud as a "psychological determinist" with an "abiding faith in the principle of cause and effect" (Sulloway, *Freud, Biologist of the Mind*, 1979, p. 94; see also pp. 94–97, 138, 356). For a conflicting "hermeneutical" view claiming that psychoanalysis "speaks not of causes but motives [although] its explanations resemble causal explanation" (p. 360), see Ricoeur, *Freud and Philosophy* (1977, pp. 360–363), and Habermas, *Knowledge and Human Interests* (1971). And for a critical reading of Ricoeur's and Habermas' hermeneutical evaluations of psychoanalysis, see Grünbaum, *The Foundations of Psychoanalysis* (1984, in particular pp. 69–74).
18. "Rüya tahlillerinden istihraç olunan deliller, hergünkü hayatin psikopatolojisi denilen mevzudan olunan deliller, gayrı meşura ehemmiyet vermek yolunu takip ederek hastaları tedavi eden tıbbi usulden çıkarılan deliller, posthypnotic husule gelen bazı fıkirlerin hatıraların, hatta müşkül meselelerin halli gibi hadiselerin davetsizce ani olarak tezahür, eromdem çıkarılan deliller" (Şadan, "Akıl Hastalıkları," 1937a, p. 16).
19. Although Şadan early on considered Freud's psychoanalytic approach unscientific, Freud defined psychoanalysis as a natural science and an offspring of modern scientific revolution. See Freud,

New Introductory Lectures (1933a). Freud was also considered "an ideal type of Enlightenment scientist" (Cohler & Galatzer-Levy, "What kind of science is psychoanalysis?", 2007, p. 550), as well as "the true heir of the Enlightenment" (Gay, *The Freud Reader*, 1995, p. 685; quoted in Kapila, "The 'godless' Freud," 2007, p. 134). On Freud's commitment to empiricism and biology, as highlighted by his lifelong friend, colleague, and biographer Ernest Jones, see Jones, "Psychoanalysis and biology" (1930). Freud's image as the "psychoanalytic hero" who defied positivism is a product of the second half of the twentieth century, propounded by hermeneutical reading of his works by Ricoeur and others. In contrast, Freud was also defined as a "biologist of the mind" whose work fundamentally relied on Darwinian evolutionary biology. See Sulloway, *Freud, Biologist of the Mind* (1979). There is also a vibrant literature that in various different but convincing ways problematizes the scientific nature of Freud's psychoanalytic claims and scrutinizes the persuasive power that Freudian psychoanalysis attained by and through its scientific garb. See Popper, *Conjectures and Refutations* (1963, p. 37). Wittgenstein, who criticizes Freud for "propounding a new myth" and for being "clever, but not wise" is also particularly interesting. See Wittgenstein, *Lectures and Conversations on Aesthetics, Psychology and Religious Belief* (1967, p. 41). For more on Wittgenstein's take on the issue, see Bouveresse, *Wittgenstein Reads Freud* (1995), and Cioffi, *Wittgenstein on Freud and Frazer* (1998).

20. See Jones, *Traité théorique et pratique de psychoanalyse* (1925). Şadan later translated Jones' book *Psycho-Analysis* (London, 1929) into Turkish. See Jones, *Psikanaliz.*
21. Şadan, "Hatırat" (1968, p. 77). He particularly defines two of A. A. Brill's books, *Psychoanalysis* (1912) and *Freud's Contribution to Psychiatry* (1944), as "essential to understand the evolution of psychiatry" (op. cit.).
22. Although it was a common practice to publish patient cases in that period, it is not possible to find any patient case Şadan published in which he employed either psychoanalytic or descriptive psychiatry methodology to cure a patient. For psychoanalytic examples of such published cases, see Freud's case studies including Anna O. (with Josef Breuer), the "Rat Man," the "Wolf Man," and Dora. For example, of the published patient cases from Turkey in the same period, see Mazhar Osman [Uzman]'s serialized articles, titled "Mecnunlar Arasında Mücrim Tipleri," in the medical journal İstanbul Seririyati, as well as his books such as *Akıl Hastalıları* (1928) and *Tababet-i Ruhiye* (1947).
23. "[Freud] *Eros' a boyun eğdi. Libido'ya Eros adını Verdi*" ("[Freud] complied with Eros, and named Libido as Eros") (Şadan, "Eros (Aşk) ile Mücadele," 1936a, p. 11). It must be noted that writing this article series in the popular literary-cultural magazine *Yeni Adam*, Şadan rarely offers direct references to Freud's publications. Yet his interpretation of Freud's take of "libido as Eros" plausibly derived from a reading of Freud's 1925 paper "The resistances to psycho-analysis," in which Freud, responding to critiques of psychoanalysis, stressed that the psychoanalytic concept of sexuality is "by no means identical with the impulsion toward a union of the two sexes or toward producing a pleasurable sensation in the genitals; it had far more resemblance to the all-inclusive and all-preserving Eros of Plato's *Symposium*" (Freud, "The resistances to psychoanalysis,", 1925e, p. 218). Publishing in medical journals to introduce some Freudian concepts, Şadan nonetheless defined the "libido" as exclusively the sex drive (*cinsi garize*), predicated on

genital activity. Şadan, "Freud'un Nevroz Nazariyesi". In these publications, he referred to English and French translations of Freud's works, including *Introduction à la psychanalyse: Three Essays on Sexuality, Civilized Sexual Morality and Modern Nervous Illness* as well as works of some of Freud's followers, such as Jones *Psychoanalysis, Traité théorique et pratique de psychanalyse*, and Brill, Psychoanalysis. See Şadan, "*Freud'un Nevroz Nazariyesi*" (1933a); Şadan, "*Freud'un Nevroz Nazariyesi-2*" (1933b); Şadan, "Psikanalize Göre Nevrozların Etiyolojisi" (1933c). Also see Şadan's definition of libido as purely sexual (*cinsi*) in its early phases yet losing its sexual orientation and being sublimated (*sublime olur*) once taken under control by the ego and superego (*ben and yüksek ben*). Şadan, "Akıl Hastalıkları" (1937b, p. 16).

24. Here I employ the concept of tradition not as an antonym of modern, or a category belonging to the past that can only be reinvented within modernity, but rather as a living and constantly reconfigured entity. For more on tradition as being reconfigured and practiced differently under different historical contexts, as well as sustaining relationships both to the "past" and the "future," yet keeping the "present" at its center, see MacIntyre, "The virtues, the unity of a human life" (1981, pp. 221–223), and Asad, *Formations of the Secular* (2003, pp. 222–223). For a study that historically analyzes Islamic tradition as a living one, see Haj, *Reconfiguring Islamic Tradition* (2009).
25. Şadan, "Eros (Aşk) ile Mücadele" (1936a, p. 11).
26. Ibid. Also see Şadan, "Aşkla Mücadele" (1936d, p. 10). On love as a sui generis sickness, see Şadan, "Aşkla Mücadele" (1936f, p. 10).
27. Şadan, "Eros (Aşk) ile Mücadele" (1936a, p. 11).
28. Ibid., pp. 11–12.
29. Şadan, "Eros (Aşk) ile Mücadele" 1936b, p. 5.
30. See Freud, *Totem and Taboo* (1912–13), and Freud, *Moses and Monotheism* (1939a). For Freud's treatment of religion as a "mass-delusion," see Freud, *Civilization and Its Discontents* (1930a, p. 36); for religion as an illusion, causing a collective delirium that would be overcome by science, see Freud, *The Future of an Illusion* (1927c). Science, in contrast, is not illusionary, and it has given us "evidence by its numerous and important successes" (ibid., p. 70). Also see Gay, *A Godless Jew* (1989).
31. "*Müslümanlar cins garizesini bukadar şiddetli bir ihtibasa tutmamışlardır*" (Şadan, "Eros [Aşk] ile Mücadele," 1936a, p. 12). Tracing Şadan's argument here also displays a plausible dialogue with Freud's analysis of civilization as a source of discontent because of its oppressive dynamics over the sex drive. Freud, *Civilization and Its Discontents* (1930a, pp. 72–78). Şadan emphatically refutes this argument by emphasizing the differences between Islamic and Christian approaches to sexuality and pleasure.
32. "Müslümanlıkta hıristiyanlığın mazohist temayüllerine benziyecek, yalaşacak şekillere girdikçe, mazohistlenimş ihtibasa tutulmuş, ve marazi bir hal almiştır" (Şadan, "Eros [Aşk] ile Mücadele," 1936a, p. 12).
33. Musallam, *Sex and Society in Islam* (1983, pp. 10–12, 31–37).
34. Şadan, "Bir Müslüman Efsanesi" (2007, pp. 23, 29).

35. Şadan, *Birsam-ı Saadet* (1943, p. 20).
36. Ibid., pp. 20–21.
37. Şadan, "Bir Müslüman Efsanesi" (2007, p. 22).
38. See Pandolfo, "The thin line of modernity" (2000). On criticisms of Sufism within the Islamic tradition for its self-mortification, seclusion, and celibacy, which were considered deviations from the Islamic sunna, see Schimmel, *Mystical Dimensions of Islam* (1975, p. 16); N. Green, *Sufism* (2012, p. 20); and Wilde, "Monasticism" (2006, p. 507). It is nonetheless impossible to find any explicit references to key concepts or hallmarks of the Islamic tradition in Şadan's writing. Şadan clearly appears as a secular, if not secularist, republican man of science, rejecting past traditions as obsolete and backward in accordance with the Kemalist project of Turkish secularism, yet continuously haunted by them. In this regard, Şadan differs from "Muslim" psychoanalysts such as Yusuf Murad (1902–66), who produced a local psychoanalytic discourse in Egypt in which he overtly referred to and rearticulated key ideas and concepts of the Islamic tradition. On Murad and his reliance on the concepts of Islamic thinkers such as Ibn 'Arabî and al-Ghazali while engaging with Western psychoanalysts, including Freud, Karen Horney, Ian Suttie, and Western philosophers such as Henri Bergson and Victor Cousin, see El Shakry, "The Arabic Freud" (2014).
39. Şadan, "Aşk (Eros) ile Mücadele," 121: 5,11.
40. Ibid., 11.
41. Şadan, "Aşk (Eros) ile Mücadele," 124: 1936c, p. 5.
42. Ibid., p. 5.
43. Ibid.
44. TBMM (The Grand National Assembly of Turkey), *Zabıt Ceridesi* [Minutes Journal], *2*(19): 311–312, quoted in Shaw and Shaw, *History of the Ottoman Empire and Modern Turkey, Vol. 2* (1977, p. 385); Berkes, *The Development of Secularism in Turkey* (1964, pp. 465–467); and Zürcher, *Turkey* (2004, pp. 172–173).
45. For the concept of "horizon of expectations," see Koselleck, "Space of experience" (2004).
46. Here my understanding of Judeo-Christian secularism is directly inspired by Talal Asad's genealogical evaluation of secularism as a discourse embedded in the (Judeo-) Christian culture and its tradition of liberalism. See Asad, *Formations of the Secular* (2003), and Anidjar, *Semites* (2007, pp. 39–63).
47. Şadan, *Birsam-ı Saadet* (1943, p. 8). Thus the first chapter of *Birsam-ı Saadet* appears to be a direct critique of this hostility toward individualism in Turkey, which Şadan considers to be one of the major neuroses within Turkish society.
48. Şadan, *Birsam-ı Saadet* (1943, pp. 31, 37–38, 53–54).
49. Nevertheless, as various historians argue, Ottomanism proved to be fruitless in an era of emerging ethnic nationalism among different communities of the empire, diverting the modernizing Ottoman state from clinging to the idea of Turkish nationalism to redefine itself. For more on Ottomanism and the emergence of Turkish nationalism, see Somer, "Osmanlı Reform Çağında Osmanlıcılık Düşüncesi" (2001), and Hanioğlu, "Turkish nationalism and the

young Turks" (2002). Hasan Kayalı is particularly interesting with his analysis of a persistent and resilient supernational ideology of Islamism hindering the prevalence of Arab and Turkish ethnic nationalism during the Young Turk Period; see Kayalı, *Arabs and Young Turks* (1997). Comparative studies on the emergence of modern nations and ethnic identities include Anderson, *Imagined Communities* (2006), Wimmer, *Waves of War* (2013), and Brubaker, *Ethnicity without Groups* (2006).

50. Şadan, *Birsam-ı Saadet* (1943, p. 38).
51. Ibid., pp. 37–38; see also pp. 31–32.
52. Ibid., p. 52.
53. Ibid., p. 36. It should be noted that Freud belonged to a period when definitions and perceptions regarding communities were shaped by the paradigm of nationalism. Thus, one cannot ignore his transhistorical perception of various communities as nations within his writings. However, Freud maintained a very reserved stance on the issue of Zionism during his lifetime as an intellectual identifying himself as a European Jew. His writings have the contours of a universalist rather than a nationalist. Thus, Isaac Deutscher claims that Freud was a "non-Jewish Jew," who (together with Baruch Spinoza, Karl Marx, and Heinrich Heine) "believe in the ultimate solidarity of man" at a time when horrors and tragedies were compelling Jews to embrace the idea of a nation state (Deutscher, *The Non-Jewish Jew*, 1968, pp. 35, 40). Moreover, as Edward Said argues, Freud's depiction of Moses, the prophet of Judaism and the originator of Jewish identity, as a non-European Egyptian is a "way of refusing to resolve identity into some nationalist or religious herds" (Said, *Freud and the Non-European*, 2004, p. 53).
54. "Milliyetçilik hissi ise, yine Freud'dan öğrendiğimize nazaran yalnız ferdi değil, cemyeti de en yakın olan muhite intibak ettirmesi dolayısile nevrozdan kurtaran bir mihanikiyettir" (Şadan, *Birsam-ı Saadet*, 1943, p. 50).
55. "Ferdi yükselten her iktisa, narsisizmi doyurur ve binnetice şahsı mésut kılar" (ibid., pp. 50–51).
56. Ibid., p. 51.
57. Şadan, "Milliyetin Felsefesi" (1942, p. 59).
58. Freud, *Group Psychology and the Analysis of the Ego* (1921c).
59. Şadan, *Birsam-ı Saadet* (1943, pp. 51–52).
60. Ibid., p. 52. Also see Şadan, "Türk Milliyetçileri Diyorlar ki" (1958, pp. 20–21), and Şadan, "Milliyetin Felsefesi" (1942, pp. 59–60).
61. See "Turks teach new theories," *New York Times*, February 9, 1936; Aytürk, İ. (2004). Turkish linguists against the West: the origins of linguistic nationalism in Atatürk's Turkey, *40*(6), pp. 1–25.
62. Şadan, *Birsam-ı Saadet* (1943, p. 52).
63. "Ve madem ki milliyet duygusu, psikolojinin narsisik mihanikiyetine istinad eder. O halde bu narsisistik hali rahnedar eden hersey insanları felakete yani manevi ve ruhi ızdıraba sürükiyecektir. Ruhi ıztırap bir hastalıktır. Bu ise ancak tababeti ruhiye usulile tetkik ve bertaraf edilebilir. Bu da bana gösteriyor ki: Saadet ancak milliyetçiliktedir" (ibid., p. 60).
64. For internationalism in particular, see Şadan, "Milliyetin Felsefesi" (1942, p. 59).

65. Şadan, *Birsam-ı Saadet* (1943, p. 59).
66. "*Milliyet cereyanını bulandırmak vatan mefhumunu bulandırmaktır*" (ibid., p. 61).
67. Turanism is the ultranationalist, racist ideology that is predicated on the idea of the existence and unity of a Turanid (Ural-Altaic) race. It played a significant role in the emergence of Turkish nationalism as well as other national narratives such as Hungarian nationalism. For more on Turanism, see Landau, *Pan-Turkism* (1995), and Özdoğan, "*Turan'dan 'Bozkurt'a*" (2001, pp. 15–42). For a study on the construction of republican official history of the "Turkish nation," which locates Turkish identity historically in Central Asia as well as in Anatolia, see Ersanlı, *İktidar ve Tarih* (2003).
68. For a study on Turanism in early republican Turkey that takes this legal incident as its starting point, see Özdoğan, "*Turan'dan 'Bozkurt'a*" (2001). See also Koçak for an elaboration of the relationships between this Turanist group and the Nazi government in Germany, which considered antisocialist sentiments of Turanism as a possible weapon to stimulate the Turkic populations living under the Soviet rule. Koçak, *Türkiye'de Milli Şef Dönemi* (1996, pp. 660–695). For the list of ultranationalists in the lawsuit file, see "V. Ek," (Appendix V) in Sefercioğlu, 3 *Mayıs 1944* (2009).
69. Şadan, *Birsam-ı Saadet* (1943, pp. 10–11, 23–24).
70. Şadan, "Eine Mohammadanische Legende" (1932), and Şadan, "Bir Müslüman Efsanesi" (2007).
71. Şadan, "Notes" (1948, pp. 572–573).
72. On the issue of modernity as multidimensional, see T. Mitchell, "The stage of modernity." For situating Europe not as the center but as a province of modern history, see Chakrabarty, *Provincializing Europe* (2007); for modern science and its multidimensionality, see Prakash, *Another Reason* (1999).
73. See Bose, "Letter dated 11.4.29 from Dr. G. Bose to Prof. Dr. Freud" (1964). For some suggestive studies on Bose and the challenge he posed for certain Freudian concepts, see Nandy, "The savage Freud" (1995); Kapila, "The 'godless' Freud" (2007); and Hartnack, *Psychoanalysis in Colonial India* (2001).

Chapter 3

1. I am grateful to Dr. Şahap Erkoç, a serious scholar of the history of psychiatry in Turkey, for providing me with a copy of parts of İzeddin Şadan's memoirs, and Hale Uşak-Şahin for sharing her research on this man's role in introducing psychoanalysis to Turkey (Uşak-Şahin, 2009a, 2009b).

Chapter 7

1. She was one of the thousands of victims of the US-supported military coup in Turkey on March 12, 1971. During that period, the United States was involved in several controversial actions worldwide, including organizing or supporting military coups in Turkey, Argentina, Chile, and other countries. The military coups in Turkey in 1971 and 1980 are now viewed critically, having

left a legacy of hundreds of dead and missing, along with thousands who suffered physical and psychological injuries.

2. An illusion is not a delusion. This distinction is crucial because a delusion is incompatible with reality, whereas an illusion may not always be so; it can be realized and can be compatible with reality. Furthermore, an illusion is also distinct from a hallucination, because a hallucination involves perception without an object.
3. However, some parents struggle with this because they have either not allowed themselves the opportunity to create illusions supported by their own ego ideals, or they have not accepted that these illusions must eventually yield to the dominance of external reality. These individuals often lack a fully realized adolescence within their adult psyche.

Chapter 10

1. Controversies over the notion of "the banality of evil" also have a political character, namely the role of Jewish institutions in the deportations and the ironic tone used by Arendt (1951) in the aftermath of the disaster. In the course of writing this chapter, we have left out this aspect, which does not relate directly to our purpose. For more details on this topic, see Leibovici (2002).

References

Abazov, R. (2009). *Culture and Customs of Turkey.* Westport, CT: Greenwood.

Abram, J. (1996). *The Language of Winnicott: A Dictionary of Winnicott's Use of Words.* London: Karnac.

Abram, J. (2013). On Winnicott's area of formlessness: The pure female element and the capacity to feel real. *European Psychoanalytic Bulletin, 67*: 43–57.

Abram, J. (2021). On Winnicott's concept of trauma. *International Journal of Psychoanalysis, 102*: 778–793.

Açıkgöz, A., Örsal, O., Örsal, Ö., & Balcı-Alparslan, G. (2014). Traditional practices used by Turkish mothers in the care of their babies. *Holistic Nursing Practice, 28*: 198–207.

Adasal, R. (1964). *Medikal Psikoloji [Medical psychology], Vol. 1 and 2.* Ankara: Ankara Üniversitesi Yayınları.

Agger, E. M. (1988). Psychoanalytic perspectives on sibling relationships. *Psychoanalytic Inquiry, 8*: 3–30.

Ainsworth, M. D. S., Blehar, M. C., Waters, E., & Wall, S. (1978). *Patterns of Attachment: A Psychological Study of the Strange Situation.* Hillsdale, NJ: Lawrence Erlbaum.

Akçınar, B. (2017). *Involved Fatherhood and Its Determinants in Turkey.* Istanbul: Mother Child Education Foundation. www.acev.org/wp/-content/uploads/2019/10/1_involved-fatherhood-and-its-determinants-in-turkey-pdf (last accessed May 2, 2023).

Akhtar, S. (1991). Three fantasies related to unresolved separation-individuation: A less recognized aspect of severe character pathology. In: S. Akhtar & H. Parens (Eds.), *Beyond the Symbiotic Orbit: Advances in Separation-Individuation Theory* (pp. 261–284). Northvale, NJ: Jason Aronson.

Akhtar, S. (1992). Tethers, orbits and invisible fences: Clinical, developmental, sociocultural, and technical aspects of optimal distance. In: S. Kramer & S. Akhtar (Eds.), *When the Body Speaks: Psychological Meanings in Kinetic Clues* (pp. 21–57). Northvale, NJ: Jason Aronson.

Akhtar, S. (1995). A third individuation: Immigration, identity, and the psychoanalytic process. *Journal of the American Psychoanalytic Association, 43*: 1051–1084.

Akhtar, S. (1999). *Immigration and Identity: Turmoil, Treatment, and Transformation.* Northvale, NJ: Jason Aronson.

Akhtar, S. (2005). *Freud Along the Ganges: Psychoanalytic Reflections on the People and Culture of India.* New York: Other Press.

Akhtar, S. (Ed.) (2008). *The Crescent and the Couch: Cross-Currents between Islam and Psychoanalysis.* New York: Jason Aronson.

Akhtar, S. (2009). *Comprehensive Dictionary of Psychoanalysis.* London: Karnac.

Akhtar, S. (2010). *Freud and the Far East: Psychoanalytic Perspectives on the People and Culture of China, Japan, and Korea.* Northvale, NJ: Jason Aronson,

Akhtar, S. (2011). *Immigration and Acculturation: Mourning, Adaptation, and the Next Generation.* Lanham, MD: Jason Aronson.

Akhtar, S. (2012a). What does a mother do? In: *The Mother and Her Child: Clinical Aspects of Attachment, Separation, and Loss* (pp. 1–14). Lanham, MD: Jason Aronson.

Akhtar, S. (2012b). *The African American Experience: Psychoanalytic Perspectives.* Lanham, MD: Jason Aronson.

Akhtar, S., & Bertoglia, S. M. (Eds.) (2015). *The American Latino: Psychodynamic Perspectives on Culture and Mental Health.* Lanham, MD: Jason Aronson.

Akhtar, S., & Kramer, S. (1999). *Brothers and Sisters: Developmental, Dynamic, and Technical Aspects of the Sibling Relationship.* London: Jason Aronson.

Akhtar, S., & Parens, H. (1991). *Beyond the Symbiotic Orbit: Advances in Separation-Individuation Theory: Essays in Honor of Selma Kramer.* London: Routledge.

Akhtar, S., & Powell, A. (2004). Celluloid fathers: the depiction of paternal function in some recent movies. In: S. Akhtar & H. Parens (Eds.), *Real and Imaginary Fathers: Development, Transference, and Healing* (pp. 77–78). Lanham, MD: Jason Aronson.

Althusser, L. (1982). *Freud ve Lacan.* Istanbul, Turkey: Yazko Felsefe Yazıları.

Altınay, A. R. (2005). *Kadınlar Saltanatı.* Istanbul, Turkey: Tarih Vakfı Yayınları.

Ammaniti, M., & Gallese, V. (2014). *The Birth of Intersubjectivity.* New York: W. W. Norton.

Andersen, H. C. (1843). *Le Rossignol de l'Empereur de Chine.* Paris: Gallimard, 1990.

Anderson, B. (2006). *Imagined Communities: Reflections on the Origin and Spread of Nationalism.* Revised edn. London: Version.

Anidjar, G. (2007). *Semites: Race, Religion, Literature.* Stanford, CA: Stanford University Press.

Anzieu, D. (1984). *The Group and the Unconscious.* B. Kilborne (Trans. from the French). London: Routledge.

Arendt, H. (1951). *Les Origines du Totalitarisme*. I. Birksted (Trans.). Paris: Gallimard, 2002.

Arendt, H. (1963a). *Eichmann in Jerusalem: A Report on the Banality of Evil*. New York: Viking.

Arendt, H. (1963b). Letter of 24 July 1963 to Gershom Scholem. In: R. H. Feldman (Ed.), *The Jew as Pariah* (pp. 250–251). New York: Grove, 1978.

Arlow, J. (1980). The revenge motive in the primal scene. *Journal of the American Psychoanalytic Association, 28*: 519–541.

Artvinli, F. (2013). *Delilik, Siyaset ve Toplum: Toptaşı Bimarhanesi* (1873–1927) [*Madness, Politics, and Society: The Toptaşı Asylum*, 1873–1927]. Istanbul, Turkey: Boğaziçi Üniversitesi Yayınevi.

Asad, T. (1986). The concept of cultural translation in British social anthropology. In: J. Clifford & G. E. Marcus (Eds.), *Writing Culture: The Poetics and Politics of Ethnography* (pp. 141–164). Berkeley, CA: University of California Press.

Asad, T. (2003). *Formations of the Secular: Christianity, Islam, Modernity*. Stanford, CA: Stanford University Press.

Asch, S. S. (1976). Varieties of negative therapeutic reaction and problems of technique. *Journal of the American Psychoanalytic Association, 24*: 383–407.

Atsız, Y. (2008, September 14). İzzeddin Şadan ve Fetullah Gülen. *Star*.

Aytürk, İ. (2004). Turkish linguists against the West: The origins of linguistic nationalism in Atatürk's Turkey. *Middle Eastern Studies, 40*: 1–25.

Balsam, R. (2000). The mother within the mother. *Psychoanalytic Quarterly, 69*: 465–492.

Bank, S., & Kahn, M. D. (1980). Freudian siblings. *Psychoanalytic Review, 67*: 493–504.

Baranger, M., & Baranger, W. (2008). The analytic situation as a dynamic field. *International Journal of Psychoanalysis, 89*: 795–826.

Baranger, M., Baranger, W., & Mom, J. M. (1983). Process and non-process in analytic work. *International Journal of Psychoanalysis, 64*: 1–15.

Barnett, J. (1971). Narcissism and dependency in the obsessional-hysteric marriage. *Family Process, 1*: 75–83.

Baruzzi, A. (1981). Bion on self-expression. *Rivista di Psicoanalisi, 27*: 640–650.

Bassen, C. R. (2007). Telephone analysis (Panel report). *Journal of American Psychoanalytic Association, 55*: 1033–1041.

Bayrakceken, A., & Randall, D. (2005). Meetings of East and West: Orhan Pamuk's Istanbullite perspective. *Critique Studies in Contemporary Fiction, 46*: 191–204.

Beebe, B., & Lachmann, F. (1994). Representation and internalization in infancy: Three principles of salience. *Psychoanalytic Psychology, 11*: 127–165.

Bektaş, G., Boelsma, F., Gündüz, M., & Klaassen, E. (2022). A qualitative study on the perspectives of Turkish mothers and grandmothers in the Netherlands regarding the influence of grandmothers on health related practices in the first 1000 days of a child's life. *BMC Public Health, 22*: 1364–1377.

Belge, M. (2003, December 30). Ana düşünce akımı ırkçılık [Main ideological approach: Racism]. *Radikal.*

Benedict, R. (2008). Continuity and discontinuities in cultural conditioning. In: R. A. LeVine & R. S. New (Eds.), *Anthropology and Child Development: A Cross-Cultural Reader* (pp. 42–48). Hoboken, NJ: Blackwell.

Benjamin, W. (1968). The task of the translator: An introduction to the translation of *Baudelaire's Tableaux Parisiens.* In: H. Arendt (Ed.), H. Zohn (Trans.), *Illuminations* (pp. 69–82). New York: Schocken.

Bergman, A. (1996). Identifications on the way to constancy. In: S. Akhtar, S. Kramer, & H. Parens (Eds.), *The Internal Mother: Conceptual and Technical Aspects of Object Constancy* (pp. 61–76). Northvale, NJ: Jason Aronson.

Bergstein, A. (2013). Transcending the caesura: Reverie, dreaming and counter-dreaming. *International Journal of Psychoanalysis, 94*: 621–644.

Bergstein, A. (2018). The psychotic parts of the personality: Bion's expeditions into unmapped mental life. *Journal of the American Psychoanalytic Association, 66*: 193–220.

Berkes, N. (1964). *The Development of Secularism in Turkey.* Montreal, Canada: McGill University Press.

Bibring, E. (1938). Report of the International Training Commission. *Bulletin of the International Psychoanalytical Association, 19*: 271–289.

Bick, E. (1964). Notes on infant observation in psycho-analytical training. *International Journal of Psychoanalysis, 45*: 558–566.

Bion, W. R. (1957). Psikotik kişiliklerin psikotik olmayanlardan ayrımı [Distinguishing psychotic from non-psychotic personalities]. P. Padar (Trans.). *Psikanaliz Yazıları, 30*: 35–53.

Bion, W. R. (1959). Attacks on linking. *International Journal of Psychoanalysis, 40*: 308–315.

Bion, W. R. (1961). *Experiences in Groups and Other Papers.* London: Tavistock.

Bion, W. R. (1962). *Learning from Experience.* London: Karnac, 1984.

Bion, W. R. (1963). *Elements of Psychoanalysis.* London: Karnac.

Bion, W. R. (1965). *Transformations: Change from Learning to Growth.* London: Tavistock.

Bion, W. R. (1970). *Attention and Interpretation: A Scientific Approach to Insight in Psychoanalysis and Groups.* London: Tavistock.

Bion, W. R. (1984). *Second Thoughts: Selected Papers on Psychoanalysis.* London: Routledge.

Bion, W. R. (1989). *Two Papers: The Grid and Caesura.* London: Karnac.

Blessing, D. (2007). Hiding in plain sight: The sibling connection in eating disorders. *Journal of Child Psychotherapy, 33*: 36–50.

Blos, P. (1967). The second individuation process of adolescence. *Psychoanalytic Study of the Child, 22*: 162–186.

Boas, F. (2008). Plasticity in child development. In: R. A. LeVine & R. S. New (Eds.), *Anthropology and Child Development: A Cross-Cultural Reader* (pp. 18–21). Hoboken, NJ: Blackwell.

Boccara, P., Gaddini, A., & Riefolo, G. (2009). Authenticity and the analytic process. *American Journal of Psychoanalysis, 69*: 348–362.

Bollas, C. (1987). *The Shadow of the Object*. New York: Columbia University Press.

Bollas, C. (2000). *Hysteria*. London: Routledge.

Bolognini, S. (2008). Intrapsychic-interpsychic. *International Journal of Psychoanalysis, 85*: 337–357.

Bose, G. (1964). Letter to Sigmund Freud dated 11.4.1929, cited in Ramana, C. V. (1964). On the early history and development of psychoanalysis in India. *Journal of the American Psychoanalytic Association, 12*: 110–134.

Botella, S., & Botella, C. (2005). *The Work of Psychic Figurability: Mental States Without Representation*. London: Routledge.

Bouveresse, J. (1995). *Wittgenstein Reads Freud: The Myth of the Unconscious*. C. Cosman (Trans.). Princeton, NJ: Princeton University Press.

Bowlby, J. (1960). Grief and mourning in infancy and early childhood. *Psychoanalytic Study of the Child, 15*: 9–52.

Bowlby, J. (1969). *Attachment and Loss: Vol. 1*. New York: Basic Books, 1982.

Bowlby, J. (1980). *Attachment and Loss, Volume III: Loss—Sadness and Depression*. New York: Basic Books, 1982.

Bowlby, J. (1988). *A Secure Base: Parent-Child Attachment and Healthy Human Development*. New York: Basic Books.

Brainsky, S. (2003). Adapting to, or idealizing technology? *Insight, 12*: 22–24.

Breidenthal, S. M. (2010). Lacan's critique of Freud's case of Dora and the therapeutic action of working in the symbolic: A project based upon an independent investigation. [Unpublished thesis.] Smith College, Northampton, MA.

Brill, A. A. (1912). *Psychoanalysis: Its Theories and Practical Application*. Philadelphia, PA: W. B. Saunders.

Brill, A. A. (1944). *Freud's Contribution to Psychiatry*. New York: W. W. Norton.

Britton, R. (1989). The missing link: Parental sexuality in the Oedipus complex. Reprinted in: R. Schafer (Ed.), *The Contemporary Kleinians of London* (pp. 239–242). Madison, CT: International Universities Press, 1997.

Britton, R. (1998). *Belief and Imagination: Explorations in Psychoanalysis*. London: Routledge.

Bronfen, E. (1998). *Knotted Subject: Hysteria and Its Discontents*. Princeton, NJ: Princeton University Press.

Brubaker, R. (2006). *Ethnicity without Groups*. Cambridge, MA: Harvard University Press.

Bucci, W. (1997). *Psychoanalysis and Cognitive Science: A Multiple Code Theory*. New York: Guilford.

Büken, N. (2016). The silence of women, the silence of language, the language of silence. [Unpublished manuscript.] HÜTF Tıp Tarihi ve Etiği AD, Hacettepe University, Turkey.

Burnham, D. L., Gladstone, A. E., & Gibson, R. W. (1969). *Schizophrenia and the Need-Fear Dilemma*. New York: International Universities Press.

Cahen, C. (1968). *Pre-Ottoman Turkey*. J. Jones-Williams (Trans.). New York: Taplinger.

Çalışlar, I., (2019). *Latife Hanım*. Istanbul, Turkey: Yapı Kredi Yayınları.

Campbell, J. (1949). *The Hero with a Thousand Faces*. Cleveland, OH: Meridian.

Cavasola, R. (2015). A reading of contemporary hysteria from Lacan's teachings. *European Journal of Psychoanalysis, 2*(1).

Çelik, H. (2020). Mothers and parents' marital adaptations: Influential agents in father-child relations. *World Journal of Education, 10*: 164–177.

Chakrabarty, D. (2007). *Provincializing Europe: Postcolonial Thought and Historical Difference*. Princeton, NJ: Princeton University Press.

Chao, R. K. (1994). Beyond parental control and authoritarian parenting style: Understanding Chinese parenting through the cultural notion of training. *Child Development, 65*: 1111–1119.

Chasseguet-Smirgel, J. (1969). Le rossignol de l'empereur de Chine. In: *Pour une psychanalyse de l'art et de la créativité* (pp. 183–216). Paris: Payot, 1971.

Chasseguet-Smirgel, J. (1984). *Creativity and Perversion*. New York: W. W. Norton.

Chasseguet-Smirgel, J. (1985). The ego ideal and the psychology of groups. *Free Associations, 1*: 31–60.

Choi-Kain, L. (2009). Second generation Korean Americans. In: S. Akhtar (Ed.), *Freud and the Far East: Psychoanalytic Perspectives on the People and Culture of China, Japan, and Korea* (pp. 215–234). Lanham, MD: Rowman and Littlefield.

Chopra, D. (1993). *Ageless Body Timeless Mind*. New York: Harmony.

Chopra, D. (1994). *The Seven Spiritual Laws of Success*. San Rafael, CA: Amber-Allen & New World Library.

Christensen, L. W. (1999). Suffering and the dialectical self in Buddhism and relational psychoanalysis. *American Journal of Psychoanalysis, 59*: 37–57.

Chu, J. Y. (2009). The Chinese-American family: Some psychoanalytic speculations. In: S. Akhtar (Ed.), *Freud and the Far East: Psychoanalytic Perspectives on the People and Culture of China, Japan and Korea* (pp. 199–214). Lanham, MD: Jason Aronson.

Çiçek, C. (2021). Türk sinemasında kadın ve anlatı: Arım, Balım, Peteğim'den On Kadın'a. *Ulak Bilge Sosyal Bilimler Dergisi, 56*: 30–40.

Cioffi, F. (1998). *Wittgenstein on Freud and Frazer*. Cambridge: Cambridge University Press.

Clulow, C. (1991). The chronically ill child and the parents' marriage: Interactive effects. *British Journal of Psychotherapy, 7*: 331–340.

Cohler, B., & Galatzer-Levy, R. (2007). What kind of science is psychoanalysis? *Psychoanalytic Quarterly, 27*: 547–582.

Coleman, D. (1996). Positive sibling transference: Theoretical and clinical dimensions. *Clinical Social Work Journal, 24*: 377–387.

Coles, P. (2003). *The Importance of Sibling Relationships in Psychoanalysis*. London: Karnac.

Colonna, A. B., & Newman, L. M. (1983). The psychoanalytic literature on siblings. *Psychoanalytic Study of the Child, 38*: 285–309.

Corey, G. (2008). *Theory and Practice of Counseling and Psychotherapy*. Belmont, CA: Wadsworth.

Cündioğlu, D. (2007, November 26). Freud'un Türk Talebesinden İlginç (Psiko) Analizler [Interesting (psycho)analysis from Freud's Turkish pupil]. *Yeni Şafak*.

Daniel, K. (2009). Dialogues between feminists and Jacques Lacan on female hysteria and femininity. Doctoral dissertation submitted to Duquesne University, Pittsburgh, PA.

Davids, M. F. (2002). Fathers in the internal world: From boy to man to father. In: A. Etchegoyen & J. Trowell (Eds.), *The Importance of Fathers: A Psychoanalytic Re-evaluation* (pp. 67–92). Hove, UK: Brunner-Routledge.

De Cortinas, L. P. (2011). Science and fiction in the psychoanalytical field. In: C. Mawson (Ed.), *Bion Today* (pp. 121–150). London: Routledge.

Deniz, T. (2017). *Biraz mağrur biraz mağdur: Türk sinemasında kahramanlar*. Istanbul, Turkey: Küre Yayınları.

Deutscher, I. (1968). *The Non-Jewish Jew and Other Essays*. Oxford: Oxford University Press.

Diatkine, R. (1985). Devenir adolescent, rester adolescent. In: A. M. Alléon, O. Morvan, & S. Lebovici (Eds.), *Adolescence Terminée, Adolescence Interminable* (p. 61). Paris: Presses Universitaires de France.

Doğan, H. (2013). Türk sinemasinda 1980'li yıllar ve "Dulluk" teması etrafında üretilen geleneksel cinsiyet rolleri. *Folklor/Edebiyat, 76*: 9–20.

Doi, T. (1962). Amae: A key concept for understanding Japanese personality structure. In: R. J. Smith & R. K. Beardsley (Eds.), *Japanese Culture: Its Development and Characteristics* (pp. 121–129). Chicago, IL: Aldine.

Doi, T. (1973). *The Anatomy of Dependence*. Tokyo: Kodansha.

Dor, J. (2013). *The Clinical Lacan*. New York: Other Press.

Dorsay, A. (1995). *12 Eylül Yılları ve Sinemamız: 160 Filmle 1980–90 Arası Türk Sinemasına Bakışlar*. Istanbul, Turkey: İnkılâp Kitabevi.

Eagle, M. N. (1981). Interests as object relations. *Psychoanalysis and Contemporary Thought, 4*: 527–565.

Ebadi, H. (1988). Psikososyal faktörlerin konversiyon reaksiyon üzerinde etkileri. Doctoral dissertation submitted to İstanbul Üniversitesi, Istanbul, Turkey.

Ekici, A. (2017). *1980–1990 arası Türk sinemasında kentsel ailede kadının konumu* [Yayımlanmamış yüksek lisans tezi]. Ankara: Ankara Üniversitesi.

El Shakry, O. (2014). The Arabic Freud: The unconscious and the modern subject. *Modern Intellectual History, 11*: 89–118.

Elshakry, M. (2013). *Reading Darwin in Arabic, 1860–1950*. Chicago, IL: University of Chicago Press.

Emde, R. (1983). The re-representational self and its affective core. *Psychoanalytic Study of the Child, 38*: 165–192.

Erikson, E. H. (1959). *Identity and the Life Circle*. New York: International Universities Press.

Erkoç, S. (2004). Osmanlı'dan günümuze İstanbul'da psikiyatri kurumları [Psychiatric foundations in Istanbul from the Ottoman period to today]. *Istanbul, 48*: 76–79.

Ersanlı, B. (2003). *İktidar ve Tarih: Türkiye'de "Resmi Tarih" Tezinin Oluşumu (1929–1937) [Power and History: The Emergence of the "Official History" Thesis in Turkey, 1929–1937]*. Istanbul, Turkey: İletişim.

Erten, Y. (2017). Psike Istanbul and the training of psychoanalysts in Turkey. *Türkiye Klinikleri, 7*: 94–100.

Eshel, O. (2019). *The Emergence of Analytic Oneness: Into the Heart of Psychoanalysis*. London: Routledge.

Etchegoyen, A. (2002). Psychoanalytic ideas about fathers. In: A. Etchegoyen & J. Trowell (Eds.), *The Importance of Fathers: A Psychoanalytic Re-evaluation* (pp. 20–42). Hove, UK: Brunner-Routledge.

Etezady, H. (2001). The mourning after: A concluding overview. In: S. Akhtar (Ed.), *Three Faces of Mourning: Melancholia, Manic Defense and Moving On* (pp. 200–224). Northvale, NJ: Jason Aronson.

Faimberg, H. (2005). *The Telescoping of Generations*. London: Routledge.

Feldman, M. (1992). Splitting and projective identification. In: R. Anderson (Ed.), *Clinical Lectures on Klein and Bion* (pp. 71–85). London: Routledge.

Ferenczi, S. (1933). On the confusion of tongues between adults and the child. In: *Final Contributions to the Problems and Methods of Psychoanalysis* (pp. 155–167). New York: Basic Books, 1955.

Ferenczi, S. (1949). Notes and fragments [1930–32]. *International Journal of Psychoanalysis, 30*: 231–242.

Ferro, A. (2002). Some implications of Bion's thought. *International Journal of Psychoanalysis, 83*: 597–607.

Ferro, A. (2005). *Seeds of Illness, Seeds of Recovery: The Genesis of Suffering and the Role of Psychoanalysis*. London: Routledge.

Ferro, A. (2006). *Psychoanalysis as Therapy and Storytelling*. London: Routledge.

Ferro, A. (2009). Transformations in dreaming and characters in the psychoanalytic field. *International Journal of Psychoanalysis, 90*: 209–230.

Ferro, A., & Basile, R. (2004). The psychoanalyst as individual: Self-analysis and gradients of functioning. *Psychoanalytic Quarterly, 73*: 659–682.

Fink, B. (1997). *A Clinical Introduction to Lacanian Psychoanalysis: Theory and Technique*. Cambridge, MA: Harvard University Press.

Fischer, R. M. S. (2004). Fathers, history, and psychoanalysis. In: S. Akhtar & H. Parens (Eds.), *Real and Imaginary Fathers: Development, Transference, and Healing* (pp. 1–12). Lanham, MD: Jason Aronson.

Fliess, R. (1942). The metapsychology of the analyst. *Psychoanalytic Quarterly, 11*: 211–217.

Fonagy, P., & Target, M. (1996). Playing with reality: I. Theory of mind and the normal development of psychic reality. *International Journal of Psychoanalysis, 77*: 217–233.

Fonagy, P., Gergely, G., Jurist, E., & Target, M. (2004). *Affect Regulation, Mentalization and the Development of the Self.* New York: Other Press.

Frank, A. (1969). The unrememberable and the unforgettable: Passive primal repression. *Psychoanalytic Study of the Child, 24*: 48–77.

Freeman, D. M. A. (1981). Mythological portrayal of developmental processes and major intrapsychic restructuralizations. In: W. Muensterberger, L. B. Boyer, & S. A. Grolnick (Eds.), *The Psychoanalytic Study of Society, Vol. IX* (pp. 319–340). New York: Psychohistory Press.

Freeman, D. M. A. (1994). Some Aspects of Japanese Female Development Reflected in the Female Story Line in Mythology and Folklore, Parts I and II. Presented at The American Psychoanalytic Association Discussion Group and Interdisciplinary Colloquium, December 1994.

Freeman, D. M. A. (1998). Emotional refueling in development, mythology, and cosmology: The Japanese separation-individuation experience. In: S. Akhtar & S. Kramer (Eds.), *The Colors of Childhood: Separation Individuation across Cultural, Racial, and Ethnic Differences* (pp. 17–60). Northvale, NJ: Jason Aronson.

Freud, A. (1946). The psychoanalytic study of infantile feeding disturbances. *Psychoanalytic Study of the Child, 2*: 119–132.

Freud, A. (1958). Çocuklarin ruh hayatında vücut hastalıklarının rolü [The effects of physical illness on children's psychic lives]. *Tıpta Yenilikler, 4*: 24–31.

Freud, A. (1963). The concept of developmental lines. *Psychoanalytic Study of the Child, 18*: 245–265.

Freud, A. (1965). *Normality and Pathology in Childhood.* New York: International Universities Press.

Freud, S., with Breuer, J. (1895d). *Studies on Hysteria. S. E., 2*: 1–335. London: Hogarth.

Freud, S. (1896b). Further remarks on the neuro-psychoses of defence. *S. E., 3*: 162–185. London: Hogarth.

Freud, S. (1900a). *The Interpretation of Dreams. S. E., 4–5*: 1–626. London: Hogarth.

Freud, S. (1901b). *The Psychopathology of Everyday Life. S. E., 6*: 1–310. London: Hogarth.

Freud, S. (1905d). *Three Essays on the Theory of Sexuality. S. E., 7*: 130–243. London: Hogarth.

Freud, S. (1905e). Fragment of an analysis of a case of hysteria. *S. E., 7*: 7–124. London: Hogarth.

Freud, S. (1908c). On the sexual theories of children. *S. E., 9.* London: Hogarth.

Freud, S. (1908d). "Civilized" sexual morality and modern nervous illness. *S. E., 9*: 177–204. London: Hogarth.

Freud, S. (1908e). Creative writers and day-dreaming. *S. E., 9*: 141–154. London: Hogarth.

Freud, S. (1909b). Analysis of a phobia in a five-year-old boy. *S. E., 10.* London: Hogarth.

Freud, S. (1909d). Notes upon a case of obsessional neurosis. *S. E., 10.* London: Hogarth.

Freud, S. (1910h). A special type of choice of object made by men. *S. E., 11*: 163–177. London: Hogarth.

Freud, S. (1911b). Formulations on the two principles of mental functioning. *S. E., 12*: 215–226. London: Hogarth.

Freud, S. (1912e). Recommendations for physicians practising psycho-analysis. *S. E., 12*. London: Hogarth.

Freud, S. (1912–13). *Totem and Taboo. S. E., 13*: 1–161. London: Hogarth.

Freud, S. (1914c). On narcissism: An introduction. *S. E., 14*: 67–103. London: Hogarth.

Freud, S. (1914d). On the history of the psycho-analytic movement. *S. E., 14*: 3–66.

Freud, S. (1915d). Repression. *S. E., 14*. London: Hogarth.

Freud S. (1916–17). *Introductory Lectures on Psycho-Analysis (Part I and Part II). S. E., 15–16*: 1–240; 3–463. London: Hogarth.

Freud, S. (1917b). A childhood recollection from *Dichtung und Wahrheit. S. E., 17*: 145–157. London: Hogarth.

Freud, S. (1917e). Mourning and melancholia. *S. E., 14*: 237–258. London: Hogarth.

Freud, S. (1918b). From the history of an infantile neurosis. *S. E., 17*: 1–122. London: Hogarth.

Freud, S. (1921c). *Group Psychology and the Analysis of the Ego. S. E., 18*: 65–144. London: Hogarth.

Freud, S. (1922b). Some neurotic mechanisms in jealousy, paranoia and homosexuality. *S. E., 18*: 221–233. London: Hogarth.

Freud, S. (1923b). *The Ego and the Id. S. E., 19*: 1–66. London: Hogarth.

Freud, S. (1924d). The dissolution of the Oedipus complex. *S. E., 19*: 171–180. London: Hogarth.

Freud, S. (1925d). An autobiographical study. *S. E., 20*: 3–76.

Freud, S. (1925e). The resistances to psycho-analysis. *S. E., 19*: 211–224. London: Hogarth.

Freud, S. (1926d). *Inhibitions, Symptoms and Anxiety. S. E., 20*: 75–176. London: Hogarth.

Freud, S. (1927c). *The Future of an Illusion. S. E., 21*: 5–56. London: Hogarth.

Freud, S. (1930a). *Civilization and Its Discontents, S. E., 21*: 59–145. London: Hogarth.

Freud, S. (1931b). Female sexuality. *S. E., 21*: 223–243. London: Hogarth.

Freud, S. (1933a). *New Introductory Lectures on Psycho-analysis. S. E., 22*: 3–182. London: Hogarth.

Freud, S. (1939a). *Moses and Monotheism. S. E., 23*: 1–137. London: Hogarth.

Freud, S. (1940a). *An Outline of Psycho-analysis. S. E., 23*: 141–208. London: Hogarth.

Fulghum, R. (1988). *All I Really Need to Know I Learned in Kindergarten*. New York: Ivy.

Furman, E. (1982). Mothers have to be there to be left. *Psychoanalytic Study of the Child, 37*: 15–41.

Gabbard, G. O. (1993). Hysterical personality style and the histrionic personality disorder, revised. *American Journal of Psychiatry, 150*: 1120–1121.

Gaddini, R. (2004). Thinking about Winnicott and the origins of the self. *Psychoanalysis and History, 6*: 225–235.

Gallese, V. (2009). Mirror neurons, embodied simulation, and the neural basis of social identification. *Psychoanalytic Dialogues, 19*: 519–536.

Gay, P. (1989). *A Godless Jew: Freud, Atheism, and the Making of Psychoanalysis.* New Haven, CT: Yale University Press.

Gay, P. (1995). *The Freud Reader.* London: Vintage.

Gessert, A. (2014). Where have the hysterics gone? Lacan's reinvention of hysteria. *European Society of Cardiology, 40*: 47–70.

Giovacchini, P. L. (1967). The frozen introject. *International Journal of Psychoanalysis, 48*: 61–67.

Glasser, M. (1986). Identification and its vicissitudes as observed in the perversions. *International Journal of Psychoanalysis, 67*: 9–16.

Glasser, M. (1992). Problems in the psychoanalysis of certain narcissistic disorders. *International Journal of Psychoanalysis, 73*: 493–503.

God's Word: *The Bible* (1995). Grand Rapids, MI: World Publishing.

Gökay, F. K. (1969). Ruh hekimliği sahasında Türklerin çalışmaları [Turks' studies in the field of mental illness]. *Tıp Dünyast, 42*: 526–536.

Goldin, D. (2015). The storied self: The search for coherence amidst constant change. *Psychoanalytic Dialogues, 2*: 661–679.

Goldstein, J. (2013). Neutralizing Freud: The Lycée philosophy class and the problem of the reception of psychoanalysis in France. *Critical Inquiry, 40*: 40–82.

Graham, I. (1988). The sibling object and its transferences: Alternate organizer of the middle field. *Psychoanalytic Inquiry, 8*: 88–107.

Green, A. (1975). The analyst, symbolization and absence in the analytic setting (on changes in analytic practice and analytic experience) in memory of D. W. Winnicott. *International Journal of Psychoanalysis, 56*: 1–22.

Green, A. (1980). The dead mother. In: *Life Narcissism, Death Narcissism.* A. Weller (Trans.). London: Free Association.

Green, N. (2012). *Sufism: A Global History.* Malden, MA: Wiley-Blackwell.

Greenacre, P. (1952). Pregenital patterning. *International Journal of Psychoanalysis, 33*: 410–415.

Greenacre, P. (1958). Problems of identity, abstracted in panel: Problems of identity (reported by D. L. Rubinfine). *Journal of the American Psychoanalytic Association, 6*: 131–142.

Greenacre, P. (1960). Considerations regarding the parent–infant relationship. *International Journal of Psychoanalysis, 41*: 571–584.

Greenson, R. R. (1968). Disidentifying from the mother. *International Journal of Psychoanalysis, 49*: 370–374.

Grinberg, L., & Grinberg, R. (1989). *Psychoanalytic Perspectives on Migration and Exile.* N. Festinger (Trans.). New Haven, CT: Yale University Press.

Grotstein, J. S. (2009). Dreaming as a "curtain of illusion": Revisiting the "royal road" with Bion as our guide. *International Journal of Psychoanalysis, 90*: 733–752.

Grünbaum, A. (1984). *The Foundations of Psychoanalysis: A Philosophical Critique.* Berkeley, CA: University of California Press.

Gu, M. D. (2006). The filial piety complex: Variations on the Oedipus theme in Chinese literature and culture. *Psychoanalytic Quarterly*, *75*: 163–196.

Günergün, F. (2006, November 3). Ikinci Dünya Savaşı ve Türkiye [The Second World War and Turkey]. *Cumhuriyet Gazetesi, Science and Technology Supplement.*

Gürdal Küey, A. (2009). *Œdipe à Istanbul, l'Écriture du Divan.* Paris: Éditions des Crépuscules.

Gurman, A. S., & Messer, S. B. (Eds.) (1995). *Essential Psychotherapies: Theory and Practice.* New York: Guilford.

Gutton, P. (1991). *Le Pubertaire.* Paris: Presses Universitaires de France.

Gutton, P. (1996). *Adolescens.* Paris: Presses Universitaires de France.

Gutton, P. (2008). *Le Génie Adolescent.* Paris: Odile Jacob.

Güzel, H. (2018). Pain as performance: Re-virginisation in Turkey. *Medical Humanities*, *44*: 89–95.

Habermas, J. (1971). *Knowledge and Human Interests.* J. Shapiro (Trans.). Boston, MA: Beacon.

Habip, B. (2004). Psychoanalysis Transfer and Psychoanalysis Turkey. Why Did Psychoanalysis Practice Come to Turkey Late? Presentation made in symposium of Gokce Cansever, Bosphorus University, Istanbul.

Hagman, G. (1995a). Bereavement and neurosis. *Journal of the American Psychoanalytic Association*, *23*: 635–653.

Hagman, G. (1995b). Mourning: A review and reconsideration. *International Journal of Psychoanalysis*, *76*: 909–925.

Haj, S. (2009). *Reconfiguring Islamic Tradition: Reform, Rationality and Modernity.* Stanford, CA: Stanford University Press.

Hanioğlu, S. (2002). Turkish nationalism and the young Turks. In: F. M. Göçek (Ed.), *Social Constructions of Nationalism in the Middle East* (pp. 85–94). Albany, NY: State University of New York Press.

Hartnack, C. (2001). *Psychoanalysis in Colonial India.* Oxford: Oxford University Press.

Haspolat, N. K. (2022). Psikanalizin içinden bir kavram "özdeşleşme." *Muş Alparslan Üniversitesi Eğitim Fakültesi Dergisi*, *2*: 1–9.

Hathaway, J. (2018). The chief harem eunuch of the Ottoman empire. In: A. Höfert, M. M. Mesley, & S. Tolino (Eds.), *Celibate and Childless Men in Power Ruling Eunuchs and Bishops in the Pre-Modern World* (pp. 211–225). London: Routledge.

Haute, P. V. (2018). Freud against Oedipus? In: J. A. Godley & J. Goldbach (Eds.), *Inheritance in Psychoanalysis* (pp. 274–289). Buffalo, NY: State University of New York Press.

Havlıoğlu, D., & Uysal, Z. (2023). *Handbook of Turkish Literature.* London: Routledge.

Hekimoğlu, E. C., & Bilik, M. Z. (2020). Freud'dan Lacan'a kaygı. *Ayna Klinik Psikoloji Dergisi.*

Hendrickx, D. (2017). Freud and Lacan on fetishism and masochism/sadism as paradigms of perversion. Doctoral dissertation submitted to Ghent University, Faculty of Psychology and Educational Sciences, Ghent, Belgium.

Hillman, J. (1992). *The Myth of Analysis.* New York: Harper Perennial.

Holmes, M. (2010). Subject of focus: The lives of emigrants: Düsseldorf-Berlin-Ankara-Washington: The life of Edith Weigert (née Vowinckel) (1894–1982). C. S. Noel (Trans.). *Psychiatry: Interpersonal and Biological Processes, 73*: 1–33.

Homer, S. (2005). *Jacques Lacan*. Abingdon, UK: Routledge.

Hooke, M. T., & Akhtar, S. (Eds.) (2007). *The Geography of Meanings: Psychoanalytic Perspectives on Place, Space, Land, and Dislocation*. London: International Psychoanalytical Association.

Horney, K. (1923). *Feminine Psychology*. H. Kelman (Ed.). New York: W. W. Norton.

Horowitz, M. J. (1990). A model of mourning: Change in schemas of self and other. *Journal of the American Psychoanalytic Association, 38*: 297–324.

Hortaçsu, N., Kalaycıoğlu, S., & Rittersberger-Tilic, H. (2003). Intrafamily aggression in Turkey: Frequency, instigation, and acceptance. *Journal of Social Psychology, 143*: 163–184.

Huxley, A. (1994). *The Perennial Philosophy*. New York: Harper & Row.

Isakower, O. (1963a). Minutes of New York Psychoanalytic Institute Faculty Meeting. October 14, unpublished.

Isakower, O. (1963b). Minutes of New York Psychoanalytic Institute Faculty Meeting. November 20, unpublished.

Itzkowitz, N. (2001). Unity out of diversity. *Mind and Human Interaction, 12*: 173–175.

Izeddin, A. (1932). Eine Mohammedanische Legende [A Mohammedan legend]. *Imago, 18*: 189–213.

Izeddin, A. (1948). Notes. *Psychoanalytic Quarterly, 17*: 572–573.

Jacobs, T. J. (2007). Listening, dreaming and sharing: On the uses of the analyst's inner experiences. In: S. Akhtar (Ed.), *Listening to Others: Developmental and Clinical Aspects of Empathy and Attunement* (pp. 93–112). Lanham, MD: Jason Aronson.

Jaspers, K. (1954). *Way to Wisdom*. New Haven, CT: Yale University Press.

Jeammet, P. (2000). Gérer la place de l'infantile. *Adolescence, 36*: 426–427.

Johnson, J. T. (1992). *Mothers of Incest Survivors*. Bloomington, IN: Indiana University Press.

Jones, E. (1925). *Traité théorique et practique de psychanalyse* [*Theory and Practice of Psychoanalysis*]. S. Jankélévitch (Trans.). Paris: Payot.

Jones, E. (1929). *Psycho-Analysis*. Republished as *Psikanaliz*. İ. Şadan (Trans.). Istanbul, Turkey: Sebat, 1941.

Jones, E. (1930). Psycho-analysis and biology. In: A. W. Greenwood (Ed.), *Proceedings of the Second International Congress for Sex Research. London 1930* (pp. 601–623). Edinburgh, UK: Oliver and Boyd.

Kağıtçıbaşı, Ç. (1980). *Çocuğun Değeri: Türkiye'de Değerler ve Doğurganlık* [*Value of the Child: Values and Fertility in Turkey*]. İstanbul, Turkey: Boğaziçi University Publications.

Kağıtçıbaşı, Ç. (2013). *Family, Self, and Human Development Across Cultures: Theory and Applications*. New York: Psychology Press.

Kağıtçıbaşı, Ç. (2017, April). Turkish early enrichment precept. www.Ace.or (last accessed July 2003).

Kağıtçibaşı, C., & Ataca, B. (2005). Value of children and family change: A three-decade portrait from Turkey. *Applied Psychology: An International Review, 54*: 317–337.

Kağıtçibaşı, Ç., Ataca, B., & Diri, A. (2005). The Turkish family and the value of children: Trends over time. In: G. Trommsdorff & B. Nauck (Eds.), *The Value of Children in Cross-cultural Perspective* (pp. 91–120). Berlin: Pabst Science.

Kahya, H. (1975). Histeri. *Atatürk Üniversitesi Tıp Bülteni, 4*: 415–420.

Kakar, S. (1990a). *Intimate Relations: Exploring Indian Sexuality.* Chicago, IL: University of Chicago Press.

Kakar, S. (1990b). *The Inner World: A Psychoanalytic Study of Child and Society in India.* London: Oxford University Press.

Kakar, S. (1993). *Identity and Adulthood.* London: Oxford University Press.

Kakar, S. (2024). *The Indian Jungle: Psychoanalysis and Non-Western Civilizations.* London: Karnac.

Kandiyoti, D. (1996). *Cariyeler, Bacılar, Yurttaşlar: Kimlikler ve Toplumsal Dönüşümler* [*Concubines, Sisters, Citizens: Identities and Social Transformations*]. İstanbul: Metis.

Kang, W. (2020). *Korean Culture Dictionary.* Los Angeles, CA: New Ampersand.

Kanwal, G. S. (2017). Death: The last chapter. In: S. Akhtar & G. S. Kanwal (Eds.), *Bereavement: Personal Experiences and Clinical Reflections* (pp. 169–190). London: Karnac.

Kapila, S. (2007). The "godless" Freud and his Indian friends: An Indian agenda for psychoanalysis. In: S. Mahone & M. Vaughan (Eds.), *Psychiatry and Empire* (pp. 124–152). Basingstoke, UK: Palgrave Macmillan.

Karasu, T. B. (1977). Psychotherapies: An overview. *American Journal of Psychiatry, 138*: 851–863.

Karasu, T. B. (1992). *Wisdom in the Practice of Psychotherapy.* New York: Basic Books.

Kawai, H. (1996). *Buddhism and the Art of Psychotherapy.* College Station, TX: Texas A&M University Press.

Kayalı, H. (1997). *Arabs and Young Turks: Ottomanism, Arabism, and Islamism in the Ottoman Empire, 1908–1918.* Berkeley, CA: University of California Press.

Kayatekin, M. S. (2008). Christian–Muslim relations: The axis of Balkans and the West. In: S. Akhtar (Ed.), *The Crescent and the Couch: Crosscurrents between Islam and Psychoanalysis* (pp. 199–216). Northvale, NJ: Jason Aronson.

Kayatekin, M. S. (2022, November 11). Black money and love. A country of people with unintegrated pasts. *Birikim, Socialist Journal of Culture*, pp. 62–72.

Kayatekin, M. S. (2023, April 24). In search of a new concept of "citizenship." *Birikim, Socialist Journal of Culture.*

Kelly, M. (1998). *Imaging Desire.* Boston, MA: MIT Press.

Kelman, H. (1975). The "day precipitate" of dreams: The Morris hypothesis. *International Journal of Psychoanalysis, 56*: 209–218.

Kernberg, O. F. (1980). *Internal World and External Reality: Object Relations Theory Applied.* New York: Jason Aronson.

Kernberg, O. F. (1991). The psychopathology of hatred. *Journal of the American Psychoanalytic Association, 39S*: 209–238.

Kernberg, O. F. (1992). *Aggression in Personality Disorders and Perversions*. New Haven, CT: Yale University Press.

Kernberg, O. F. (2010). Some observations on the process of mourning. *International Journal of Psychoanalysis, 91*: 601–619.

Khamsi, R. (2022). Unpicking the link between smell and memories. *Nature, 606*: 2–4.

Kieffer, C. C. (2008). On siblings: Mutual regulation and mutual recognition. *Annual of Psychoanalysis, 36*: 161–173.

Kılıç, R. (2013). *Deliler ve Doktorları: Osmanlı'dan Cumhuriyet'e Delilik* [*The Mad and Their Physicians: Madness from the Ottomans to the Republic*]. Istanbul, Turkey: Tarih Vakfı Yurt Yayınları.

Kim, S., Conway-Turner, K., Sherif-Trask, B., & Woolfolk, T. (2009). Reconstructing mothering among Korean immigrant working class women in the United States. *Journal of Comparative Family Studies, 37*(1): 43–58.

Kinston, W., & Cohen, J. (1986). Primal repression: Clinical and theoretical aspects. *International Journal of Psychoanalysis, 67*: 337–353.

Kıraç, M. E. (2022, May 13). Lideri iyi ama çevresi kötü [Leader is good but advisors are bad]. *Yeniçağ*.

Klein, M. (1921). The development of a child. In: *Love, Guilt and Reparation and Other Works, 1921–1945* (pp. 1–53). New York: Simon & Schuster, 1975.

Klein, M. (1928). Early stages of the Oedipus conflict. *International Journal of Psychoanalysis, 9*: 167–180.

Klein, M. (1929). Infantile anxiety-situations reflected in a work of art and in the creative impulse. *International Journal of Psychoanalysis, 10*: 436–443.

Klein, M. (1932). *The Psychoanalysis of Children*. New York: Free Press, 1975.

Klein, M. (1933). The early development of conscience in the child. In: *Love, Guilt and Reparation and Other Works, 1921–1945* (pp. 262–289). New York: Free Press, 1984.

Klein, M. (1935). A contribution to the psychogenesis of manic-depressive states. In: *Love, Guilt and Reparation and Other Works, 1921–1945*. New York: Free Press, 1975.

Klein, M. (1937). Love, guilt, and reparation. In: *Love, Guilt and Reparation and Other Works, 1921–1945* (pp. 306–343). New York: Free Press, 1975.

Klein, M. (1940). Mourning and its relation to manic-depressive states. *International Journal of Psychoanalysis, 21*: 125–153.

Klein, M. (1946). Notes on some schizoid mechanisms. In: *Envy and Gratitude and Other Works, 1946–1963*. New York: Free Press, 1975.

Klein, M. (1948). On the theory of anxiety and guilt. In: *Envy and Gratitude and Other Works, 1946–1963* (pp. 25–42). London: Hogarth, 1975.

Klein, M. (1957). *Envy and Gratitude and Other Works*. New York: Free Press, 1975.

Klein, M. (1975). *The Collected Works of Melanie Klein*. London: Hogarth.

Koçak, C. (1996). *Türkiye'de Milli Şef Dönemi (1938–1945)* [*The National Chief Era in Turkey, 1938–1945*], *Vol. I*. Istanbul, Turkey: İletişim.

Kohut, H. (1971). *The Analysis of the Self*. New York: International Universities Press.

Kohut, H. (1972). Thoughts on narcissism and narcissistic rage. *Psychoanalytic Study of the Child, 27*: 360–400.

Kohut, H. (1977). *The Restoration of the Self*. New York: International Universities Press.

Kohut, H. (1982). Introspection, empathy, and the semi-circle of mental health. *International Journal of Psychoanalysis, 63*: 395–407.

Kongar, E. (1998). *21. Yüzyılda Türkiye: 2000'li yıllarda Türkiyenin toplumsal yapısı* [*Turkey in the 21st Century: Structure of Turkish Society in the 2000s*]. İstanbul, Turkey: Remzi Kitabevi.

Korkmaz, A. (2021). Lacanyen psikanalizde travma ve düşlem. *Ayna Klinik Psikoloji Dergisi, 2*: 161–185.

Koselleck, R. (2004). "Space of experience" and "horizon of expectation": Two historical categories. In: *Futures Past: On the Semantics of Historical Time*. K. Tribe (Trans.) (pp. 255–275). New York: Columbia University Press.

Kovel, J. (1991). *History and Spirit*. Boston, MA: Beacon.

Kramer, S. (1983). Object coercive doubting: A pathological defensive response to maternal incest. *Journal of the American Psychoanalytic Association, 31S*: 325–351.

Kristeva, J. (1984). *Revolution in Poetic Language*. New York: Columbia University Press.

Krohn, A. (1978). *Hysteria: The Elusive Neurosis*. New York: International Universities Press.

Kücükkaya, İ. (2008). *Cumhuriyetimize Dair* [*About Our Republic*]. Ankara: Aşina Kitaplar.

Kulin, A. (2000). *Füreya*. Istanbul, Turkey: Remzi Kitabevi.

Kulin, A. (2014). *Handan*. Istanbul, Turkey: Everest Yayınları.

Künüçen, H. (2001). Türk sinemasında kadının sunumu üzerine. *Kurgu Dergisi, 18*: 51–64.

Kushner, H. S. (1981). *When Bad Things Happen to Good People*. New York: Avon.

Lacan, J. (1962–63). *Anxiety: The Seminar of Jacques Lacan, Book X*. A. Price (Trans.). Cambridge: Polity.

Lacan, J. (2006). *Écrits: The First Complete Edition in English*. New York: W. W. Norton.

Lacan, J. (2014). *Anxiety: The Seminar of Jacques Lacan, Book* X. J.-A. Miller (Ed.). Paris: Polity.

Lacan, J., & Gallagher, C. (2002). *Family Complexes in the Formation of the Individual*. Eastbourne, UK: Antony Rowe.

Laçiner, Ö. (2016, March 24). Ibretlik bir hikaye. *Birikim, Socialist Journal of Culture*.

Landau, J. M. (1995). *Pan-Turkism: From Irredentism to Cooperation*. Bloomington, IN: Indiana University Press.

Laplanche, J. (1989). *New Foundations for Psychoanalysis*. Oxford: Blackwell.

Laplanche, J., & Pontalis, J.-B. (1973). *The Language of Psychoanalysis*. London: Karnac.

Larmo, A. (2007). Sibling rivalry and the structuring of the mind. *Scandinavian Psychoanalytic Review, 30*(1): 22–30.

Lasch, C. (1978). *The Culture of Narcissism*. New York: W. W. Norton.

Lebovici, S. (1983). *Le Nourrison, la mere et le psychanalyste. Les interactions precoces*. Paris: Le Centurion.

Leibovici, M. (2002). *Hannah Arendt, une juive Expérience politique et histoire*. Paris: Gallimard.

Lechevalier, B. (2004). *Psikanalitik Anne-Çocuk Tedavisi*. Psike İstanbul Psikanaliz Kitaplığı. İstanbul, Turkey: Bilgi Üniversitesi Yayınları.

Lemma, A. (2015). Psychoanalysis in times of technoculture: Some reflections on the fate of the body in virtual space. *International Journal of Psychoanalysis, 96*: 569–582.

Levin, C. (2008). The sibling complex: Thoughts on French–English "translation". *Canadian Journal of Psychoanalysis, 16*: 262–274.

Levin, S. (1966). Depression and object loss. *Journal of the American Psychoanalytic Association, 14*: 142–153.

Levine, H. (2022). The logic of the field. In: H. Levine (Ed.), *The Post-Bionian Field Theory of Antonino Ferro*. London: Routledge.

Lewis, R. (1971). *Everyday Life in Ottoman Turkey*. London: B. T. Batsford.

Lichtenstein, H. (1961). Identity and sexuality: A study of their interrelationship in man. *Journal of the American Psychoanalytic Association, 9*: 179–260.

Lindemann, E. (1944). Symptomatology and management of acute grief. *American Journal of Psychiatry, 101*: 144–148.

Lindon, J. A. (1967). A psychoanalytic view of the family. *Psychoanalytic Forum, 3*: 13–65.

Liu, L. (1995). *Translingual Practice: Literature, National Culture, and Translated Modernity—China, 1900–1937*. Stanford, CA: Stanford University Press.

Loewald, H. W. (1951). Ego and reality. In: *Papers on Psychoanalysis* (pp. 3–20). New Haven, CT: Yale University Press.

Loewald, H. W. (1960). On the therapeutic action of psychoanalysis. *International Journal Psychoanalysis, 41*: 16–33.

Loewald, H. W. (1979). The waning of the Oedipus complex. *Journal of the American Psychoanalytic Association, 27*: 751–775.

Lüleci, Y. (2016). 27 Mayıs ve 12 Eylül askeri darbelerinin Türk sinema sektörüne etkileri. *Muhafazakâr Düşünce Dergisi, 49*: 183–208.

Lunbeck, E. (2003). Psychiatry. In: T. M. Porter & D. Ross (Eds.), *The Cambridge History of Science, Vol. 7* (pp. 663–677). Cambridge: Cambridge University Press.

MacIntyre, A. C. (1981). The virtues, the unity of a human life and the concept of a tradition. In: *After Virtue: A Study in Moral Theory* (pp. 204–225). Notre Dame, IN: University of Notre Dame Press, 1984.

MacIntyre, A. C. (1988). Tradition and translation. In: *Whose Justice? Which Rationality?* (pp. 370–388). Notre Dame, IN: University of Notre Dame Press.

Mahler, M. S. (1942). Pseudoimbecility: A magic cap of invisibility. *Psychoanalytic Quarterly, 11*: 149–164.

Mahler, M. S. (1958). On two crucial phases of integration of the sense of identity: Separation-individuation and bisexual identity. *Journal of the American Psychoanalytic Association*, *6*: 136–139.

Mahler, M. S. (1965). On the significance of the normal separation-individuation phase with reference to research in symbiotic child psychosis. In: M. Schur (Ed.), *Drives, Affects, Behavior - Vol. II* (pp. 161–169). New York: International Universities Press.

Mahler, M. S. (1975). *The Psychological Birth of the Human Infant*. London: Routledge.

Mahler, M. S., & Gosliner, B. (1955). On symbiotic child psychosis: Genetic, dynamic and restitutive aspects. *Psychoanalytic Study of the Child*, *10*: 195–212.

Mahler, M. S., Pine, F., & Bergman, A. (1975). *The Psychological Birth of the Human Infant: Symbiosis and Individuation*. New York: Basic Books.

Makari, G. J. (1997). Between seduction and libido: Sigmund Freud's masturbation hypotheses and the realignment of his etiologic thinking, 1897–1905. *Bulletin of the History of Medicine*, *72*: 638–662.

Malawista, K. L. (2017). Death of mother. In: S. Akhtar & G. S. Kanwal (Eds.), *Bereavement: Personal Experiences and Clinical Reflections* (pp. 33–55). London: Karnac.

Malinowski, B. (2008). Childhood in the Trobriand Islands, Melanesia. In: R. A. LeVine & R. S. New (Eds.), *Anthropology and Child Development: A Cross-Cultural Reader* (pp. 28–33). Hoboken, NJ: Blackwell.

Mariotti, P. (2012). General introduction. In: P. Mariotti (Ed.), *The Maternal Lineage: Identification, Desire and Transgenerational Issues* (pp. 1–45). London: Routledge.

Marty, P., & de M'Uzan, M. (1963). La Pensée Opératoire. *Revue Française de Psychanalyse*, *XXVII* (spécial Congrès des psychanalystes de langues romanes): 345–356.

Marvasti, J. A. (1986). *Psychiatric Treatment of Sexual Offenders*. Springfield, IL: Charles C. Thomas.

Maslow, A. (1970). Neurosis as a failure of human growth. In: W. S. Sahakian (Ed.), *Psychopathology Today: Experimentation, Theory, and Research* (pp. 122–130). Itasca, IL: Peacock.

Massicard, E., & Watts, N. F. (2012). *Negotiating Political Power in Turkey in Reconsidering Parties, Power, and Social Forces Breaking up the Party*. London: Routledge.

McDougall, J. (1990). *Plea for a Measure of Abnormality*. London: Routledge.

Mead, M. (2008). The ethnography of childhood. In: R. A. LeVine & R. S. New (Eds.), *Anthropology and Child Development: A Cross-Cultural Reader* (pp. 22–27). Hoboken, NJ: Blackwell.

Menon, A. (2022). Dora's mother: A housewife's psychosis. *British Journal of Psychiatry Bulletin*, *47*: 1–5.

Merchant, J. (2016). The use of Skype in analysis and training: A research and literature review. *Journal of Analytical Psychology*, *61*: 309–328.

Meyers, H. (1996). Mapping out the internal world. In: S. Akhtar, S. Kramer, & H. Parens (Eds.), *The Internal Mother: Conceptual and Technical Aspects of Object Constancy* (pp. 47–61). Northvale, NJ: Jason Aronson.

Micco, V. D. (2017). The Skin I Live in, the Name I Bear. Cultural Fractures and Transgenerational Bonds: Familiar and Unfamiliar in Migrant Children. Presentation at EPF meeting, Den Haag, the Netherlands.

Michel, B. (2022). Hysteria and its deceptive masks. *Archives of Depression and Anxiety, 8*: 12–18.

Miller, D. (1973). Gods and games: *Toward a Theology of Play*. New York: Harper & Row.

Miller, T. (1995). *How to Want What You Have*. New York: Henry Holt.

Milner, M. (1949). Review of "Painting and Personality: A Study of Young Children" by R. H. Alschuler and L. B. W. Hattwick. *International Journal of Psychoanalysis, 30*: 139–141.

Mitchell, J. (2003). *Siblings: Sex and Violence*. Cambridge: Polity.

Mitchell, J. (2006). From infant to child: The sibling trauma, the *rite de passage*, and the construction of the "other" in the social group. *Fort Da, 12*: 35–49.

Mitchell, J. (2011). *Kardeşler: Cinsellik ve Şiddet [Siblings: Sex and Violence]*. P. Padar & B. C. Yılmazyiğit (Trans.). Istanbul, Turkey: Bilgi Üniversitesi Yayınları.

Mitchell, J. (2013). The Law of the Mother: Sibling trauma and the brotherhood of war. *Canadian Journal of Psychoanalysis, 21*: 145–159.

Mitchell, T. (2000). The stage of modernity. In: T. Mitchell (Ed.), *Questions of Modernity* (pp. 1–34). Minneapolis, MN: University of Minnesota Press.

Modell, A. (1965). On aspects of the superego's development. *International Journal of Psychoanalysis, 46*: 323–331.

Monribot, P. (2013). "There is no sexual relation." What does it mean? Clinical consequences of Lacan's formulae of sexuation. *ICLO-NLS Annual Seminar "The Names of the Real in the 21st Century"*, Dublin.

Moore, T. (1992). *Care of the Soul*. New York: Harper Perennial.

Moore, T. (1994). *Soul Mates*. New York: Harper Perennial.

Mottram, S. A., & Hortaçsu, N. (2005). Adult daughter aging mother relationship over the life cycle: The Turkish case. *Journal of Aging Studies, 19*: 471–488.

Musallam, B. F. (1983). *Sex and Society in Islam: Birth Control before the Nineteenth Century*. Cambridge: Cambridge University Press.

Nandy, A. (1995). The savage Freud: The first non-Western psychoanalysts and the politics of secret selves in colonial India. In: *The Savage Freud and Other Essays on Possible and Retrievable Selves* (pp. 81–144). Princeton, NJ: Princeton University Press.

Nayar-Akhtar, M. (2015). *Identities in Transition: The Growth and Development of a Multicultural Therapist*. London: Karnac.

Neri, C. (2009). The enlarged notion of field in psychoanalysis. In: A. Ferro and R. Basile (Ed.), *The Analytic Field—A Clinical Concept* (pp. 45–80). London: Karnac.

Neruda, P. (1994). *Odes to Common Things*. New York: Little, Brown.

Neumann, D. (2013). The frame for psychoanalysis in cyberspace. In: J. S. Scharff (Ed.), *Psychoanalysis Online: Mental Health, Teletherapy, and Training*. London: Karnac.

New York Times (1936, February 9). Turks teach new theories.

Oberoi, R. (2013). Dreams—delving into the abyss of memory. *International Journal of English and Literature (IJEL)*, *3*: 77–86.

Oflu, A. (2020). Weaning practices of Turkish mothers: A mixed-model research. *Breastfeeding Medicine*, *15*: 109–113.

Ogden, T. H. (1982). *Projective Identification and Psychotherapeutic Technique*. London: Routledge.

Ogden, T. H. (1995). Analyzing forms of aliveness and deadness of the transference-countertransference. *International Journal of Psychoanalysis*, *76*: 695–709.

Ogden, T. H. (2004). This art of psychoanalysis: Dreaming undreamt dreams and interrupted cries. *International Journal of Psychoanalysis*, *85*: 857–877.

Ogden, T. H. (2012). *Creative Readings: Essays on Seminal Analytic Works*. London: Routledge.

Ogden, T. H. (2014). Fear of breakdown and the unlived life. *International Journal of Psychoanalysis*, *95*: 205–223.

Öğüt, D. T., & Güvenç, G. (2023). What do Turkish mothers have to say about motherhood? In: Z. Golen (Ed.), *Interpretive Research: Humanities and Social Sciences* (pp. 139–168). Lyon, France: Livre de Lyon.

Olinick, S. L. (1964). The negative therapeutic reaction. *International Journal of Psychoanalysis*, *45*: 540–548.

Onaylı, S., & Erdur-Baker, O. (2013). Mother-daughter relationship and daughter's self-esteem. *Procedia—Social and Behavioral Sciences*, *84*: 327–331.

O'Shaughnessy, E. (1983). Words and working through. *International Journal of Psychoanalysis*, *64*: 281–289.

Özdemir, M. N. (2017, February 12). İzzettin Şadan' ın Dünya Görüşü [İzzettin Şadan's Worldview]. *Yeni Şafak*.

Özdoğan, G. G. (2001). *"Turan"dan "Bozkurt"a: Tek Parti Döneminde Türkçülük*, 1931–1946 [*From "Turan" to "the Grey Wolf": Turkism during the Single-Party Era*, 1931–1946]. Istanbul, Turkey: İletişim.

Öztürk, O. M. (2022). *Biat Toplumunun Ruhsal Kökenleri Özerk Benlik Kul Benlik* [*Psychological Roots of the Subservient Society. Autonomous Self, Subservient Self*]. Istanbul, Turkey: Cumhuriyet Kitaplari.

Öztürk, O. M., & Volkan, V. D. (1971). The theory and practice of psychiatry in Turkey. *American Journal of Psychotherapy*, *25*: 240–271.

Pamuk, O. (2006). Nobel lecture. https://nobelprize.org/prizes/literature/2006/pamuk/lecture/

Pandolfo, S. (2000). The thin line of modernity: Some Moroccan debates on subjectivity. In: T. Mitchell (Ed.), *Questions of Modernity* (pp. 115–147). Minneapolis, MN: University of Minnesota Press.

Parkes, C. (1972). *Bereavement: Studies of Grief in Adult Life*. New York: International Universities Press.

Parlayandemir, P. (2022). *Türk sinemasından örneklerle sinema sosyolojisi*. Istanbul, Turkey: Eğitim Yayınevi.

Parsons, M. (2007). Raiding the inarticulate: The internal analytic setting and listening beyond countertransference. *International Journal of Psychoanalysis, 88*: 1441–1456.

Peck, M. S. (1978). *The Road Less Traveled*. New York: Touchstone.

Peirce, L. (1993). *The Imperial Harem: Women and Sovereignty in the Ottoman Empire*. New York: Oxford University Press.

Pines, D. (1993). *A Woman's Unconscious Use of Her Body*. London: Virago.

Pirsig, R. M. (1974). *Zen and the Art of Motorcycle Maintenance*. New York: Bantam New Age.

Pollock, G. H. (1961). Mourning and adaptation. *International Journal of Psychoanalysis, 42*: 341–361.

Pollock, G. H. (1987). The mourning-liberation process in health and disease. *Psychiatric Clinics of North America, 10*: 345–354.

Pontalis, J.-B. (2001). *Pencereler*. İstanbul, Turkey: Bağlam Yayınları.

Poo, C., Agarwal, G., Bonacchi, N., & Mainen, Z. F. (2022). Spatial maps in priform cortex during olfactory navigation. *Nature, 601*: 595–599.

Popp, N. (2015). The concept and phenomenon of psychological boundaries from a dialectical perspective: An empirical exploration. Doctoral dissertation submitted to Harvard Graduate School of Education, Cambridge, MA.

Popper, K. R. (1963). *Conjectures and Refutations: The Growth of Scientific Knowledge*. London: Routledge.

Prakash, G. (1999). *Another Reason: Science and the Imagination of Modern India*. Princeton, NJ: Princeton University Press.

Ragland-Sullivan, E. (1982). Jacques Lacan: Feminism and the problem of gender identity. *SubStance, 11*(3): 6–20.

Ragland-Sullivan, E. (1989). Dora and the name-of-the-father: The structure of hysteria. Doctoral dissertation. Australian Centre for Psychoanalysis, Carlton South, Victoria.

Ragland-Sullivan, E. (2004). Logic of sexuation. From Aristotle to Lacan. Doctoral dissertation. State University of New York Press, Albany, NY.

Rahman, S. A. (2003). *A Dictionary of Muslim Names*. Waterloo, ON: Laurier.

Rank, O. (1924). *The Trauma of Birth*. New York: Robert Brunner.

Raphael-Leff, J. (2014). *Dark Side of the Womb: Pregnancy, Parenting, and Persecutory Anxieties*. London: Anna Freud Centre.

Reisman, A. (2006). *Turkey's Modernization: Refugees from Nazism and Atatürk's Vision*. Washington, DC: New Academia.

Restivo, G. (2013). Jouissance & the sexual reality of the (two) unconscious. Doctoral dissertation submitted to The Auckland University of Technology, New Zealand.

Ricoeur, P. (1977). *Freud and Philosophy: An Essay on Interpretation*. D. Savage (Trans.). New Haven, CT: Yale University Press.

Rinpoche, S. (1994). *The Tibetan Book of Living and Dying.* San Francisco, CA: Harper San Francisco.

Roland, A. (1988). *In Search of Self in India and Japan: Toward a Cross-cultural Psychology.* Princeton, NJ: Princeton University Press.

Rosenfeld, H. A. (1965). Note on the psychopathology of confusional states in chronic schizophrenia. *International Journal of Psychoanalysis, 31*: 132–137.

Rosenfeld, H. A. (1971). Contribution to the psychopathology of psychotic states: The importance of projective identification in the ego structure and object relations of the psychotic patient. In: E. B. Spillius (Ed.), *Melanie Klein Today* (pp. 117–137). London: Routledge.

Roussillon, R. (1999). *Agonie, clivage et symbolisation.* Paris: Presses Universitaires de France.

Roussillon, R. (2006). History and theory of the psychoanalytic framework. Presentation at the Symposium Psychoanalytic Perspectives 2: Psychoanalytic Framework, Psike Istanbul Psychoanalytical Library, Turkey.

Russell, G. I. (2019). Review of "The Digital Age on the Couch" by Alessandra Lemma. *Contemporary Psychoanalysis, 55*: 132–138.

Russell, G. I. (2020). Remote working during the pandemic: A Q&A with Gillian Isaacs Russell, questions from the editor and editorial board of the *BJP. British Journal of Psychotherapy, 36*: 364–367.

Rustin, M. (2007). Taking account of siblings: A view from child psychotherapy. *Journal of Child Psychotherapy, 33*: 21–35.

Şadan, İ. (Dr. A. Izeddin) (1925). Freudizmin Sırr-ı Muvaffakiyeti [The secret behind Freudianism's success]. *Istanbul Serririyali, 8*: 1939–1942.

Şadan, İ. (1932). Eine Mohammedanische Legende: Ein psychoanalytischer Versuch [A Muslim legend: A psychoanalytic attempt]. *Imago, 18*: 189–213.

Şadan, İ. (1933a). Freud'un Nevroz Nazariyesi [Freud's neurosis theory]. *Poliklinik, 1*(1): 20–22.

Şadan, İ. (1933b). Freud'un Nevroz Nazariyesi-2 [Freud's neurosis theory 2]. *Poliklinik, 1*(1): 53–55.

Şadan, İ. (1933c, August 15). Psikanalize Göre Nevrozların Etiyolojisi [The etiology of neuroses according to psychoanalysis]. *Klinik Tıbbı Gazete, 2.*

Şadan, İ. (1936a, February 6). Eros (Aşk) ile Mücadele [Combating love-Eros]. *Yeni Adam, 110.*

Şadan, İ. (1936b, February 27). Eros (Aşk) ile Mücadele: Meryem Ana ve Donkişot [Combating love-Eros: Virgin Mary and Don Quixote]. *Yeni Adam, 113.*

Şadan, İ. (1936c, May 14). Aşk (Eros) ile Mücadele [Combating love-Eros]. *Yeni Adam, 124.*

Şadan, İ. (1936d, June 25). Aşkla Mücadele [Combating love]. *Yeni Adam, 130.*

Şadan, İ. (1936e, July 9). Psikopatoloji [Psychopathology]. *Yeni Adam, 132.*

Şadan, İ. (1936f, July 23). Aşkla Mücadele [Combating love]. *Yeni Adam, 134.*

Şadan, İ. (1937a, March 4). Akıl Hastalıkları: Nevrozlar, Psikonevrozlar, Psikozlar [Mental disorders: Neuroses, psychoneuroses, and psychoses]. *Yeni Adam, 166.*

Şadan, İ. (1937b, April 22). Akıl Hastalıkları: Topografik, Ekonomik ve Dinamik Telekkilerin Bugünkü Sistematizasyonu [Mental disorders: Contemporary systematization of topographic, economic, and dynamic considerations]. *Yeni Adam, 173.*

Şadan, İ. (1942). Milliyetin Felsefesi [Philosophy of nation]. In: İ. Mete (Ed.), *Milliyetin Felsefesi ve Türklerde Ulusal İnanç (National Belief and Philosophy of Nation among the Turks)* (pp. 59–60). Istanbul, Turkey: Türkiye Basımevi.

Şadan, İ. (1943). *Birsam-ı Saadet [Hallucinations of Happiness]*. Istanbul, Turkey: Işık Dizgievi.

Şadan, İ. (1948). Notes. *Psychoanalytic Quarterly, 17*: 572–573.

Şadan, İ. (1958). Türk Milliyetçileri diyorlar ki [What the Turkish nationalists say]. *Toprak, 5*(5): 20–21.

Şadan, İ. (1968). Hatırat [Memoirs]. In: *İstanbul Bakırköy Akıl ve Sinir Hastalıkları Yıllığı: Bakırköy'de 40 Yıl [Yearbook of Istanbul Bakırköy Psychiatric Hospital: 40 Years at Bakırköy]* (pp. 74–80). Istanbul: Cezaevi Matbaası.

Şadan, İ. (2007). Bir Müslüman Efsanesi: Psikoanalitik Bir Deneme [A Muslim legend: A psychoanalytic attempt]. T. Kutlar & Ş. Erkoç (Trans.). *Bilim Tarihi Araştırmaları, 15*: 19–32.

Said, E. W. (2004). *Freud and the Non-European*. London: Verso.

Salo, F. T. (2018). *Infant Observation: Creating Transformative Relationships*. London: Routledge.

Sanchez, N. (1986). *L'observation des bebes*. Paris: Clancier-Guenaud.

Sandler, J. (1987). *From Safety to Superego: Selected Papers of Joseph Sandler*. New York: Guilford.

Sandler, J., Holder, A., & Dare, C. (1970). Basic psychoanalytic concepts: Acting out. *British Journal of Psychiatry, 117*: 329–334.

Scharff, J. S. (2010). Telephone analysis: Panel report. *International Journal of Psychoanalysis, 91*: 989–992.

Scharff, J. S. (2012). Clinical issues in analyses over the telephone and the internet. *International Journal of Psychoanalysis, 93*: 81–95.

Scharff, J. S. (2013). Technology-assisted psychoanalyses. *Journal of the American Psychoanalytic Association, 61*: 491–509.

Scheffer, A. (2016). The hysterical substrate: An analysis of the hysterical mode of representation underlying surrealism. Unpublished doctoral dissertation. University of Pretoria, South Africa.

Schimmel, A. M. (1975). *Mystical Dimensions of Islam*. Chapel Hill, NC: University of North Carolina Press.

Schlesinger, H. (1995). The process of interpretation and the moment of change. *International Journal of Psychoanalysis, 43*: 662–685.

Schlesinger, H. (2001). Technical problems in analyzing the mourning patient. In: S. Akhtar (Ed.), *Three Faces of Mourning: Melancholia, Manic Defense and Moving On* (pp. 116–139). Northvale, NJ: Jason Aronson.

Schore, A. (1994). *Affect Regulation and the Origin of the Self: The Neurobiology of Emotional Development*. Hillsdale, NJ: Lawrence Erlbaum.

Schuon, F. (1975). *The Transcendent Unity of Religions*. New York: Harper & Row.

Scull, A. (2015). *Madness in Civilization: A Cultural History of Insanity, from the Bible to Freud, from the Madhouse to Modern Medicine*. Princeton, NJ: Princeton University Press.

Seelig, B. J., & Rosof, L. S. (2001). Normal and pathological altruism. *Journal of the American Psychoanalytic Association, 49*: 933–959.

Sefercioğlu, N. (2009). *3 Mayıs 1944 ve Türkçülük Davası* [*The Trial of Turkism, May 3, 1944*]. Ankara: Türk Ocakları Ankara Şubesi.

Segal, H. (1957). Notes on symbol formation. In: *The Work of Hanna Segal: A Kleinian Approach to Clinical Practice* (pp. 49–68). New York: Jason Aronson, 1981.

Segel, N. P. (1969). Repetition compulsion, acting out, and identification with the doer. *Journal of the American Psychoanalytic Association, 17*: 474–488.

Settlage, C. (1993). Therapeutic process and developmental process in the restructuring of object and self constancy. *Journal of the American Psychoanalytic Association, 41*: 473–492.

Settlage, C. F., Rosenthal, J., Spielman, P. M., Gassner, S., Afterman, J., Bemesderfer, S., & Kolodny, S. (1990). An exploratory study of mother-child interaction during the second year of life. *Journal of the American Psychoanalytic Association, 38*: 705–731.

Shaw, S. J., & Shaw, E. K. (1977). *Reform, Revolution, and Republic: The Rise of Modern Turkey, 1808–1975. Vol. 2 of History of the Ottoman Empire and Modern Turkey*. Cambridge: Cambridge University Press.

Sheikh, A. A., & Sheikh, K. S. (1989). *Healing East and West: Ancient Wisdom and Modern Psychology*. New York: John Wiley.

Shields, R. (1964). The "too good" mother. *International Journal of Psychoanalysis, 45*: 85–88.

Shorter, E. (1997). *A History of Psychiatry: From the Era of the Asylum to the Age of Prozac*. New York: John Wiley.

Siegel, A. (2003). Studying psychoanalysis in Turkey. *American Psychoanalyst, 37*: 10, 12.

Silver, C. B. (2007). Womb envy: Loss and grief of the maternal body. *Psychoanalytic Review, 94*: 409–430.

Slipp, S. (1976). Interpersonal factors in hysteria: Freud's seduction theory and the case of Dora. *Journal of the American Academy of Psychoanalysis, 5*: 359–376.

Soler, C. (1996). Hysteria and obsession. In: R. Feldstein, B. Fink, & M. Jaanus (Eds.), *Reading Seminars I and II: Lacan's Return to Freud* (pp. 248–282). Albany, NY: State University of New York Press.

Somer, S. A. (2001). Osmanlı Reform Çağında Osmanlıcılık Düşüncesi (1839–1913) [The idea of Ottomanism during the Ottoman reform era, 1839–1913]. In: *Modern Türkiye'de Siyasî Düşünce* [*Political Thought in Modern Turkey*], *1* (pp. 88–116). Istanbul, Turkey: İletişim.

Steiner, J. (1993). *Psychic Retreats: Pathological Organization of the Personality in Psychotic, Neurotic, and Borderline Patients*. London: Routledge.

Stenslie, S. (2011). Power behind the veil: Princesses of the House of Saud. *Journal of Arabian Studies, 1*: 69–79.

Stern, D. (1998). *The Birth of a Mother*. London: Routledge.

Stern, D., Bruschweiler-Stern, N., & Freeland, A. (2013). *Bir Annenin Doğuşu: Annelik Deneyimi Sizi Sonsuza Dek Nasıl Değiştirir*. İstanbul, Turkey: İstanbul Bilgi Üniversitesi Yayınları.

Stoller, R. J. (1968). *Sex and Gender, Vol. 1*. New York: Science House.

Stoller, R. J. (1976). *Perversion: The Erotic Form of Hatred*. New York: Pantheon.

Storr, A. (1988). *Solitude. A Return to Self*. New York: Ballantine.

Sulloway, F. J. (1979). *Freud, Biologist of the Mind: Beyond the Psychoanalytic Legend*. New York: Basic Books.

Sunar, D. (2009). Mothers' and fathers' child rearing practices and self-esteem in three generations of urban Turkish families. In: S. Bekman & A. Aksu-Koc (Eds.), *Perspectives on Human Development, Family and Culture* (pp. 126–139). New York: Cambridge University Press.

Sutter, J. (1983). *L'anticipation*. Paris: Presses Universitaires de France, 1990.

Sutter, J., & Berta, M. (1991). *L'anticipation et ses applications cliniques*. Paris: Presses Universitaires de France.

Swales, S. S. (2012). *Perversion: A Lacanian Psychoanalytic Approach to the Subject*. London: Routledge.

Szönyi, G., & Štajner-Popović, T. (2008). Shuttle analysis, shuttle supervision, and shuttle life: Some facts, experiences, and questions. *Psychoanalytic Inquiry, 28*: 309–328.

Target, M., & Fonagy, P. (2002). Fathers in modern psychoanalysis and in society: the role of the father and child development. In: A. Etchegoyen & J. Trowell (Eds.), *The Importance of Fathers: A Psychoanalytic Re-evaluation* (pp. 45–67). Hove, UK: Brunner-Routledge.

Taştan, C. (Ed.) (2011). *Türkiye'de Psikanaliz Hakkında En Eski Metinler-I, 1917–1928 [The Oldest Texts on Psychoanalysis in Turkey-I]*. Istanbul, Turkey: Bağlam.

Thomas, N. (2018). Interrogating interpassivity: Do androids dream of electric sheep? *Continental Thought and Theory: A Journal of Intellectual Freedom, 2*: 159–190.

Triandis, H. C. (1995). *Individualism & Collectivism*. Boulder, CO: Westview.

Tronick, E., Adamson, L., Wise, S., & Brazelton, T. B. (1978). The infant's response to entrapment between contradictory messages in face-to-face interaction. *Journal of the American Academy of Child Psychiatry, 17*: 1–13.

Trowell, J. (2002). Setting the scene. In: A. Etchegoyen & J. Trowell (Eds.), *The Importance of Fathers: A Psychoanalytic Re-evaluation* (pp. 3–19). Hove, UK: Brunner-Routledge.

Tunaboylu İkiz, T. (2011). A brief look at the development of psychoanalysis in Turkey. *Journal of Sociology*, Series 3: 22.

Tunaboylu İkiz, T., & Arkonaç, S. (2004). Les raisons divers pour comprendre 100 ans de retard de psychoanalyse en Turquie. *Topic, 89*.

Ünver, A. S. (1943). *Tip Tarihi [History of Medicine]*. Istanbul, Turkey: Istanbul Üniversitesi Yayınları.

Üre, P. (2014). Byzantine heritage, archaeology, and politics between Russia and the Ottoman Empire: Russian archaeological institute in Constantinople (1894–1914). A dissertation submitted to the Department of International History of the London School of Economics and Political Science for the degree of doctor of philosophy, London, September.

Uşak-Şahin, H. (2009a). *Zur Geschichte und Gegenwart der Psychoanalyse in der Türkei* [On the history and present of psychoanalysis in Turkey]. Doctoral dissertation submitted to Leopold Franzens Universität, Innsbruck, Austria.

Uşak-Şahin, H. (2009b). Perspectives on Freudian psychoanalysis from Central Europe, Turkey and the United States. Paper presented at the symposium "After Freud left: Centennial reflections on his 1909 visit to the United States". New York Academy of Medicine, New York, October 4.

Uşak-Şahin, H. (2012). Another dimension of the émigré experience: From Central Europe to the United States via Turkey. In: J. Burnham (Ed.), *After Freud Left: A Century of Psychoanalysis in America* (pp. 125–153). Chicago, IL: University of Chicago Press.

Uysal, Y. (2021). The representation of women in the films of the 1980s with Hülya Avşar. *Journal of International Social Research, 14*: 81.

Uzman, M. O. (1928). *Akıl Hastalıkları* [*Mental Disorders*]. Istanbul, Turkey: Kader Matbaası.

Uzman, M. O. (1947). *Tababet-ı Ruhiye* [*Psychiatry*], *Vol. 2*, 3rd edn. Istanbul, Turkey: Kader Basımevi.

Vermote, R. (2018). *Reading Bion*. London: Routledge.

Vivona, J. M. (2010). Siblings, transference, and the lateral dimension of psychic life. *Psychoanalytic Psychology, 27*: 8–26.

Volkan, V. D. (1975). Turkey. In: J. G. Howells (Ed.), *World History of Psychiatry* (pp. 383–399). New York: Brunner/Mazel.

Volkan, V. D. (1981). *Linking Objects and Linking Phenomena: A Study of the Forms, Symptoms, Metapsychology, and Therapy of Complicated Mourning*. New York: International Universities Press.

Volkan, V. D. (1984). Complicated mourning. *Annual of Psychoanalysis, 12*: 323–348.

Volkan, V. D. (1985). Becoming a psychoanalyst. In: J. Reppen (Ed.), *Analysts at Work: Practice, Principles and Techniques* (pp. 251–231). New York: Analytic Press.

Volkan, V. D. (1997). *Bloodlines: From Ethnic Pride to Ethnic Terrorism*. New York: Farrar, Straus and Giroux.

Volkan, V. D. (1999). Childhood sibling rivalry and unconscious womb fantasies in adults. In: S. Akhtar & S. Kramer (Eds.), *Brothers and Sisters: Developmental, Dynamic, and Technical Aspects of the Sibling Relationship* (pp. 115–133). London: Jason Aronson.

Volkan, V. D. (2009). Some psychoanalytic views on leaders with narcissistic personality organization and their roles in large-group processes. In: R. H. Klein, C. A. Rice, & V. L. Schermer (Eds.), *Leadership in a Changing World: Dynamic Perspectives on Groups and Their Leaders* (pp. 67–89). New York: Lexington.

Volkan, V. D., & Ast, G. (1997). *Siblings in the Unconscious and Psychopathology.* New York: International Universities Press.

Volkan, V. D., & Çevik, A. (1989). Turkish fathers and their families: A study of fathers and their families in a transitional society. In: S. H. Cath, A. Gurwitt, & L. Gunsberg (Eds.), *Fathers and Their Families* (pp. 347–364). Hillsdale, NJ: The Analytic Press.

Volkan, V. D., & Corney, R. T. (1968). Some considerations of satellite states and satellite dreams. *British Journal of Medical Psychology, 41*: 283–290.

Volkan, V. D., & Itzkowitz, N. (1984). *The Immortal Atatürk: A Psychobiography*, Chicago, IL: University of Chicago Press.

Volkan, V. D., & Kayatekin, M. S. (2006). Extreme religious fundamentalism and violence: Some psychoanalytic and psychopolitical thoughts. *Psyche & Geloof, 17*: 71–91.

Wahl, C. W. (1960). The psychodynamics of consummated maternal incest. *Archives of General* Psychiatry, *3*: 96–101.

Waugaman, R. M. (1990). On patients' disclosure of parents' and siblings' names during the treatment. *Journal of the American Psychoanalytic Association, 38*: 167–194.

Weigert, O. (1937). New Turkish Labour Code. *International Labor Review, 35*: 753–774.

Weil, A. (1970). The basic core. *Psychoanalytic Study of the Child, 25*: 442–460.

Weisel-Barth, J. (2015). Multiple cultures, multiple selves, and analytic influence: A response to Goldin's "The Storied Self". *Psychoanalytic Dialogues, 6*: 680–686.

Welldon, E. (1988). *Mother, Madonna, Whore: The Idealization and Denigration of Motherhood.* London: Routledge.

Wilde, C. E. (2006). Monasticism. In: J. W. Meri (Ed.), *Medieval Islamic Civilization: An Encyclopedia* (pp. 507–508). New York: Routledge.

Wimmer, A. (2013). *Waves of War: Nationalism, State Formation, and Ethnic Exclusion in the Modern World.* Cambridge: Cambridge University Press.

Winnicott, D. W. (1931). *Clinical Notes on Disorders of Childhood.* London: Heinemann.

Winnicott, D. W. (1945). Primitive emotional development. *International Journal of Psychoanalysis, 26*: 137–143.

Winnicott, D. W. (1946). Some psychological aspects of juvenile delinquency. In: *The Child and the Outside World: Studies in Developing Relationships* (pp. 181–187). London: Tavistock, 1957.

Winnicott, D. W. (1949). Mind and its relation to the psychosoma. In: *Collected Papers: Through Paediatrics to Psychoanalysis* (pp. 243–255). New York: Brunner/Mazel, 1992.

Winnicott, D. W. (1953). Transitional objects and transitional phenomena: A study of the first not-me possession. *International Journal of Psychoanalysis, 34*: 89–97.

Winnicott, D. W. (1954). Metapsychological and clinical aspect of regression within the psychological set-up. In: L. Caldwell & A. Joys (Eds.), *Reading Winnicott.* (New Library of Psychoanalysis Teaching Series.) London: Routledge, 2011.

Winnicott, D. W. (1956). Primary maternal preoccupation. In: *Collected Papers: Through Paediatrics to Psychoanalysis.* London: Tavistock.

Winnicott, D. W. (1958a). *Collected Papers: Through Paediatrics to Psycho-Analysis*, London: Tavistock.

Winnicott, D. W. (1958b). The capacity to be alone. *International Journal of Psychoanalysis*, *39*: 416–420.

Winnicott, D. W. (1958c). Psikanalizde ilerlemeler [Advances in psychoanalysis]. *Tıpta Yenilikler*, *4*: 17–19.

Winnicott, D. W. (1960a). The theory of the parent–infant relationship. In: *The Maturational Processes and the Facilitating Environment* (pp. 37–55). New York: International Universities Press.

Winnicott, D. W. (1960b). Ego distortion in terms of true and false self. In: *The Maturational Processes and the Facilitating Environment: Studies in the Theory of Emotional Development* (pp. 140–152). New York: International Universities Press, 1965.

Winnicott, D. W. (1962). Ego integration in child development. In: *The Maturational Processes and the Facilitating Environment* (pp. 45–53). New York: International Universities Press.

Winnicott, D. W. (1963). On communication. In: *The Maturational Processes and the Facilitating Environment: Studies in the Theory of Emotional Development*. London: Hogarth.

Winnicott, D. W. (1964). The importance of the setting in meeting regression in psychoanalysis. In: C. Winnicott, R. Shepherd, & M. Davis (Eds.), *Psycho-analytic Explorations* (pp. 96–102). Cambridge, MA: Harvard University Press, 1989.

Winnicott, D. W. (1967). The mirror-role of the mother and family in child development. In: *Playing and Reality* (pp. 130–138). London: Penguin, 1971.

Winnicott, D. W. (1969). The use of an object. *International Journal of Psychoanalysis*, *50*: 711–716.

Winnicott, D. W. (1971). *Playing and Reality*. New York: Basic Books.

Winnicott, D. W. (1974). Fear of breakdown. *International Review of Psychoanalysis*, *1*: 103–107.

Winnicott, D. W. (1978). *The Piggle: An Account of the Psychoanalytic Treatment of a Little Girl*. London: Hogarth and the Institute of Psycho-Analysis.

Wittgenstein, L. (1951). *Tractatus Logico-philosophicus*. New York: Humanities.

Wittgenstein, L. (1967). *Lectures and Conversations on Aesthetics, Psychology, and Religious Belief*. C. Barrett (Ed.). Berkeley, CA: University of California Press.

Yalçıner, B., & Hanoğlu, L. (2001). *İç Bahçe: Toptaşı'ndan Bakırköy'e Akıl Hastanesi* [*The Courtyard: The History of the Mental Hospital from Toptaşı to Bakırköy*]. Istanbul, Turkey: Okuyanus.

Yalçınkaya, A. M. (2015). *Learned Patriots: Debating Science, State, and Society in the Nineteenth-Century Ottoman Empire*. Chicago, IL: University of Chicago Press.

Yamin Habib, L. E. (2003). Physical presence: A sine qua non of analysis? *Insight*, *12*: 25–27.

Yerlikaya, B. (2020). 1980 sonrası Türk Sineması'nda özel ve kamusal alan kıskacındaki kadın temsillerinin değişimi, dayanışması ve toplumsal cinsiyetçi söylenceleri reddi: Mine nasıl kurtulur? *Gaziantep University Journal of Social Sciences*, *19*: 1286–1303.

Yorukoglu, A., & Kemph, J. P. (1964). Children not severely damaged by incest with a parent. *Journal of the American Academy of Child Psychiatry*, *5*: 111.

Yorulmaz, A. (2020). Bulutların İz'inde: Anna O. ve Öteki'nin arzusu. [Unpublished paper.]

Zeavin, L. (2016). Commentary on Levy and Finnegan. *Journal of the American Psychoanalytic Association*, *64*: 85–91.

Zetzel, E. (1968). The so-called good hysterics. *International Journal of Psychoanalysis*, *49*: 256–260.

Žižek, S. (1989). *The Sublime Object of Ideology*. London: Verso.

Zürcher, E. J. (2004). *Turkey: A Modern History*. London: I. B. Tauris.

Index

Note: Entries with "n" refer to notes.

Abram, J., 190, 191, 257, 258, 261
acting out, 129
Adasal, R., 33
Adler, A., 74
adolescence, 49, 52, 62, 86, 96–98, 102
  adolescent-ish, 101–102
  adolescent-like, 98–102
  creativity, 97–101
adolescens, 96–97
Agger, E. M., 74
Ahmet İzeddin Şadan Biril *see* Şadan, İ.
Ainsworth, M. D. S., 42, 63
Akçınar, B., 68
Akhtar, S., 27, 49, 51, 108, 118
  father's role, 63–64
  sibling relationships, 78, 80, 81
  smell, 202
  tether fantasy, 220
  third individuation, 121
al-Ghazali, 9, 267n38
alpha function, 154, 191, 203
amorphousness, 190, 191
analyst
  metapsychology of, 192–193
  psychic working metabolism of, 193
  work of, 256
analytic instrument, 193–194
analytic psychotherapy, 247
analyzing instrument, 203
Anatolian Group of Psychoanalytic Psychotherapies, 18, 20, 21, 25
Andersen, H. C., 149
Anlı, İ., 20
anticipation, 98–99 *see also* mourning
anxiety
  anxieties of grouping, 86–87
  castration, 15, 62
  paranoid–schizoid anxieties, 77
Anzieu, D., 73, 86
Apprey, M., xv, 36
Arendt, H., 150–152, 153, 270n1
Arkonaç, S., 24
Asad, T., 267n46
Ast, G., 79
Atatürk, K., 5, 28–33
Atsız, N., 14
attachment, 63, 72, 80, 236, 241, 245
Avicenna (Ibni Sina), 28
Avşar, H., 124

Balsam, R., 42, 43
banality of evil, 150–152, 270n1
Bank, S., 74, 80
Baranger, M., 24, 194, 203

Baranger, W., 24, 194, 203
Baruzzi, A., 195
Basile, R., 204
Bayrakceken, A., 66
Beebe, B., 42, 63
believing
  in sacred, 238–239
  in transformation, 240–242
  in unity, 239–240
belonging, 237–238
Bergman, A., 222
Bergstein, A., 214
Bernanos, G., 99
Beyazid II, 28
Bibring, E., 31
Bick, E., 195, 199
Bion, W. R., 163, 202–203, 204, 214
  alpha function, 191
  basic assumption, 88
  caesura, 213
  catastrophic change, 190
  containment, 42, 43, 45, 251
  denial, 179
  group and gang formations, 88
  mother's reverie, 154
  negative capability, 191
  projective identification, 192
  psyche beta elements, 191
  psychosis, 178, 181
  siblings, 79
  theory of thinking, 153
bi-personal field theory, 203
Birsam-ı Saadet (Şadan), 11–14, 267n47
The Birth of a Mother (Stern), 198
Blessing, D., 82
Bollas, C., 131, 142, 189
Bolognini, S., 189, 195
Bose, G., 15, 269n73
Bowlby, J., 41, 46, 63, 216
Brel, J., 103
Breuer, J., 145, 265n22
Brill, A. A., 7, 265n21, 266n23
Britton, R., 62
Bucci, W., 202
Bumke, O., 263n2

caesura, 213–214
Campbell, J., 235, 240, 246
Camus, A., 239
castration anxiety, 15, 32, 62, 130, 137
causality, 6, 10, 264n17
Çevik, A., 66, 67
Chasseguet-Smirgel, J., 49, 85, 86, 148, 149, 153, 168
Chopra, D., 233, 241, 244
Christensen, L. W., 242
Civilization and Its Discontents (Freud), 7, 61, 266n30, 266n31
clinical withdrawal, 186
Clulow, C., 217
Cohen, G., 30
Cohen, J., 190
Coleman, D., 81
Coles, P., 82
collective
  memory, 146
  Turkish psyche, 4
Colonna, A. B., 80
concentrated analysis, 35
conditioned daydreaming, 193
containing, 42
  dead womb to containing womb, 210–212
  psychic pain, 204–205
Corney, R. T., 67
creative survival, 185–187
The Crescent and the Couch: Crosscurrents between Islam and Psychoanalysis (Akhtar), 27
cura animarum, 235

Dante, 241
Davids, M. F., 65
Davies, D., 19
daydreams, 138, 193, 194, 214
dead mother, 54, 224
death, 216–218, 223, 225, 226, 227, 240–242
De Cortinas, L. P., 204–205
defense mechanisms, 146, 148, 179
delusion, 187, 270n2
de M'Uzan, M., 153
denial, 179
Denzler, B., 36
desexualized love, 8, 10
dialectical self, 242
Diatkine, R., 102
Dispaux, M.-F., 20, 36
Divina Commedia (Dante), 241
Dora, 75, 127, 129–130, 138 *see also* Freud, S.
dreams, 73–74, 190, 194, 223
  Ferenczi, 155
  Freud, 73–74, 127
  Zeavin, 221

Eagle, M. N., 237
Efendi, M., 15
efsuncu, 28
ego, 243
adult, 96
ideal, 85–86, 101
super-, 85, 86
Eğrilmez, A., xxiv
Eichmann, A., 150–152, 153
Eichmann in Jerusalem (Arendt), 150
Einstein, A., 30
electronic setting *see* remote psychoanalytic practice
Emde, R., 42
empty space, 184–185
enactment, 129
environment mother, 42
Envy and Gratitude (Klein), 77
Erikson, E. H., 34, 45, 108
Erkoç, Ş., 28, 269n1
eros, 5, 7, 8, 9
Erten, Y., 25
Etchegoyen, A., 60, 62, 64
Etezady, H., 225
European Psychoanalytical Federation (EPF), 26, 35
existential therapy, 246–247

Faimberg, H., 201–202, 204, 205
Fairbairn, W. R. D., 41
faith, 238, 240, 247
false self, 129, 154–155, 181, 186, 256
Family, Self, and Human Development Across Cultures (Kağıtçıbaşı), 65
fantasy
hysterical, 134
intrauterine, 207
tether, 220
father(s) *see also* Dora; Name of the Father; *Nefret* (film)
categories of, 68
genital, 168
incest, 161, 163, 175
killing of, 23–24, 76, 81, 83–84
mother's role, 46, 48–49, 51, 56
myth of Myrrha, 159–160
parental couple, 72
in psychoanalysis, 61–65, 85, 86, 89–90
respect towards, 46, 48–49
role of, 60–61
as symbol, 59–60
fear of breakdown, 83, 190
feeling alive, 154, 181
feelings of suffocation, 204–205
female sexuality, 49
femininity, repressed, 52
Ferenczi, S., 97, 162, 164
dreams, 155
Ferro, A., 191, 202, 203, 204, 214
Fliess, R., 192–193
Fonagy, P., 42, 65, 204
formative murder, 83
formlessness, 191
Frank, A., 190
free-floating attention, 193
Freud, A., 33, 41, 55, 162, 163–164, 174
Freud, S., 6, 15, 243, 268n53
acting out, 129
adolescent contribution to adulthood, 96
adult mourning, 215
caesura, 213
castration anxiety, 15, 62
conditioned daydreaming, 193
determinism and causal methodology, 264n17
displacement of sensation, 130
Dora case, 75, 127, 129–130, 138
dreams, 73–74, 127
ego ideal, 85–86
father's role, 61–62
fetishism of perversion, 148–149
formative murder, 83
free-floating attention, 193
The Future of an Illusion (Freud), 7
Group Psychology and the Analysis of the Ego, 76, 84, 85, 86, 87
groups, 84
hysteria, 127–128, 138
identification, 85, 86
The Interpretation of Dreams, 41, 75, 146
libido, 265n23
Little Hans case, 75
loss of beloved object, 184–185
maternal-infant psyche, 189
maternal influence and mother-child studies, 41
maternal seduction, 167–168
melancholia, 215
memory, 145–146
Mourning and melancholia, 215
on nationalism, 12
Oedipus complex, 15, 61
An Outline of Psychoanalysis, 177
perversion, 138

primary repression, 189
psyche and object, 85
psychoanalysis, 264n19
psychosis, 177–178
published patient cases, 265n22
Rat Man case, 75
reversal of affect, 130
Şadan on, 6, 12
seduction theory, 127, 176
sibling relationship, 73–76
smell and memories, 202
society and neuroses, 7
Studies on Hysteria, 145
superego, 85
on thought, 153
Three Essays on the Theory of Sexuality, 75, 164, 174
Totem and Taboo, 76, 83, 84, 161
Wolf Man case, 76
Furman, E., 57
The Future of an Illusion (Freud), 7

Gallese, V., 196
Gampel, Y., 36
Genkoan, S., 242
Giovacchini, P. L., 223
Gods and Games (Miller), 238
Goldberg, A., 19, 34
Goldberg, C., 19
Golomb, A., 20, 36
Graham, I., 81
Green, A., 19, 44, 54, 224, 261
Green, N., 267n38
Greenacre, P., 164, 166, 168
Greenson, R. R., 44
grief, 216, 229 *see also* mourning
Group Psychology and the Analysis of the Ego (Freud), 76, 84, 85, 86, 87
Gruenthal, R., 19
Gunzberg, S., 29, 30
Gürdal Küey, A., 22
Gürışık, E., 36
Gurışık, Ü., 20
Gutton, P., 96–97

Habip, B., 22, 23, 35, 36 *see also* Psike İstanbul, 19–20, 35, 36
Hacib, Y. H., 28
Hagman, G., 217
Halime Odağ Foundation, 34, 36
hallucination, 17, 193, 270n2
of happiness, 11, 13
Han Groen-Prakken Psychoanalytic Institute, 35
Hani, A., 20, 34, 35
Hanım ağa (lady the landlord) syndrome, 115
Hartocollis, P., 35, 36
Hatred (film) *see Nefret* (film)
healer, 242
Hillman, J., 235
Hoche, A., 263n2
holding, 42
Holocaust survivors *see The Pageant* (film)
Homer, S., 64
homosexuality, 14, 76, 84, 161, 162
latent, 8
Hoover, I., 202
Horowitz, M. J., 216, 217
human diminution, 243

Ibn ʿArabî, 267n38
Ibni Sina *see* Avicenna
id, 243
identification, 85, 86, 135
illusion, 99–100, 187, 270n2
Imago, 15, 32
The Immortal Atatürk (Volkan & Itzkowitz), 264n11
inaccessible states of mind, 214
incest, 159, 174–176
clinical vignettes, 165–174
incestuous objects, 136
intergenerational repetition, 163–165
maternal sexual abuse, 165–166, 167–168
The mother and son incest, 160
mother as barrier, 56, 78
Myrrha myth, 159–160, 176
parasitic symbiosis, 166
between siblings, 74, 76, 77, 81, 90, 91
silent mothers, 162–165, 171
theoretical perspectives, 161–162
individual
and collective recollection, 145–146
memory, 146
individuation, 48, 67, 90, 121, 217, 235
individuation–separation, 66–67, 100 *see also* separation–individuation
infantile sexuality, 97
inner narcissistic gang, 179
İnönü, İ., 30, 31
independence–interdependence dimension, 66
International Psychoanalytical Association (IPA), xxiv, xxv, 17, 20, 21, 25–26, 27, 31, 33, 34–37, 263n4

The Interpretation of Dreams (Freud), 41, 75, 146
intrauterine fantasies, 207
Ipeker, E., 145 *see also The Pageant* (film)
Isakower, O., 193
Islamic
  care for mental illness, 28–29
  thinkers, 267n38
İstanbul Association for Psychoanalysis and Psychoanalytic Psychotherapies *see* Psike İstanbul
İstanbul Psychoanalytical Association, 4, 17, 19, 20, 21, 34, 35, 36, 263n4
İstanbul Psychoanalytical Group *see* İstanbul Psychoanalytical Association
Itzkowitz, N., 29, 30, 31, 216, 264n11
İzeddin, A *see* Şadan, İ.

Jacobs, T. J., 193
Jaspers, K., 233, 238, 239, 246
Jeammet, P., 96, 101
Jenkins, S., 19
Joannidis, C., 19
Johnson, J. T., 163
Jones, E., 7, 265n19
Jung, C. G., 7, 74, 243

Kaës, R., 80
Kağıtçıbaşı, Ç., 47, 61, 65
  independence–interdependence dimension, 66
  separate self, 66
  Turkish Early Enrichment Project, 67–68
Kahn, M. D., 74, 80
Kakar, S., 46, 65, 108
Kant, I., 152
Kanwal, G. S., 226
Karasu, T. B., 234, 244
Kayalı, H., 268n49
Kayatekin, M. S., 28, 108 *see also* Turkish identity
Keats, J., 191
Kemal, M. *see* Atatürk, K.
Kernberg, O. F., 45, 128, 163, 165, 171, 216, 217, 229
Kieffer, C. C., 80
Kinston, W., 190
Klein, M., 41, 62, 216, 222
  empty space, 184–185
  good breast, 43
  manic defense, 220
  paranoid–schizoid anxieties, 77, 191
  projective identification, 77, 178, 191–192
  psychic withdrawal, 178
  psychosis, 178
  sadism, 183
  theory of siblings, 76–77, 79
  unconscious phantasies, 88
Koçak, P., 20
Kogan, I., 36
Kohut, H., 18
Kolmer, S., 147–148
Kouretas, N., 36
Kovel, J., 235, 237, 238, 239, 248
Kraepelin, E., 29, 32, 33, 263n2
Kramer, S., 78, 80, 162
Kristeva, J., 210
Krohn, A., 128
Kulin, A., 117
Kulish, N., 42
Kushner, H. S., 238
Kutadgu-Bilig (Yusuf Hasi Hacib), 28

Lacan, J., 64, 128, 133
  bisexuality of hysterics, 135
  castration, 130
  fantasy, 134
  hysteria, 128–129
  hysteria and obsessive neurosis, 137
  hysterical subject, 132, 134, 141
  hysterical suffering, 140–141
  identification, 135
  Lacanian theory, 64
  Oedipus complex, 131–132
  sexual impasse, 140
lady the landlord syndrome, 115
L'anticipation (Sutter), 99
Laplanche, J., 25, 161, 190
Larmo, A., 82
Lasch, C., 233
latent homosexuality *see* homosexuality
Law of Least Effort, 233–234
Law of the Mother, 78
Lechevalier, B., 199
Leibovici, M., 198
Lemma, A., 259
Le Rossignol de l'Empereur de Chine (Andersen), 149
Levin, C., 80
Levin, S., 216
Levine, H., 203
libido, 7, 84, 265–266n23
Lichtenberg, J., 19
Lindemann, E., 216
Lindon, J. A., 91
Little Hans, 75
liturgy, 237

Loewald, H. W., 45, 63
longue durée millet system *see* multicommunal Ottoman system
loss of beloved object, 184–185
loss of soul, 236
love, 8, 236, 239–240
of belonging, 237–238
conjugal, 8
desexualized, 8, 10
of others, 236
phases of sickness of, 10
of work, 237

madness, 177, 181
madrassa, 28
Mahler, M. S., 41, 45, 63, 166, 201, 220, 222
Mahmud the Second, 111
Majority World, 61, 65
Malawista, K. L., 216
Mansion, E., 95
Marty, P., 153
Maslow, A., 243
mass memory, 146
maternal
competition, 53–54, 56
complicity and psychopathology, 161–162
enmeshment, 53–54
inaction, 54
primacy and paternal emergence, 62
responsiveness, 154
roles in incest, 162–163
seduction, 167–168
sexual abuse, 165–166
shame, 52–53
turn in psychoanalysis, 41–42
voyeurism and exhibitionism, 168–169
medrese, 28
Mehmet the Conqueror, 115
melancholia, 215 *see also* mourning
memory, 145–146 *see also The Pageant* (film)
Mercan, S., 20
metapsychology of analyst, 192–193
Meyers, H., 222
Miller, D., 238
Miller, T., 239
Milner, M., 187
mind
inaccessible states of, 214
theory of, 244–245
Mitchell, J., 78, 81, 83, 85, 89
Mitchell, T., 269n72
monolithic psychoanalysis, 14–16
Moore, T., 235, 236, 237, 241, 244, 245
Moses and Monotheism (Freud), 7, 15, 32, 61
Moses, R., 34, 35
mother *see also* Law of the Mother; *Nefret*
-baby observation, 195–199, 203
-child relationship, 33, 41–46, 60, 62–65, 74, 76, 77, 79, 82, 86, 88, 100, 154, 189, 191, 258
containing, 42, 43
-daughter relationship, 48–51, 53, 56–57, 185
dead, 54
environment, 42, 185
good/bad, 67, 183
good enough, 78, 100, 255
holding, 42, 43
hysteric's, 133
-infant relationship, 44, 45, 46, 72, 82, 100, 168, 191, 198–199, 259, 261
libidinal, 221
object, 42
overprotective and/or competitive, 55
placental paradigm, 212–214
potential space, 187, 251
primary maternal preoccupation, 43, 256
projective identification, 192
protecting and nourishing, 43
reverie, 154
silent, 162–165, 175
smell, 202–203
sultan's, 115
Mother, Madonna, Whore: The Idealization and Denigration of Motherhood (Welldon), 162
mourning, 216
acknowledging death, 225–226
adult, 215
adult mourning, 215
anticipated loss, 215–216
anticipatory grief reaction, 216
anticipatory mourning, 216–218
clinical presentation, 218–230
displacement of anger, 226–227
dreams, 221
dreams and transference, 224
dream symbols and unspoken loss, 223
grief, 216, 227–228, 229
management of anger, 231
manic defense, 219, 220
melancholia, 215
narcissistic transformation in loss, 229–230

object constancy and anticipatory grief, 221–223
optimal distance and object constancy, 220–221
projection of need and control, 219
protecting mourning process, 223–224
psychoanalytic understanding of anticipated loss, 215–216
putting death into words, 223–224
readjusting relationship, 227–228
schematic change in self and other, 217
separation guilt and sacrificial fantasies, 224–225
sounds and silence, 226
substituted identity and unmourned losses, 218–219
tether fantasy, 220
themes of death, 223
toward mending, 221–223
visual memory and work of, 228–229
within analytic process, 215, 230–231
work of, 215
Mourning and melancholia (Freud), 215
multicommunal Ottoman system, 11
Murad, Y., 267n38
Myrrha myth, 159–160, 176 *see also* incest

Name of the Father, 131–132, 140
narcissism
narcissistic parentage and ego split, 201–202
paternal, 131
phallic, 141
nationalism, 11–14, 267–268n49, 268n53, 269n67
Nayar-Akhtar, M., 108
Nefret (film), 123, 124, 142–143
alliances and chaotic borders, 134–137
father–daughter dynamics, 125–127, 130–131, 134–135, 136–137, 138, 139–141, 143
Hülya, 127–134
hysteria and desire, 127–134
hysterical denial and acting, 137–142
Lacanian analysis of filial conflict in, 127–134
mother–daughter relationship, 125–127, 129–143
oedipal tragedy in, 124–127
synopsis and tagline, 124–127
negative capability, 191
Neri, C., 194
Neruda, P., 238
Netanyahu, S., 147
New Age therapy, 247
Newman, L. M., 80
non-duality, 244
Nur, R., 14

object
constancy, 222
loss of beloved, 184–185
mother, 42
psyche and, 85
use of, 258
obsessive neurosis, 137
Odağ, C., xxiv, 34
oedipal
barrier, 51
complex, 10, 15, 61–64, 73, 76, 77, 78, 79, 80–81, 82, 86, 131, 136–137, 183
competitiveness, 53, 54
navigation, 46–47
triangulation, 81, 128
Ogden, T. H., 191, 192, 214, 256, 257
online therapy *see* remote psychoanalytic practice
Orhon, O. S., 14
origins of the self, 190–191
The Origins of Totalitarianism (Arendt), 152
Ornstein, A., 18, 19
Ornstein, P., 18
O'Shaughnessy, E., 192
Osman, M., 5, 29, 32
other, 85
love, 236
psyche and object, 85
schematic change in, 217
Ottoman Empire, 28
Ottomanism, 267n49
An Outline of Psychoanalysis (Freud), 177
OZE (Organization for the Protection of the Jewish Population), 30
Öztürk, O. M., 33–34

The Pageant (film), 145
Banality of Evil, 150–152
Bion's theory of thinking, 153
Hannah Arendt, 150–152
Holocaust survivors, 147–148
meditation on memory and meaning, 149–150
perversion and denial of primal scene, 148–149
recovery of affect, 153–155
trauma, affect, and hyper-mediatized world, 155–156
Pamuk, O., 59, 61, 66
Pandolfo, S., 9
Paracelsus, 244
Parens, H., 42, 51
parental neglect, 51–52, 55

Parkes, C., 216
Parman, T. *see* İstanbul Psychoanalytical Association
pathological splitting, 179
Peck, M. S., 239
Penot, B., 36
Perls, F., 243
perversion, 138–139, 148–149
phallic narcissism, 141
Piggle case, 77
placental paradigm, 208, 212–214
Playing and Reality (Winnicott), 187
Pollock, G. H., 216
Pontalis, J.-B., 161, 190, 205
positive science, 6
Powell, A., 63
pre-conceptualization, 79
primal scene, denial of, 148–149
primary
  maternal preoccupation, 43, 256
  nonintegration, 190–191
  repression, 189, 190
primitive
  agonies, 254
  defences, 88
primordial unity, 239
projective identification, 179, 191–192
pseudo-naiveté, 141–142
pseudo-stupidity, 201
Psikanaliz (Şadan), 32
Psike İstanbul, 19–20, 35, 36
psyche
  adolescence, 96
  beta elements, 191
  collective Turkish, 4
  maternal–infant, 189
  and object, 85
psychiatric approaches, 3
psychic
  pain, 186
  reality, 100
  withdrawal, 178
  working metabolism of analyst, 193
psychoanalysis, 17 *see also* Turkish psychoanalysis
  Anatolian Group, 18, 20, 21, 25
  anthropological, xxiii–xxv
  delayed institutionalization of, 21–25
  enlightenment-based modernization initiatives, 24
  evolution and future, 24–25
  Freud, 264n19
  generational shifts, 24–25
  genesis and evolution, 17–21
  İstanbul Psychoanalysis Meetings, 19
  monolithic, 14–16
  nationalist, 11–14
  problem of timing, 25–26
  Psike İstanbul, 20, 25
  of smell, 199–205
  Turkification of, 7–11
  Volkan Group, 17, 20
psychoanalytic discourse, 4
psychological boundary, 135
psychosis, 177–178
psychotherapeutic models, 246–248
psychotic defenses, 257
pubertaire, 96–97

radical evil, 152
Randall, D., 66
Raphael-Leff, J., 207, 208, 212, 214
Rat Man, 75
reciprocity, 196
regression, 255–256
Reign of Women, 115
remote psychoanalytic practice, 249, 260–262
  analytic environment, 250
  analytical framework, 250–251
  capacity to go back and forth, 255
  dependent transference, 255–260
  different patient groups and, 253–255, 261
  electronic setting, 250–255, 257
  impact of, 249–250
  primary maternal preoccupation, 256
  psychoanalytic frame, 250–253
  regression, 255–256
  symbolization process, 261
  unconventional healing, 255–260
  use of an object, 258
  work of the analyst, 256
repression, 179
  repressed femininity, 52
  repressed unconscious, 190
reversal of affect, 130
Rilke, R. M., 236, 239
Rinpoche, S., 239, 240, 241, 242
Roland, A., 65
Rosenfeld, H. A., 179, 192
Roussillon, R., 155, 250
Roux, M. L., 20
Russell, G. I., 252, 259
Rustin, M., 80

Sachs, D., 34, 36
sacred experience, 238–239
Şadan, İ., 4–6, 16, 32, 264n17, 265n21
  claims of priority and non-Western contributions, 14–16
  on Freud, 6, 12
  Freudian eros and Western modernity, 7–11
  intellectual evolution, 6–7
  libido, 265n23
  nationalist psychoanalysis, 11–14
  Şadanian psychoanalytic discourse, 16
  Sufism, 9
  Sunni-informed secularism, 10–11
sadism, 183
Salo, F. T., 198
Sanchez, N., 199
Sandler, J., 129, 163
Sanz, M. C., 36
satellite state, 67
Scharff, J. S., 253, 260, 262
Schlesinger, H., 217, 223, 226
Scholem, G., 152
Scull, A., 263n2
seduction theory, 127
Segal, H., 180
  symbolic equation, 180, 181
self
  dialectical, 242
  false, 154, 185–187
  origins of, 190–191
  schematic change in, 217
  separate, 66
  spiritual, 242
  true, 154, 181, 186, 235, 256
self psychology, 17
  Anatolian Group, 18, 20, 21, 25
  enlightenment-based modernization initiatives, 24
  generational shifts, 24–25
  genesis and evolution, 17–21
  İstanbul Psychoanalysis Meetings, 19
  problem of timing, 25–26
  Psike İstanbul, 20, 25
  reflection on premature, 24–25
  Volkan Group, 17, 20
Self Psychology Society *see* Anatolian Group of Psychoanalytic Psychotherapies
separation-individuation, 45, 63, 212, 220, 225 *see also* individuation; individuation-separation
Settlage, C., 222
sexual impasse, 140
sexuality
  female, 49
  infantile, 97, 127
  latent homosexuality, 8
Sheikh, A. A., 246
Sheikh, K. S., 246
shuttle analysis, 17, 21, 35
sibling relationship, 73, 93
  abandonment, 92–93
  anxieties of grouping, 86–87
  clinical setting, 81–83
  clinical vignette, 92–93
  Dora case, 75
  emotional bonds, 78–81
  formative murder, 83
  Freud's views, 73–76
  hierarchy, gender, and tradition, 89–93
  Klein's theory, 76–77
  Law of the Mother, 78
  Little Hans case, 75
  Mitchell, 78
  oedipal triangulation, 81
  Oedipus complex, 80–81
  Piggle case, 77
  positive sibling transference, 81
  pre-conceptualization, 79
  primitive defences, 88
  psychic development, 78–81
  Rat Man case, 75
  sibling dynamics and group psychology, 83–89
  sibling-peer relationships, 89
  transference-countertransference, 81
  Winnicott's approach, 77–78
  Wolf Man case, 76
Siblings: Sex and Violence (Mitchell), 78
Siegel, A., 18, 19, 20, 21, 36, 34
Siegel, R., 18, 20
silent mothers *see also* incest
  complicity, 163–165
  psychic origins of, 163–165
  types of, 162–163
Silver, C. B., 210
smell, 202–204
Socrates, 241
Solomon, D., 19
Sorter, D., 19
soul, 235, 241
soulfulness, way of, 236
  belonging, 237–238
  others, 236
  work, 237

spirit, 235, 238
spiritual existence, 234–236, 244, 246
spiritual psychotherapist, 242–244, 245
spiritual therapy, 233, 234, 246–248
  therapist, 242–246
spiritually, way of, 238
  believing, 238–242
  love, 239–240
  sacred experience, 238–239
  unfolding vision of wholeness, 239
Spitz, R., 41
splitting, 80, 88
  pathological, 179
Steiner, J.
  psychic pain, 186
  psychic retreat, 178
Stern, D., 42, 198
still face experiment, 196
Stoller, R. J., 44, 164
Storr, A., 237, 239
Studies on Hysteria (Freud), 145
Sufism (Tasavvuf), 9
Suleiman the Magnificent, 115
Sulloway, F. J., 264n17
Sultan Abdülhamid II, 29
Sultan Mahmud the Second, 111
sultans, 115
superego *see* ego
Sutter, J., 98, 99
symbolic equation, 180, 181
symbolization process, 261

Tahsin, R., 29
Talat Parman group, 36
Tanık, M., 20
Tanoğlu, L., 20
Tanzimat, 24
Target, M., 65, 204
tekkes, 10, 28, 29
tele-analysis *see* remote psychoanalytic practice
Temperley, A., 64–65
Terbas, O., 20
tether fantasy, 220–221
Tevetoğlu, F., 14
therapeutic relationship, 245
thought, 153
Three Essays on the Theory of Sexuality (Freud), 32, 75, 164, 174
The Tibetan Book of Living and Dying (Rinpoche), 240
Togan, Z. V., 14
Tokgöz, G., 20
Topkapi Hospital, 29
Toptaşı Asylum, 5
Totem and Taboo (Freud), 7, 61, 76, 83, 84, 161
tradition, 266n24
traditional fatherhood, 68
Traité théorique et pratique de psychoanalyse (Jones), 7
transcendence and healing, 234–236
transference, 22–23, 130, 187, 193, 222, 226, 230, 245, 247, 254
  counter-, 194
  -countertransference, 81–83, 93, 212, 213, 214, 221, 224, 250
  dependent, 254, 255, 256, 257, 259, 260, 261
transgenerational
  knots, 201–202
  trauma, 202–204
transitional
  field, 180–181
  space, 99
transpersonal love, 239
Tronick, E., 196
true self, 154, 181, 186, 235, 256
Tunaboylu İkiz, T., 24
Turanism, 14, 269n67
Turkish nationalism, 267n49, 269n67
Turkish psychiatry, 264n6
Turkish psychoanalysis, 3–4, 16, 29–35 *see also* psychoanalysis
  anthropological psychoanalysis, xxiii–xxv
  challenging monolithic psychoanalysis, 14–16
  cultural translation, 3–4
  descriptive psychiatry to psychoanalysis, 6–7
  eros, 7
  evolution of psychiatry, 28–29
  historical overview, 27
  international collaboration and local development, 29–35
  IPA's involvement, 35–37
  İzzettin Şadan, 4–6
  love, 8, 10
  mental healthcare, 28–29
  Mustafa Kemal Atatürk, 28, 29–35
  narrative of positivism, 6–7
  nationalism, 11–14
  neuroses, 11–14
  Sufism, 9
  Turkification of psychoanalysis, 7–11

unconscious
forces, 245
repressed, 190
unrepressed, 190–191
unfolding vision of wholeness, 239
unity, 239–240
unrepressed unconscious, 190–191
unspeakable, 190–191
unthought known, 189
use of an object, 258
US-supported military coups, 269n1

Vahip, I., 36
Value of the Child research, 47–48
Vivona, J. M., 80
Volkan, V. D., 28, 29, 30, 32, 66, 67, 79, 216, 223, 263, 264
Volkan Group, 17, 20–21

Way to Wisdom (Jaspers), 233
Weigert, E. V., 5, 30, 31
Weigert, O., 5, 30
Welldon, E., 162, 167
Weltanschauung, 48
Widlöcher, D., 36
Winnicott, D. W., 33, 37, 41, 45, 46, 50, 90, 166, 251, 204
art as therapy, 177
capacity to go back and forth, 255
concept of fear of breakdown, 83
creative survival, 185–187
development of sense of reality, 185
facilitating environment, 62
false self, 154, 185–187
fear of breakdown, 83, 190
feeling alive, 154
formlessness, 191
holding, 42, 62, 251
illusion, 99–100
not me, 135
omnipotent illusion, 257
Piggle case, 77
Playing and Reality, 187
primary maternal preoccupation, 43, 256
primitive agonies, 254
psychological boundary, 135
regression, 255–256
siblings, 77–78
subject and object, 185
symbolization process, 261
transitional field, 180–181
transitional space, 99
true self, 154
use of an object, 258
view of father's role, 62
Wittgenstein, L., 246, 265n19
Wolf, E., 17, 18
Wolf Man, 76
women depictions in Turkish cinema, 123–124, 142
see also Nefret (film)
working with preverbal, 205

Yazıcı, A., 36
Yeşilçam' (Turkish cinema), 123 *see also Nefret* (film); *The Pageant* (film)
Young Turk, 5, 113, 268n49
Yücel, H. A., 31

Zeavin, L., 221
Zetzel, E., 128